CAMBRIDGE

Official Cambridge Exam Preparation

CB082255

OPEN WORLD

B1

PRELIMINARY

STUDENT'S BOOK WITH ANSWERS

with Online Practice

Niamh Humphreys and Susan Kingsley

with Sheila Dignen

Cambridge University Press
www.cambridge.org/elt

Cambridge Assessment English
www.cambridgeenglish.org

Information on this title: www.cambridge.org/9781108759199

First published 2019

20 19 18 17 16 15 14 13 12 11 10 9 8 7

Printed in Poland by Opolgraf

A catalogue record for this publication is available from the British Library

ISBN 978-1-108-75919-9 Student's Book with answers with Online Practice

CONTENTS

Map of the book 4
How to use this book 6

Starter Personal profile 8
Unit 1 Getting away 14
Unit 2 Entertain me 26
Progress check 1 38
Unit 3 Dining out, eating in 40
Unit 4 City living? 52
Unit 5 Picture of health 64
Progress check 2 76
Unit 6 Online, offline 78
Unit 7 What's your style? 90
Unit 8 Into the wild 102
Progress check 3 114
Unit 9 Always learning 116
Unit 10 Travelling well 128
Unit 11 A great location 140
Progress check 4 152
Unit 12 The perfect job 154
Unit 13 Get involved! 166
Unit 14 On top of the world 178
Progress check 5 190

Communication activities 192
Grammar reference 196
Irregular verb list 223
Phrasal verb bank 224
Writing bank 226
Speaking bank 234
Exam information 244
Answer keys 245

UNIT	READING	LISTENING	WRITING
Starter **Personal profile** p. 8	A blogger	Celebrity profiles	A personal profile
1 **Getting away** p. 14	**Part 2** Holiday destinations A trip to Paris	A trip to Madagascar	A review
2 **Entertain me** p. 26	TV-watching habits	**Part 2** Short dialogues	**Part 1** An email
Progress check 1 p. 38			
3 **Dining out, eating in** p. 40	**Part 4** An unusual restaurant A world of differences	A visit to a restaurant	Describing a restaurant
4 **City living?** p. 52	Countryside and city living	**Part 1** Short dialogues and monologues	**Part 2** A story
5 **Picture of health** p. 64	**Part 6** A record-breaking runner The benefits of laughter **Part 1** Short texts	**Part 3** A health club A bike hire club	An email of advice
Progress check 2 p. 76			
6 **Online, offline** p. 78	**Part 3** Social media rules Digital detox	Planning a weekend trip	A blog post
7 **What's your style?** p. 90	**Part 5** Tricks of the trade The oldest sweet shop in the world	**Part 4** A fashion vlogger A mystery shopper	A review
8 **Into the wild** p. 102	Extreme sports challenges	Running in the jungle	**Part 2** An article
Progress check 3 p. 114			
9 **Always learning** p. 116	**Part 3** Free schools Sanjeev Kanwar	**Part 2** Short dialogues	A formal email
10 **Travelling well** p. 128	**Part 4** A fabulous flight Joe's surprise holiday	Bands and the environment B2 Listening for opinions	**Part 2** A story
11 **A great location** p. 140	Different types of homes	**Part 1** Short dialogues and monologues	**Part 1** An email
Progress check 4 p. 152			
12 **The perfect job** p. 154	**Part 5** Young pilots Dream Jobs	**Part 3** A good job A digital artist	A job advertisement
13 **Get involved!** p. 166	**Part 2** Weekend sports courses Winter sports holidays	A hobby	An article
14 **On top of the world** p. 178	**Part 1** Short texts **Part 6** Call a friend and talk What is happiness?	**Part 4** An interview with an actress An interview with a yoga teacher	A profile of a person you like
Progress check 5 p. 190			

SPEAKING	GRAMMAR	VOCABULARY	REAL WORLD
Introducing yourself Intonation	Present simple and present continuous Adverbs of frequency Present continuous with *always*	Personal interests Habits and routines Occupations	
Part 3 Making suggestions, asking for opinions, agreeing and disagreeing **Part 4** A holiday Sports and outdoor activities	Comparatives and superlatives *so* and *such*, *too* and *enough* Pronouncing *too* and *to*	Holiday activities Easily confused travel words Weather B2 Environment	Where can I stay in Auckland?
Likes and dislikes	*used to* Present perfect and past simple *for* and *since* *yet* and *already* Linking /w/	Entertainment B2 Phrasal verbs	At a festival in California
Part 2 Describing a photo	Verbs + adjectives Quantifiers Articles Pronouncing the schwa /ə/	Easily confused restaurant words Cooking B2 Food idioms	Eating out in Bangkok
Making and responding to suggestions	Past simple and past continuous Past perfect B2 Mixed tenses Pronouncing /wəz/ and /wə/	Town and country	Things to do in Amsterdam
Asking about problems, showing sympathy and giving advice	Ability and advice Obligation	Parts of the body Aches and pains B2 Health expressions Vowel sounds	Preparing to travel to Marrakesh
Part 1 Introducing yourself	Plans and intentions Predictions B2 Future certainty and uncertainty Pronouncing *going to*	Social media Phrasal verbs	Meeting people in Paris
Expressing preferences Pronouncing *clothes/close*	Reported speech B2 Reporting verbs	Fashion Buying and returning goods Shopping	Shopping in Istanbul
Part 2 Describing a photo	Modals of speculation Elision	Environments and landscapes Adjectives with *-ed* and *-ing* Animals and their habitats B2 Animals' bodies	Visiting a national park in Wyoming
Likes and dislikes Word stress	Passive B2 Passive in other tenses	Education Higher education Education collocations	Booking onto a language course in Oxford
Speculating	Zero and first conditionals Second conditional Pronouncing *'ll* and *'d*	Transport words Phrasal verbs with *get*	Getting through the airport in London
Informal reactions	Relative clauses *Have/Get something done*	Homes Furniture and furnishings B2 Adjectives for homes Pronouncing /ʌ/ and /æ/	Finding student accommodation in Grenoble
Agreeing and disagreeing	Modals of permission *make* and *let* B2 *be able to*	Jobs and occupations People in the workplace Qualities and qualifications for a job Leaving out syllables	Getting a summer job in Florida
Part 1 What you do in your free time **Parts 3 and 4** Asking for opinions Stress in questions	Gerunds Verb + *to* infinitive	Sports verbs People in sport *Do/Go/Play* + sports and hobbies B2 Phrasal verbs	Using sports facilities on holiday in Greece
Finding out information	Conditionals Reported speech Modal verbs Relative clauses	Emotions Appearance and personality B2 Compound adjectives Spellings and the /ʃ/ sound	Having a job interview in Tenerife

HOW TO USE THIS BOOK

WELCOME TO OPEN WORLD

THE COURSE THAT TAKES YOU FURTHER

Learn about the features in your new Student's Book

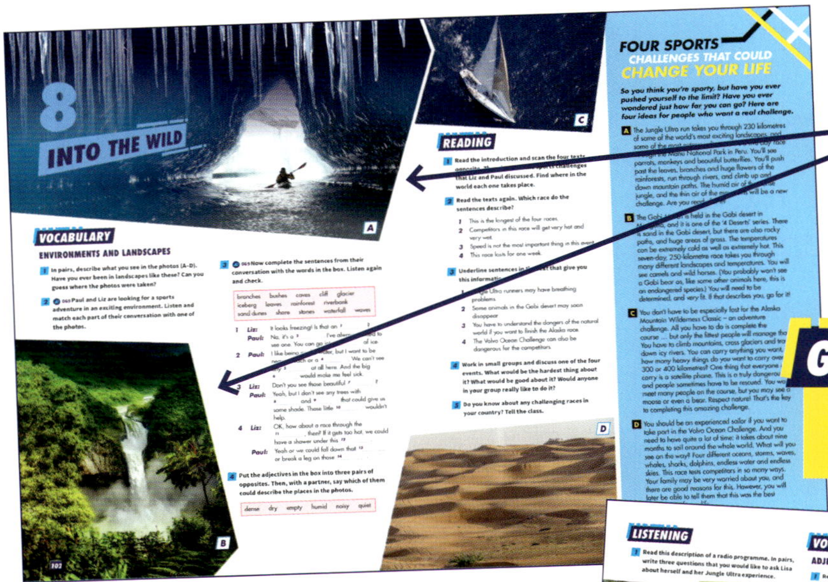

Large images at the start of each unit introduce the topic and get you talking

GRAMMAR ON THE MOVE

Scan the QR codes to watch grammar animations in your free time to learn about each grammar point

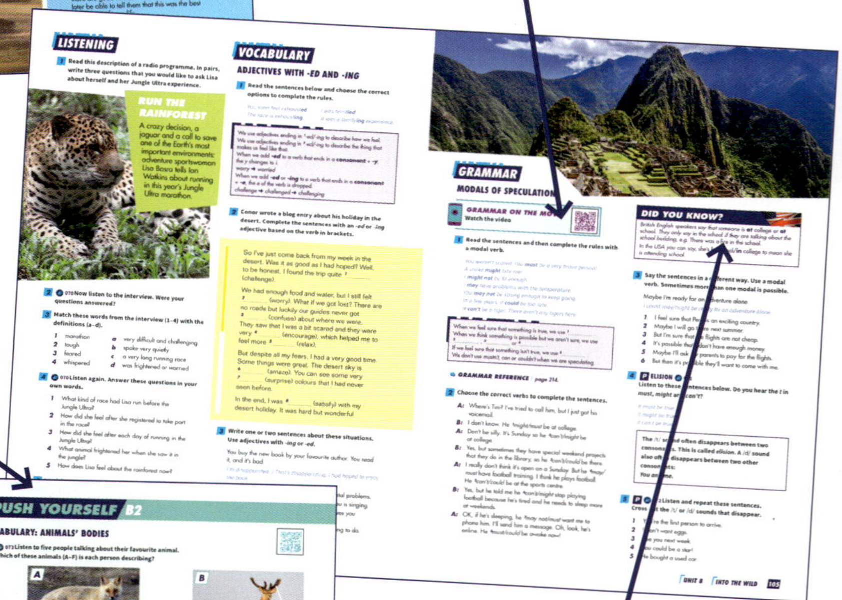

PUSH YOURSELF

Learn and practise more challenging language and skills that take you to the next level

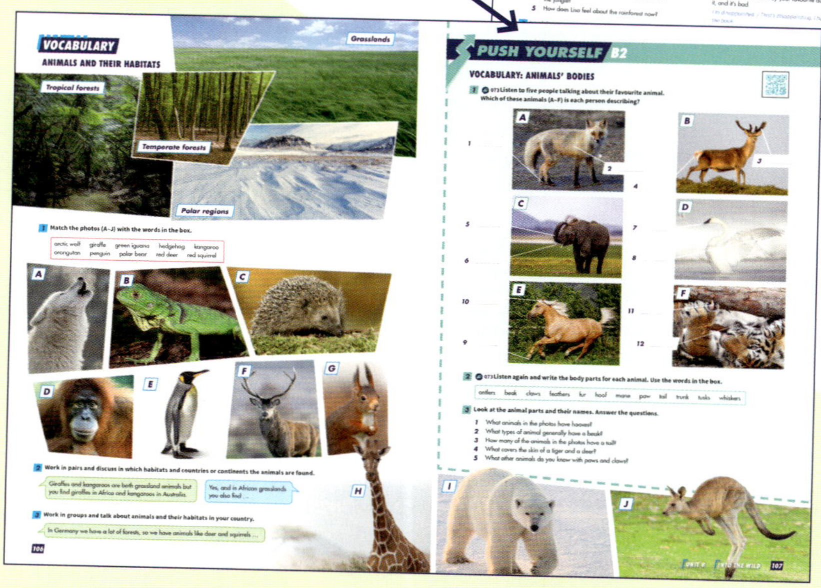

DID YOU KNOW?

Learn the differences between British English and American English

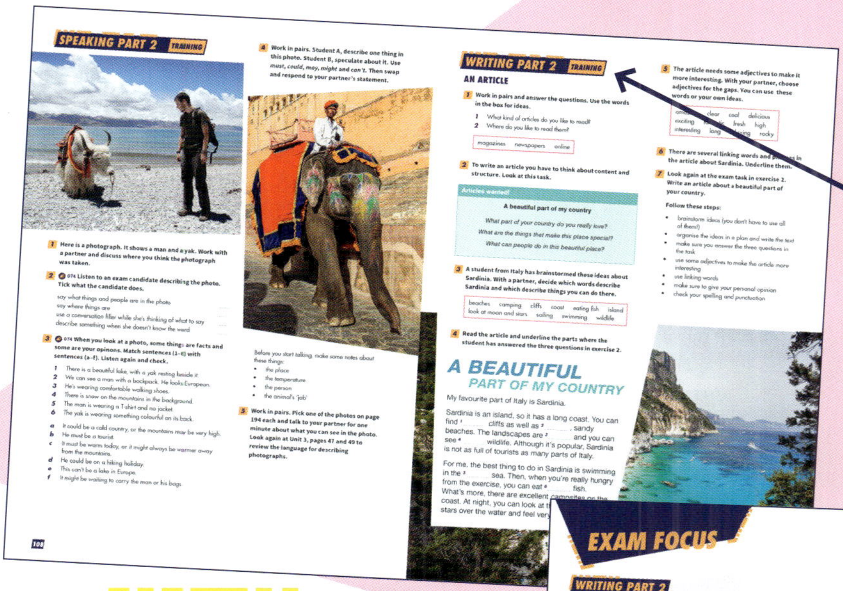

EXAM TRAINING

'Training' exam tasks provide guidance and tips on each part of the exam

EXAM CHECKS

test what you remember about the exam

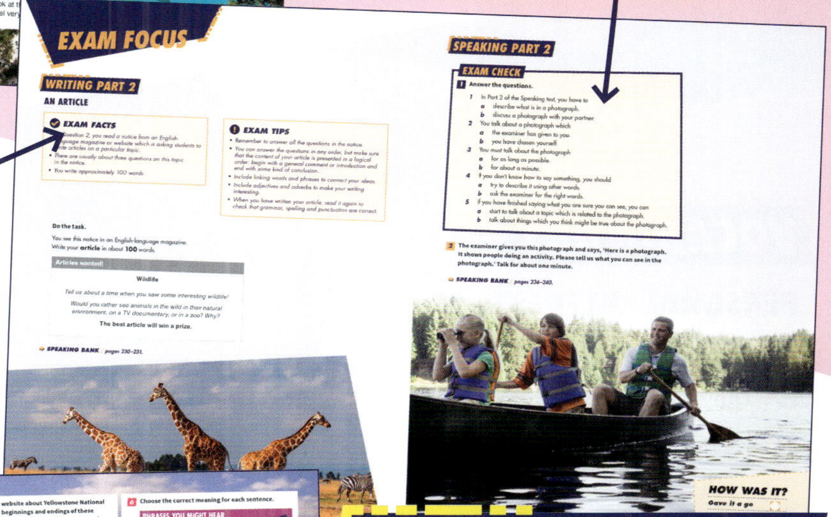

EXAM FOCUS

Read exam tips and facts and do two complete practice exam tasks after every unit

REAL WORLD

pages take you outside the classroom and into the real world

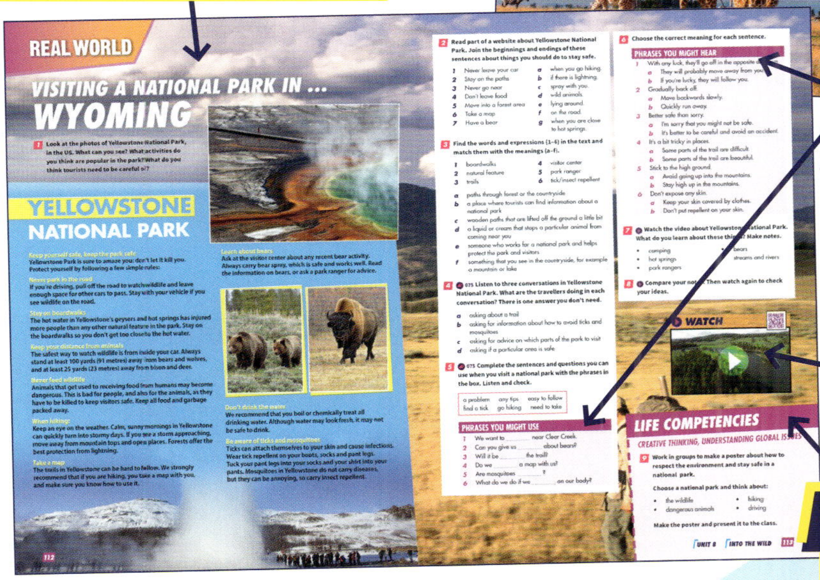

PHRASES YOU MIGHT USE AND HEAR

Learn and practise phrases you might use and hear when you are using English in the real world

Scan the QR codes to watch videos of different locations around the world on your mobile phone or tablet

LIFE COMPETENCIES

Develop important skills, knowledge and attitudes that you can use in your daily life

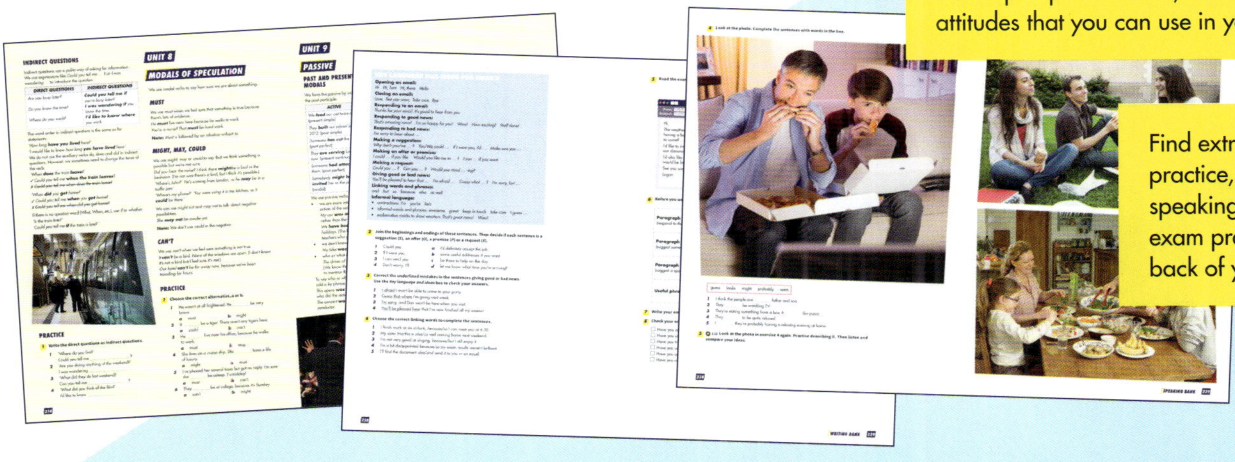

Find extra grammar practice, and extra speaking and writing exam practice at the back of your book

S PERSONAL PROFILE

A

VOCABULARY

PERSONAL INTERESTS

1 **Look at the photos. What interests and activities do they show?**

2 **Read the article and match the words in purple with the photos.**

3 **Work in groups and write down as many personal interests and hobbies as you can in two minutes.**

4 **Read the sentence and complete the rule.**

*I really enjoy listen**ing** to music, but I don't like danc**ing**.*

> To say how we feel about an activity, we can use ***like/love/enjoy***, etc. and a verb with ....

5 **What types of blog are you interested in and why?**

TELLING YOUR STORIES, SHARING YOUR TALENTS

Blogs. So many people write them and even more people read them, but why?

Some people write a blog just for their friends and family. Maybe they want to share stories about their hobbies, such as dancing or music. Other bloggers want more readers and choose popular topics. For example, **travel** blogs or blogs about **sports** and fitness are often interesting for a lot of people. For some writers, blogging is a full-time occupation. Many blogs, about **fashion** or cooking for example, appear quickly in online search results and really make money. **Arts and crafts** blogs can also be successful. If you can make things yourself, why not show other people how to do that? A blog is a great way to share your talents!

B

C

D

READING

1 **Read the blog entry and write the word which best fits in the gap.**

every in my of to with

2 **Work in groups and discuss the questions.**

1 Do you think Martina's life is unusual?
2 Would you like to have her life?

A day in the life of a blogger

Hello! I'm Martina, an IT student. I share a nice little flat [1] ________ some good friends, and I'm a blogger in my spare time.

Lectures at university usually start at nine o'clock, but I get up at five. I make a cup [2] ________ coffee and check my emails and all my other messages. Then I start to write. Why do I get up so early? I just love this quiet time. It's half past five now, and I'm sitting at my desk and feeling very happy.

I have a shower and then have breakfast at about eight o'clock. Then I go to university and I forget about my blog until 5 p.m. A lot of young people hang out with their friends [3] ________ the evenings. Not me. I never go out during the week. I have to work! I read and write for the whole evening, but I don't go to bed late.

My friends are always telling me I should go out more, but during the holidays, I'm out all the time. My blog is a travel blog and I go out [4] ________ day when I'm travelling.

It's the autumn term now, and I'm not travelling. So what am I writing? I'm creating pages on my blog that give people useful tips. I want [5] ________ tell everyone how to have a wonderful holiday in [6] ________ favourite places. Eventually, I'd like to be a full-time blogger.

VOCABULARY

HABITS AND ROUTINES

1 **Look at the vocabulary. Put the words in the correct columns for you.**

eat out get up go to school/work/college
hang out with have a shower/bath
have breakfast/lunch/dinner make lunch/dinner
meet up work out

EVERY DAY	MOST DAYS	SOMETIMES
get up	*go to college*	*eat out*

2 **Complete the sentences with the correct form of the phrasal verbs and collocations from exercise 1. You don't need to use all the words.**

1 George cooks a lot at home, but he ________ when he is on holiday.
2 I sometimes wake up early, but I never ________ before nine o'clock.
3 Julie ________ her friends all day every Saturday.
4 Let's ________ on Friday afternoon. We could go to the cinema or just have a coffee together.
5 Lou and Fiona ________ at the gym three times a week.

3 **Now tell your classmates three 'facts' about your daily or weekly routine. One of them is not true.**

I usually get up at five o'clock in the morning.

I eat out with my friends on Friday evenings.

I play ice hockey every weekend.

Your classmates ask questions until they can guess which 'fact' is not true.

Why do you get up so early?

What restaurant do you go to?

Where do you play ice hockey?

GRAMMAR

PRESENT SIMPLE AND PRESENT CONTINUOUS

GRAMMAR ON THE MOVE
Watch the video

1 **Match the sentences (1–3) with the descriptions (a–c), then complete the rules.**

1 *Martina **gets up** early.*
2 *She**'s creating** information pages for her blog.*
3 *She**'s sitting** at her desk and feeling very happy.*

a It's happening right now.
b It's a temporary activity.
c It's a habit.

> We use the present [1] .... to talk about habits and things that are generally true.
> We use the present [2] .... to talk about things that are happening now or around now.
> We use the present [3] .... to talk about temporary activity.

2 **Look at Martina's blog on page 9. Find a question in the present simple and a question in the present continuous. Complete the rules.**

> For questions in the present simple, we use [1] .... or [2] .... + **the subject** + **the main verb**.
> For questions in the present continuous, we use a form of the verb [3] .... + **the subject** + **the main verb with -ing**.

3 **Complete the questions. Use the present simple or present continuous and the verb in brackets.**

1 What .... you .... ? (do)
I'm a student.
2 Where .... Toby .... ? (work)
In an office in the city centre.
3 It's Sunday. Why .... Sue .... today? (work)
Because she's preparing for a meeting tomorrow.
4 Who .... Emma .... coffee with? (have)
She's having coffee with friends.

4 **Look at Martina's blog again. Find a negative sentence in the present simple and a negative sentence in the present continuous. Complete these sentences with *isn't* or *doesn't*.**

1 Martina .... go to bed late.
2 She .... travelling at the moment.

> In the present simple, we use ***don't*** or ***doesn't*** to make negative sentences.
> In the present continuous, we use ***isn't*** and ***aren't*** in negative sentences.

➜ ***GRAMMAR REFERENCE*** / *page 196.*

5 **Complete the interview with another blogger. Use the present simple or present continuous.**

Reporter: Joey, you're 18 and you've just finished school. Are you a full-time blogger now?
Joey: Yes! I [1] .... (write) about celebrity sports people.
Reporter: But it's not really a job, is it? How [2] .... (you/earn) money with your blogs?
Joey: It *is* a job, and I earn money when I recommend sports products, for example. At the moment I [3] .... (not earn) a lot of money, but I have a plan. I [4] .... (work) on an amazing new blog.
Reporter: Exciting! So, you write about sports celebrities. [5] .... (you/interview) them?
Joey: It's hard to get interviews. Some sports people [6] .... (not/understand) that it's good to talk to bloggers. The blogging world [7] .... (get) bigger and popular blogs are really important nowadays.

6 **Discuss in pairs. Is blogging a real job? Do you know anyone who writes a blog?**

VOCABULARY

OCCUPATIONS

1 **Match each photo (A–F) with an occupation in the box and the description of what the person does (1–6).**

chef	gardener	hairdresser	mechanic
police officer	sales assistant		

1 She tries to stop crime and make the streets safe.
2 He cuts and styles hair.
3 She cooks at a restaurant.
4 She works in a garden.
5 He repairs cars.
6 He works in a shop.

2 002 **Listen to a man talking about his day at work. What do you think his job is?**

3 **Now think of a job. Make some notes and then tell your classmates about your day. They guess your job.**

LISTENING

1 003 **Look at the photos below. Do you know who these people are? Listen and write the first name and surname of the celebrity in each information panel.**

2 **Can you spell the names? Check with your partner and then with the teacher.**

How do you spell … ?

I think it's …

3 004 **Now listen to the profile of each celebrity and write the information. Listen again and check.**

1 First name:
2 Surname:
3 Occupation: *gymnast*
4 Date of birth:
5 Place of birth:
6 Nationality: *Belizean and …*
7 Siblings:
8 Interests:

1 First name:
2 Surname:
3 Occupation:
4 Nationality:
5 Date of birth:
6 Place of birth:
7 Siblings:
8 Interests:

4 **Work in pairs. Write a short profile of a celebrity from your country. Read it to your partner, but don't say the person's name. Can they guess who the celebrity is?**

GRAMMAR

ADVERBS OF FREQUENCY

GRAMMAR ON THE MOVE
Watch the video

1 **Look at these sentences and answer the questions.**

*Lectures at university **usually** start at nine o'clock.*
*I **never** tell reporters about my plans!*
*A blogger's life is **sometimes** hard.*

1 Where does the adverb of frequency usually go in a sentence?
2 Where does it go if the verb is *be*?

2 **Put the words in the box on the line in the correct order.**

~~always~~	hardly ever	~~never~~	
often	rarely	~~sometimes~~	usually

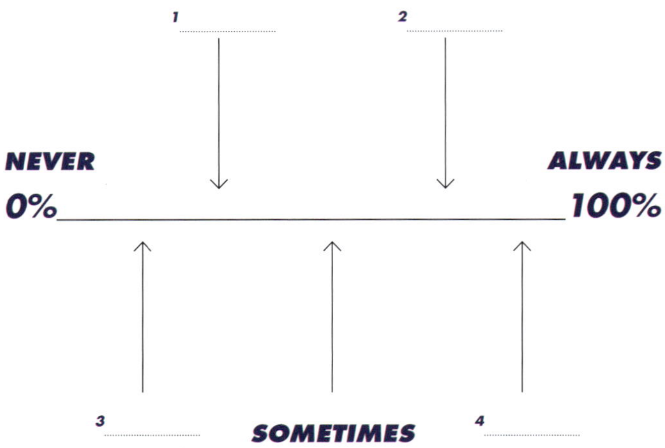

3 **What's true for you? Complete the sentences with adverbs of frequency.**

1 I .... get up before six o'clock.
2 I .... have breakfast before I go out.
3 I .... go to school/university/work by bus.
4 I .... have time to relax in the afternoons.
5 My friends .... visit me at home.
6 We .... hang out together in the evenings.

4 **Work in pairs. Ask three questions each about your partner's habits. Use *How often ... ?* or *When ... usually ... ?***

How often do you usually go to the cinema?

I hardly ever go to the cinema.

PRESENT CONTINUOUS WITH *ALWAYS*

5 **Read the sentences and complete the rule.**

*Mark is **always** talk**ing** about himself.*
*My friends are **always** tell**ing** me I should go out more.*

To say that something happens too often, and that we don't like it, we can use the present [1] .... with ***always***. We put ***always*** between **be** and the [2] .... with ***-ing***.

➔ ***GRAMMAR REFERENCE*** / *pages 197–198.*

6 **Write sentences using the present continuous and *always*.**

1 I / always / forget / my telephone number.
2 My sister / always / take / my phone.
3 Our teacher / always / give / us extra homework.
4 He / always / complain / about my work.

7 **Tell the class about a person who is always doing something that you don't like.**

My brother is always complaining about food.

WRITING

A PERSONAL PROFILE

1 **Imagine you are starting to write your own blog. You need to write a short profile of yourself on the *About Me* page.**

Include

- your name, age, nationality and occupation
- some information about your everyday routines
- some information about your interests and things you love doing

Begin like this:

Hello! My name .... Welcome to my blog.

SPEAKING

INTRODUCING YOURSELF

1 **Work in pairs and discuss the questions.**

1. When do you introduce yourself with your first name only?
2. When do you tell people your first name and your surname?
3. When do you say 'Nice to meet you'?
4. What are some simple answers to 'How are you?'

2 **Choose the topics you think are good for small talk when you meet a new person.**

your school/university/job
your problems
people you both know
music/TV shows/films that you like
politics
your hobbies

3 **005 Listen to two women talking at a party and tick the expressions that you hear.**

Nice to meet you. ....
How are you? ....
Where are you from? ....
Really? ....
Me too. ....
What do you do? ....
I agree. ....
Do you like …-ing? ....
That sounds interesting. ....

> *Intonation* is the way our voices go up and down when we speak. If your intonation is very flat, you don't sound interested.

4 **P INTONATION 006**
You will hear three short dialogues twice. In which dialogue does the second speaker, Sam, sound interested? Tick *a* or *b*.

1. ***Karen:*** I go swimming every morning.
   Sam: Really?
   a ☐ ***b*** ☐
2. ***Karen:*** I think everyone should have a hobby.
   Sam: I agree.
   a ☐ ***b*** ☐
3. ***Karen:*** I love watching winter sports on TV.
   Sam: Me too.
   a ☐ ***b*** ☐

5 **Work in pairs. You and your partner are at a party. You don't know each other, but you want to start talking. Role-play the conversation. Begin like this:**

Hi! I'm … . What's your name?

1 GETTING AWAY

VOCABULARY

HOLIDAY ACTIVITIES

1 **What are the people in the photos doing? Match the photos (A–D) with the activities in the box.**

buying souvenirs	hiking	sightseeing
sunbathing	taking photos	

2 007 **Listen to some people talking about holiday activities. Which photo is each person talking about? There is one photo you don't need.**

3 **How many of these things do you do when you are on holiday?**

4 **Do the quiz.**

5 **Ask your partner the questions from the quiz, then ask some of your own questions. Are you the same kind of holidaymaker?**

What kind of places do you like to explore on holiday?

Quiz: What kind of holidaymaker are you?

1 When you're packing to go on holiday, what do you like to take?
- ***a*** a good book to read
- ***b*** plenty of party clothes
- ***c*** strong walking shoes

2 What's your ideal way of spending time when you're on holiday?
- ***a*** lying next to the swimming pool
- ***b*** playing games or sports with friends
- ***c*** discovering exciting places

3 Where do you like to eat when you're on holiday abroad?
- ***a*** at your hotel
- ***b*** in a lively café
- ***c*** at a restaurant which serves unusual local dishes

4 In most of your holiday photos, what are you doing?
- ***a*** sunbathing
- ***b*** dancing
- ***c*** exploring

➡ *Turn to page 192 to find out what kind of holidaymaker you are!*

READING PART 2 TRAINING

1 **Read about two friends, Lauren and Abby, and think about the three things which they want in orange. Then look at the phrases in orange in the descriptions of the six holiday destinations (A–F). Which holiday best matches what the friends want?**

1 Lauren and Abby love to relax on the beach when the weather is hot. They also enjoy shopping for clothes. When it gets dark, they want to go somewhere they can dance.

ANSWER: E

Options B, C and D each have only one of the things that Lauren and Abby want. Only option E has all three things. Now read about a couple called Birgit and Oscar, and look at the texts with the words in blue.

2 Birgit and Oscar are fond of the countryside and like to go hiking when they are on holiday. They also want to find some interesting souvenirs.

ANSWER: ....

Do you think the correct answer is B, D or F? Or another option? Why? Which option has everything that they want? Underline the phrases in this option which have the same meanings as the blue words in the text above.

Now answer questions 3 and 4. Underline the three things which the people want, and for each question, choose the correct answer.

3 Tomasz and Marta are interested in sightseeing. They want to go somewhere that's suitable for their small children and where they can buy food to cook their own meals.

ANSWER: ....

4 Ricardo and Paolo would like to do some watersports and meet new people. They're also keen to try some typical dishes from the region.

ANSWER: ....

2 **Which of these people are most similar to you? Which people like to do the same things as you on holiday?**

HOLIDAY DESTINATIONS BY THE SEA

A St Lucy's Bay

This pretty spot is popular with painters, photographers and anyone who loves nature, and the green hills and valleys around the bay are ideal for walkers. Don't forget to visit the artists' shops on the waterfront where you can buy food, drinks and some unusual gifts to take home made out of local rocks and stones.

B Blackstowe

Anyone who likes being active on holiday will love it here. There's something for everyone – sailing, windsurfing and waterskiing on the sea, and hiking, cycling and horseriding up on the cliffs. If you like dancing and getting to know new people, there's a party every night on the beach.

C Westhaven

The beach club here is a great place to make friends from all over the world, and both children and adults can learn how to surf, windsurf and dive with the club's qualified instructors. Or, if you prefer, you can just relax on the sunny beach. The restaurants here are famous for their traditional local cooking – not to be missed!

D Helmston-on-Sea

This village has everything you need, including a café, a grocery store selling local fruit, vegetables and fresh fish, and another shop where you can get beach clothes, watersports equipment, and some great souvenirs. The beach is quiet and safe for all the family. It's also the perfect spot for exploring the castles and interesting historic places in the area.

E Capstone Cove

If you're looking for fun, this is the place for you. The nightlife and music are fantastic, with nightclubs and discos open until the early hours. In the daytime, why not go and sunbathe on the soft sand by the edge of the sea? There's also a market where you can buy food and drink, as well as all the latest fashions.

F Swanmouth

This 17th-century town on the coast is the ideal destination for culture lovers. Take a sightseeing trip around the historic centre, and then relax at one of the waterside cafés and taste the delicious fish dishes that this region is famous for. The surrounding countryside is also well worth a visit.

GRAMMAR

COMPARATIVES AND SUPERLATIVES

GRAMMAR ON THE MOVE
Watch the video

1 008 **Listen to a couple, Emma and Tim, talking about travelling from London to Edinburgh. How are they going to travel?**

2 008 **Listen again. Which type of transport is:**

1 the fastest? ....
2 the slowest? ....
3 the cheapest? ....
4 the most expensive? ....
5 the greenest? ....

> **Superlatives**
> Use ***-est*** with short adjectives and adverbs of one syllable, e.g. ***slow/fast → the slowest/the fastest***
> Use ***the most*** with adjectives and adverbs of more than one syllable, e.g. ***expensive/slowly → the most expensive/the most slowly***

3 Choose the correct words to complete these sentences.

1 Tim thinks it is *easy/easier* to drive than to go by public transport.
2 It is *more/most* expensive to buy two train tickets than to drive.
3 You can travel more *quickly/quicker* by train than by car.
4 Emma says it's *better/best* for the environment to go by train than by car or plane.

> **Comparatives**
> Use ***-er*** with short adjectives and adverbs of one syllable, e.g. ***quick/fast → quicker/faster*** + ***than***
> Use ***more*** with adjectives and adverbs of more than one syllable, e.g. ***expensive/quickly → more expensive/more quickly*** + ***than***

4 Complete these sentences. Use a comparative or a superlative of the adjective or adverb in brackets.

1 Milan is .... than Edinburgh. (big)
2 What's .... city in your country? (large)
3 Can you speak .... please? (slowly)
4 That's .... car journey I've ever had. (bad)
5 I prefer this car to the other one. It's .... (comfortable)
6 Our hotel was .... than the others in the town. (good)
7 Please talk .... I'm trying to work. (quietly)
8 Pietro plays tennis .... than I do. (well)

5 Look at the sentences below and choose the correct option to complete the rules (1–3).

The journey by car is ***less expensive than*** *the journey by plane.*
The journey by car is ***not as expensive as*** *the journey by plane.*
The journey by car is ***as long as*** *the journey by train.*

> 1 We use ***less … than*** to say something is *a smaller amount/the same.*
> 2 We use ***not as … as*** to say something is *a different amount/the same.*
> 3 We use ***as … as*** to say something is *a different amount/the same.*

→ **GRAMMAR REFERENCE** / *pages 199–201.*

REVIEWS

We spent three great days in Salzburg. **Although** the train journey was quite expensive, it was fast **and** comfortable. Our hotel was comfortable, **too**. The castle is so interesting, and it is **also** good value for money. **What's more**, there's a beautiful view from it. **As well as** visiting the castle, Mozart's birthplace and the Mirabel Gardens, we went to Salzburg Zoo. It's a long way from the city centre, **but** it is definitely worth a visit. We'd really recommend Salzburg to anyone who likes lively historic cities. Take warm clothes, **though**. It can be cold in Austria!

5,853 reviews

WRITING

A REVIEW

1 **Read a review of a trip to Salzburg. Did the reviewer enjoy the trip?**

2 **Look at the words and phrases in purple in the text. Which ones add more information, and which ones show a contrast?**

3 **Complete the sentences using the linking words in the review.**

The flight to New York was very long, [1]b______ we watched a couple of movies, so it wasn't too boring. [2]A______ the city is very large, the transport system is cheap [3]a______ reliable. [4]W______ , you can get a city card, which gives you a discount on museum entry and city transport. [5]A______ visiting all the famous sights in New York, we did lots of shopping and watched a show on Broadway, [6]t______ . The clothes shops are great and they are [7]a______ cheaper than at home. I didn't like some of the cafés, [8]t______ . The tea and coffee were a bit weak.

4 **Now write a review of a trip you have made. Use these linking words and phrases in your review.**

VOCABULARY

EASILY CONFUSED TRAVEL WORDS

Let's talk about our **trip** to Edinburgh next month.

I really want to take a **tour** of Edinburgh castle.

What about **transport**? How shall we go?

Air **travel** costs a lot.

The **journey** will take us at least seven hours.

1 **Look at the speech bubbles and use the words in bold to complete these sentences.**

1. Would you rather go on a weekend ______ to a city or to the countryside?
2. What's the best type of ______ to use to get across your city?
3. When you visit a new place, would you rather take an organised ______ or explore it by yourself?
4. What's the longest ______ that you have ever been on?
5. Would you like to have a job which involves some foreign ______ ?

2 **Work in pairs and discuss the questions in exercise 1.**

GRAMMAR

SO AND SUCH, TOO AND ENOUGH

GRAMMAR ON THE MOVE
Watch the video

1 **Read these online reviews of three hotels. Which has the best food? Which is the smallest? Which has the worst service?**

2 **009 Listen to Emma and Tim talking about hotels. Which one of the reviewed hotels will they choose? Why?**

3 **Read the sentences and complete the rules with *too*, *enough*, *so* and *such*.**

*If we book early **enough**, we can get cheaper tickets.*
*I hate it when you can't get **enough** sleep at night.*
*I guess it's not **so** important.*
*We shouldn't stay anywhere that's **too** far from a station.*
*The city centre has **such** great places to eat.*

> ***so* and *such***
> Use [1] .... (a/an) before an adjective + noun and [2] .... before an adjective without a noun.
>
> ***too* and *enough***
> Use [3] .... before an adjective without a noun and [4] .... before a noun or after a verb or adjective.

→ **GRAMMAR REFERENCE** / *page 201.*

4 **Choose the correct words to complete these sentences.**

1. I'm *enough/so* excited about going on holiday!
2. They decided not to drive because it was *such/too* a long journey.
3. Did you have *enough/such* time to visit the museum?
4. If it's warm *such/enough* we can go swimming in the sea.
5. Our bags won't be *too/enough* heavy to carry.
6. It was *such/too* far to walk.

5 **Complete the sentences about the hotel reviews using *so*, *such*, *too* and *enough*.**

1. Guests say that the food at Campbell House is .... good.
2. Visitors think that Campbell House is .... noisy to stay in.
3. Visitors think that Drumcraig Lodge is .... a friendly hotel.
4. The service isn't good .... at Hotel Glenross.
5. The Hotel Glenross is .... far for guests to walk to from the city centre.

Hotel Glenross

10 km from city centre 42 rooms

Comfort ★★★★★ Service ★★ Food ★★★★

It's really comfortable here. The food's nice, but it's a shame the service isn't very good.

●●●◐○ 853 reviews

Campbell House

1 km from city centre 75 rooms

Comfort ★★★ Service ★★★★ Food ★★★★★

The food is fantastic, and the service is good, too. Unfortunately it's on a busy road so you can hear the traffic.

●●●◐○ 573 reviews

Drumcraig Lodge

3 km from city centre 20 rooms

Comfort ★★★★ Service ★★★ Food ★★

This is a friendly hotel, and it's also lovely and quiet. We were disappointed with the food, though.

●●●○○ 763 reviews

6 **When you go on holiday, do you like to stay in hotels? Why? / Why not?**

7 **P *TOO* AND *TO* 010**
Listen to these words. Do they sound the same or different?

too to

8 **P 011 Now listen to this sentence. Which word is shorter when it's in a sentence – *too* or *to*?**

It's too far to drive.

9 **P 012 Listen and repeat these sentences. Pay attention to the correct pronunciation of *too* and *to*.**

It's too small to stay in.
It's too far from the city centre.
Do you want to go by car?
That's not too bad.

LISTENING

1 **What do you know about the island of Madagascar? Look at the photos (A–C) and match them with the landscapes.**

rainforest ....
high and mountainous ....
dry and rocky ....

A

2 **Work in pairs. What do you think tourists can do there? What do you think the weather is like?**

B

3 **013 Listen to a student talking about her trip to Madagascar. Match the photos with the different parts of the island in the box. There is one you don't need.**

the south	the northwest
the centre	the east

C

4 **013 Listen again and decide if the sentences are true or false.**

1. The island has three seasons.
2. The climate in Madagascar varies according to which part of the island you're in.
3. It's warm and wet in the south of the island.
4. It's very cold in the northwest.
5. There are lots of rainforests on the east coast.
6. The centre of the island has got mountains.

5 **Work in pairs. Would you like to go to Madagascar? Which part would you like to go to? Why?**

VOCABULARY

WEATHER

1 **Match the words in the box with the meanings below.**

breeze	chilly	climate	cool	damp
dull	fine	humid	lightning	showers

1. not so warm
2. short periods of rain
3. a light wind
4. the weather conditions that an area usually has
5. not sunny
6. hot and slightly wet weather or air
7. pleasant and dry
8. a sudden flash of light in the sky during a storm
9. quite cold
10. rather wet conditions that are cold or unpleasant

2 **Complete the sentences with five of the words from exercise 1.**

1. In the afternoon, there are storms with thunder and ....
2. There are also heavy .... in the afternoon.
3. The most interesting thing about Madagascar's .... is the incredible variety.
4. Because the weather is so .... , there are thick rainforests in this part of the island.
5. It's fairly .... between May and September, with temperatures falling to around 15 or 16°C.

3 **Complete the weather forecast below with the other five words from exercise 1.**

And now for tomorrow's weather forecast for the Auckland region of New Zealand. It's going to rain heavily in the early hours, so there'll be a [1] .... start to the day. There's also going to be a cold wind, so it'll feel quite [2] .... , with temperatures of only around 5 or 6°C. The clouds are going to be around all morning, which means that it will stay rather grey and [3] .... until around midday. But after that, the sun's going to come out, and it's going to be a [4] .... , bright afternoon. Those cold winds will change to just a gentle [5] .... , and it will feel quite pleasant for the time of year.

4 **What is the weather like where you are today?**

PUSH YOURSELF B2

VOCABULARY: ENVIRONMENT

1 **What global problems can be caused by travel and tourism? Do you know what 'green tourism' is?**

2 **Read this text about green tourism, and then complete the sentences below using the words in green.**

GREEN TOURISM

How can you see the world without damaging the environment?
Here are some tips on being an eco-tourist:

Travelling:

Try to keep your **carbon footprint** small by avoiding unnecessary air and car travel.

This helps to:

- reduce the amount of **fossil fuels** burned
- limit the level of **climate change**

At your destination:

- buy products that are locally produced and **environmentally friendly**
- support the **conservation** of the local environment
- try to limit the amount of **waste** that you leave behind

1. Gas, coal and oil are types of ....
2. Things which don't harm the planet are ....
3. .... is a way of protecting nature.
4. Unwanted things which we throw away are ....
5. A person's .... is the amount of CO_2 produced by their lifestyle.
6. .... is the way that the Earth's weather is changing.

3 **Work in pairs and discuss the questions. Do you try to be an eco-tourist? Do you think they are good tips? Can you think of more?**

DID YOU KNOW?

*British English speakers say **holiday** to talk about long summer breaks and enjoyable trips away from home. American English speakers say **vacation**. They use the word **holiday** only to talk about days off work or school for celebrations such as Christmas and Independence Day.*

SPEAKING PART 3 TRAINING

MAKING SUGGESTIONS, ASKING FOR OPINIONS, AGREEING AND DISAGREEING

1 **Where do people go for weekend breaks in your country? What kind of things can visitors do there?**

2 **014 Listen to two candidates discussing the most suitable place for a weekend trip away for teenagers. Answer the questions.**

1. Do the candidates sound interested? Why?
2. Does the woman make suggestions?
3. Does the man respond to the woman's ideas?

3 **014 Listen to the conversation again and tick the phrases you hear.**

....	....	....	....
I think they'd enjoy going to …	What do you think?	Yes, you're right.	Sorry, but I don't agree (with you).
I think they should go to …	What's your opinion?	I agree (with you).	Do you think so?
Perhaps they could go to …	Do you agree?	That's true.	Really?
I think the … . is the best place for them to go.		I think that's a great idea.	I'm afraid I disagree (with you).
They might like going to …			

4 **Put the headings below in the correct column in exercise 3.**

agreeing asking for an opinion
disagreeing making a suggestion

5 **Complete the sentences using words in exercise 3.**

1. They .... like going to the city.
2. I'm afraid I don't .... with you. I think cities are too noisy for young children.
3. I think that's .... They'll love swimming in the sea.
4. I think the countryside is the best place for them to go. Do .... ?

6 **A family with two children want to go away for a weekend trip. Here are some places they could go to. Talk together about the different places they could go, and say which would be most suitable for them.**

Make sure you give reasons for your opinions, and use some of the phrases from exercise 3 during the conversation.

SPEAKING PART 4 TRAINING

In Speaking Part 4 the examiner will ask you some questions on the same topic as Part 3.

7 015 **Match the questions with the candidate answers and reasons. Then listen and check.**

QUESTIONS	ANSWERS	REASONS
1 Do you like holidays in the city or at the seaside?	I'd rather go on holiday with my family than with my friends	because I love shopping and visiting museums.
2 What's your ideal holiday destination?	I prefer holidays in the city	because I really enjoy dancing.
3 Do you prefer to go on holiday with your family or with friends?	Autumn is my favourite time of year to go on holiday	because the weather might be cold and wet.
4 What time of year do you like to go on holiday?	I like the countryside, but I'd rather stay in a hotel than a tentv	because I prefer cooler weather and there aren't so many people.
5 What do you think about camping holidays in the countryside?	My ideal holiday destination is somewhere lively that has good nightlife	because we have a lot of fun together.

8 **Now work in groups of three. One of you is the examiner and the other two are candidates. Take turns to ask and answer the questions below.**

Do you enjoy holidays at the seaside or in the mountains?
What's your favourite holiday destination?
Who do you like to go on holiday with?
What time of year would you rather go on holiday? Why?
What kind of accommodation do you prefer to stay in? Why?

EXAM FOCUS

READING PART 2

For each question, choose the correct answer.
The people (1–5) below are going to visit Paris, and are looking for a guidebook to the city.
Below are reviews of eight guidebooks (A–H).
Decide which guidebook would be the most suitable for the people.

A **SEE PARIS** This is a great guidebook if you want tips from local people about where to eat out and go shopping, as well as helpful information about places suitable for disabled visitors. And with its clear descriptions of the contents of famous museums and art galleries, it is especially good for lovers of culture.

B **PARIS ... AND MORE** If you're going to Paris for only a few days, but don't want to miss anything, this guidebook is ideal. There are tours suitable for everyone, including families and children, as well as the elderly. You'll also find restaurant suggestions – however much or little you want to spend. And for those with more time, there are also ideas for trips outside the city.

C **PARIS: A VISITOR'S HANDBOOK** This guidebook contains some excellent walking tours, together with information about the city's history and information on when to visit its attractions at a discount or for free. There's also a section with basic words and phrases to help you communicate in French, as well as some detailed maps.

D **GUIDE TO PARIS** Whatever recommendations you need – restaurants, concert halls or clothes stores – you'll find them here. And anyone who needs to travel around Paris, on foot, by public transport or car, will find this book very helpful. There's also useful information about places to visit in the areas surrounding Paris.

E **PARIS FOR EVERYONE** The author of this guide is a travel writer who uses a wheelchair, so there's plenty of information for visitors who want to know which locations they can access, including tips on accommodation, transport and sightseeing. And for anyone who wants to practise speaking with locals, the book includes some excellent language tips.

F **TRAVELLERS' PARIS** This guidebook is highly recommended, whether you're visiting Paris to buy designer clothes, look at famous paintings, eat fine food, learn the French language, or just walk around looking at the sights. It also includes some useful advice about driving in the city centre.

G **PARIS, CITY OF LIGHTS** Written by an architecture expert, this will tell you everything you need to know about Paris from ancient Roman times up to the present. There are suggestions of tours taking in all the main sights, suitable for the longest or the shortest of trips, along with tips to help you find good food, good music and all the latest fashions.

H **ALL ABOUT PARIS** You'll find everything you need to know here about getting around by bus and underground (metro). There are suggestions for activities for every age group. It also has lots of information about where to stay, from simple student hostels to the finest hotels – there's something for everyone.

EXAM FACTS

- *You read five descriptions of people (Questions 1–5).*
- *You also read eight descriptions of places or things (Options A–H).*
- *You have to match each question with one of the eight options.*

EXAM TIPS

- *Read the questions carefully, and underline all the different things that the people require. Each person will have three requirements.*
- *Read the options quickly and look for words and phrases which have the same meaning as those which you have underlined or highlighted.*
- *For each person/profile, find the option which matches all their requirements. Remember that this option will probably not have the same words as the question. It will contain the same information, but will use different words and phrases.*

1 Jack is a student, so he wants to spend as little money as possible in Paris, and would like to explore the city on foot. He's also keen to learn a little French to speak to local people.

2 Emily is looking for things to do in Paris with her six-year-old daughter. She needs to choose some accommodation, and would also like to know how to use the city's public transport.

3 Ray wants to visit Paris with his wife Carole, who uses a wheelchair. They want a guidebook that recommends good restaurants as well as giving details about well-known paintings on display.

4 Ali wants to know about driving in Paris and about making trips outside the city. He'd also like suggestions about the best places to listen to music.

5 Katarina wants to see as much as possible of Paris in just two days. She'd like to discover about the history of the city, and also wants some ideas on where to buy stylish clothes and shoes.

SPEAKING PART 3

EXAM FACTS

- *The examiner describes a situation to you and shows you some pictures.*
- *You have to discuss your views and opinions with another student.*
- *You will need to make suggestions and reply to the suggestions which the other student makes.*

EXAM TIPS

- *Look at and talk to the other student, not the examiner.*
- *Show interest in what the other student says, and respond to his or her ideas.*
- *At the end of the conversation, you should either agree or agree to disagree with the other student.*

A group of students are on holiday together and they want to spend a day in the countryside.
Here are some things which they could do.
Talk together about the different activities they could do, and say which would be most interesting for them.

➡ ***SPEAKING BANK*** / ***pages 241–242.***

SPEAKING PART 4

EXAM FACTS

- *The examiner asks you questions about the same topic as in Part 3.*
- *You need to talk for about three minutes.*

EXAM TIPS

- *Don't worry too much about making mistakes.*
- *Remember you don't always need to tell the truth – just try to keep talking and give reasons for your answers.*

In pairs, ask and answer the questions below. Take turns.

1. Do you like spending time in the countryside?
2. If you go into the countryside, what do you like doing there?
3. Do you prefer to relax or be active when you're on holiday?
4. What sports do you like doing when you're on holiday?
5. Are there any sports or outdoor activities which you would like to try?
6. Do you think it is important for young people to do sports and outdoor activities in their free time?

➡ ***SPEAKING BANK*** / ***page 243.***

HOW WAS IT?

- ***Gave it a go*** ☐
- ***Getting there*** ☐
- ***Aced it!*** ☐

REAL WORLD

WHERE CAN I STAY IN ... AUCKLAND?

1 **Who do you usually go on holiday with? What kind of accommodation do you usually stay in when you are away? What are the advantages of this kind of accommodation?**

2 **Look at the photos of types of accommodation in New Zealand and read the tourist information text. Match five of the types of accommodation with the photos.**

PLANNING YOUR STAY:

ACCOMMODATION TYPES IN NEW ZEALAND

HOSTELS

This kind of accommodation is great value if you just want a bed for the night. Hostels often provide information about their area, and are usually happy to book activities for you. Some hostels have single and double rooms, but most have just dormitories.

MOTELS

Motels are more common than hotels in New Zealand. Most rooms have a small kitchen and the rooms are usually en suite. They're a good place to stay if you're travelling by car, and you don't usually need to book ahead.

HOTELS

There aren't as many hotels in New Zealand as other countries, but you'll find something for all tastes, including luxury, boutique and historic hotels. Most offer single, double and twin rooms.

CAMPSITES

Campsites are an inexpensive way to stay in a place overnight, and they get you right into the beautiful landscape. Most places have shared kitchen and bathroom facilities, and there are usually barbecues too. A few even have swimming pools. Some campsites also have cabins or lodges to stay in if you don't have a tent.

BED AND BREAKFASTS AND HOMESTAYS

These allow you to see how the local people live, often staying in very comfortable houses with extremely nice gardens. Breakfast is always included in the price, and many homestays also offer home-cooked evening meals with the family.

DOC HUTS

The Department of Conservation (DOC) looks after hundreds of huts in the countryside. You can stay in a basic hut for free, but some huts with more facilities charge a fee. They certainly aren't luxury accommodation – there aren't usually bathrooms or places to cook, bed sheets or even hot water. But you are close to nature. Booking is usually required.

APARTMENTS

Normally only available for a week at a time, not for single nights, you can really live and feel like a local person on holiday. They're great if you want a base to really explore an area, and you can also save money by cooking your own meals.

3 **Read the text again. Write the correct accommodation type for each sentence.**

1 There isn't usually a bathroom or kitchen. ....
2 You usually have to book for at least seven days. ....
3 Breakfast is already in the price you pay. ....
4 There are fewer of these in New Zealand than in other countries. ....
5 You can learn about the area you are staying in here. ....

4 **Look at the words in pink in the text. Match them with the meanings.**

1 a room for two people, with two separate beds
2 a room with its own bathroom and toilet
3 a room for one person
4 a large room where several people sleep
5 a room for two people, with one large bed

5 **016 Listen to three conversations with tourists. Match each conversation (1–3) with what the person is doing (a–d). There is one answer you don't need.**

a arriving at a motel they have booked in advance
b asking about accommodation at a Tourist Information Office
c asking someone in the street about places to stay in a town
d phoning a hotel to book in advance

6 **016 Decide if the sentences are true or false. Then listen again and check.**

1 Queen Street Backpackers is in the city centre.
2 The hostel only has mixed dorms.
3 The rooms at the Auckland city hotel all have their own bathroom.
4 You have to pay more for breakfast at the hotel.
5 The room in the motel is en suite.

7 **Complete the sentences about accommodation with the correct words.**

booked for | by card | go for | how much | information on | looking for | price include | rooms available | sounds

PHRASES YOU MIGHT USE

1 Do you have any .... accommodation?
2 We're .... somewhere close to the city centre.
3 And .... is it?
4 That .... good. We'll .... that.
5 Do you have any .... for tonight?
6 Does the .... breakfast?
7 We've got a room .... tonight.
8 I'll pay ...., please.

8 **Match the sentences (1–6) with the meanings (a–f).**

PHRASES YOU MIGHT HEAR

1 If you could just fill in your details here.
2 Would you like to go ahead with that?
3 So, if I can just take your name?
4 I've got you down for a value twin room.
5 If you could just pop your card in there for me.
6 That's all gone through for you.

a You have booked a value twin room.
b Your card payment was successful.
c Please write your name, etc. here.
d Please put your bank card in this machine.
e Do you want to book the room?
f Please tell me your name.

9 **Watch the video about New Zealand. What do you learn about these things? Make notes.**

- the country
- wildlife
- camping
- hostels
- homestays
- motels

10 **Work in pairs and compare your notes. Then watch again to check your ideas. Would you like to try bungee jumping? Why? / Why not?**

WATCH

LIFE COMPETENCIES

EVALUATING IDEAS, UNDERSTANDING CULTURES

11 **Work in pairs to plan a trip. Think about:**

- the town, city or region you would like to visit
- the advantages of different types of accommodation
- the location of the accommodation

Tell the class about what you chose and why.

2 ENTERTAIN ME

SPEAKING

TALKING ABOUT LIKES AND DISLIKES

1 **It is Saturday evening. Where would you like to be? Look at the photos and rate them from 1 to 8.**

1 = that looks like a lot of fun
8 = that looks boring

2 **017 Listen to four people talking about what they did last Saturday night. Match each speaker with one of the photos (A–H).**

3 **017 Now complete the extracts. Then listen again and check.**

1. I can't [1] ________ big crowds, but last Saturday my favourite band played live in my town. I'm [2] ________ about their music so of course I went to see them.
2. Sometimes, I [3] ________ just staying in and relaxing. I'm really [4] ________ detective shows and this one is set in Copenhagen.
3. I'm comfortable on my sofa, and I don't [5] ________ having only a small screen. I'm not a [6] ________ of comedies.
4. Parties are not my [7] ________ , and I have to work on Sunday mornings. That's why I'm not [8] ________ about going out on Saturday nights, and I often stay at home with a good book.

4 **Complete the table with the phrases.**

I'm into …
I can't stand …
I don't mind …
I'm crazy about …
I'm not bothered about…
I'm not a fan of …
I really enjoy …
… is not my thing.

🙂	😐	😣

5 **Work in pairs and discuss why you like or don't like the activities in exercise 1. Use the phrases in exercise 4.**

> My number 1 is the concert, but for you it's number 6. Why do you dislike music?

> Oh, I really enjoy music, but concerts are not my thing. There are too many people …

6 **Tell the class about your partner.**

> Paul is into music, but his favourite thing here is watching a good TV series. He sometimes watches four or five episodes of his favourite series during a weekend.

READING

1 **Work in pairs and discuss these questions.**

1. How much TV do you watch?
2. How and where do you watch it?
3. Who do you watch TV with?

2 **Have you heard the word *binge-watching*? What do you think it means? Read the article and check.**

3 **Choose the best introduction to the article.**

A Lucy Drew explains why TV watching was much more fun in the past.

B Lucy Drew considers the advantages and disadvantages of modern TV habits.

C Lucy Drew tells readers about the benefits of watching TV series late at night.

4 **Look at the words in blue in the text and match them with these meanings.**

1. Information that tells you too much about a TV programme before you watch it.
2. Put something from the internet, for example a TV show, onto your phone or tablet.
3. A way of watching TV programmes after they were first on television.
4. One after the other, without a break.

5 **Decide if the sentences are true or false. Correct the false sentences.**

1. Lucy can choose when she wants to watch her favourite TV programmes.
2. When she was younger, she didn't watch the same TV programmes as her classmates.
3. She enjoyed talking to people about television.
4. Now she watches one episode of a series and then turns her tablet off.
5. She does not watch television as regularly as her parents.

6 **Write a paragraph about your TV-watching habits. Say whether your habits have changed and whether your habits are different from your parents' habits.**

Just one more episode ...

That's me in the photo. I should be in bed, but I'm enjoying a TV series on my tablet. This is the way I watch TV now. In some ways, it's much better than the way I used to watch just a few years ago. There are some great series now, and it doesn't matter if I miss a new episode. I can **download** several episodes and watch them **back to back** whenever I have time.

When I was younger, things were different. My friends and I used to watch the same things at the same times. For example, there was one series that we all watched on Thursday evenings. We didn't use to make plans for Thursdays because that was a TV night. When the week's episode was over, I used to phone my best friend and talk about it for hours. The next day, we discussed it with our friends at school. It was fun. Nowadays I can't talk about all the episodes I've seen because people hate **spoilers**!

What did we use to do if we couldn't be at home on a Thursday? We missed our favourite programme and that was annoying. I am so happy that we have **catch-up TV** now. However, there is a problem: binge-watching. I watch one episode of a series, and then I want to know what happens next. So, I watch one more, and then one more ... until I notice that it's very late and I *must* get some sleep. Late-night binge-watching is not a healthy habit.

So, were things better in the past? I'm not sure. My parents used to watch TV every evening. They always switched on the television after dinner. Personally, I think that's boring! I have other things to do, and watching TV is for when I am tired. I just have to make sure that I don't watch for too long.

GRAMMAR

USED TO

GRAMMAR ON THE MOVE
Watch the video

1 Look at these sentences and complete the rule.

*My friends and I **used to watch** the same things at the same times.*
*We **didn't use to make** plans for Thursdays because that was a TV night.*
*What **did** we **use to do** if we couldn't be at home on a Thursday?*

We use ________ + **verb** for talking about things that were true in the past but are not true now.
To make negative sentences or questions with ***used to***, we use ***did/didn't* + *use to***. The verb after ***used to/didn't use to*** is always in the infinitive form, without ***to***.

➜ **GRAMMAR REFERENCE** / *page 202.*

2 Complete this dialogue with *used to* or *did/didn't use to* and one of the verbs below.

enjoy sit tell watch

Mum: You never watch TV with me! When I was young, the whole family [1] ________ down together to watch TV.
Son: But [2] ________ you ________ the same programmes as your parents? Did you really all like the same things?
Mum: Well, we [3] ________ *everything* together, but a really good series is interesting for younger and older people.
Son: You aren't interested in the things I watch. I [4] ________ you about them, but you never listened.
Mum: Really? Sorry! Then tell me again now. What are you enjoying at the moment? Maybe I would like it too.

3 How have things changed in your family? Tell the class about something that your parents or grandparents used to do and that you don't do now.

My grandparents used to work on their parents' farm in the school holidays …

VOCABULARY

ENTERTAINMENT

1 What type of entertainment is each person talking about? Choose the correct word.

1. The atmosphere was great and everyone in the **audience** danced.
   a play a concert
2. I've watched five **episodes** but I still don't know who the killer is.
   a detective series a soap opera
3. It was such an exciting **thriller**, from the first page to the last.
   a book a film
4. Have you seen your favourite singer live on **stage**?
   a play an opera
5. I went to bed early and listened to a **documentary** about wild animals in London.
   a film a radio programme
6. It was almost three hours long, but I enjoyed every minute because the **soundtrack** was so good.
   a TV series a film
7. It was a very funny **comedy**, but it was hard work for the actors. They looked so tired at the end.
   a play a film
8. The writer tells you all the star's secrets. I'm not surprised that the book is a **bestseller**!
   a biography a novel

2 **Complete the texts with the words in green from exercise 1. You may need a plural form.**

1

I'm crazy about going to concerts. I love being part of a big [1] ________ , and it's so exciting to see my favourite bands live on [2] ________ .

2

My favourite kind of film is an exciting [3] ________ with a surprising ending, but it's also great to watch a really amusing [4] ________ with friends. Music is important in a film. Sometimes I'm not keen on a film, but if it has a really good [5] ________ then I can enjoy it anyway.

3

I'm not really into watching TV, but my friends love it. They can watch three or four [6] ________ of their favourite series without a break! I don't mind watching some things, for example a good [7] ________ about something real that interests me. However, books are my favourite type of entertainment. I always know about the latest [8] ________ , and I try to read all of them!

3 **Tell the class about one of the things below. Say why you enjoyed or didn't enjoy it.**

a book   a concert   a film   a series or an episode

LISTENING PART 2 TRAINING

1 **Read this extract from a conversation and the two options for describing the gist of what the person is saying.**

'What a concert! The music was brilliant and they played for hours. I was really impressed.'

A The boy enjoyed the concert.
B The boy did not enjoy the concert.

The two underlined words in the extract show you that option A is correct.

2 **Now read this extract. Work in pairs, underline the key words and decide which option gives the gist.**

'The film? Well, it wasn't great, really. It was too long. To be honest, I fell asleep!'

A The girl thought the film was good.
B The girl thought the film was boring.

3 **018 Listen and for each question, choose the correct answer.**

1 You will hear a girl telling her friend about a theatre trip.
How did the girl feel when she was at the theatre?
A proud because she was wearing a lovely dress
B embarrassed because of the bad performances
C surprised because the experience was so good

2 You will hear two friends talking about a film they've seen.
What did they both enjoy about the film?
A the music
B the acting
C the story

3 You will hear a man telling his friend about a music festival.
What did he like best about it?
A the experience of sleeping in a tent
B the relaxing time with his friends
C the musicians who performed there

4 **Work in pairs and discuss the questions.**

1 What kind of entertainment is there for people in your town or city?
2 Do you ever travel to other places if you want to see a concert, film, play, etc.?

DID YOU KNOW?

British English: You see a ***film*** *or* ***movie*** *at the* ***cinema****.*
American English: You see a ***movie*** *at a* ***movie theater****.*

GRAMMAR

PRESENT PERFECT AND PAST SIMPLE

GRAMMAR ON THE MOVE
Watch the video

1 Read the conversation and complete the rules below.

Have you ever been to Glastonbury?

Yes, I have. I went last year.

We use the [1] .... to talk about experiences that have happened some time up to now. We often use it with ***ever*** and ***never***.
We use the [2] .... to talk about things that happened at a definite time in the past.
To form the past simple with regular verbs, we add ***-ed***.
For negative forms or questions in the past simple, we use ***did/ didn't*** plus the infinitive without ***to***.
To form the present perfect, we use ***have/has (not)*** + **the past participle**.

➔ **GRAMMAR REFERENCE** / *pages 202–203.*

2 Complete the conversation with the verbs in brackets in the present perfect or the past simple.

A: [1] .... (you / ever / be) to a musical?
B: Yes, I have. I [2] .... (see) *Mamma Mia*.
A: Cool! When [3] .... (you / see) it?
B: I [4] .... (go) to London last summer, and I [5] .... (see) it then.
A: And [6] .... (you / enjoy) it?
B: Yes! I [7] .... (love) it! It was really fun. How about you? Which musicals [8] .... (you / see)?
A: Me? I've never seen any!

3 Work in pairs. Ask and answer questions about entertainment. Use the ideas below.

a book (about/by …) a Bollywood film
a concert a festival a musical a play

Have you ever read a book by Charles Dickens?

Yes, I read *Oliver Twist* last year.

Connected speech **is important in English. When one word ends in a vowel sound and the next one begins with a vowel sound, we often connect them, for example with a /w/ sound.**

4 **P LINKING** /w/ 019
Listen to the start of a question and then repeat it. Where do you hear a /w/ sound?

Have you ever … ?

5 **P** 020 Now listen to these sentences and repeat them. Find at least one linking /w/ in each sentence.

1 Have you ever been to England?
2 Have you ordered a cup of coffee?
3 Have you answered his two emails?
4 Have you asked Tom to go away?

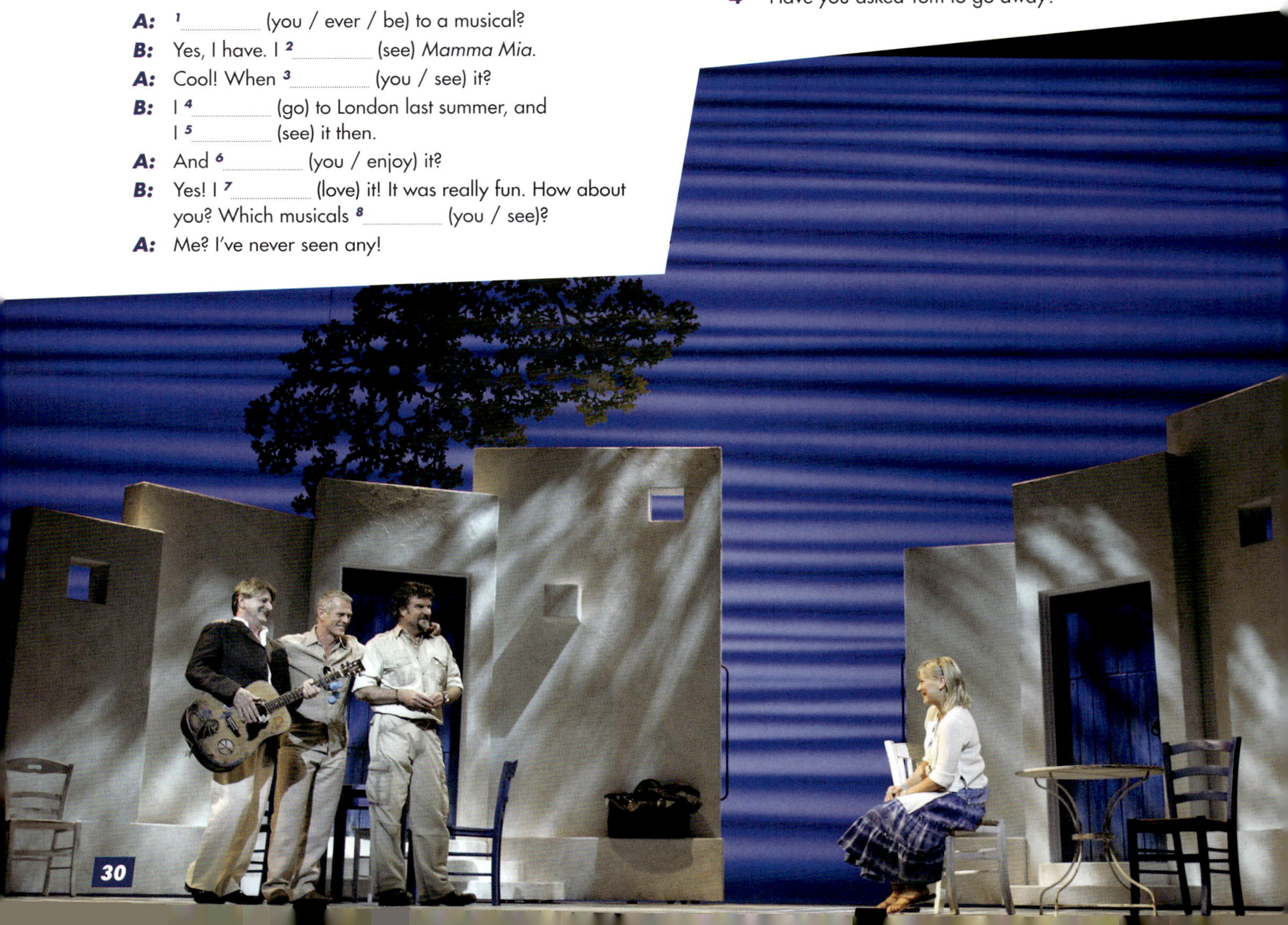

FOR AND SINCE

6 **Read this conversation and complete the rule.**

A: So you're a music journalist. How long have you had that job?
B: I've worked as a music journalist since 2016.
A: What did you do before that?
B: I was also a journalist, but I wrote about sport. What about you?
A: I'm a student. I've been at university for two years. I'm enjoying it.

We use the ________ to talk about things that started in the past and are still true now.
We use ***since*** with the present perfect and a point in time.
We use ***for*** with the present perfect and a period of time.

➩ ***GRAMMAR REFERENCE*** / *page 203.*

7 **Put these time phrases in the correct column.**

2016 a long time a week January last Monday last year three years two hours

SINCE	*FOR*

8 **Write answers to these questions. Use *for* or *since*.**

1 How long have you lived in your house or flat? *I've lived there …*
2 How long have you known your best friend?
3 How long have you had this English book?
4 How long have you been in this lesson?

9 **Now write three more questions to ask your partner using *How long …* .**

PUSH YOURSELF B2

VOCABULARY: PHRASAL VERBS

1 **Work in pairs. Do you have a favourite band? What kind of music do they play? Think of reasons why bands split up.**

2 **Read the blog entry by a singer called Mee and find phrasal verbs that fit the meanings below.**

DECEMBER 31ST – THOUGHTS ON NEW YEAR'S EVE

It's been a hard year, fans. As you know, our band, the Mighty Mees, split up and I fell out with the people who used to be my best friends – Sam the drummer and Lara the guitarist. Now we don't speak to each other. I knew that I wanted to keep on performing, but how? Our manager really let me down. He's working with Sam and Lara now, but what about me?

I took some time to travel and chill out. I got into yoga and I started to feel better. One well-known band asked me to be their singer. It was a good offer, but I turned it down. I don't think their songs are good enough, and I have to live up to *your* expectations. You want great songs, so I've decided to write them myself! See you next year … a year of great music from Mee!

1 stop being together *split up*
2 have a fight with friends
3 continue doing something
4 not help someone when help is needed
5 relax and stop worrying
6 start enjoying something
7 say no to an offer
8 be as good as people expect

3 **Complete the sentences with the correct form of the phrasal verbs in exercise 2.**

1 My uncle wanted to give me a job, but I ________ his offer.
2 Stop fighting with people. You will be lonely if you ________ all of your friends.
3 Caroline ________ jogging and now she's very fit.
4 Oh no! Kerry and Tim have ________ ! They were such a great couple.
5 I trusted Sheila. What a mistake! She really ________ me ________ when I needed help. She ________ my expectations.
6 My grandfather ________ playing in his blues band until he was 83. He said it helped him ________ and relax.

GRAMMAR

YET AND ALREADY

1 **What kind of festivals do you like? What's the most famous festival in your country? What do you need to pack when you go to a music festival?**

2 **021 Ethan and Mia are going to a music festival. There's a lot to prepare. Look at their to-do list. Listen and tick the things they have done.**

- ☐ print out the tickets
- ☐ get tent
- ☐ book the campsite
- ☐ book train tickets
- ☐ buy rubber boots (it's going to rain!)
- ☐ pack backpacks

3 **Look at the examples below and complete the rules.**

*Have you printed out our tickets **yet**?*
*I've **already** printed them out, but I haven't found our tent **yet**. Where could it be?*

We can use [1] .... when we have done something.
We can use [2] .... when we haven't done something, but we plan to do it.
We also use [3] .... in questions.

➔ **GRAMMAR REFERENCE** / *page 203.*

4 **021 Now complete the conversation with *yet* and *already* and the words in brackets. Listen again and check.**

Ethan: Have you ***printed out our tickets yet***?
Mia: Yes, ***I've already printed*** them out, but ***I haven't found our tent yet***. Where could it be?
Ethan: My brother has the tent, remember? Oh, [1] .... (I / not book / campsite).
Mia: Don't worry. [2] .... (I / do it). And [3] .... (I / book / train tickets), too.
Ethan: Great!
Mia: Oh, [4] .... (you / buy / rubber boots)? I've bought a pair for myself because it's going to rain.
Ethan: [5] .... (I / get some).
Mia: Great, so we've done everything!
Ethan: Well, [6] .... (we / not pack / our backpacks). Let's do it now!

5 **Work in pairs. You are travelling to another city with a group of friends to see a musical. There are some things you have to do in the box. Have a conversation like the one in exercise 4. Use the present perfect with *yet* and *already*.**

book tickets for the musical
collect the money for the tickets from your friends
buy train or bus tickets
find a hotel
choose a restaurant for dinner
reserve a table

WRITING PART 1 TRAINING

1 **What do you do with friends or family if they come to visit you for the weekend?**

2 **Choose three greetings for the beginning of an email to a friend.**

Hi Tina,	Dear Tina,
Hi,	Tina!
My dear Tina,	

3 **Put the words in the correct order to make closing sentences for an email.**

1 soon / See / you / .
2 to / you / Looking / forward / seeing / .
3 now / for / Bye / .

4 **Read this email from your English-speaking friend, Martin, and the notes you have made. Find these things in the email.**

1 a reference to earlier communication
2 an example of informal language
3 short forms
4 linking words
5 an invitation
6 a suggestion

From: Martin
Subject: this weekend
Reply Forward

Hi,

Thanks for your message. I'm so happy that you're coming this weekend! — *Me too!*

There's a festival on Saturday with music and some theatre performances, too. Would you like to go? — *Yes!*

We'll have jazz, electronic music and an African band, as well as some other bands. What type of music do you like? — *Tell Martin*

Are you into theatre? If you want, we could see a play and then hear some music. Let me know! — *No, just music*

See you soon,

Martin

MAKING AND RESPONDING TO SUGGESTIONS

5 **Join the beginnings and endings of these sentences. You can use one ending twice.**

1 How about
2 We could
3 Why don't we
4 Let's

a see a play and then hear some music.
b see a play and then hear some music?
c seeing a play and then hearing some music?

6 **Put the phrases in the correct columns.**

I'd love to …	… sounds great
I wouldn't like …	That's a good idea.
Sorry, but …	That's a nice idea, but …

SAYING YES	SAYING NO

7 **Write a response for each of these suggestions. Use phrases from exercise 6.**

1 How about going to see an opera?
2 We could learn to play the guitar together.
3 Why don't we cook a big meal together?
4 Let's go to the cinema this evening.

8 **Read Martin's email and the notes you have made again. Write your email to Martin, using all the notes. Write about 100 words.**

EXAM FOCUS

LISTENING PART 2

EXAM FACTS

- *For each question, you read a short question and a set of three options.*
- *You listen to a short recording of two people speaking.*
- *You hear each recording twice.*
- *You choose the correct option, A, B or C, according to what you hear.*
- *There are six questions in this section.*

EXAM TIPS

- *Before you hear the recording, read the questions and decide what information you need to listen for.*
- *Remember that the questions in this section are about gist: the main or general ideas in the conversation. The questions often focus on opinions and feelings rather than details.*
- *Remember to listen carefully to both speakers. Sometimes you have to decide what they agree about.*
- *When you hear the recording for the second time, look at the options again to check that the answer you've chosen is correct and that the other two answers are wrong.*

022 **For each question, choose the correct answer.**

1 You will hear two friends talking about a television drama.

They agree that

A the story was clever.

B the acting was good.

C the music was suitable.

2 You will hear two colleagues talking about jazz music.

Why does the woman want to talk to the man?

A to invite him to a concert

B to ask him to recommend a concert

C to give him advice about going to a concert

3 You will hear two friends talking about going to the cinema.

Why has the man stopped going to the cinema?

A He doesn't have enough money.

B He doesn't have time.

C The films don't interest him.

4 You will hear a woman telling a friend about a concert she attended.

What does the woman say was disappointing about the concert?

A the choice of songs

B the quality of the sound

C the length of the performance

5 You will hear two friends talking about a computer game.

They agree that

A it is easy to play.

B it is good value for money.

C it is better than the previous version.

6 You will hear two friends talking about a TV talent show.

How did the man feel about it?

A pleased with the judges' choice of winner

B surprised at how good the performers were

C annoyed by the way the contest was organised

WRITING PART 1

EXAM FACTS

- *You read an email.*
- *You also read four notes written on the email.*
- *You have to write a reply to the email using all the notes.*

EXAM TIPS

- *Remember to imagine that you received this email and that you made the notes.*
- *Look carefully at the sections of the email highlighted by the lines from the notes – sometimes the writer is asking you a question and sometimes the writer is making a suggestion which you need to respond to.*
- *Write an email of about 100 words in total, making sure that you use all the notes. You will have to invent some extra information. For example, you may need to explain why you think something is a good idea.*
- *You can write the four parts of your reply in the order that you think is best.*
- *Remember to begin and end your email using suitable words and expressions.*

Read this email from your English-speaking friend Alex and the notes you have made.

From: Alex
Subject: Music Festival

Reply Forward

Hi!

I'm really looking forward to going to the music festival next weekend! — *Me too!*

The festival's on Friday, Saturday and Sunday. Do you want to go for two days or three days? I'll let you choose. — *Tell Alex*

How do you think we should travel to the festival? I don't think that there'll be many parking spaces there. — *I think …*

It's going to be fun camping at the festival. Should I bring my tent? It's quite small, but it's OK. — *No, because …*

See you soon!

Write your email to Alex using all the notes.
Write about 100 words.

➡ ***WRITING BANK*** / *pages 227–229.*

HOW WAS IT?

Gave it a go	☐
Getting there	☐
Aced it!	☐

REAL WORLD

AT A FESTIVAL IN ... CALIFORNIA

1 Do you ever go to music festivals? Would you like to go to one? Why?

2 Look at photos (A–E) from the Coachella music festival in California and read the website. Match each photo with one of the sections on the website.

Coachella

LINEUP PASSES GUIDES TRIP PLANNING

Getting there

There are plenty of ways to get to the festival, either by car or by public transportation, including services from airports. There are regular shuttles between LAX airport and the festival campground. The Any Line, Anytime Shuttle Pass allows you to get on or off at any shuttle stop between the airport and the festival. You can use it to come and go during the festival.

See the map for car and taxi **pick-up** and **drop-off** sites.

Festival rules and general information

The **venue** opens at 11:00 each day.

All **attendees** must wear their festival wristbands.

The show will take place even if conditions are wet.

Line-up and **set times** may change.

Ins and outs are allowed, as long as festival wristbands are worn.

On-site camping

Tent-only camping spots are available. You can have as many people camp in your spot as you like. Each tent camping spot comes with an overnight-parking place to leave your car.

Lake Eldorado's teepees are already set up and ready to go, with two beds, sleeping bags and pillows. Four-person tents also have additional features, such as a cooler and chairs.

Eat and drink

Coachella offers a wide variety of delicious food and drinks for all tastes and budgets. Food is available throughout the main festival area and campground. There are over 100 vendors on-site, who will be glad to serve you food that is quick and delicious.

Coachella mobile

The Coachella Mobile App gives you all the information you need about the festival in your pocket, with the most up-to-date set times, maps and listings of food vendors. You can use the app to update your schedule and receive reminders of when one of your favourite stars is about **to hit the stage**.

3 **Read the website again and decide if the sentences are true or false.**

1. There is only one bus from the airport to the festival site each day.
2. You can't leave the festival and come back in later.
3. Small tents are for a fixed number of people.
4. In bigger tents, there is also somewhere to keep your food fresh.
5. The food vendors are all on one part of the festival site.
6. The Coachella App will tell you when a band that you want to see is going to perform.

4 **Look at the purple words in the text and match them with the meanings.**

1. the people who come to an event
2. the full list of all the bands and singers at the festival
3. to start performing
4. the place where an event takes place
5. a place where cars and buses stop to leave or collect people
6. the times when bands or singers will perform

5 **023 Listen to three conversations. Match the speakers (1–3) with the information they want (a–d). There is one answer you don't need.**

a where to camp
b where to charge a mobile phone
c where to get a new wristband
d how to get to a supermarket

6 **023 Complete the phrases with the words in the box. Then listen and check.**

Can I	charge	Is there	looking for	out of

PHRASES YOU MIGHT USE

1. My phone's ______ battery.
2. Is there somewhere I can ______ it?
3. ______ get a new one?
4. We're ______ a supermarket.
5. ______ one here?

7 **Match the sentences (1–6) with the meanings (a–f).**

PHRASES YOU MIGHT HEAR

1. Are you camping on-site?
2. Which zone are you in?
3. the wide avenue running down the centre
4. just off the main avenue
5. If you head for the camping area, …
6. They'll fix you up with a replacement.

a the wide street in the middle
b They will give you a new one.
c Are you camping at the festival?
d Go towards the camping area.
e next to the main street
f Which camping area are you staying in?

8 **Watch the video about the Coachella Festival. Make notes on extra things you learn about the festival:**

- the venue
- kinds of music
- getting there
- food and drink
- on-site camping

9 **In groups, compare your notes. Then watch again to check your ideas.**

WATCH

LIFE COMPETENCIES

TAKING CONTROL OF LEARNING, WORKING TOWARDS A RESOLUTION

10 **Work in pairs. Find information about a festival in your country and plan your visit. Think about:**

- how to get there
- where to stay
- what kinds of food you will eat
- which bands and musicians you want to see

Tell the class about what you chose and why.

PROGRESS CHECK 1

OCCUPATIONS

1 **Match the quotes with the occupations in the box. There are three occupations you don't need.**

actor	blogger	chef	gardener	hairdresser
journalist	mechanic	police officer	sales assistant	

1. 'I work outside. That's sometimes hard, but luckily I don't have much work in winter.'
2. 'I've always been interested in news and love asking people difficult questions.'
3. 'My kitchen at work is big and modern. I love working there.'
4. 'I'm always busy. We have thousands of customers a day in our shop.'
5. 'I love cars, and I love repairing things. I have my dream job!'
6. 'I help people to look more beautiful. I also listen to people's stories. My customers usually talk a lot while I'm working!'

PRESENT SIMPLE AND PRESENT CONTINUOUS

2 **Choose the correct options.**

Home About Search

I'm a student and I love my life. [1]*I go/I'm going* to university every day, and I have a lot to do there. My best friend Paula studies at the same university, so [2]*we usually have/we're usually having* lunch together. At the moment we can't do that because [3]*she studies/she's studying* in France for a few weeks. Unfortunately, she [4]*doesn't enjoy/isn't enjoying* it. She sent me this message last night: 'I want to go home! I'm sharing a room with another girl and she's horrible! [5]*She always is borrowing/She's always borrowing* my clothes and she never asks first.' Poor Paula. She says the other girls in her class hang out together, but [6]*they never invite/they're never inviting* her to join them.

ADVERBS OF FREQUENCY

3 **Put the adverbs of frequency into the sentences in the correct position.**

1. My friends and I meet up on Saturday evenings. (usually)
2. We eat out. (sometimes)
3. My brother goes to bed before midnight. (never)
4. He is at home. (hardly ever)
5. I get up very early. (usually)
6. I am tired! (always)

HOLIDAY WEATHER

4 **Complete the text with the words in the box. There are two words you don't need.**

breeze	chilly	climate	cool
dull	fine	lightning	showers

For a good holiday, you need to choose a place with the right [1] ________ . For a beach holiday, you need a warm place with a lot of [2] ________ weather, of course. I like hiking, so for my holidays [3] ________ weather can be better than hot weather. If you go hiking in the mountains, summer is usually the best time. The weather is not too hot, but mostly sunny and dry, with just a few [4] ________ . After the rain, there is often a lovely, cool [5] ________ . I really enjoy walking in that weather. However, you need to be careful if the sky is suddenly dark and cloudy as there are often thunderstorms. Both the heavy rain and the [6] ________ can be very dangerous.

COMPARATIVES AND SUPERLATIVES

5 **Rewrite the sentences. Use comparative and superlative forms.**

1. Iceland is not as cold as Greenland.
   Greenland ________
2. Madagascar is warmer than Ireland.
   Ireland is ________
3. No country has more tourists than France.
   France has ________
4. Skiing holidays are more expensive than hiking holidays.
   Hiking holidays are not ________
5. City holidays are not as relaxing as beach holidays.
   Beach holidays are ________
6. No beaches are longer than the beaches in Brazil.
   The beaches ________

ENTERTAINMENT

6 Match the quotes (1–8) with the types of entertainment (a–h).

1. 'The sound was good, but I couldn't see the orchestra.'
2. 'It was three hours long, and the only good thing in it was the soundtrack.'
3. 'It's so exciting. That's why it's a bestseller.'
4. 'I watched five episodes without a break!'
5. 'I was disappointed. It really wasn't very funny.'
6. 'The acting was great and everyone in the audience enjoyed it.'
7. 'I learned a lot. They showed some amazing places.'
8. 'My parents always listen to it after dinner.'

a a book
b a comedy
c a concert
d a documentary
e a film
f a play
g a radio programme
h a series

PRESENT PERFECT AND PAST SIMPLE

7 Put the verbs in brackets in the correct tense. Use the present perfect or past simple.

My name is Sylvio and I'm an author. I [1] ______ (write) five bestsellers. I [2] ______ (write) my first book when I was 16, but it wasn't very good. When I was 20, I [3] ______ (go) to Paris and I got some good ideas for a novel there. [4] ______ you ever ______ (visit) a really exciting city? Cities give me energy. I [5] ______ (be) to Paris, New York, Mexico City, Rome … and each city gave me an idea for a book. I [6] ______ (not visit) Rio de Janeiro yet, but that's the next city on my list. My mother was a writer too, but she [7] ______ (not write) novels. She wrote poems. When I was a child we [8] ______ (live) in the countryside because she loved writing in quiet places. Now I'm an adult, I love writing in busy places. Everyone is different!

USED TO

8 Rewrite the sentences with *used to*.

1. When I was a child, I watched television with my family. *When I was a child, I used …*
2. We sat together in the living room.
3. My sister and I argued about what programme to watch.
4. My father didn't enjoy watching television.
5. He read his book while we were watching our favourite shows.
6. Did you spend evenings with your family when you were younger?

SAYING WHAT YOU ENJOY

9 Complete the text with the words in the box.

crazy	enjoy	fan	into	stand	thing

I'm [1] ______ plays. I'm [2] ______ about the theatre. I love the atmosphere before a play begins. It's always so exciting. However, I'm not a [3] ______ of every kind of play. For example, I can't [4] ______ musicals. I don't know why. I really [5] ______ Shakespeare plays and I like modern dramas, but musicals are just not my [6] ______ .

COMMON MISTAKES

10 Find one mistake in each sentence and rewrite the sentences.

1. Martin enjoy playing football.
2. I like Katrin because she very kind.
3. She always is happy.
4. I'm never go to the theatre.
5. We had a so great holiday.
6. He is here since last week.
7. I never saw a musical.
8. I use to go to work on foot but now I go by car.

A REVIEW

11 Complete the text with the word which best fits each gap.

Raffia is the [1] ______ exciting film I've ever seen. It's about a young woman called Maureen who [2] ______ always dreamed of going to Africa. When the film begins, Maureen [3] ______ planning a trip to Madagascar with her friend Henry. He has [4] ______ been there several times and he knows that Maureen will love it. However, things start to go wrong on the plane and they get [5] ______ when the two arrive in Madagascar.

I don't want to tell you what happens, but if you haven't seen this film [6] ______ , then see it today! Actress Kerry O'Neil is better [7] ______ she has been in any other film. You also see how beautiful Madagascar is. I've gone online and looked at a lot of hotels there [8] ______ I saw *Raffia* last Saturday.

3 DINING OUT, EATING IN

A

LISTENING

1 **How often do you go to restaurants? Who do you go with?**

2 **Look at the restaurants in the photos and answer the questions.**

1. Which do you think is … the most expensive? the least expensive? the friendliest?
2. Which one is best for … a family celebration? a romantic date? a business lunch? a quick meal?

3 024 **Look at the words in the box. Which do you think describe each restaurant? Listen to three people talking and check your answers.**

cheap and cheerful	family run	good value for money	home-cooked	junk food	smart	stylish	traditional

4 025 **Listen to a man called Tim describing a visit to one of the restaurants with his wife, Sarah. Which restaurant is it?**

5 025 **Read these statements and choose *Yes* or *No*. Listen again and check.**

1. It was Tim's first visit to this restaurant.
   a Yes ***b*** No
2. Tim and Sarah were surprised by the number of dishes on the menu.
   a Yes ***b*** No
3. Tim was disappointed by the taste of the food.
   a Yes ***b*** No
4. Sarah's favourite part of the meal was the soup.
   a Yes ***b*** No
5. Tim and Sarah ordered different desserts.
   a Yes ***b*** No
6. Tim thought that the restaurant was good value for money.
   a Yes ***b*** No

6 **What kind of restaurants do you like going to? Why?**

C

B

VOCABULARY

EASILY CONFUSED RESTAURANT WORDS

1 **Look at these sentences from the recording. In pairs, discuss what you think the words in bold mean.**

1. My favourite **dish** is beef lasagne.
2. We usually have a quick **meal** of a burger and chips.
3. Our dinner began with a nice **starter**.
4. We both had a **bowl** of really tasty vegetable soup.
5. For our **main course**, we had a large **plate** of grilled fish.
6. The **bill** was quite big.
7. Because the service was good, we also left a **tip** for the waiters.

2 **Complete this text with the words in bold in exercise 1.**

My friends and I had a really nice [1] .... at Da Maria last night. We often have a light [2] .... , like a tomato salad, and cheese to begin with. But there was a special [3] .... with spaghetti and fish on the menu yesterday, so we had that instead.
Our [4] .... was a large steak with a [5] .... of chips. There was so much food on my [6] .... that I couldn't finish it, even though it was delicious.
Da Maria isn't an expensive restaurant, so the [7] .... at the end of the evening wasn't too large, but we added a big [8] .... We always do that, because the staff are so friendly and the food is great!

3 **Choose the correct word to complete the sentences.**

1. We decided to *go/take* out for dinner.
2. It's a restaurant that *serves/brings* good food.
3. We *kept/reserved* a table for eight o'clock.
4. The waiter *picked/took* our coats.
5. The waiter *showed/offered* us to our table.
6. Another waiter *brought/carried* us the menu.
7. We *asked/ordered* our meal.
8. I *decided/asked* for the bill.
9. We *left/shared* the waiter a tip.

4 **Discuss in pairs.**

1. Do people often go out to eat with family or friends in your country?
2. What sort of restaurants do you like?
3. Do you usually leave a tip?

READING PART 4 TRAINING

1 **Are there any unusual restaurants in your town or city?**

2 **Read this text about a very unusual restaurant. What is special about it?**

Last weekend it was my friend Clara's birthday, and we went with a group of friends to a rather special restaurant. When we arrived at the restaurant, everything looked quite normal. **(1)** .... The only strange thing was that they took our bags, phones and watches and put them into locked cupboards.
Next, we followed our blind waiter, Serge, down a long and fairly dark corridor. **(2)** .... It was totally black in there. Fortunately, Serge showed us to our table and helped us to sit down. There were no menus. Serge just put some things down on the table and told us to enjoy our meal. **(3)** .... But **after a while**, we got used to it. Everything smelled and tasted so good that it didn't matter that nobody could see anything.
(4) .... So we all had a really good time, laughing and trying to guess what we were eating. There was a relaxed atmosphere, and we were soon chatting and joking with all the other customers.
At the end of the meal, Serge took us back to the reception area. The staff there told us what we'd eaten. It was certainly an unusual experience!

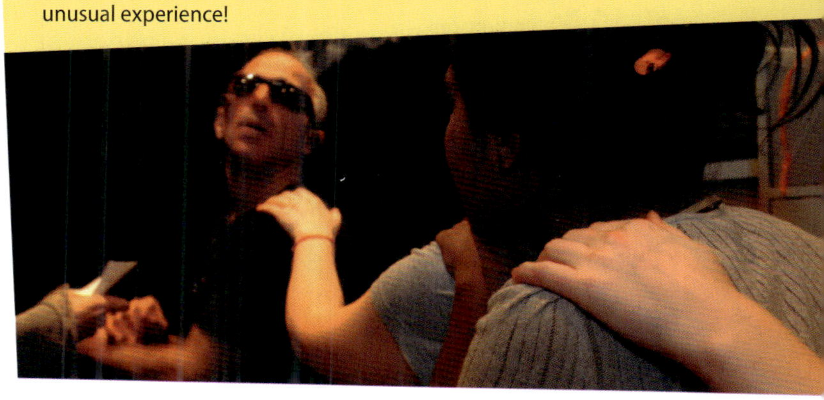

3 **Read the tip.**

> *Remember to think about what comes before and after the gap. Check for words or phrases which refer back to information which has been removed. Check for pronouns such as 'this', 'that', 'he', 'she', 'it' or 'they' which might refer to people or things in the missing sentence.*

Which sentence (A–E) in exercise 4 describes a normal restaurant and introduces the people who took the customers' things? Look at the first paragraph in the text. Which of the sentences fits best in gap 1?

4 **Now complete the rest of the text. There is one sentence you don't need.**

A Then he led us into another room.
B In fact, it made the meal a lot of fun.
C There was a nice reception area with comfortable seats, and the staff were very friendly.
D But Serge told us that it wasn't possible to change our table.
E At first, we found it difficult to eat and drink in complete darkness.

5 **Would you like to eat at this restaurant? Why? / Why not?**

GRAMMAR

VERBS + ADJECTIVES

*Everything **looked normal**.*
*Everything **smelled** and **tasted good**.*

> Look at the examples above. What kind of word comes after the **verbs**?
> *look/taste/smell/sound/feel +* ....

➡ ***GRAMMAR REFERENCE** / page 205.*

1 **Look at these words for describing food in the box, and group them 1–5 from very negative to very positive. Some words have already been added.**

all right	delicious	disappointing
enjoyable	horrible	nice	OK

1 disgusting …
2 unpleasant …
3 …
4 tasty …
5 fantastic …

2 **Match these questions (1–5) with the answers (a–e).**

1 Have you ever tried chocolate chip cookies?
2 Would you like one of these cakes?
3 Have you really eaten all those sweets?
4 Do you want some vegetable soup?
5 You can buy chocolate insects, can't you?

a Mmm. Yes, please. It smells fantastic.
b Yes … and I feel sick now!
c Yes, I have. They taste lovely.
d Really? That sounds horrible.
e No, thanks. They look delicious, though.

3 **Do you know what these foods are? Do you know where they are from?**

A

B

4 **Now read the texts and match them with the photos.**

But do they taste as weird *as they look?*

1 Jackfruit is a **very large** fruit, which grows on trees and can weigh up to 55 kg. It looks **quite strange** and feels **fairly rough**. When it's ready to pick, the smell is **extremely strong**. However, it tastes **quite sweet**, a bit like a mix of pineapple and bananas. In fact, lots of people think it tastes **absolutely delicious**. It grows in tropical areas around the world, but it's becoming very popular in many other countries.

2 Haggis is a large sausage, usually shaped like a ball, and is made from minced sheep's meat, onion and spices. It doesn't sound **very nice** and it looks **quite unpleasant**, so lots of people aren't keen to try it the first time. However, people are often **very surprised** to find that it tastes **really good**. It is traditionally made and eaten in Scotland.

5 026 **Listen to some people talking about the foods in exercise 4. What are they eating?**

6 **Look at the words in green in the texts in exercise 4. What words can we use before an adjective to make it stronger or weaker?**

quite/fairly/really/very/extremely + neutral or mild adjectives
It looks ***quite strange****.* ~~*It's absolutely good.*~~
really/absolutely + strong adjectives
It tastes ***absolutely delicious****.* ~~*It's extremely delicious.*~~

7 **Read the conversation between Cody from the USA and Laura from Italy. Choose the correct word to complete the sentences.**

Laura: Clam chowder's a kind of soup, isn't it?
Cody: That's right. It's from the USA. It's [1]*really/absolutely* popular there.
Laura: So what's it like? It sounds [2]*absolutely/quite* nice.
Cody: Well, it's made with seafood and there's lots of garlic and cream in it, too.
Laura: Mmm, that sounds [3]*very/absolutely* tasty. It's like an Italian dish called 'cozze alla panna'.
Cody: It's [4]*really/very* delicious. You should try it!

8 **Have you ever tried any unusual food or drink?**

WRITING

1 **Look at the text on page 41 again. Which paragraph has information about:**

a the meal?
b when and why the writer visited the restaurant?
c what the writer thought about the visit?

2 **Look at the words and phrases in purple in the text on page 41. What do these words and phrases tell us?**

3 **Join the beginnings and endings of these sentences.**

1 Last weekend,
2 When we arrived at the restaurant,
3 Then,
4 Next,
5 After a while
6 At the end of the meal

a she showed us to a table near the window.
b we looked at the menu and ordered our meal.
c I went to a Chinese restaurant with my friends.
d we paid the bill and went home.
e a waitress said, 'Good evening' and took our coats.
f we ordered dessert and coffee.

4 **Work in pairs and write down some adjectives for describing a restaurant visit.**

Place … People … Food …

5 **Now write about your own visit to a restaurant. Plan three paragraphs and make notes about:**

- when and where the visit was
- who you were with
- the meal and your thoughts about the restaurant

Use the time linkers in exercise 3 and adjectives with words like *quite*, *fairly* and *extremely*, etc.

GRAMMAR

SOME, ANY, MUCH, MANY, A LOT OF, A LITTLE, A FEW, NO

GRAMMAR ON THE MOVE
Watch the video

1 **Work in pairs and discuss the questions.**

1. Do you prefer eating at home or eating out?
2. How often do you cook?
3. What kinds of dishes do you cook?

2 **Read the texts. Look at the underlined words. Are they countable or uncountable? Think about whether the words have a plural form or *a/an* in front of them to help you.**

EATING OUT OR STAYING IN?

How **many** times have you eaten out recently? I love trying new places to eat, but I don't get to eat out often, as I live in a really small town. We don't have **many** restaurants and we don't have **any** really special ones at all. That's why I always go on holiday to cities with **lots of** great places to eat. Last year, a friend and I went to San Sebastian in northern Spain, and I was in food heaven! Within **a few** minutes of arriving in the city, we met **some** students who told us the best places to eat. We had a great time and I tried **lots of** wonderful food. We only went for a long weekend, so we didn't have **much** time to explore the city before it was time to fly home again.

3 **Now look at the blue words in the texts and complete the table.**

~~a/an~~ any a few a little a lot of many much no some

UNCOUNTABLE	SINGULAR	PLURAL
	a/an	

4 **Look at the texts again and complete the rules with *some* and *any*.**

We use [1] .... in positive sentences with countable and uncountable nouns.
We use [2] .... in negative sentences with countable and uncountable nouns.
We use [3] .... in questions with countable and uncountable nouns.

5 **Now complete the rules with *much, many, a lot of, a few, a little* and *no*.**

We use [1] .... and [2] .... to talk about large amounts in negative sentences and questions. We use [3] .... with uncountable nouns and [4] .... with countable ones.
We use [5] .... to talk about large amounts in positive sentences.
We use [6] .... and [7] .... to talk about small amounts.
We use [8] .... with uncountable nouns and [9] .... with countable ones.
We use [10] .... + noun to mean none. We do not use it with a negative verb.

➡ GRAMMAR REFERENCE / pages 204–205.

People often ask me: 'Haven't you got **any** favourite restaurants?', but to be honest, I prefer cooking for friends at home. How **much** money does eating out cost? Too much! All you need is **some** time and **a little** imagination and you can create a great meal. I love sitting in the garden with my friends, listening to **some** music and eating delicious food. **No** restaurant is as relaxing as that. I have **a lot of** fantastic memories connected to meals I've cooked, and I know my friends and family do too.

6 **Choose the correct words to complete the sentences.**

1 How *much/many/any* books do we need?
2 There's *no/any/a* garlic.
3 We don't need very *much/many/few* money.
4 There are a *little/few/lot* biscuits in the cupboard.
5 I haven't got *no/much/any* friends there.
6 There's *some/any/many* cream in the fridge.
7 We need a *lot/few/little* juice.
8 I've got a *little/many/lot* of information now.

7 **Some nouns can be both countable and uncountable, especially for food and drink. Look at these photos and complete the sentences using some of the words in the box.**

a	an	any	few	little
many	much	some		

1 How .... chocolate should we put on the cake?

2 You can use .... of that chicken for a sandwich.

3 I don't want .... ice cream, thank you.

4 We cooked .... whole chicken for Sunday lunch.

5 Take a .... of these chocolates if you want.

6 Would you like .... ice cream?

8 **Which sentences in exercise 7 are about countable things? Which are about uncountable things?**

9 **Tell your partner what you ate yesterday, using the words in the box in exercise 7.**

PUSH YOURSELF B2

VOCABULARY: FOOD IDIOMS

1 **In pairs, discuss what these expressions mean.**

a I'm not going to watch that film. Horror films are really **not my cup of tea**.

b I was so worried about the exam, but **it was a piece of cake**.

c **Take** everything he says **with a pinch of salt**. He's always telling fantastic stories.

d It was supposed to be a secret, but my sister **spilt the beans**.

e I thought my holiday was organised, but **it's all gone pear-shaped**.

f **It's no good crying over spilt milk**. We can't change it now.

2 **Now match the idioms (a–f) with the questions (1–6). Which idiom can we use when …**

1 we don't believe everything that someone is saying?
2 something is not the type of thing that you like?
3 a plan has gone wrong?
4 you think that something is very easy to do?
5 someone is upset about something that is too late to change?
6 someone says something that they should keep secret?

DID YOU KNOW?

Lots of food words are different in American and British English.

American English	British English
chips	*crisps*
cookies	*biscuits*
candy	*sweets*
soda	*soft drinks*
French fries	*chips*

VOCABULARY

COOKING

1 **What is your favourite dish? When do you eat it and why do you like it?**

2 **027 Listen to a woman called Bella talking about how to make her favourite dish, a snack from Britain called Welsh rarebit. Which photo shows the dish?**

A

B

C

3 **027 Complete these instructions using the verbs below. Listen and check.**

add	fry	grate	grill	heat	mix	pour	put

To make Welsh rarebit, you need cheese, butter and milk. First, you take the cheese, and you [1] __________ it. After that, you [2] __________ it in a small saucepan, [3] __________ it with the other ingredients, and [4] __________ it gently. You then [5] __________ salt, pepper and a little Worcester sauce. Next, you [6] __________ a slice of bread on both sides, [7] __________ the mixture over the bread, and then put it back under the grill for a few moments until it goes nice and brown. If you like, you can get an egg and [8] __________ it. Then finally, you put the egg on top of the Welsh rarebit.

4 **Look at the photos (A–F) and match them with the verbs in exercise 3. There are two verbs you don't need.**

A

B

C

D

E

F

GRAMMAR

ARTICLES: *A, AN, THE, Ø* (ZERO ARTICLE)

GRAMMAR ON THE MOVE
Watch the video

1 **Look at these things that Bella says. Why don't we use an article in sentences 1 and 2? Why do we use *the* in sentences 5 and 6?**

1. *I love cheese.*
2. *I like eggs.*
3. *You need cheese.*
4. *You can get an egg.*
5. *First, you take the cheese.*
6. *You put the egg on top of the Welsh rarebit.*

2 **Complete the rules using *a*, *an*, *the*, or *Ø* (zero article).**

Indefinite articles
We use:
[1] __________ with uncountable and plural nouns to talk about things in general.
[2] __________ or __________ with singular nouns when we aren't being specific about which one.

Definite article
We use [3] __________ with all nouns to talk about a specific or known thing or things.

➡ ***GRAMMAR REFERENCE*** / *pages 205–206.*

3 **Look at these five sentences. There is a mistake in three of the sentences. Which two are correct?**

1. I prefer to drink coffee without the sugar.
2. Please could I have glass of water?
3. Apples are my favourite fruit.
4. Would you like a bread with your meal?
5. I usually have toast and jam for breakfast.

4 **Now correct the mistakes in the other three sentences.**

5 **Work in pairs. Explain how to make a dish from your country. Use the verbs in the recipe for Welsh rarebit and the expressions below to help you. Say what ingredients you need and explain what you need to do.**

To make … , you need …
First, … Then … Next … After that …
Finally …

6 **P** **SCHWA /ə/** 028

Listen to these four words.

a slice of bread

7 **P** 029 **Now listen to this question.**

Would you like a slice of bread?

Can you hear a difference? How are the words *of* and *a* pronounced in a sentence?

> **In natural speech, we stress the most important words. Small grammar words, such as articles and prepositions, usually become shorter and weaker. This short, weak sound is called a *schwa*.**

8 **P** 030 **Listen to these phrases and underline the schwa sounds that you hear.**

a cup of tea some fries to go a table for two
a piece of cake

9 **Now practise saying the phrases.**

SPEAKING PART 2 TRAINING

- *In the Speaking section of the Preliminary exam, you have to talk about what you can see in a photo for about a minute. You should mention the people, what they are doing and what they are wearing, and describe the place and any other things you can see. If it is outside, remember to talk about the weather and the landscape.*
- *If you don't know how to say something, try to say it using different words. For example, if you don't know the word 'waitress', you can say 'The woman who works in the restaurant'.*

1 **Look at the photo below. It shows people in a kitchen. Think of words you could use to talk about the photo and add them in the correct column in the table.**

ADJECTIVES	PEOPLE / THINGS	POSITION	VERB
large	*students*	*on the right*	*looking*

2 031 **Now listen to a student talking about the photo and complete the text using the phrases below.**

USEFUL LANGUAGE

Describing position

In the middle, there's … at the back/front of …
On the left/right of the photo … , I can see …

Opinion

I think … I'm not sure what it is, but … Maybe …

Describing what's happening

This is a photo of … he's wearing …
He's holding … they are looking …

Unknown words

I don't know what they are called, but …

[1] .... a large kitchen. [2] .... it's in a restaurant or perhaps in a college. [3] .... a large black table and there are some pots and knives [4] .... [5] .... a man behind the table. Maybe he's a chef or teacher because he's showing the other people something and [6] .... a white apron. [7] .... a knife and he is cutting something. [8] .... it looks like a small onion. Some people are standing [9] .... the photo and they are watching the chef. There are some big wooden things in front of the people. [10] .... people use them when they're cutting up vegetables.

3 031 **Listen again and check your answers.**

4 **Look at the photos on pages 192 and 193 and use the phrases above to tell your partner what you can see in the photos. Remember to:**

- say where people and things are
- say what they are doing
- use adjectives and adverbs

EXAM FOCUS

READING PART 4

Five sentences have been removed from the text below. For each question, choose the correct answer. There are three extra sentences which you do not need to use.

A But in France, the opposite is true.
B For example, not everybody eats with a knife and fork.
C But in some countries, this is actually seen as a good thing.
D It is polite to arrive on time for meals.
E In many countries, people only give one if the service has been especially good.
F Eating everything that is given to you is considered rude.
G There are differences in the times that people eat, too.
H In Germany, however, it is divided up according to how much each person has eaten.

EXAM FACTS

- *You read a text which has five gaps in it. Five sentences have been removed from the text.*
- *You also read eight sentences (A–H).*
- *You must match five of the sentences (A–H) to the gaps in the text. You don't need to use the other three sentences.*

EXAM TIPS

- *Read the whole text. You will be able to follow it even though there are sentences missing.*
- *Now look at each gap and think about the information that is missing.*
- *Read the sentence before the gap. Look at the ideas it introduces and think about what kind of information might come next.*
- *Look at the eight sentences and find the one which contains the missing information. Put the sentence into the gap and check that it fits, looking both forwards and backwards in the text.*
- *Check that none of the other sentences also fits into the gap.*
- *When you have filled the five gaps, look at the three remaining sentences. Check these again to make sure that none of these sentences fits into any of the gaps.*
- *Read the whole text again with the five sentences inserted to check that it all makes sense.*

A world of differences

People enjoy eating together with family and friends in every corner of the world. However, customs to do with good behaviour around the dinner table vary greatly. What is seen as polite in one country may be seen as impolite in another. In many parts of the world, people think it is rude to eat your food noisily or to make any noise when you drink. **1** ______ In China, for example, it is considered polite to eat and drink noisily, because this is a sign that you are enjoying your meal. Chinese people also show respect to their hosts by always leaving a little food in their bowls. **2** ______ Meanwhile, in India, people show respect to their hosts by finishing all their food.

There are even differences regarding how you sit at the dinner table. For instance, in Britain it is bad manners to put your elbows on the table, and children are taught to keep their hands under the table when they're not eating. **3** ______ There, people are expected to keep their hands on the table at all times.

And what about when the meal is over and the restaurant bill arrives? In France, the custom is for one person to pay the whole bill. **4** ______ Then, finally, there is the problem of whether or not to leave a tip for the staff. **5** ______ In Japan, people almost never tip, while in the USA, you are expected to leave at least 15–20%. So, before you travel anywhere, make sure you know the local customs!

SPEAKING PART 2

EXAM FACTS

- *The examiner gives you a photo and tells you what the photograph shows.*
- *The examiner then says, 'Please tell us what you can see in the photograph.'*
- *You have about a minute to describe what you can see in the photo.*

EXAM TIPS

- *Start by saying where the photo was taken or what the photo shows.*
- *Describe where all the things and people are in the photo, and say what the people are doing.*
- *If you don't know how to say something, try to say it using different words.*
- *You can give your opinion about people and things. Try to use adjectives to describe people, things and the atmosphere in the place. You can also give a reason for your opinion.*
- *You can add information such as what time of day or year you think it is, or why the people are there.*
- *You can use words such as 'OK ...', 'Well ...' to begin with and 'What else?' while you're thinking of what to say next.*
- *Finally – keep talking. If you stop talking too soon, the examiner may ask you questions about the photo, but you shouldn't wait for these questions.*

The examiner gives you this photograph. It shows people in their free time. Describe what you can see in the photograph. Talk for about one minute.

SPEAKING BANK / *pages 236–240.*

HOW WAS IT?

- **Gave it a go** [ ]
- **Getting there** [ ]
- **Aced it!** [ ]

REAL WORLD

EATING OUT IN ... BANGKOK

1 **Look at the photos of places to eat in Bangkok. Which place would you choose for a meal? Why?**

Eating out in **Bangkok**

Bangkok restaurants cater to all price ranges and are open all hours, so the city is certainly heaven for food lovers. There are plenty of eating options day or night, with Thai-style dining, trendy restaurants and food markets all available.

A Bangkok has an amazing range of local restaurants serving authentic Thai food in open-fronted shops. If you're lucky, there may even be a fan to cool you. Thipsamai Pad is one of the best local restaurants in Bangkok. Ingredients are incredibly fresh and portions are large and filling. Plus, a row of woks, with food being tossed over flames, is a classic snapshot of Bangkok food culture. Expect a queue and take any table you can find, either inside the restaurant or on the benches outside.

B Street food in Bangkok provides convenient, delicious and cheap meals and it's one of the best ways to get in touch with the local culture. Street food might be a humble cart on the side of the road, or it could be a collection of stalls in a local market. Our tip is to eat at busy places as the ingredients will be fresh. Try SomTam, (papaya salad) Khao Pad (fried rice) or Pad Thai Kung (noodles with shrimp).

C When it comes to where to eat in Bangkok, you can certainly aim high. Vertigo is a restaurant 61 floors above the bustling streets of Bangkok, looking out over a magnificent cityscape of lights and movement. It's a great feeling to walk out on a rooftop with absolutely nothing above you. The 360 degree view is striking and there's a chance to watch the sunset from a comfortable sofa. As well as local food, the restaurant also serves imported steaks, lamb and seafood. Spending a romantic evening at Vertigo is all about eating and feeling on top of the world.

2 **Read the website about eating out in Bangkok. Match the headings with the paragraphs.**

1 Street food for beginners
2 A great dining experience
3 A local Thai restaurant

3 **Read the website again. For each sentence write *TP* (Thipsamai Pad), *SF* (street food) or *V* (Vertigo).**

1 You get enough food to make you feel full.
2 Some of the food does not come from the local area.
3 It's best to eat where a lot of other people are eating.
4 You might have to wait before you can go in.
5 The food is very nice, and it doesn't cost much.

4 **Find the phrases in the texts and choose the correct meaning for each.**

1 cater to all price ranges
 a are all expensive
 b are all different prices
2 open-fronted shops
 a shops with the door at the front
 b shops with no wall at the front
3 a classic snapshot of Bangkok food culture
 a a typical photo of how people eat there
 b a perfect place to take a photo of local food
4 a magnificent cityscape
 a a great view of the city
 b a great way to escape from the city

5 **032 Listen to four conversations. What is each person doing? There is one answer you don't need.**

a asking about something on the menu
b booking a table
c ordering food
d paying for a meal
e complaining about a dish

6 **032 Complete the phrases with the correct words and phrases in the box. Then listen and check.**

fine	gluten	help me	isn't cooked
suitable	the bill	to book	very happy

PHRASES YOU MIGHT USE

1 I'd like ________ a table for tonight, please.
2 Yes, eight o'clock is ________ .
3 I'm not ________ with my meal.
4 My meat is tough and it ________ properly.
5 Can you ________ with the menu, please?
6 Is it ________ for vegetarians?
7 And is it ________ free?
8 Can we have ________ , please?

7 **Match the sentences (1–6) with the meanings (a–f).**

PHRASES YOU MIGHT HEAR

1 How many for?
2 We could do eight o'clock.
3 I'll get it sorted for you.
4 We could do you a fresh salad.
5 If you could just check the details.
6 It takes a while to go through.

a Please check the amount on the card reader.
b It takes time to process the payment.
c How many people do you want to book for?
d I will bring a fresh meal for you.
e We can make a salad for you.
f You can have a table at eight o'clock.

8 **Watch the video about eating out in Bangkok. What else do you learn about street food and restaurants in the city? Take notes.**

9 **Work in pairs and compare your notes. Then watch again. Where would you most like to eat? Why? What dishes would you like to try?**

WATCH

LIFE COMPETENCIES

SYNTHESISING INFORMATION, MAKING DECISIONS

10 **Work in pairs. Choose another city and find out about eating out there:**

- choose a restaurant
- look at the menu online
- decide what you would like to try

Then make a poster about the food and restaurants in the city you chose.

4 CITY LIVING?

READING

1 Do most people in your country live in towns and cities or in the countryside?

2 Work in pairs and do the quiz. Compare your answers.

WERE YOU MADE FOR THE CITY STREETS OR THE OPEN AIR?

Complete the sentences and then read what we think!

1 My perfect home would have …
a a balcony with a view of skyscrapers.
b a garden with a view of the mountains.

2 It is important for me to have …
a efficient public transport near my home.
b a reliable car or a good bike.

3 The best pet for me would be …
a something small. I don't have much time for a pet.
b a big, energetic dog.

4 The best place to get vegetables is …
a at the supermarket.
b from a garden.

5 I'm planning a perfect weekend with friends. I'll need …
a fashionable clothes and a lot of money!
b a tent, my sleeping bag, and sun cream.

➜ *Turn to page 193 to find out your results.*

3 **Read Jason's blog and then answer the questions.**

I'm from New York. I've lived in an apartment block in Manhattan since I was born and until last summer, I had never wanted to leave the city. Who needs nature? I had Central Park! Then my friend sent me a message that changed my life: 'Let's do volunteer work on a nature reserve this summer.' Despite my doubts, I decided to do it.

We stayed on a campsite next to a stream just outside the nature reserve. Every night, we sat outside and looked at the stars. Of course, I had seen stars before but not like this! During the day, we helped visitors, however, there was also a lot of free time. We climbed mountains, explored valleys and saw amazing scenery. We swam in lakes below waterfalls and had so much fun, but we learned to respect nature, too.

Early one morning while I was walking in the forest I saw a moose. At first, I thought she was alone, and then I saw that she was a mother with a calf. She was so beautiful, and the moment was magical. I'd never been so close to a wild animal before. I knew that something had changed. I never wanted to live in the city again.

1. Why did Jason go to work on a nature reserve?
2. Why did he enjoy it?
3. When did he realise that he wanted to live in the countryside?

DID YOU KNOW?

In the Preliminary exam, it does not matter whether you use British or American spelling, but you should try not to mix the two.

American English	British English
-or	**-our**
neighborhood	*neighbourhood*
favorite	*favourite*
-er	**-re**
center	*centre*
theater	*theatre*

4 **Read Mona's blog and answer the questions.**

I'm from Greenville. It's a normal village, but for me it used to be the best place in the world. I had never wanted to live in a city until I spent a summer in New York. My aunt invited me to her home in Manhattan. I didn't want to go but my friends said, 'Are you crazy? This is a fantastic opportunity!' They were right.

At first, I felt nervous on New York's busy streets because I had never seen so many people in one place. However, I soon learned to love it. I loved the skyscrapers and the smaller, older buildings, too. I loved the bright lights of Times Square and I had a favorite quieter square, where I used to sit and eat tacos from a food truck. I took the subway to neighborhoods in Manhattan and Brooklyn, and then I walked and walked. I never got lost because there are signposts everywhere.

My favorite place in the city was Brooklyn Bridge because the view is amazing. One morning, my mother called me while I was standing there looking at the skyline. 'Where are you?' asked Mom. I answered, 'I'm exactly where I want to be!'

Share Like Comment

1. Why did Mona spend a summer in New York?
2. Why did she enjoy it?
3. When did she realise that she wanted to live in the city?

5 **Work in pairs. Would you prefer to live in New York City or on a nature reserve? Why?**

VOCABULARY

TOWN AND COUNTRY

1 **Work in pairs. Look at these words from the blogs in the box. Put them in the correct column. If you don't understand a word, discuss it with your partner.**

apartment block food truck nature reserve neighbourhood scenery signpost skyline skyscraper ~~stream~~ subway valley waterfall

USUALLY IN CITIES	USUALLY IN THE COUNTRY
	stream, ...

What's a stream?

It's a small river.

2 **Match the words in exercise 1 with the definitions below.**

1. a big building with flats in it
2. a small river
3. a very tall building
4. the appearance of part of the countryside
5. a vehicle that sells things to eat
6. an American English word for an underground train system
7. water that drops from high up
8. a part of the city where people live
9. an area where plants and animals are protected
10. a low area of land between mountains or hills
11. a notice giving information about where something is
12. the shape of tall buildings with sky behind them

3 **Look at the adjectives below. Do they make you think of the city or the country?**

beautiful exciting noisy peaceful

4 **Think of a city or town and a place in the countryside that you know well. Write a list of things you like and dislike about those places.**

My village
☺ peaceful, friendly ...
☹ a bit boring, no cinema, no sports centre ...
Berlin
☺ fantastic museums, cafés ...
☹ noisy, not always friendly ...

5 **Work in pairs and tell your partner about the places you have chosen and what you like and dislike about them.**

I love my village, but sometimes it's a bit boring. We don't have ...

GRAMMAR

PAST SIMPLE AND PAST CONTINUOUS

GRAMMAR ON THE MOVE
Watch the video

1 **Look at these sentences and complete the rules.**

*While I **was walking** in the forest I **saw** a moose.*
*My mother **called** me while I **was standing** there.*
*Where **was** Jason **living** when he **decided** to work on a nature reserve?*
*He **was living** in New York. He **wasn't living** in the country.*

We use the **past** [1] .... to talk about things that were happening at a certain time in the past. They are often the background to the main event, or they are interrupted by an event. When we describe an event that happened at one point of time in the past, we use the **past** [2] ....

To make the past simple, we add ***-d/-ed*** to a regular verb, or use an irregular form.
We use ***did*** and ***didn't*** to make questions and negative forms.
To make the past continuous, we use ***was/were*** and the main verb with ***-ing***.

➔ ***IRREGULAR VERB LIST*** / *page 223.*

➔ ***GRAMMAR REFERENCE*** / *pages 206–207.*

2 **Choose the correct verb options to complete the text.**

A strange thing happened one day while I [1]*waited/was waiting* for a train. I [2]*read/was reading* a news story on my phone when suddenly I [3]*heard/was hearing* beautiful music. I [4]*looked/was looking* up and saw a woman. She [5]*played/was playing* a piano. There was a piano right there in the station. I wanted to play the piano too but then my train [6]*arrived/was arriving* and I had to go home. Next time!

3 Look at the picture. Complete the sentences with the verbs in the box in the past continuous.

do	draw	laugh	sleep	talk	write

What were the people doing when the bus arrived?

1. One girl was ________ a picture.
2. Two girls were ________ to each other.
3. One woman ________ a message on her phone.
4. Two boys ________ .
5. What ________ the man ________ ?
6. I think he ________ .

If an activity in the past is interrupted by an event, we often introduce the event with **when**.

*I was having my lunch **when** Mark called me.*

Or, we can introduce the background with **while**.

*Mark called me **while** I was having my lunch. / **While** I was having my lunch, Mark called me.*

➡ ***GRAMMAR REFERENCE*** / *page 207.*

4 Complete the text with *when* or *while*.

I live in a big city and I spend a lot of time on public transport. Yesterday, [1] ________ I was waiting for my bus to college, a friend called me and we had a good chat. [2] ________ the bus arrived I was really enjoying the conversation and I nearly forgot to get on! Then, [3] ________ the bus stopped outside my college, I was reading, and I missed the stop. I noticed three stops later and I jumped off the bus. I ran back to my college but [4] ________ I was running, some books fell out of my bag and I had to stop and pick them up. I felt so silly. I want a car!

5 P /wəz/ AND /wə/ 033

Listen to five sentences and count how many words you hear in each.

In past continuous sentences, *was* and *were* are usually heard in their weak forms: /wəz/ and /wə/.

6 P 034 Now say these sentences. Listen and check.

1. I was reading when she called.
2. Why were you laughing?
3. I made dinner while Lisa was sleeping.
4. They were reading all day in the library.
5. Who was shouting so angrily?

LISTENING PART 1 TRAINING

In Part 1 of the Listening exam you will have to identify key information in seven short listening texts, and choose the correct picture.

1 035 **Here is an example. Listen to the conversation and answer the question.**

Where does the woman live now?

A

B

C

2 035 **Listen again and check. Then answer these questions.**

1 Has the woman ever lived on a farm?
2 Would she like to live in a house with a garden?
3 Why can't she have a house in the city?

- *All of the things in the pictures may be mentioned in the listening text, so read the question very carefully before you listen.*
- *Underline key words to help you focus on the information you need.*

3 036 **Listen to two more examples and for each question, choose the correct answer.**

1 What has the girl bought for Lisa?

A

B

C

2 Where is the boy now?

A

B

C

GRAMMAR

PAST PERFECT

GRAMMAR ON THE MOVE
Watch the video

1 Read the sentences and choose the correct word to complete the rule.

*Until last summer, I **had never wanted** to leave the city.*
*Of course, I **had seen** stars before but not like this!*
*I **had never wanted** to live in a city until I spent a summer in New York.*

We use the past perfect to talk about something that happened *before/after* another past event.
We make the past perfect with ***had/hadn't*** + **the past participle**.
We often use the past perfect with ***never, ever, already*** and ***just***. We put these words between ***had*** and the main verb.

➔ **GRAMMAR REFERENCE** / *page 208.*

2 Find one more example of the past perfect in Jason's blog, and one in Mona's blog on page 53.

3 Add the words in brackets in the correct place in these sentences.

1 The party had started when Sam arrived. (already)
2 Fiona felt nervous because she had been on a plane before. (never)
3 I didn't meet Henry because when I arrived at the café, he had left. (just)
4 Had you tried sushi before you ate it yesterday? (ever)

4 Read Marta's travel blog about her arrival in Berlin and put the events in the correct order.

I had never been to Berlin before so my Aunt Katrin met me at the airport. We went to her home by bus. She had sold her car before she moved to the city. 'Public transport is great here!' she told me. We arrived at her apartment and I saw that she had prepared a beautiful room for me. Her son – my cousin Daniel – had gone to live in Los Angeles the month before and she had made his room into a lovely guest room. I looked out of my window and saw some beautiful old buildings and a little park. I knew I was going to love it here.

Share Like Comment

Marta's Aunt Katrin met her at the airport.
Katrin sold her car. *1*
Katrin prepared a room for Marta.
Daniel moved to Los Angeles.
Marta looked out of a window and felt happy.

5 **Complete the text with the verbs in brackets in the past simple or past perfect.**

Daniel [1] ________ (fly) to Los Angeles on 30th May. He [2] ________ (visit) the city once before and he was in love with it. His first visit [3] ________ (be) in January. They don't have a cold winter in LA and when he arrived in May, the weather [4] ________ (be) only a little warmer than it had been in January. When the plane landed he [5] ________ (feel) very happy. He [6] ________ (travel) a long way from home but he knew it was the right thing for him.

6 **Work in pairs and discuss the questions. Use the past perfect and the ideas in the boxes.**

Marta, the travel blogger, did not feel happy at the end of her first day in Berlin. What had she done and seen that day? What had been difficult?

bad food   got lost   language problems
ugly neighbourhoods   unfriendly people

I think she had gone out alone and had got lost.

Yes, or maybe someone had been unfriendly to her.

At the end of her second day in Berlin, Marta felt much happier. What had she done and seen? What had been better?

beautiful neighbourhoods   friendly people
good food   interesting museums   new friends

PUSH YOURSELF B2

GRAMMAR: MIXED TENSES

Complete the conversation between Rob and his friend Lewis. Use the correct form of the verbs in the past simple, past continuous or past perfect.

be   decide   do   happen   hear   leave
lie   look   not finish   read   sleep (x2)

Lewis: Did you enjoy sleeping in a tent every night?
Rob: Well, on the first night I [1] ________ quite frightened.
Lewis: Why? The campsite is safe, isn't it?
Rob: Yes, but I [2] ________ never ________ in a tent before. On the first night I was awake until morning. On the second night I was more relaxed because nothing bad [3] ________ the night before. At about 11 p.m. I [4] ________ in my sleeping bag, feeling quite happy, when suddenly I [5] ________ an animal outside the tent, right next to me.
Lewis: Oh! What was it? A bear?
Rob: No! It was just a fox, but I didn't know that. It was eating the dinner that I [6] ________ because I had been so tired.
Lewis: But you mustn't leave food outside at night! Even I know that! So what [7] ________ you ________ ?
Rob: Nothing! I waited until the animal [8] ________ and then I waited some more, and finally I opened my tent and [9] ________ out. It was late and most other people on the campsite [10] ________ , but I could see a light in my friend's tent. He [11] ________ a book, so I [12] ________ to go and sleep there!

WRITING PART 2 TRAINING

A STORY

In the exam, you will write a story of about 100 words. You are given the first sentence of the story.

1 **Look at this first sentence and then at the story that a student wrote. There are no vocabulary or grammar mistakes in the story, but it is not perfect. What are the problems?**

My friend did not look happy.

My friend did not look happy. I saw her and called her name. She didn't answer. What was the problem? At first I walked away, but then I decided to go and talk to her. 'What's wrong, Stefanie?' I asked. 'Nothing,' she said, but I knew it wasn't true. Then my phone went 'ping!' I looked at the words on the screen: 'Stefanie's birthday.' Finally I understood. 'I'm so sorry!' I said. 'I forgot, again. Happy birthday!' Later we went out together and had fun. Next year, I won't forget.

2 **Find places to put these phrases into the story to add interest.**

when I was walking home from college
She had heard me but
she wasn't smiling and

3 **A story is easier to read if you can see where the beginning, the main part and the ending are. Divide the story into three paragraphs.**

4 **You need time linkers in a story to say when things happened. Here are some examples. Underline the time linkers in the story.**

after that at first finally in the end later
next the next day then when while

5 **Choose the best time linkers to complete the sentences.**

1 *When/While* I was doing the shopping, I saw my friend.
2 First we went out for dinner, and *after that/in the end* we saw a film.
3 Our homework was hard, but I *finally/later* understood it when Laria helped me.
4 *Then/At first* I didn't like Conny, but now I think she's nice.
5 Mark had a great party, but *next/the next day* he had to clean the whole apartment.

6 **Now write a story beginning *My friend did not look happy.* Plan your story first. Remember to do these things:**

- introduce the situation (beginning paragraph)
- describe what happened (main part – usually one paragraph)
- say how things ended (final paragraph)

SPEAKING

MAKING AND RESPONDING TO SUGGESTIONS

1 037 **Listen to five short dialogues. Number the places in the correct order.**

art gallery	covered market	monument
nightclub	shopping mall	

2 **Work in groups. You are going to design a small town with 10 of the facilities in the box below or in exercise 1. Agree on which things you want in your town.**

bank   book shop   café   cinema
department store   factory   library   museum
park   playground   police station   post office
restaurant   sports centre   swimming pool   theatre

3 038 **Listen to some students designing their town. Tick the phrases that you hear for making and responding to suggestions.**

we could … ……
I'm not sure ……
Let's … ……
yes that's great ……
I think that's a great/better idea ……
What about … ? ……
that sounds good ……
Shall we … ? ……
I don't really like that idea ……
… is a nice idea ……

4 **In your group, draw a simple map of your town and agree on where to put things. Use the map below for ideas.**

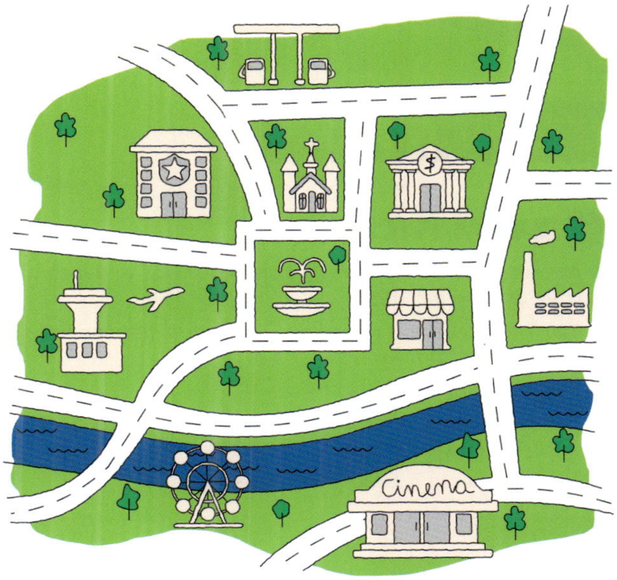

USEFUL LANGUAGE

the cinema is near/next to/opposite in the centre of …
on the left/right there is a …
let's have a big park on this road

5 **Present your town to the class. When all the groups have presented their towns, vote to decide which one would be the best place to live.**

This is our town. It's a lively place with culture and a lot of facilities. Here in the centre we have a cinema and a theatre …

EXAM FOCUS

LISTENING PART 1

EXAM FACTS

- *For each question, you read a short question and look at a set of three pictures.*
- *You listen to a short recording. You hear either one or two people speaking.*
- *You hear each recording twice.*
- *You choose the correct picture, A, B or C, according to what you hear.*
- *There are seven questions in this section.*

EXAM TIPS

- *Before you hear the recording, look at the pictures and note the differences between them.*
- *The speakers usually mention the things you can see in all three pictures. Don't just focus on single words or phrases – you need to listen to everything the speakers say and wait until the end before you choose the answer.*
- *The speakers may mention something twice. But watch out! If the speakers talk about something again, they may use a pronoun, such as 'there', 'that' or 'it' – so listen carefully so that you know what this pronoun means. Remember: the information you need often comes in a sentence where the speakers refer back to something that they have already mentioned.*

  When you hear the recording for the second time, look at the pictures again to check that the answer you've chosen is correct and that the other two pictures are wrong.

039 **For each question, choose the correct answer.**

1 Where will the man and woman go for the weekend?

A B C

2 Where is the girl at the moment?

A B C

3 Where did the family spend the first night of their holiday?

A B C

4 Which place did the woman like best?

A B C

5 Where will the boy meet his friends?

A B C

6 What will the family do this afternoon?

A B C

7 Where will the coach pick up the visitors?

A B C

WRITING PART 2

A STORY

EXAM FACTS

- *For Part 2 of the Writing paper, you answer only ONE question.*
- *You can choose whether to write an article (Question 2) or a story (Question 3).*
- *For Question 3, you are given the first line of a story.*
- *You must write approximately 100 words for your story.*

EXAM TIPS

- *Make sure that your story has a beginning, a middle and an end.*
- *Use past tenses to tell your story.*
- *Use linkers to help your story flow well.*
- *Use adjectives and adverbs to make your story interesting and 'colourful'.*
- *When you've written your story, read it again to check that your grammar, spelling and punctuation are correct.*
- *Don't waste time counting words – it doesn't matter if you don't write exactly 100 words!*

Your English teacher has asked you to write a story.

- Your story must begin with this sentence.
  John looked out of the train window and saw the bright lights of the city.
- Write your **story** in about 100 words.

➡ ***WRITING BANK** / pages 232–233.*

HOW WAS IT?

- Gave it a go
- Getting there
- Aced it!

REAL WORLD

THINGS TO DO IN ... AMSTERDAM

1 **Look at the photos. Which of these activities do you enjoy doing when you visit a city? What other activities do you enjoy?**

AMSTERDAM,

ONE OF THE MOST BEAUTIFUL CITIES IN EUROPE

HOME THINGS TO DO ABOUT FOOD

Often called the 'Venice of the North', Amsterdam has over 100 kilometres of canals and over 1,500 bridges. A canal cruise offers the perfect way to enjoy the city, taking you on a journey along the main waterways and also the many smaller canals, to discover hidden corners of the city. Many boats offer a Hop-On Hop-Off option, allowing you to get off and visit famous sights as you pass them before continuing your trip.

The Rijksmuseum is one of Amsterdam's must-see attractions. The museum first opened its doors to the public in 1800, and now has a magnificent collection of more than 8,000 works of art, including works by artists such as Rembrandt and Rubens.

The Albert Cuyp Market is one of the best-known and busiest street markets in Europe. It began trading in 1904, and now over 300 stalls line the street, selling everything from fruit, vegetables, cheese and fish to clothes and cosmetics. It is also a good place to find souvenirs, offering some of the lowest prices in the city.

Rembrandtplein in the heart of the old city is lined with cafés, restaurants and hotels, making it a magnet for tourists. In the summer, the seats outside cafés are packed with people enjoying a drink, chatting or just watching the world go by. There is also a small park in the centre of the square, where you can relax and admire a statue of the famous Dutch painter Rembrandt.

2 **Read part of a tourist website about things to do in Amsterdam. Which photo is not mentioned?**

3 **Read the text again. Answer the questions.**

1. Why is Amsterdam similar to Venice?
2. What can you do on a Hop-On Hop-Off canal boat?
3. How old is the Rijksmuseum?
4. What can you learn about at the museum?
5. What foods can you buy at the Albert Cuyp Market?
6. Where can you find a statue of a famous Dutch painter?

4 **Find the words in the text (1–5) and match them with their meanings (a–e).**

1	magnificent	**a**	has things all along its sides
2	trading	**b**	selling things
3	is lined with	**c**	very good
4	magnet	**d**	are full of
5	are packed with	**e**	something that attracts a lot of people

5 **040 Listen to three conversations in the Tourist Information Office in Amsterdam. What information does each person want? There is one answer you don't need.**

a information about transport
b information about prices at museums
c ideas for places to visit
d directions to a well-known attraction

6 **040 Complete the questions with the correct words and phrases in the box. Listen and check.**

buy	far	get around	get to	learn about	recommend

PHRASES YOU MIGHT USE

1. Can you .... some places to visit?
2. We'd like to .... the history of the city.
3. Can you tell me how to .... the Albert Cuyp Market?
4. How .... is it?
5. What's the best way to .... the city?
6. Can we .... a City Card here?

7 **Match the sentences (1–6) with the meanings (a–f).**

PHRASES YOU MIGHT HEAR

1. It's like stepping back in time.
2. You can't leave Amsterdam without going on a canal trip.
3. There are loads of points around the city where you can pick one up.
4. It's a bit of a hike.
5. The quickest thing would be to hop on a tram.
6. You might want to consider getting a City Card.

a It's a long way to walk.
b You should go on a canal trip.
c There are lots of places in the city where you can get on a canal boat.
d The quickest thing would be to go by tram.
e It gives you a clear idea of what life was like in the past.
f I think you should get a City Card.

8 **Watch the video about Amsterdam. What helpful advice does it give about these things? Make notes.**

- seeing the old city
- getting around the city
- museums
- street markets
- eating and drinking

9 **Compare your notes in groups. Then watch again to check your ideas.**

LIFE COMPETENCIES

UNDERSTANDING CULTURES, CREATIVE THINKING

10 **Work in groups to make a tourist leaflet for your town or city. Think about:**

- tourist attractions
- why they are interesting
- opening times
- how to get there

Prepare the leaflet and present it to the class.

5 PICTURE OF HEALTH

VOCABULARY

PARTS OF THE BODY

1 **Discuss in pairs. Are you fit? How often do you do sports or take exercise?**

2 041 **Listen to three people, Callum, Anna and Greg, talking about sport. Answer the questions.**

1. Which one is the fittest?
2. Which one is the least fit?
3. Which person is most similar to you?

3 041 **Listen again and write who mentions the body parts below.**

ankle	bone	elbows	knees	lungs
muscles	shoulders	skin	tongue	wrists

4 042 **Decide if the sentences are true or false. Then listen and check.**

IS THAT REALLY TRUE?

1. You can't kiss your **elbow**.
2. Both of your **lungs** are the same size.
3. Adults have more **bones** than babies.
4. The total area of an average man's **skin** is nearly two square metres.
5. You need 100 **muscles** to take just one step.
6. Doctors see more injuries to **shoulders** than to any other part of the body.
7. Most people in the world wear their watch on their left **wrist**.
8. Your knees are different from any other person's **knees**.
9. **Ankle** injuries are the most common problem among sports people.
10. It's possible for a person's **tongue** to be over 10 centimetres long.

5 **Choose the correct words to complete the sentences.**

1. It's important to make sure your *muscles/bones/elbows* are warm before you do exercise.
2. Be careful if you do extreme sports – it can be painful if you break a *tongue/bone/lung*.
3. It you hurt your *knee/wrist/ankle*, it can be difficult to write.
4. Small children sometimes like to sit on their parents' *wrists/ankles/knees*.
5. If you hurt your *shoulder/ankle/lung*, it can be difficult to walk.
6. When people go hiking, they often carry a rucksack on their *shoulders/knees/wrists*.
7. When you breathe in, you fill your *muscles/bones/lungs* with air.
8. When you talk, your *tongue/ankle/wrist* moves in your mouth.
9. If you cut yourself, you break your *skin/elbow/tongue*.
10. Your *elbows/knees/ankles* help your arms to bend.

READING PART 6 TRAINING

1 **Look at the photo of a man called Sam Green. How would you describe him? What is he doing?**

2 **Look at the news article about Sam below. How many parts of the body can you find in the article?**

3 **Read the article again and answer these questions. Don't fill in the gaps.**

1 How far did Sam run?
2 How long did it take him?
3 Why did he do this run?
4 How did he feel after the run?

SAM GREEN –
A RECORD-BREAKING RUNNER

Twenty-year-old student Sam Green **(1)** ________ just become one of the youngest people to run the whole length of Great Britain. That's a total distance of nearly 1,400 km, or the same **(2)** ________ running 38 marathons one after the other.

Superfit Sam says, 'I only started running a few years **(3)** ________ when I injured my shoulder and had to stop playing tennis.' Amazingly, he was able to to do the run in only 31 days. He did this to raise money for a charity **(4)** ________ helps young people and their families.

When he had finished, Sam said, 'It was brilliant. It was a great experience and I enjoyed every minute, although it was painful. My knees are a bit sore, and I've torn a muscle, but I'm fine apart **(5)** ________ that.'

Look at gap 1. The words 'just become' after the gap tell us that this is a verb in the present perfect tense talking about a recent event. The subject before the gap is 'Sam Green', so the missing word is HAS.

4 **Now look at gaps 2–5. Read the tip and think about the kind of words which are missing. For each question, write the correct answer. Write one word for each gap.**

5 **Work in pairs and discuss the questions.**

1 Do you think that doing challenges like this are a good way to help charities?
2 Have you ever done a sporting activity for charity?
3 Do you think that long-distance running is a good way to keep fit?
4 What other ways are there to keep fit?

GRAMMAR

ABILITY AND ADVICE

GRAMMAR ON THE MOVE
Watch the video

1 **Read this online post from a young woman called Emily and answer the question below.**

Wall Friends Photos Profile

Can anyone help me? I've got a problem. I'm tired all day, but I **can't** sleep at night! When I go to bed, it takes me ages to fall asleep. I can only fall asleep if I watch TV in bed, but then I wake up after a short time, and **I'm not able to** go back to sleep again. I **could** sleep really well when I was younger, but I haven't been able to sleep for months now! What do you think I should do? *Emily*

Share Like Comment

What is Emily's problem?

A She can't wake up in the morning.
B She falls asleep in the daytime.
C She is awake during the night.

2 **Look at the words in bold in Emily's post and complete the rules.**

> To talk about present ability, we use [1] ……………… /***can't*** or ***be (not)*** [2] ……………… ***to*** before the main verb. But ***can/can't*** is more usual.
> To talk about past ability, we use [3] ……………… /***couldn't*** for general ability but ***was*** (***not***) ***able to*** to talk about a specific situation:
> *I **could** sleep really well when I was younger.*
> *He **was able to** do the run in only 31 days.*
> We only use ***can*** in the present simple and ***could*** in the past simple. For all other tenses, we use ***be able to***.

3 **Can you find an example of another tense in the text above?**

GRAMMAR REFERENCE / *page 208.*

4 **Complete the sentences using the words below. There are three words you don't need.**

am	can	can't	could	couldn't
have been	haven't been	was		

1 I live in the mountains where it snows a lot, so I ……………… ski quite well.
2 Because I ……………… swim when I was a child, I never enjoyed holidays at the seaside.
3 I broke a bone in my foot last month, so I ……………… walk very fast at the moment.
4 Unfortunately I've had lots of work to do this week, so I ……………… able to go to the gym.
5 Because I'd trained a lot, I ……………… able to win the race quite easily.

5 **Read the advice that people have given Emily. Which do you think is the best piece of advice?**

Wall Friends Photos Profile

You **should** have a warm bath before you go to bed. That will relax you! *Gabriella*

You **ought to** do a sport, like running or cycling. The fresh air and exercise will help you fall asleep. *Peter*

You **shouldn't** drink coffee after dinner. Coffee keeps people awake. *Ksenia*

Share Like Comment

6 **Look at the words in bold above and complete the rule.**

> To give advice, we use ***should/shouldn't*** or ……………… before the main verb. Most of the time, we can use both.
> We don't usually use ***ought to*** in the negative.

GRAMMAR REFERENCE / *page 209.*

7 **Complete each sentence with one word.**

1 You ……………… have so many sugary drinks – they're bad for your teeth.
2 My doctor says that I ……………… to take more exercise.
3 You ……………… train every day if you want to run a marathon.
4 I think I ……………… join a gym and try to get fitter.

8 **Write a reply to Emily. Tell her how you feel, give her some advice, and then say what you hope.**

I'm sorry to hear about your problem.
You shouldn't … I think … You should/ You ought to …
I hope this helps. / I hope you sleep well tonight.

VOCABULARY

ACHES AND PAINS

1 043 **Match the sentences (1–8) with the photos (A–H). Then listen and check.**

1. I've got **backache**.
2. My tooth **hurts**.
3. I've got **a cough**.
4. I **injured** my ankle.
5. I've got **a cold**.
6. I've got **a pain** in my stomach.
7. I've got **a sore** throat.
8. My knee is **painful**.

A

B

C

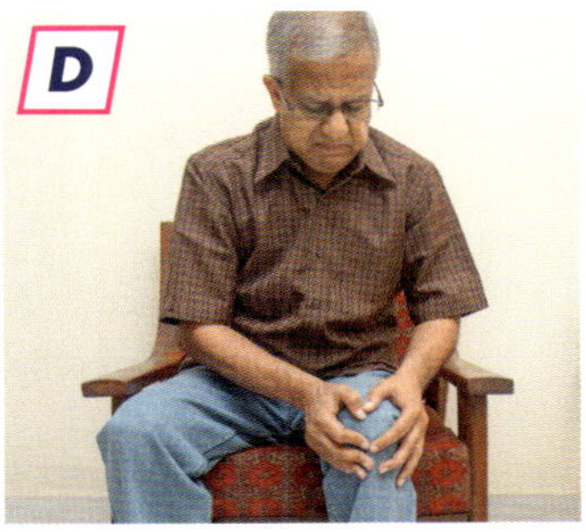
D

E

F

G

H

2 Look at the words in bold in exercise 1 and complete the sentences. There are three words you don't need.

1. I've got a .... in my foot.
2. My throat .... when I talk.
3. I .... my neck when I was doing gymnastics.
4. I've written so much that I've got .... fingers.
5. I can't bend over. I've had .... all day.

3 P VOWEL SOUNDS 044

Look at these words. Which one has the same sound as the word in bold? Which two words in bold have the same sound? Listen and check.

1	**ache**	make	match
2	**cough**	up	off
3	**sore**	four	on
4	**hurt**	but	skirt
5	**pain**	plane	plan

4 045 **Listen to the conversations. You will hear the words in the box. Match the words with the meanings.**

patient infection tablet prescription emergency

a. a serious situation that needs immediate action
b. a disease in a part of your body
c. a person who is looked after by a doctor, nurse or other health professional
d. a piece of paper where a doctor writes details of the medicine that you need
e. a small, round type of medicine that you put in your mouth

5 Complete these sentences using the words in exercise 4.

1. The chemist's won't give you this medicine unless you have a .... from your doctor.
2. An ambulance on the road can only drive faster than the speed limit if there is an ....
3. I was the only .... in the doctor's waiting room today, so I didn't have to wait very long.
4. If you have an .... in a part of your body, you sometimes have to take .... to make it go away.

DID YOU KNOW?

*British English speakers say they are **ill** if they aren't well, but American English speakers say they are **sick**.*

6 Work in pairs and discuss the questions.

1. Have you ever broken a bone or had an injury?
2. What were you doing when it happened?
3. How did it happen?

PUSH YOURSELF B2

VOCABULARY: HEALTH EXPRESSIONS

1 **046 What do you think these expressions mean? Match the expressions (A–H) with the questions (1–7). Then listen and check.**

A I've got a splitting headache.
B I think I'm coming down with flu.
C My feet are killing me.
D I'm a bit under the weather.
E I'll call in sick.
F There's a bug going round.
G I'm on the mend.
H I'm back on my feet.

2 **Which expression could you use when …**

1. you've got a high temperature and you're beginning to feel more and more ill?
2. you're feeling tired and a little unwell?
3. you phone work because you're ill?
4. you've been ill but you're starting to get better now?
5. a lot of people that you know have been getting ill recently?
6. you've recovered from an illness or injury and you're well again now?
7. something is hurting you a lot? (two expressions)

3 **Work in pairs. Ask your partner some of these questions. Try to think of suitable answers using the expressions in exercise 1. There may be more than one possible answer.**

1. How are you feeling?
2. Are you going to work today?
3. Do you want to sit down?
4. Are you the only person in your class who's ill?
5. Should I turn the music down?
6. Are you still feeling ill?

SPEAKING

ASKING ABOUT PROBLEMS, SHOWING SYMPATHY AND GIVING ADVICE

1 **Who do you speak to when you're ill? What advice do people give you?**

2 **047 Listen to a man called Tom talking to a friend and a doctor about how he feels. Answer the questions.**

1. Where does Tom want to go tonight?
2. Why can't he go there?
3. What does the friend tell him to do?
4. What does the doctor tell him to do?

3 **048 Listen to the first conversation again and tick the phrases that you hear. Check with your partner.**

1	2	3 ....
How are you? What's the matter? How are you doing? What's wrong?	I'm sorry to hear that. Take care. Poor you. Get well soon. I hope you feel better soon. Look after yourself.	You should … You ought to … Why don't you have … ? How about having … ? It's a good idea to … If I were you, I'd …

4 **Work in pairs and answer the questions.**

1. Put the headings in the box in the correct column in exercise 3.

   Giving advice Asking about problems Showing sympathy

2. Look at the phrases you have ticked in columns 1 and 2. Can you find another phrase in the column which has the same meaning?

5 **Complete this conversation using expressions in exercise 3 on page 68.**

A: Hi, how [1] .... ?
B: I don't feel [2] .... , actually.
A: [3] .... the matter?
B: My head really [4] ....
A: I'm sorry to [5] .... Why [6] .... lie down and have a rest?
B: Yes, I will.
A: Well, take [7] ....
B: Thanks.

6 **Work in pairs and practise the conversation in exercise 5, then create conversations of your own. Choose a problem from the box below and use the expressions in exercise 3 on page 68.**

earache	headache	stomach ache	toothache

GRAMMAR

OBLIGATION

GRAMMAR ON THE MOVE
Watch the video

1 **Look at these sentences and complete the rules.**

*I **need to** rest.*
*You **don't need to** say sorry.*
*You **have to** take these tablets four times a day.*
*You **don't have to** take them with food.*
*You **mustn't** forget to take your tablets.*
*You **must** take them for five days.*

If it's necessary for us to do something, we use [1] .... , [2] .... or [3] .... If it's not necessary for us to do something, we use [4] .... or [5] .... If it's important for us not to do something, we use [6] ....
We use ***must***, ***need to*** and ***have to*** with the infinitive form of the verb.
To form the negative and questions with ***need to*** and ***have to***, we use ***do/does*** (***not***).
To form the negative with ***must***, we add ***not***.
To form questions about necessity we usually use ***have to*** instead of ***must***.
*Do I **have to** … ?*

GRAMMAR REFERENCE / *page 209.*

2 **Choose the correct words to complete these sentences.**

1 In my country, you *don't have to/mustn't* pay for medicine if you're under 18.
2 Tom's doctor said that he *doesn't have to/mustn't* play rugby with an injured shoulder.
3 If you want to lose weight and get fit, you *need/must* stop eating so much chocolate.
4 You *don't need to/mustn't* be a member of the gym to use the pool.

3 **Complete this text about running with the words in the box.**

don't have to	must	mustn't	need

Running is a good way of keeping healthy. It's quite a cheap way to stay fit because you [1] .... buy equipment or join a club. You [2] .... have a good pair of running shoes, though. You [3] .... go running without warming up your muscles first, and you [4] .... to make sure that you drink plenty of water while you're running.

4 **Do you go to a gym, sports club, or swimming pool? Are there any rules there? Discuss in pairs.**

1 What can people do there?
2 What do people have to do when they are there?
3 What don't people have to do?
4 What mustn't you do there?

READING PART 1 TRAINING

1 **Look at the notice below, and think about the questions.**

1. Where do you think you might see this sign?
2. Who might be interested in it?
3. What extra information would people need?

2 **Read the notice. Underline an expression that means 'necessary' and an expression that means 'not necessary'.**

3 **Look at these three sentences. Only one of them contains the same information as the notice above. Is it A, B or C?**

A You don't have to reserve a place for this course.
B You must have some experience of learning to dance.
C You can come to these lessons alone.

The notice says, 'no need to bring a partner'. This means 'you can go to classes on your own', so sentence C is correct. Sentences A and B don't match the notice.

4 **Now read the label and the message. For each question, choose the correct answer.**

1

Adults and over 12s:
Take 1–2 tablets, up to a maximum of four times daily

A Teenagers shouldn't take these tablets.
B You mustn't take these tablets more than four times a day.
C You have to take at least two of these tablets at a time.

2

Hi Laura
Do you know Oasis Health Club? I was thinking of going next weekend and wondered if you'd like to come too.
Let me know what you think!
Sophie

Why is Sophie writing this text?
A to give Laura some advice
B to make a suggestion to Laura
C to ask for some information from Laura

LISTENING PART 3 TRAINING

1 **Work in pairs. Which of the things in the box do you think are most important for customers who go to health clubs? Put them in order of importance.**

comfortable facilities	friendly staff	good food
a large pool	a relaxing atmosphere	
a well-equipped gym	a wide range of activities	

2 **Look at the notes about a day at Oasis Health Club on page 71 and think about the missing words. Which gap needs information about: A time? A place? Something you can learn to do? Something to eat or drink?**

3 049 **Look at gap 1 in exercise 4. Read and listen to part of a talk by a health club manager who is welcoming customers for the weekend, and think about how to fill the gap.**

In the mornings, we normally have a **tennis** class, but unfortunately the tennis court is out of use today. So instead we have an hour's **yoga** outside in the garden – that class will be taught by Annie, one of our fitness instructors.

The speaker mentions two classes – tennis and yoga – but says that there is no tennis class today. So you should write **yoga** *in gap 1.*

4 050 **Now listen to the whole talk. For each question, write the correct answer in the gap. Write one or two words or a number or a date or a time.**

You'll hear two or more possible words that could fill each gap – but only one answer is correct.

Oasis Health Club

Today's programme:

This morning: (1) .... class

Lunch: Salad bar opens at (2) .... o'clock

Afternoon: Talk by food expert on the health benefits of (3) ....

(4) .... lesson in the indoor swimming pool

Bike ride to the (5) ....

5 Discuss the questions in pairs.

Would you like to go to a health or fitness club like this? Why / Why not? What would you like to do there?

WRITING

1 Read this email. Why is Alex writing to Chris?

Hi Chris

How are you? Could I ask you for some advice? I really want to get healthier and fitter, but I'm not sure how to do this. Do you have any ideas? I'd be really grateful for any tips you could give me.

Thanks for your help. I'm looking forward to hearing your ideas!

Alex

2 Now read Chris' answer to Alex. Find phrases he uses to give advice, an expression to start an email with, and an expression to end an email with.

Hi Alex

Thank's for your email. It's great that you want to get fitter and healthier! So here's my advice:

The best way to get healthier is to eat a lot of fresh fruits and vegetables. Theyre much better for you than fast food and ready meals. Why don't you try cooking your own food? It can be a lot of fun! You shouldn't to eat too much sugar because it's not good on your health.

How about joining a gym to get fitter? If I were you, I'd join Lifestyle Fitness on High Street. It's a great gym and its swiming pool is fantastic. The staff who work there are realy friendly people, too. It doesn't matter if you're not able to go there every day. Just two or three times a week is enough.

It was great to hear from you. Tell me how it goes!

Write soon!

Chris

3 Read Chris' email again. Chris has made two punctuation errors, two spelling errors, one preposition error, and one modal verb error. Can you find them and correct them?

4 Now write your answer to Alex's email. In your email, you should:

- say how you feel about Alex's email
- give Alex some advice about health and fitness
- recommend a place where Alex can go to get fit

Use your own ideas and write about 100 words. When you have written your reply, read it through carefully and check that there are no mistakes with punctuation, spelling, prepositions or modal verbs.

EXAM FOCUS

READING PART 1

EXAM FACTS

- *You read five short texts. These can be signs, labels, notices, advertisements, messages or emails.*
- *After each text there are three options: three statements or a question with three answers.*
- *You must choose the option which means the same as the text.*

EXAM TIPS

- *Read each text carefully. Make sure that you understand the whole message of the text.*
- *Read each option carefully and think about what it means. Don't just focus on individual words or phrases – consider the whole statement.*
- *The correct answer is the one which expresses the same information as the text in a different way.*
- *When you've chosen your answer, check that the other two options are wrong.*

For each question, choose the correct answer.

1

Take this medicine before each meal.
Keep in refrigerator after opening and use before 30 September.

This label has information about

A how much medicine you should take.

B how long you should keep this medicine.

C where you should put this medicine before it's opened.

2

Hi Amy
Sorry, I can't give you a lift to our dance practice tonight. I've got a bad headache, so I'm staying at home. I've let the teacher know.
Olivia

Why is Olivia writing this text?

A to offer Amy a lift to their dance practice

B to ask Amy to give a message to the teacher

C to tell Amy that she isn't going out tonight

3

The volleyball court is closed today.
Volleyball classes are taking place in the gym today.

This notice is telling volleyball students

A why the volleyball court is not open.

B when their class will take place.

C where to go for their lesson.

4

Hi Joe,
Have you finished that book about athletics that I lent you? If you have, could you bring it into work for me some time next week? Thanks!
Harry

What does Harry want Joe to do?

A return a book to him

B lend a book to him

C recommend a book to him

5

Children aged under eight must not use this pool alone
An adult must accompany them at all times

A This pool is only for children of under eight and their parents.

B Nobody under the age of eight is allowed in this pool on their own.

C Each adult can only take one child under eight into the pool with them.

READING PART 6

EXAM FACTS

- *You read a text of about 120 words which has six gaps in it. Six words have been removed from the text.*

EXAM TIPS

- *Before you try to fill the gaps, read each sentence carefully. Look at the words before and after the gap and think about what kind of word is missing. Think about the grammar of the word: Does it have to agree with a singular or plural noun? You will find the answers to these questions by looking at the rest of the sentence.*
- *Read the sentence again with the word you have chosen. Check that it makes sense and that it fits grammatically.*
- *When you have filled in the gaps, read the whole text again to make sure that you have chosen the correct words.*

For each question, write the correct answer.
Write one word for each gap.

The Health Benefits of Laughter

We all know that it's fun to laugh. But did you know that laughing is good for you, too?

Several recent studies **(1)** .... shown that laughter has health benefits. Laughing not only makes people feel happy and relaxed, but it reduces stress, too. What's more, it helps our blood to flow, and so protects **(2)** .... from heart disease. According to scientific research, people **(3)** .... spend a lot of time laughing with family and friends are likely to be healthier **(4)** .... other people. In fact, a study done at a university in Japan suggests that people with a good sense **(5)** .... humour may even live longer.

It seems that laughter really is **(6)** .... best medicine.

LISTENING PART 3

EXAM FACTS

- *You listen to a person giving information: for example, details about a place, an event or an experience.*
- *You read a list of notes or short sentences which have six gaps in them.*
- *You hear the information twice, and you fill in the gaps with words that you hear while you are listening.*
- *The answer is usually one word or number, or occasionally two words. Sometimes you have to write down a name which is spelled out.*

EXAM TIPS

- *Before you hear the recording, read the notes or sentences and try to predict the type of word which you need to write in each gap. Is it a number, or the name of a place, a person, or an object, for example? Check whether a singular or plural word is needed.*
- *Look at the words before or after the gap. These will tell you when you should start to listen carefully for each answer.*
- *Listen for the first time and try to fill each gap. If you don't catch the word, don't worry – just move straight on to the next question.*
- *Be careful of words which could fit in the gap but are not the correct answer. You hear these words either before or after the correct word.*
- *Listen for the second time to check that you heard correctly and to fill in any words which you missed the first time.*
- *Check what you've written. Have you spelled the word correctly? Does it fit correctly in the gap?*

051 For each question, write the correct answer in the gap. Write one or two words or a number or a date or a time. You will hear a radio announcement about a new bike hire club.

City Bike Hire Club

You join at the beginning of: **(1)** ....

Colour of bikes for adults: **(2)** ....

Unlock bikes by using a **(3)** ....

Collect and leave bikes at city's **(4)** ....

Cost of annual membership: **(5)** €............

Get information from www. **(6)** ....

HOW WAS IT?

Gave it a go ☐

Getting there ☐

Aced it! ☐

REAL WORLD

PREPARING TO TRAVEL TO ... MARRAKESH

1 **Look at the photos of Marrakesh. Have you ever been to the city? What do you know about it? What can you learn from the photos?**

2 **What do you think about when you are preparing to travel abroad? Read part of a health website. Can you think of any more tips?**

Before you **travel abroad**

There's a lot to think about before you travel abroad. Here are some tips to help you.

- Look online and find the latest health advice for the country you're travelling to.
- Find out if you need any vaccinations, and arrange to have these before you leave.
- If there are diseases such as malaria in the country you are visiting, you may need to start taking tablets before you travel.
- Make sure you take high-factor sunscreen, painkillers and antiseptic. It's also useful to take a bottle of hand sanitiser.
- It's very important to have travel insurance, both for longer periods of travelling and short family holidays.

FOOD AND DRINK IN MARRAKESH

Morocco has some delicious traditional dishes, but sometimes when you try unusual food in a foreign country, you can experience an upset stomach. As with any country, follow these few simple steps to stay safe and enjoy some amazing food in Marrakesh!

- Always wash your hands before eating and after using the bathroom.
- Carry a small bottle of hand sanitiser, which is helpful in places where it isn't possible to wash your hands.
- When you buy street food, remember that hot food is usually safe to eat, but avoid food that has been in the sun for a long time.
- It's easy to find bottled water when you're out and about. However, remember the plastic from water bottles causes a lot of pollution. Most hotels have filtered water for their guests. This water is usually free.

3 **Find the words below in the webpage and match them with their meanings.**

antiseptic	filtered water	painkiller	sanitiser
sunscreen	travel insurance	vaccination	

1. a liquid or cream you put on your skin to keep it clean when you have cut it
2. this prevents you from catching an illness
3. an agreement with a company that they will pay the costs if something bad happens to you while you are on holiday
4. water that has been cleaned so that it is safe to drink
5. a liquid or cream to put on your skin to clean it before you eat food
6. a medicine to stop you feeling pain
7. a cream or liquid that protects your skin from the sun

4 **Read the information about food and drink in Marrakesh. Answer the questions.**

1. When should you use hand sanitiser?
2. What street food should you not eat?
3. What is the problem with bottled water?
4. What can you drink in most hotels?

5 **052 Listen to two tourists talking to a travel agent about the holiday they are planning in Marrakesh. Tick the topics they discuss.**

1 flights ....
2 vaccinations ....
3 the weather ....
4 luggage ....
5 the water ....
6 food ....
7 the local currency ....
8 dealing with illness ....

6 **052 Complete the questions you can ask when you are preparing to travel with words in the box. Listen and check.**

do we need	is there anything	
safe to drink	the food like	we do

PHRASES YOU MIGHT USE

1 .... any vaccinations?
2 .... we should take with us?
3 Is the water .... ?
4 What's .... in Morocco?
5 What should .... if we're ill?

7 **Choose the correct meanings.**

PHRASES YOU MIGHT HEAR

1 That's all the details sorted.
 a We have discussed all the facts and information.
 b We need to discuss some more details.
2 It's only an issue in the very rural areas.
 a It's only a problem in the big cities.
 b It's only a problem in the countryside.
3 They can be a nuisance.
 a They are sometimes annoying.
 b They are sometimes dangerous.
4 It doesn't hurt to be cautious.
 a You don't need to worry.
 b It's a good idea to be careful.
5 Stick to hot dishes.
 a Only choose hot dishes.
 b Don't eat hot dishes.
6 Your hotel's your first port of call for any problems.
 a Your hotel might cause some problems.
 b Ask at your hotel if you have problems.

8 **Watch the video about travelling to Marrakesh. What do you learn about these things? Make notes.**

- the old city of Marrakesh
- hotels in Marrakesh
- restaurants and cafés
- street food
- health advice

9 **Compare your notes. Then watch again to check your ideas.**

LIFE COMPETENCIES

SYNTHESISING INFORMATION, TAKING CONTROL OF LEARNING

10 **Make a list of information and tips to help travellers prepare for a visit to your country. Think about:**

- the weather
- vaccinations
- how to avoid getting ill
- getting medical help

Present the information to the class.

PROGRESS CHECK 2

COOKING WORDS

1 Complete the conversation with the words in the box.

saucepan	grate	oven	put	slices

Ken: What shall we do with all these potatoes?
Pete: Let's fry them. Wait! They'll be better if we boil them first. We need a big [1] .... of water.
Ken: Really? OK. Give me a knife and I'll start to peel them and cut them into [2] ....
Pete: No, we do that later. First we [3] .... them in the pot … Oh, these are really big potatoes. I have another idea: let's bake them. And then we can [4] .... some cheese over them.
Ken: That sounds delicious. I'll switch on the [5] .... 200 degrees, is that hot enough?

EATING OUT

2 Complete this waiter's social media post with the words below. There are three words you don't need.

bill	bowl	course	delicious	disgusting
meal	piece	starter	tip	

What an evening! Our customers usually say our food is absolutely [1] .... , but this evening we had a couple who didn't like anything. First, they had a [2] .... of soup and then for the main [3] .... they had steak. They said it was really horrible but they ate all of it! I think they didn't want to pay for their [4] .... In the end, they paid their [5] .... , but we gave them a bottle of wine for free. I was really nice to them and then they didn't even give me a [6] .... !

Share Like Comment

SOME, ANY, MUCH, MANY, A LOT OF, A LITTLE, A FEW, NO

3 Join the beginnings and endings of these sentences.

1 I want to cook a delicious meal but I don't have much
2 You need a lot
3 Maria wants to cook some
4 The children want some
5 We need to buy a few
6 I like to put a little
7 Is there any
8 Are there any

a of flour if you want to make bread.
b sugar in my tea.
c carrots in the cupboard?
d milk in the fridge?
e time.
f sweets, but they've already had cakes.
g meat for dinner.
h new plates for our dinner party.

PLACES IN THE CITY AND THE COUNTRY

4 Complete the names of the things described by the sentences.

1 You can study here or borrow books to read at home.
a l............
2 You can stay here on holiday if you have a tent.
a c............
3 This is one building with many homes in it.
an a............ b............
4 People come here to look at art.
an a............ g............
5 This is a kind of river that is not very big.
a s............
6 It's a part of a town or city that people live in.
a n............
7 This is one big shop for food, clothes and many other things.
a d............ s............

PAST SIMPLE, PAST CONTINUOUS AND PAST PERFECT

5 Choose the correct words to complete the text.

Last year I [1]*went/was going* to New York for a week with my friend Cathy. Cathy [2]*was/had been* there before, but for me it was the first visit. It was great but unfortunately, two bad things [3]*happened/had happened*. On the first afternoon, while I [4]*took/was taking* photos of the skyline, a thief stole my bag. Another tourist told me that exactly the same thing [5]*happened/had happened* to her the day before. I also [6]*had/was having* a problem while we [7]*were travelling/had travelled* to Staten Island on the ferry. I fell and [8]*broke/had broken* my camera! However, my trip to New York was still absolutely fantastic!

ILLNESS AND INJURY

6 Complete the telephone conversation with the words below in the box. There are three words you don't need.

earache	emergency	injure	muscle	painful
patients	prescription	shoulder	sore	

Joe: Hi, Meg. You don't sound good. What's the matter?

Meg: Everything. First, I've got a cough and a really [1] ________ throat.

Joe: You should go to the chemist's and buy some medicine. You don't need a [2] ________ from your doctor to get medicine for a cold.

Meg: I did that, but on the way back I fell in the snow and hurt my [3] ________ . It was really [4] ________ so I went directly to the doctor's. Of course, there were a lot of other [5] ________ , so I had to wait for ages.

Joe: But when it's an [6] ________ , you should go to a hospital!

Meg: Yeah, but in the end it wasn't that bad. I just have to stay at home and rest.

MODAL VERBS

7 Choose the correct words to complete the sentences.

1. I've injured my foot. I *can/must/should* walk but it hurts.
2. Last year, I broke my leg and I *mustn't/can't/couldn't* walk for three months.
3. If you've got a toothache then you *must/could/are able to* go to the dentist's.
4. You look so tired. I think you *have to/ought to/able to* stay in bed today.
5. I've been at home all day because I'm sick, but I've *could/been able to/ought to* do lots of work on my computer.
6. Please don't phone me. I've got a sore throat and I *mustn't/don't have to/don't need to* talk.

COMMON MISTAKES

8 Find one mistake in each sentence and rewrite the sentences.

1. I'd like a rice, please.
2. I need a few time to finish my homework.
3. Last weekend we have a party.
4. Sarah gave Chris a present that he has always wanted.
5. You must to do your homework!
6. It's Saturday so I don't must go to work.
7. Sorry, but I couldn't go to the English lesson today.
8. You don't have to eat too many sweets.

A MEAL IN THE COUNTRY

9 Choose the correct word (a–d) for each gap (1–6).

One day we decided to drive out to the countryside for a meal. I wanted my favourite [1] ________ : *longaniza*, a kind of sausage. We drove through a beautiful [2] ________ of hills and streams, and found a restaurant. There were not [3] ________ customers there. Now I know why! The restaurant looked [4] ________ nice, but the food was absolutely [5] ________ ! It's really not difficult to cook a sausage, but this one was grilled until it was black. The waiter served it to me with one slice of [6] ________ . No salad, no chips … and it wasn't cheap. How disappointing.

1. **a** plate **b** dish **c** bowl **d** course
2. **a** neighbourhood **b** skyline **c** landscape **d** nature
3. **a** much **b** few **c** little **d** many
4. **a** quite **b** absolutely **c** totally **d** completely
5. **a** bad **b** tasty **c** delicious **d** disgusting
6. **a** fish **b** bread **c** rice **d** wine

6 ONLINE, OFFLINE

LISTENING

1 **Answer the quiz questions. Work in groups and discuss your answers.**

1 You want to have a fun day out with some friends. How do you organise it? Why?

- ○ I use email.
- ○ I write messages to individual people.
- ○ I create a group on a messaging app.
- ○ I phone people.

2 If you are going to be late to meet a friend, how do you tell him or her? Why?

- ○ I send a written message.
- ○ I send a voice message.
- ○ I phone the person.
- ○ I don't do anything. My friend is probably late too!

2 **Work in groups and discuss the questions.**

1. Do you live in or have you ever visited your country's capital city?
2. How would you spend a day there with friends?

3 053 **Three friends are going to visit Dylan, a young man who lives in London. Listen to this short voice message and answer the questions.**

1. When are the three friends going to London?
2. What is the main purpose of Dylan's message?

4 054 **Listen to messages from Dylan's three friends. Who suggests which activity? Write *Rafi*, *Megan* or *Sue* under each photo.**

A

B

C

5 054 **Listen again. Which speaker …**

1. will have less time in London than the others?
2. needs to buy things for people they like?
3. may spend some time alone?
4. is not travelling home on Sunday afternoon?
5. is more interested in seeing Dylan than in seeing London?

6 055 **Now listen to Dylan's plan for the weekend and put the photos in the order he talks about them.**

A

B

C

D

E

7 **Work in pairs and discuss the questions. What kind of places do you like visiting with friends? Do you visit the same kinds of places with family?**

DID YOU KNOW?

British English: *You write* ***to*** *somebody, e.g. Please write to me when you arrive in New York.*

American English: *You write somebody (no* ***to****), e.g. Please write me or The college wrote him about his exam results.*

British English: *Visit a friend, visit your aunt*

American English: *Visit a friend or visit* ***with*** *a friend*

SPEAKING PART 1 TRAINING

In Part 1 of the Speaking test, the examiner will ask you some questions about yourself. You may need to talk about where you live, what you do, your hobbies, people in your life, etc.

The questions are simple, but avoid one-word answers, and make sure what you say is relevant.

1 056 **Listen to these four answers to one question. Do you think they are good? Why? / Why not?**

2 **Work in pairs. Ask and answer these questions that can come up in the Speaking test.**

1. Where do you live?
2. What do you do?
3. How do you get to school/work every day?
4. Do you enjoy learning English? Why? / Why not?
5. Do you think English will be useful for you in the future?

3 057 **Listen to candidates answering the questions below.**

1. Can you tell us about your family?
2. What does your family do together?
3. Where do you meet your friends?
4. Tell us about a teacher that you like or liked.

Which candidate uses which phrase or strategy to gain time to think while forming an answer?

USEFUL LANGUAGE

Let me see, … Well, … So, …
repeating part of the question

4 **Work in pairs and ask and answer the questions from exercise 3.**

GRAMMAR

PLANS AND INTENTIONS

GRAMMAR ON THE MOVE
Watch the video

1 **Look at the two sentences below and complete the rules with *will* or *be going to*.**

*I'**m going to** meet you at the station.*
*I forgot to book a table! I'**ll** call the restaurant later.*

We use [1] .... + infinitive to talk about things that we plan to do.
We use [2] .... + infinitive when we make decisions about the future at the time of speaking.

- The negative form of ***will*** is ***will not***, but we usually shorten it to ***won't***. We also often shorten ***will*** to ***'ll***, particularly for decisions made now. To make questions, we put ***will*** before the subject and the verb: ***Will** you call me tomorrow?*
- We use ***going to*** with ***be***. To make a negative sentence we use a form of ***be*** + ***not***:
*I'**m not going to** visit the art gallery.*

To make a question we put the form of ***be*** before the subject:
***Are** you **going to** visit your parents tomorrow?*

GRAMMAR REFERENCE / *page 210.*

2 **Complete the conversation with the words in the box.**

going	to	will (x2)	won't

Jim: I'm afraid I'm not going [1] .... have dinner with you and Marie tomorrow.
Lou: Why not? I know you don't like spaghetti. I [2] .... make pasta, OK?
Jim: That's not the problem. It's just because I don't have time. I have to finish an essay.
Lou: Oh. When are you [3] .... to meet us, then?
Jim: Maybe about 8 or 9 p.m.
Lou: That's fine. [4] .... you send me a message when you're on the way to my house?
Jim: Yes, I [5] .... See you tomorrow.

3 **Complete the conversation with the correct form of *will* or *be going to*. Use the contractions *'ll* or *won't* if possible.**

Karen: What [1] .... do on your birthday?
Jasmine: I [2] .... do anything. I'm too busy.
Karen: What? But you have to do something! Your friends want to celebrate with you.
Jasmine: Oh, OK then, I [3] .... have a little party. But I [4] .... invite many people. It's just before the exams, you see. I've made a study plan. I [5] .... study for eight hours every day. I really need to get good marks this year.
Karen: I have an idea. I [6] .... organise the party for you.
Jasmine: Great! [7] .... you clean up the next day, too?
Karen: Uh, well … OK. Yes, I [8] ....

4 **We often use the tenses in the examples below for talking about the present, but here they are used for talking about the future. Read the sentences and complete the rules.**

*I'**m meeting** my cousin Meera on Saturday afternoon.*
*We'**re seeing** a play on Saturday night.*
*The concert **starts** at eight this evening.*
*Your train **gets** in at five o'clock.*

We can use the **present** [1] .... for talking about arrangements we have made for the future, e.g. a plan to meet a person at a fixed time.
We can use the **present** [2] .... for a 'timetable future', e.g. for talking about when things begin and end, or when public transport leaves and arrives.

GRAMMAR REFERENCE / *page 210.*

5 **Complete the messages with the correct form of the verb in brackets in the present simple or present continuous.**

Hi! I'm getting the early bus at 7. It [1] .... (arrive) at 10:30. I [2] .... (see) the doctor at 11 and after that we can have lunch. OK?

No! It's Thursday. College [3] .... (finish) at 3, so I can't meet you before then. [4] .... you .... (go) back home in the evening?

No, I [5] .... (stay) in town with my sister. Can we meet in the evening? Or afternoon? I [6] .... (do) anything in the afternoon.

My sister [7] .... (play) in a concert in the afternoon. Do you want to come?

What time [8] .... it .... (start)?

6 **Work in groups of four. Talk about plans and arrangements that you already have and what time your activities start/finish. Is it possible to find a time when you could all meet this weekend?**

VOCABULARY

SOCIAL MEDIA

1 **Read what Matt says about communicating and sharing through technology. Then work in groups and discuss the questions.**

1. Do you agree with Matt?
2. What social media or messaging apps do you use? Why?

I love my messaging apps. I use them to chat with people, to **post status updates** and **selfies** with funny **filters**, and to **tag** my friends in photos. However, I don't really like the kind of social media site where you post something and everyone can see it forever. I'm a fan of apps where **stories** disappear. Then I can share everything, and people who send me friend **requests** can **follow** me and **comment**, but I don't have to worry about maybe being embarrassed later. And if I really don't want people to see my posts, I can still **unfriend** them or **block** them.

2 **Complete the second sentences so that they have the same meaning as the first sentences. Use some of the words in blue from Matt's text.**

1. James is always posting photos of himself.
   He's always posting ....
2. I always see Beyoncé's updates on Instagram.
   I .... Beyoncé on Instagram.
3. My mum posted a photo of me and added my name to it.
   She .... me in a photo.
4. I need to stop being friends with some people online.
   I need to .... some people.
5. I've stopped Carl from being my friend or seeing my posts.
   I've .... Carl.
6. I like adding funny extras to photos of my face.
   I like using face ....

3 **Choose the correct words to complete the sentences.**

1. I've *requested/updated* to follow you on Instagram.
2. I *update/post* my status at least once a day.
3. He enjoys posting *stories/statuses* because they disappear after one day.
4. When my friends upload photos, I like *posting/requesting* comments on them.
5. I don't update my *status/story* very often.

GRAMMAR

PREDICTIONS

GRAMMAR ON THE MOVE
Watch the video

1 **Read this text about the future of technology. Work in pairs and discuss whether you believe what it says.**

TELEPATHIC TECHNOLOGY

In the future we'll use technology for all of our communication. We won't need to speak. Our phones (or maybe watches or glasses) will know what we are thinking and will be able to send our thoughts to other people. Social media companies are already working on ways for computers and humans to communicate. This is called telepathic technology and one day it will allow you to communicate using only your mind.
Of course, we won't stop speaking completely, but conversation will become a special free-time activity. We'll enjoy it the way we enjoy a good meal or a hobby today.
When will this happen? Well, some day. However, the technology to make this real has not been fully developed yet, so it's not going to happen next week or next year.

Our phones ***will*** *know what we are thinking.*
It's not ***going to*** *happen next week.*

We use **will** for making predictions. Sometimes, we can also use **be going to** for predictions. We use **be going to** when there are signs in the present that something is (or is not) going to happen in the future.

GRAMMAR REFERENCE / *page 211.*

2 **Read the grammar box and complete the text using *will* or *won't*. For one sentence, use *be going to* instead of *will*.**

Classrooms without teachers

We [1] .... need teachers in the future, but we [2] .... be with them in the classroom all the time. Colleges [3] .... use technology much more than they do today. Students [4] .... write by hand very much. Most writing will be done on keyboards. However, this can only work if every student *has* some kind of computer. In the future, people [5] .... think that computers are a right, like food and water.
A secondary school in my town has already started buying computers for students, and everyone in the school [6] .... get one next term!

3 **Work in groups. Write down all of the positive and negative points you can think of about telepathic technology. Then discuss your ideas.**

4 **P** ***GOING TO*** 058
Listen to the way that *going to* is pronounced in these sentences. Repeat the sentences.

1. It's going to rain.
2. Be careful! You're going to fall!
3. I'm not going to be on time for the meeting.
4. Are we going to see you at the party?

Going to **is sometimes pronounced *gonna*. Do not use *gonna* in written English, as it is not a real word. Some people may write it in short messages to friends, but you should certainly never write it in an exam.**

PUSH YOURSELF B2

GRAMMAR: FUTURE CERTAINTY AND UNCERTAINTY

1 **We can't always predict the future. Rank these phrases according to how sure the speaker feels that something will happen. 1 = very sure, 6 = they don't believe that it will happen. There is more than one possible correct ranking.**

- **a** It will probably happen.
- **b** It will definitely happen.
- **c** I doubt that it will happen.
- **d** It certainly won't happen.
- **e** There's a good chance that it will happen.
- **f** There's not much chance that it will happen.

2 **Discuss these predictions in pairs. How sure do you feel they will happen?**

1. Everybody in the world will be connected on social networks.
2. There will only be one social network because the biggest one will buy all of the other ones.
3. We will stop learning languages. Social media will automatically translate everything for us.
4. We will have to pay for our social networks and messaging apps.

I doubt that everyone will be connected on social networks. What about in places where people don't have internet access?

I think that social network companies will probably make sure that everyone in the world has internet!

WRITING

A BLOG POST

1 **Here is some advice on writing a blog. One of the sentences does not offer good advice. Which one is it?**

- **A** Personality is important, so try to have your own personal style.
- **B** Readers can get bored quickly, so don't write very long paragraphs.
- **C** Writing is not speaking, so use a formal tone.
- **D** Invite comments on your post.

2 **Which of these openings would make you keep reading the post? Why?**

- **A** In this post I am going to discuss the different ways in which we can be friends with people.
- **B** Friends. Who can live without them? I know I can't. But what is really important in a friendship?
- **C** Let me tell you a story about a day when I really needed a friend.
- **D** Friends are more important than family. My family is boring. I never talk to my parents.

3 **Now read this blog about friendship and find three phrases that the writer uses to involve readers.**

Let me tell you a story about a day when I really needed a friend. I was on holiday with my parents and my sister. It was quite a cold day and we had stopped in a café to have a rest and a hot drink. I was carrying the drinks to our table, when I slipped and dropped them. The drinks spilt all over my sister's new jacket! It was an accident, but she was really angry and wouldn't talk to me any more. I didn't know what to do, so I texted my best friend. He said, 'Just say sorry to your sister even though it isn't your fault.' Luckily, she accepted my apology, and later that day we went shopping for a new jacket. Have you ever been in a similar situation? What did you do? I can't wait to hear your stories!

4 **Write a blog post about friendships. You should write about 150 words. Write about either what you think is important in friendships or a time when you were able to rely on a good friend.**

READING PART 3 TRAINING

1 **Can young people usually be good friends with their parents? Why? / Why not?**

2 **The article below was written by a young woman. Look at the title. Choose what you think she will say. Then read and check.**

1. Young people don't usually get on with their families.
2. She likes her family but doesn't want to share everything with them.
3. She wants her family to stop following her to restaurants.
4. She would like to go travelling with her family.

WORLD NEWS UK NEWS SPORT CULTURE TRAVEL BUSINESS BLOGS

→ BLOG/TECH/KATH MOORE

WE'RE FAMILY, NOT FRIENDS – SHOULD WE REALLY 'FOLLOW' EACH OTHER EVERYWHERE?

On social media, I accept friend requests from everyone: parents, aunties, my boyfriend's granny … There are so many networks and apps now and some of them are mainly orientated towards young people. They are for everyday communication, not to help you stay in touch with your Uncle James in Edinburgh, for example. But what if Uncle James doesn't understand that? He loves you and he wants to see *every* post, *every* story, *every* status update. It's a problem many of us have faced: how do we keep different social worlds apart on social networks?

Personally, I get on with my parents, and I see most of my relatives a few times a year. We have fun together, but not in the same way that I have fun with my friends. My relatives actually understand this very well. If I leave a family party a bit early because I'm going out with my best friends, everyone understands that I'm leaving one social world and entering a different one. They wouldn't follow me to a restaurant or club. However, many of them do want to follow me online, and I'm not very happy about that.

Most of us would prefer not to share everything with our families. Also, we don't want them to share everything about us. That means, for example, our families shouldn't share photos of us with everyone. When I was a teenager, my mum shared a photo of me getting angry when I was three years old. Her friends thought it was sweet but I didn't. I was furious! My life belongs to me and some things are private. Or, *I* decide who sees them.

So please stop and think before you ask to be part of someone's online world. It isn't always right to request to follow someone from your family on a social network. Maybe you could ask them in real life first. Or, if you send a friend request and nothing happens, don't request again. You wouldn't normally ask people of a different generation if you could go out with them or their friends, so don't ask to be part of their social group online, either.

In Part 3 of the Reading test you have to answer five multiple-choice questions about a text. The text will express an opinion or attitude. One of the questions will test your understanding of global meaning, for example by asking you to choose an introduction.

3 **What does an introduction usually tell the reader?**

A The main topic or idea of the whole article.
B One or two of the most important points in the article.

4 **What would be a good introduction to this article?**

A Kath Moore uses a lot of different social media. Here, she explains which social networks are best for friends, and which are best for families.
B Young people often get on well with their relatives. Kath Moore explains that it's still important for families not to share everything on social media.
C Kath Moore once had an argument with her mother. Here, she tells us how we can use social media more for better relationships within families.
D Parents never respect their children's privacy online. Kath Moore tells us why she was angry when her mother shared a photo of her.

5 **Look at the three introductions which are wrong. Underline the parts of them which do not describe the content of the article.**

The other questions in Reading Part 3 will test your understanding of information and opinions within the text.

6 **For each question, choose the correct answer.**

1 What does Kath say about her relatives?
   A They want to go with her when she meets friends.
   B They want her to talk to them about all her friends.
   C They want to see her stories and updates online.
   D They want her to stop using so many social networks.
2 Why did Kath once get angry with her mother?
   A Her mother posted an embarrassing photo of her.
   B Her mother talked too much about how sweet she was.
   C Her mother's friends are not nice people.
   D Her mother was not kind to her when she was three.

7 **Work in groups and discuss the questions.**

1 Do you think parents should post photos of their children online? Why? / Why not?
2 Should people ask for permission before they tag their friends in photos?

VOCABULARY

PHRASAL VERBS

1 **Look at the sentence and answer the questions.**

Personally, I get on with my parents.

1 Underline the phrasal verb in the sentence.
2 Does it describe a positive or a negative relationship?

2 **These sentences include more phrasal verbs for relationships. Say whether they describe a positive or negative situation.**

1 I can *rely on* him.
2 We met and we immediately *hit it off*.
3 Ed and Lea slowly *grew apart* and now they don't speak.
4 We often argue, but then we *make up*.
5 We used to be in love, but we *broke up* yesterday.
6 I know I can always *turn to* you.

3 **Say these sentences in another way. Use a phrasal verb from exercise 2.**

1 Jenny and Brian liked each other as soon as they met.
   They hit …
2 They sometimes fight, but then they forgive each other and become friends again.
3 My parents are always there for me when I need help.
4 You can ask me if you need support.
5 Lucy and Lee have separated.
6 Mary and Pia were school friends but at college they slowly stopped being friends.

4 **Work in groups and discuss if you agree with these sentences or not.**

1 You can hit it off with a person online but then dislike them when you meet in person.
2 The most important thing in a friendship is that you can rely on your friend.
3 It's more important to get on with a lot of people than to have one best friend.

EXAM FOCUS

READING PART 3

EXAM FACTS

- *You read a text of about 330–360 words.*
- *You also read five questions.*
- *Some of the questions test your understanding of people's feelings, attitudes and opinions.*
- *Each question has four options, A, B, C and D.*
- *You choose the correct answer to each question by finding information in the text.*

EXAM TIPS

- *Read each question carefully and find the section of the text which contains the information needed to answer that question.*
- *Choose the option which has the same meaning as information in the text. Remember that the answer probably uses different words and phrases from the text.*
- *Each of the first four questions is usually about one section of the text. The questions are in the same order as the information in the text, so you should answer the questions in that order.*
- *The fifth question has longer options and a more general focus. You should answer this question last, as you need to look at the whole text to find the answer.*

For each question, choose the correct answer.

Digital Detox

Sophie Nelson describes a technology-free weekend

I'm Sophie, and I want to tell you about an interesting weekend I spent with my friends, Chloe and Ella. The three of us have been friends since we were at college. Chloe's quiet and likes reading, Ella's cheerful and mad about sports, while I'm confident and love music, but we're all really close. Although we often argue about things, we always have a good time together. I can always rely on them to tell the truth and support me whatever happens, and they can rely on me, too.

Not long ago, I was having a dull week at work. While I was browsing some websites on my computer, I saw an article about the dangers of spending too much time on social media. By the time I got to the end of the article, I felt quite anxious. Like most people of our generation, my friends and I are always blogging, tweeting and commenting on each other's status. So, I asked them if they fancied going on a break called Digital Detox – three whole days without technology!

I explained this was a weekend in a countryside hotel where laptops, tablets and phones are forbidden. I said that it might be challenging, but it would also be good for us. Chloe and Ella weren't convinced but agreed straight away because they said it would be fun to do something different. So, we put away our phones and set off for our technology-free weekend.

It was a fantastic experience. Everybody at the hotel went for walks, swam in the pool and played tennis. A few people couldn't stand being out of contact and went home, but most stayed and loved it. Chloe, Ella and I spent hours just talking and laughing, and we didn't miss our smartphones at all. The most amazing thing, though, was the lack of stress: we couldn't believe how calm and chilled out we were. By the end of the weekend, I understood that technology can spoil your enjoyment of simple pleasures. It's very useful for keeping in touch with people, but you shouldn't look at screens all the time. Sometimes it's good to just switch off!

1 What does Sophie say about her relationship with her two best friends?
- **A** They share a lot of interests.
- **B** They all have similar characters.
- **C** They always get on well together.
- **D** They know that they can trust each other.

2 Why did Sophie suggest going on the Digital Detox break?
- **A** She was tired of working at her computer all week.
- **B** She was worried by something she had read on the internet.
- **C** She was bored with the usual things that she did with her friends.
- **D** She was embarrassed by how much time she spent on social media.

3 How did Sophie's friends feel before they went on the Digital Detox break?
- **A** keen to try an unusual experience
- **B** confident that they would benefit from it
- **C** upset at having to leave their phones at home
- **D** unsure about whether they would enjoy it

4 What was the biggest surprise for Sophie and her friends during the weekend?
- **A** how relaxed they felt
- **B** how quickly the time passed
- **C** how much fun they had together
- **D** how easy it was to be without technology

5 What might Sophie write in her diary at the end of the weekend?
- **A** I'm so glad Chloe and Ella persuaded me to go on the Digital Detox break. It was great to spend a weekend without electronic equipment.
- **B** The Digital Detox break has completely changed my attitude to my smartphone, so I'm going to give up using social media!
- **C** After going on the Digital Detox break with my friends, I've realised that there are both advantages and disadvantages to technology.
- **D** We all had fun on the Digital Detox weekend. In fact, everyone who went on the break agreed that it's good to spend time away from technology.

SPEAKING PART 1

EXAM FACTS

- *The examiner introduces himself or herself, tells you the name of the other examiner who is in the room, and asks your name.*
- *There is another student in the room with you, but you don't need to talk to them in Part 1.*
- *The examiner asks you some simple questions about yourself and your life.*
- *You need to answer all the questions.*

EXAM TIPS

- *Smile and look at the examiner when you introduce yourself.*
- *Give answers that are as full as possible. Don't give one-word answers or just say 'yes' or 'no'.*
- *If you don't understand something, you can ask the examiner to repeat it. You can say 'I'm sorry' or 'Excuse me', and then 'I don't understand' or 'Could you repeat the question, please?'*
- *Avoid silences. If you are not sure what to say, you can use fillers such as 'Well', 'In fact' or 'Let me see'.*

Work with a partner and ask and answer these questions as fully as possible.

1 Hello, I'm Tom Wilson. What's your name?
2 Where do you live?
3 How long have you lived there?
4 Do you work or are you a student?
5 Do you take English classes?
6 Do you like studying English?
7 How often do you meet up with your friends?
8 What did you do last weekend?
9 Tell us about the people you live with.

➡ **SPEAKING BANK** / *pages 234–235.*

HOW WAS IT?

- **Gave it a go** ☐
- **Getting there** ☐
- **Aced it!** ☐

REAL WORLD

MEETING PEOPLE IN ... PARIS

1 **Look at the photos of Paris. What do you know about the city? How easy do you think it is to meet people and make friends when you're travelling?**

Home | About | Destinations | Search

Imagine beautiful scenery and the feel of the wind in your hair, or the sights, sounds and smells of a new city – there's nothing like the feeling of exploring new places! Whether your holiday is a hike across the Rocky Mountains or a long weekend in Paris, the best thing about travelling is often the people that you meet. However, meeting people isn't always easy. Below are some social networks to help you meet people, get to know a country's culture and make some amazing memories.

Travelmates

Never travel alone again. With Travelmates, you can contact possible travel friends and read and write reviews for hotels, restaurants and popular tourist sights. You can also contact locals before you visit a new place, and receive updates when someone travels to your hometown. You can search for people your own age or with the same interests as you, or just for people travelling to the same place at the same time.

Localfriends

Localfriends connects you with locals in the place you're visiting, making sure you always have a tour guide, a place to crash or just someone with insider tips when you're in a new place. Many members offer their guests opportunities to cook together, compare recipes from their home countries and even practise the local language together.

Freesofas

Freesofas is one of the best travel websites, and is a really useful site for anything a traveller may need. You can find friends to travel with, a place to crash and recommendations for the best bars, places to eat and free open-air concerts. Why would you ever travel without it?

2 **Read part of a website about how to meet people when you are travelling. Decide which social network each sentence matches.**

1 You can choose to contact only people who are interested in the same things as you.
2 You can learn where to listen to live music in a city.
3 The people you stay with might show you how to cook local food.
4 You can also learn when travellers from other countries visit your city, so you can meet them.

3 **You might find these words and expressions on travel websites. Find them in the text and choose the correct meanings.**

1 locals
  a people who live in a place
  b tourists
2 travelmates
  a friends you can travel with
  b friends you can stay with when travelling
3 a tour guide
  a a book about a city
  b someone to show you around a city
4 a place to crash
  a somewhere you can sleep
  b a way of avoiding accidents
5 insider tips
  a advice based on personal knowledge
  b help with money

4 **How do you think you can stay safe when you use travel websites?**

5 **Read the information about how to use travel websites. Why do you think this advice is important? Can you think of any other advice? Work in pairs and compare your ideas.**

Using travel websites – Safety information

Your safety is important, so take it seriously.

Review information about other people carefully

Read what members say about themselves and what other members have said about them. If you're uncomfortable, keep looking.

Trust your own feelings

If a person or situation seems unsafe for any reason, move on. It can be a good idea to stay with families if you're travelling alone.

Always use the website to communicate and set up meetings

Never give out your phone number or email address to a new person until you meet them and feel comfortable with them. Always use the website to communicate.

6 **059 Listen to three conversations in Paris. What are the travellers doing in each conversation? There is one answer you don't need.**

a trying to find a local person who can show them the city
b arriving at someone's flat where they are going to stay
c arranging a place to meet someone
d meeting someone to go to a concert with them

7 **059 Join the beginnings and endings of these sentences and questions you can use when you meet new people. Listen and check.**

PHRASES YOU MIGHT USE

1	Have we got	a	be Xavier.
2	It's very kind of you	b	with you, we'd love to.
3	If that's OK	c	really cool people.
4	You must	d	the right address?
5	Shall we order	e	message her.
6	How long have you	f	to offer us a room.
7	I've met some	g	been in Paris?
8	OK. I'll	h	a coffee?

8 **Read the sentences and questions. What ways do you know to express these ideas?**

PHRASES YOU MIGHT HEAR

1 It's Jamie and Ian, isn't it?
2 Come on in.
3 Where are you guys from?
4 Will you be eating with us this evening?
5 That's settled, then.

9 **Watch the video about meeting people in Paris. What do you learn about visiting Paris? Make notes.**

10 **Compare your notes. Then watch again to check your ideas.**

WATCH

LIFE COMPETENCIES

SOCIAL RESPONSIBILITIES AND COMMUNICATION

11 **Work in pairs. Go online and find a social network site for travellers like the ones mentioned on page 88. Find out more information about how it works and how you can use it safely. Prepare a report for your classmates.**

7 WHAT'S YOUR STYLE?

VOCABULARY

FASHION

1 **How often do you go shopping for clothes? Who with? Where do you buy them?**

2 **Look at the title of the quiz. What do you think 'on trend' and 'stuck in a fashion rut' mean?**

3 **Do the quiz.**

ON TREND or STUCK IN A FASHION RUT?

1 For me, clothes are
- **a** how I show my personality.
- **b** just things that keep me warm and comfortable.
- **c** an essential way to stay up to date with fashion trends.

2 I buy fashionable clothes
- **a** only if I look good in them.
- **b** because I like to be on trend.
- **c** when they are the only things that I can find in the shops.

3 When I'm shopping for clothes, I
- **a** spend time looking at different things.
- **b** go straight to the things that I've seen online or in magazines.
- **c** buy the first thing I see and leave the shop as soon as I can.

4 If I see a fashionable piece of clothing that's quite expensive, I
- **a** forget about it.
- **b** buy it immediately. I need it!
- **c** wait a while until the price is reduced.

➡ *Now turn to page 193 to find out how important fashion is to you.*

4 **060 Listen to two friends doing the quiz. What is the man's score? Is it similar to yours?**

5 **Look at these phrases from the conversation in exercise 4 (1–5) and match them with the meanings (a–e).**

1 I only wear fashionable clothes if they **suit me**.
2 I **try things on** and I see how I look in them.
3 If they **fit me**, I'll buy them.
4 I don't buy clothes that I **can't afford**.
5 If they're really expensive, I'll wait until the **sales**.

a something is the right size for you
b a time when stores cut their prices
c you don't have enough money to buy something
d you look good wearing something
e you put clothes on to see if they're the right size

6 **Now choose the correct words from the audio to complete the fashion article.**

As we start the new year, it's time to look at some of the styles that are going to appear in the shops this spring. Here are just a few of the trends to know. [1]*Patterns/Sleeves* are back, so be bold with [2]*checked/striped* jackets, shirts and trousers – go for large rather than small squares. Or wear big [3]*tight/loose* tops over blue and white [4]*striped/plain* blouses with long [5]*buttons/sleeves* and [6]*tight/checked* collars. For a more casual look, leave the top [7] *button/sleeves* undone. And if you prefer [8]*plain/button* clothes, pick bright colours and wear them with confidence.

7 **Discuss the questions in pairs.**

1. Tell your partner about the types of clothes that you like to wear. What styles, colours and patterns do you like best when you are buying clothes?
2. Do you ask your friends for advice about clothes? Where else can you get tips and ideas about what to wear? Do you ever get tips online?

LISTENING PART 4 TRAINING

1 **Do you know any fashion vloggers? What do they talk about?**

2 **Look at the photo of fashion vlogger Matt Davies and the words in the box. Do you know what they mean? Which of these words could describe Matt's way of dressing?**

casual	classic	cool	old-fashioned
on trend	smart	stylish	

3 **Before you listen to an interview with Matt, read this question and think about what he might say.**

What does Matt enjoy most about being a fashion vlogger?

You'll hear Matt mention three things that he enjoys, so you'll need to listen carefully to find out which one he says that he enjoys MOST.

4 061 **Listen to the beginning of the interview and choose the correct answer. Which words does Matt use to tell us that he is going to talk about what he enjoys most?**

What does Matt enjoy most about being a fashion vlogger?

A being his own boss
B talking to his followers
C wearing the latest styles

DID YOU KNOW?

*Most American English speakers don't say **trousers**. American English uses the word **pants** instead. But in British English, **pants** are what people wear under their trousers!*

5 062 **Now listen to the rest of the interview and answer these questions.**

1. Matt became a vlogger because he wanted to
   A share his views about style.
   B get a job in the fashion business.
   C become well-known.
2. Matt says that to be successful at this job you must
   A post something new on your vlog every day.
   B be different from other vloggers.
   C talk about a variety of fashions.
3. What would Matt like to do in the future?
   A start a career in television
   B become a fashion model
   C design a range of clothes

6 **Discuss the following questions in pairs.**

1. Do you think that vloggers like Matt give useful advice?
2. Would you buy something because a vlogger recommends it? Why? / Why not?
3. When you need to buy something, whose advice do you listen to the most?

VOCABULARY

BUYING AND RETURNING GOODS

1 063 **Listen to a man telling his friend about a jacket that he has bought. Number these words in the order you hear them.**

complain damaged deliver exchange order receipt refund return

2 **Match the words in exercise 1 with the meanings below.**

1 to ask a company or employee to bring or send you something
2 to say that something is wrong or that you aren't happy
3 your money that's returned to you if you don't want what you've bought
4 to take or send something to a person's home
5 to take or send something back because you don't want it
6 to give back a product and change it for a similar one
7 when something is broken or not in a good condition
8 the piece of paper you get after you pay for something

3 063 **Complete the dialogue with the words from exercise 1. Then listen again and check your answers.**

A: Nice jacket, Mike! Is it new?
B: It's a long story, actually. I bought it last month, but I didn't like it at first. So, I went back to the shop and tried to [1] ______ it. I said that I wanted a [2] ______ . But I'd lost my [3] ______ , so they told me that they couldn't give me my money back.
A: That's a pity. So, what did you do?
B: Well, they said they would [4] ______ it for another style of jacket. But there wasn't one of the same price in the shop, so I asked if they could [5] ______ it for me. They said they could [6] ______ it to my house the next day. But when it arrived, I opened the bag and saw that it was [7] ______ !
A: Oh, what a pain! Did you [8] ______ ?
B: Yes, of course I told them that I wasn't happy. But in the end, I decided to keep the first jacket. It's OK. I quite like it now.

GRAMMAR

REPORTED SPEECH

GRAMMAR ON THE MOVE
Watch the video

1 **Look at these two sentences. Why does Mike change *can't* to *couldn't* when he's telling his friend what the shop assistant said?**

2 **Read the dialogue again and complete the rules in the box.**

Tense changes
When you are reporting what somebody said, you need to make these changes:

present simple → past simple	*go → went*
[1] ______ → past continuous	*is going → was going*
present perfect → [2] ______	*has gone → had gone*
[3] ______ → past perfect	*went → had gone*
past perfect → past perfect	*had said → had said*
can → could	
will → would	
must → must (no change)	

→ **GRAMMAR REFERENCE** / *page 211.*

3 **Complete the reported speech sentences below.**

1 'I want a refund.' → I said that ______ .
2 'Do you want to exchange it?' → They asked if ______ .
3 'Please can you order one for me?' → I asked if ______ .
4 'We'll deliver it to your house tomorrow.' → They said that ______ .
5 'I've changed my mind.' → I explained that ______ .
6 'I'm going to keep it.' → I told them that ______ .

Word order changes

Questions with question words:

*'When **will it** arrive?'* ➜ *She asked when **it would** arrive.*

Yes/No questions:

We remove *do/does* and use *if* or *whether*.

*'**Do you want** to try it on?'* ➜ *He asked **whether I wanted** to try it on.*

Pronoun and adjective changes

*'Where did **you** buy **your** watch?'* ➜ *I asked where **he** had bought **his** watch.*

Time changes

*'I bought some new shoes **yesterday**.'* ➜ *She had bought some new shoes the **day before**.*

*'They're going to the cinema **tomorrow**.'* ➜ *They were going to the cinema the **following/next day**.*

➜ **GRAMMAR REFERENCE** / *pages 212–213.*

4 **Read the rules above and write one word in each gap to complete the reported speech sentences.**

1. 'Can I borrow your scarf?' ➜ He asked me if ______ ______ borrow ______ scarf.
2. 'I'm wearing jeans and a T-shirt.' ➜ She said that ______ ______ wearing jeans and a T-shirt.
3. 'We have bought a new game.' ➜ They told me that ______ ______ bought a new game.
4. 'Do you wear a suit at work?' ➜ I asked him ______ he ______ a suit at work.
5. 'I don't like this dress.' ➜ She told him that ______ ______ like ______ dress.
6. 'I wore my new jacket.' ➜ He said that ______ ______ worn ______ new jacket.

- The verb ***tell*** focuses on the person or people who we are talking to, so we must mention who this is. We can say *'I told **them** that I wasn't happy'*, but we can't say ~~*'I told that I wasn't happy'*~~.
- The verb ***say*** focuses on the words we use, so we don't need to say who we're talking to. We can say *'I said hello'* or *'I said hello to them'*, but we can't say ~~*'I said them hello'*~~.

5 **Which of these sentences are wrong? Correct the mistakes.**

1. He told us about his favourite shop.
2. Can you say me the price of this?
3. I said the sales assistant, 'Good morning.'
4. I said that I wanted a new laptop.
5. They said us that the TV would arrive next week.

PUSH YOURSELF B2

GRAMMAR: REPORTING VERBS

We can use different reporting verbs according to the speaker's purpose.

Instruction:	'Leave the store immediately!' ➜ They **told** him to leave the store immediately.
Request:	'Could you help me, please?' ➜ I **asked** the shop assistant to help me.
Advice:	'You should buy that book.' ➜ She **advised** him to buy that book.
Warning:	'Don't trust that salesman!' ➜ He **warned** us not to trust that salesman.*
Promise:	'I'll help you choose a present.' ➜ She **promised** to help me choose a present.**
Invitation:	'Would you like to come to a party?' ➜ They **invited** me to go to a party.

* We use ***not to*** + **infinitive** if the advice, warning, etc. is negative.

** *Promise* does not need a direct object – all the other verbs do.

1 **Choose the correct reporting verb for each sentence.**

1. 'I wouldn't buy that phone if I were you.'
   He ______ me not to buy that phone.
   a promised ***b*** invited ***c*** advised
2. 'I'd like to speak to the manager, please.'
   She ______ to speak to the manager.
   a asked ***b*** told ***c*** warned
3. 'Don't buy anything from that shop.'
   I ______ them not to buy anything from that shop.
   a invited ***b*** warned ***c*** promised
4. 'Please pay at the cash desk.'
   The shop assistant ______ us to pay at the cash desk.
   a told ***b*** advised ***c*** warned
5. 'I'll definitely come shopping with you on Saturday.'
   She ______ to go shopping with him on Saturday.
   a asked ***b*** invited ***c*** promised

2 **Imagine that someone says these things to you. Complete the sentences in reported speech.**

1. 'We'll show you all the best shops.'
   They promised ______ all the best shops.
2. 'You shouldn't wear those clothes.'
   She advised ______ those clothes.
3. 'Come shopping with us.'
   They invited ______.
4. 'Don't go to that store again.'
   He told ______ to that store again.
5. 'Could you tell me how much this dress is, please?'
   She asked ______ that dress was.

READING PART 5 TRAINING

1 **Have you ever been shopping and come home with more things than you planned to buy? Why do you think that this happened?**

2 **You're going to read an article about shops called *Tricks of the Trade*. What do you think you are going to read about?**

3 **Read the first part of the article and choose the correct word for each gap.**

Read the whole sentence before you choose the word. Look carefully at the words before and after the gap. All four words have a similar meaning, but only one is correct in that sentence.

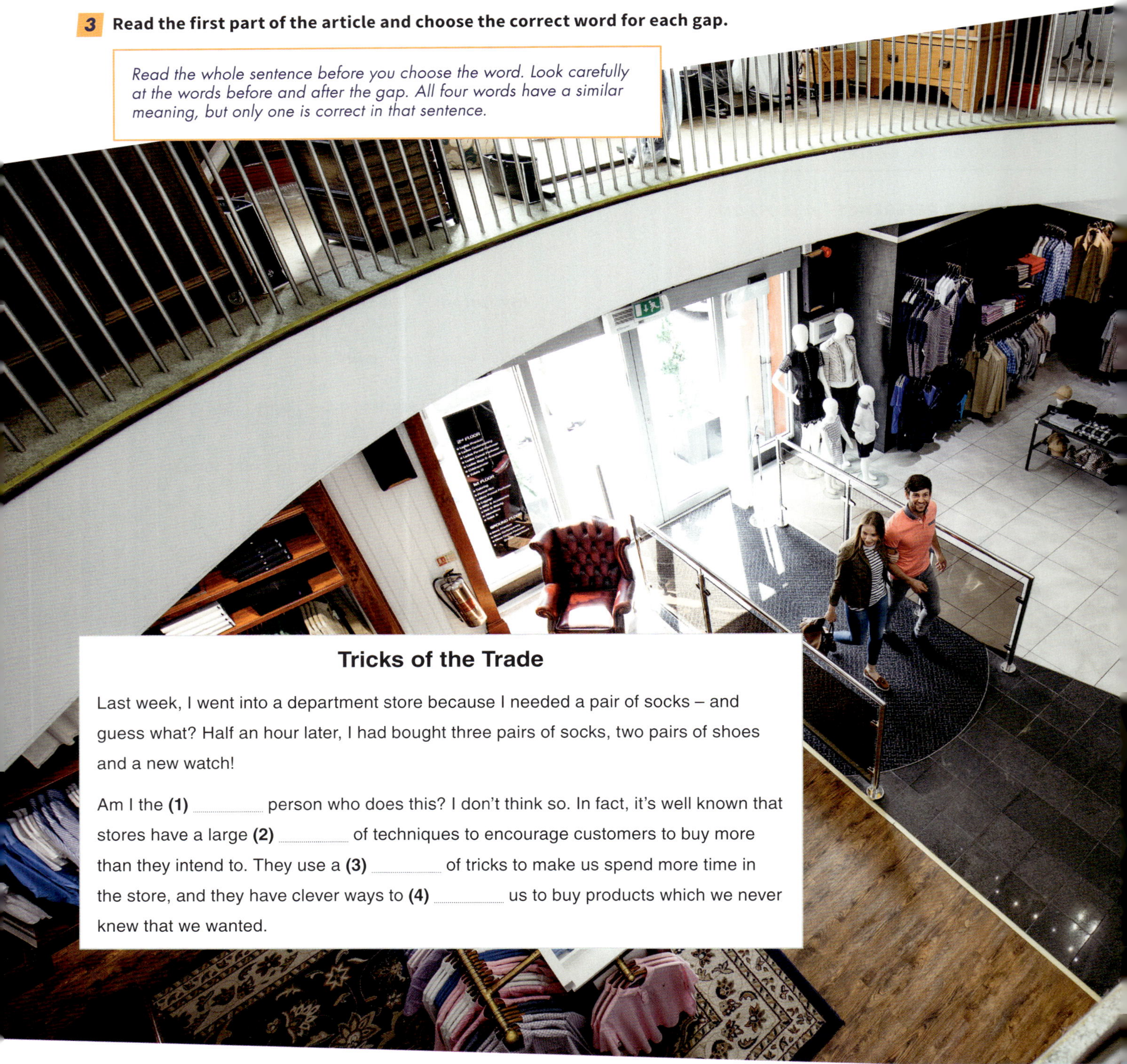

Tricks of the Trade

Last week, I went into a department store because I needed a pair of socks – and guess what? Half an hour later, I had bought three pairs of socks, two pairs of shoes and a new watch!

Am I the **(1)** .... person who does this? I don't think so. In fact, it's well known that stores have a large **(2)** .... of techniques to encourage customers to buy more than they intend to. They use a **(3)** .... of tricks to make us spend more time in the store, and they have clever ways to **(4)** .... us to buy products which we never knew that we wanted.

1	**A** alone	**B** individual	**C** only	**D** single
2	**A** number	**B** sum	**C** total	**D** amount
3	**A** group	**B** variety	**C** crowd	**D** band
4	**A** recommend	**B** persuade	**C** suggest	**D** advise

4 **Now read the rest of the article and match the questions with the bold words in the text.**

What do stores use to …

1. get people's attention?
2. change people's mood?
3. influence how people think about the price of a product?
4. make people remember pleasant experiences?

Music is one of the tricks of the trade. Cheerful music with a fast beat can make shoppers feel positive and encourage them to buy inexpensive goods quickly. Meanwhile, gentle music relaxes customers, so they stay longer in the store and consider their decisions carefully. This is why soft classical music is often played in shops where luxury goods are sold.

Colours can work in a similar way. When stores have special offers, they usually use eye-catching colours, particularly red, to make us notice these products. Supermarkets often put colourful goods like fresh fruit and vegetables at the front to attract customers into the store.

Some shops even use certain **smells** to encourage customers to buy things. For example, the smell of coconut oil is sometimes used to increase sales of holiday products, by making customers think of sun cream and so bringing back memories of their summer holidays.

How goods are displayed is also important. Research shows that customers are willing to pay more for products that are displayed in a stylish way, while an untidy arrangement makes them think that the products are very good value for money. Shoppers are often keen to search through a messy pile of clothes, for example, thinking that there's a real bargain to be found.

5 **Read the text again. Decide if the statements are true or false.**

1. The writer went into the store to buy socks, shoes and a watch.
2. Music can influence the amount of time people spend in a store.
3. Stores use bright colours to show that certain goods are now at a lower price.
4. Customers dislike buying goods which are displayed untidily.

6 **Are there any stores in your town or city that use the 'tricks of the trade' described in the article? Can you think of other 'tricks of the trade' which encourage customers to spend more money?**

VOCABULARY

SHOPPING

1 **Match the words and phrases in box A with ones in box B that have the same or similar meaning.**

A

a bargain   customers   display   goods
messy   price reductions   shops

B

arrangement   products   shoppers   special offers
stores   untidy   very good value

2 **Complete these sentences using the words or phrases from the boxes in exercise 1. In each case, more than one answer is possible.**

1. Luxury .... are usually bad value for money.
2. When stores have .... , this encourages people to spend money on things which they don't need.
3. Most people don't care whether a store creates an attractive .... or not – it's quality and price that matter.
4. People often buy something at a low price because they think that it's .... , but then they regret it later.

3 **Work in pairs and discuss the questions.**

1. Do you agree with the sentences in exercise 2?
2. What is the best bargain that you have ever bought?
3. Have you ever bought anything and then regretted it?
4. What do you do if you are not happy with something that you have bought?

SPEAKING

EXPRESSING PREFERENCES

1 **Do you do much internet shopping? What kind of things do you buy online?**

2 **064 Listen to two friends talking about shopping and tick the things that they agree about.**

1. It's better to buy clothes in normal shops. ....
2. Shopping in ordinary stores is more enjoyable. ....
3. You can get more bargains online. ....
4. Shopping online saves time. ....
5. It's useful to read online reviews. ....

3 **064 Choose the correct response to follow each statement. Then listen again and check your answers. Which response means that the speaker doesn't agree?**

1. I'd rather buy clothes in ordinary shops.
   a So would I. **b** So do I.
2. I like trying things on before I buy them.
   a Same here. **b** Me neither.
3. I prefer to buy shoes in normal shops.
   a That's a good point. **b** So do I.
4. I don't like returning things.
   a Neither do I. **b** Me too.
5. I love going to big shopping malls.
   a Do you? **b** So am I.
6. I can't stand crowded shops.
   a I do too. **b** I know what you mean.

4 **Think about your shopping habits and complete the sentences below for you.**

1. I love …
2. I like …
3. I'd rather …
4. I prefer …
5. I don't like …
6. I can't stand …

5 **Work in pairs and talk about your shopping habits in exercise 4. Use expressions from exercise 3 to agree and disagree.**

6 **P CLOTHES / CLOSE 065**
Listen to these two words. Can you hear the difference between *clothes*, which has two consonant sounds at the end, and *close* (meaning 'shut') which has only one?

clothes close

7 **P 066 Listen and circle the word that you hear.**

1. clothes close
2. clothes close
3. clothes close
4. clothes close

To pronounce *(clo)thes*:

Put the tip of your tongue between your top and bottom teeth and push the air through the gap. Pull your tongue back and say 'z'.

Make sure that there's vibration in your throat when you say these sounds, and don't pause between them!

WRITING

A REVIEW

1 **Do you read reviews online? What kind of reviews do you read? Have you ever written a review? What was it about? Was it good or bad?**

2 **Read these reviews of shopping websites. According to the reviewers, which website is the best for:**

1. price?
2. choice?
3. customer service?

A There's a good selection of products on this site, and it's easy to use, too. But the best thing about this website is that everything's such amazing value. I got a tablet that was on special offer, and I'm so pleased with it. The only thing that's not so good is that orders take a long time to arrive. But it's definitely worth checking out this site if you're looking for a bargain.

B This is quite a new website, so the range of goods is quite limited. I bought some headphones last week, and they got damaged on the way to my house. The guys on the company's help desk were great, though. They dealt with the problem quickly and also replaced my headphones straight away. Although it's not the cheapest place, I'd certainly recommend this site.

C What I like most about this website is the incredible variety of items on sale here. The products are excellent quality, and the prices are very reasonable, as well. I ordered a smartwatch from here and it arrived the next day. My only complaint is that the service is rather disappointing. If you post questions, the staff take a very long time to answer them. Apart from that, it's an excellent site.

3 **Look at the phrases (1–4) from review A, and find phrases in reviews B and C that have the same meaning.**

1. selection of products (two phrases) ....
2. the best thing about this website ....
3. the only thing that's not so good ....
4. it's definitely worth checking out this site ....

4 **Look at the phrases below. Which are positive and which are negative?**

amazing value	excellent quality	incredible variety
not the cheapest	quite limited	
rather disappointing	very reasonable	

5 **Complete the sentences using the linking words in the box.**

although	and	as well	but	though

1. This isn't the cheapest site, ... they have an incredible variety of products.
2. The staff are very friendly, ... they're extremely helpful, ...
3. .... the range of products is quite limited, the prices are very reasonable.
4. The goods here are amazing value. The service is rather disappointing, ...

6 **Complete these two reviews using the words and phrases in the box. You can use the words and phrases more than once.**

difficult	easy	excellent quality
fairly expensive	my only complaint is	
take quite a long time to arrive		
The best thing about it is		

A

There's a fantastic range of sportswear here, and it's all [1] .... , too. I found the site is quite [2] .... to use, but the customer service staff are extremely helpful. [3] .... that the prices are really low. I got a football shirt here that was amazing value. Although the things you buy [4] .... – my order took 10 days to get here – I'd still really recommend this site. It's a great place to find a bargain.

B

You can find some brilliant products on this site, but they are [5] .... You can get some bargains if you look carefully, though. What I like most about this site is that it's so [6] .... to use – I ordered some ski gloves and it only took me two minutes! [7] .... about the customer service. Unfortunately, goods [8] .... , and the staff aren't always helpful when you call them. But if you're looking for great sportswear, it's certainly worth checking out this website.

7 **Now write your own review of a website or a shop where you bought something. Say what you bought, and what you think about the store, the price and the service. Use the sentences in the texts to help you and use linking words to join your sentences.**

EXAM FOCUS

READING PART 5

EXAM FACTS

- *You read a text which has six words missing.*
- *For each question, there is a choice of four possible words to fill the gap.*
- *You have to decide on the correct word for each gap.*

EXAM TIPS

- *Read the whole text first. You should be able to understand it, in spite of the missing words.*
- *Look carefully at each sentence, paying particular attention to the words before and after the gap.*
- *Think about the meaning and structure of the sentence and choose the correct word to complete it.*
- *Check that none of the other three words fit. They will be wrong because of meaning, grammar or collocation.*
- *When you've filled in all the gaps, read the whole text again to check that it makes sense.*

Read the text below and choose the correct word for each gap.

The oldest sweet shop in the world

Keith and Gloria Tordoff live in a small town in Yorkshire, in the north of England. For the past 25 years, they have **(1)** .... a small business selling sweets and chocolates. Sweet shops, or 'candy stores' as they are **(2)** .... in American English, can be found everywhere in the world, but the Tordoffs' shop is a very special one. Their business was **(3)** .... up in 1827 and has been open ever since. In fact, the shop holds the record as being the oldest sweet shop in the **(4)** .... world.

'Everybody loves sweet shops,' says Keith. 'They **(5)** .... us of our childhood, and bring back happy memories. Recently, an old lady of 95 visited. She had last been in our shop when she was five years old, and she told me it had **(6)** .... changed at all!'

1	**A**	led	**B**	run	**C**	moved	**D**	worked
2	**A**	spoken	**B**	told	**C**	known	**D**	mentioned
3	**A**	put	**B**	given	**C**	brought	**D**	set
4	**A**	whole	**B**	complete	**C**	full	**D**	total
5	**A**	remember	**B**	recognise	**C**	remind	**D**	recommend
6	**A**	nearly	**B**	hardly	**C**	slightly	**D**	rarely

LISTENING PART 4

EXAM FACTS

- *You listen to a person being interviewed about their experiences, life, work, hobbies or interests.*
- *You read six questions about what the person is saying.*
- *While you are listening, you answer the questions by choosing the correct answer out of three possible answers.*
- *The questions are in the same order as the information in the recording.*
- *You will hear the recording twice.*

EXAM TIPS

- *Read all the questions first.*
- *As you listen to the recording, read each question and look for the key words which you need to hear.*
- *The speaker will mention all the ideas in A, B and C, but they may use different words or refer to them in a different order. Listen carefully to find out which of the three ideas is correct and which two are wrong.*
- *If you don't know the answer to one question, don't worry. Move on to the next question immediately.*
- *When you hear the recording a second time, check your answers and fill in any answers that you missed.*

067 **For each question, choose the correct answer. You will hear an interview with a woman called Tina Mackay, whose job is to write reports on the service she receives in different shops.**

1 Tina works as a 'Mystery Shopper' for

A a department store.
B a detective agency.
C a research company.

2 What is one of the things that Tina writes about in her reports?

A what the sales staff look like
B how the products are displayed
C the quality of the goods on sale

3 According to Tina, a good salesperson should

A approach the customer at the right moment.
B find out exactly what the customer wants.
C spend as much time as possible with the customer.

4 Tina says the main aim of her work is to

A compare good and bad points about different stores.
B make complaints about the service in stores.
C give an independent opinion about each company's service.

5 Tina thinks she is good at her job because she

A enjoys shopping.
B remembers things well.
C has a friendly personality.

6 Which product is Tina allowed to keep?

A clothes
B magazines
C perfume

HOW WAS IT?

Gave it a go [ ]
Getting there [ ]
Aced it! [ ]

REAL WORLD

SHOPPING IN ... ISTANBUL

1 **Have you ever been to Istanbul? Look at the photos. Which of the things below can you see? Which of these shops would you like to visit? Why?**

ceramics	cosmetics	lanterns	
leather goods	rugs	shoes	spices

ISTANBUL SHOPPING

The city of Istanbul in Turkey is a bridge between Europe and Asia. Tourists from all over the world visit the city to explore the Old Town, try the delicious cuisine and shop in the markets and malls.

MALLS

The city has an amazing range of shopping malls. You will find a great selection of international brands in the big shopping centres like Akmerkez, Nautilus, Galeria and Istinye Park. Akmerkez has 226 stores on three floors, selling everything from clothes to electronics. On the top floor, visitors can eat at the restaurants and cafés or watch the latest blockbuster at the cinema. It's a popular destination for both locals and tourists and is open seven days a week.

SHOPPING STREETS

You can also find interesting shops outside the malls. For local products, visit streets like Istiklal, Bagdat and Rumeli, where you will find handmade blankets, ceramics and locally designed clothes.

GRAND BAZAAR

The Grand Bazaar is a very popular tourist site and offers a wide variety of jewellery, antiques, souvenirs, shirts, rugs and spices. Be ready to haggle with the merchants as most of the goods don't have prices on them. It's wise to find out the average cost of local products before you visit.

SPICES

There are spice shops all over Istanbul, selling the wonderful spices that are used in Turkish and Middle Eastern food. The best place to buy them is the Egyptian Bazaar. Here you can find saffron, turmeric, cinnamon, dates, almonds, dried fruit and much more.

CERAMICS AND LEATHER

Istanbul is also the place to buy some of the finest ceramics and leather in the world. You can find potteries all over the city using Chinese and Turkish designs in their ceramics. Locals also sell leather – and the prices are definitely affordable. If you're careful, you can buy genuine leather goods much more cheaply than you would back home.

2 **Read the website about shopping in Istanbul. Decide if the sentences are true or false.**

1 There is only one main shopping mall in Istanbul.
2 Akmerkez is open every day.
3 In the Grand Bazaar, most things don't have price labels on.
4 You can only buy spices at the Egyptian Bazaar.
5 Things made of leather are usually very expensive.

3 **Find these words in the text (1–6) and match them with their meanings (a–f).**

1 international brands
2 local products
3 haggle
4 merchants
5 affordable
6 genuine

a real
b goods with company names that are known all over the world
c discuss and reach agreement on the price of something
d things that are made in the area where you are staying
e people who sell things in a market or shop
f not very expensive

4 **068 Listen to three conversations in Istanbul. What are the travellers doing in each conversation? There is one answer you don't need.**

a buying spices at the Egyptian Bazaar
b trying on clothes in a shopping mall
c haggling over souvenirs at the Grand Bazaar
d buying ceramics in a shop

5 **068 Complete the sentences and questions you can use when you are shopping with the words and phrases in the box. Listen and check.**

a fair	a small packet	can I	do you use
how much is	I'll give you	I'll leave	I'll take
in a size	taste		

PHRASES YOU MIGHT USE

1 Do you have these jeans .... 36?
2 .... try them on?
3 No. I think they'll be too big. .... it.
4 .... this top.
5 .... this wallet?
6 .... 60 lira for it.
7 That's .... price.
8 What .... it for?
9 Can I .... some?
10 Can I have .... of that, please?

6 **Match the sentences (1–6) and questions with the meanings (a–f).**

PHRASES YOU MIGHT HEAR

1 Was it the darker ones you were interested in?
2 Someone over there will sort that out for you.
3 I guarantee you won't do better than that.
4 I can't do any more than that.
5 You can't do without it.
6 It's up to you.

a This is the best price you will find.
b You really need this.
c I can't reduce the price any more.
d Do you want this colour?
e You can choose.
f An assistant in that part of the store will help you.

7 **Watch the video about shopping in Istanbul. What do you learn about these things? Make notes.**

- the Turkish currency
- Forum Istanbul
- Istiklal Street
- the Grand Bazaar

8 **Compare your notes. Then watch again to check your ideas.**

LIFE COMPETENCIES

MANAGING THE SHARING OF TASKS, SPEAKING WITH CONFIDENCE

9 **Work in groups to make a presentation about a famous market. Choose from:**

- The souks of Marrakesh, Morocco
- Chatuchak Weekend Market, Bangkok
- Marché aux Puces de Saint-Ouen, Paris
- Shilin Night Market, Taipei, Taiwan

Think about:

- how big it is
- how old it is
- what you can buy

Make the presentation to the class.

8 INTO THE WILD

A

VOCABULARY

ENVIRONMENTS AND LANDSCAPES

1 **In pairs, describe what you see in the photos (A–D). Have you ever been in landscapes like these? Can you guess where the photos were taken?**

2 **069 Paul and Liz are looking for a sports adventure in an exciting environment. Listen and match each part of their conversation with one of the photos.**

B

3 **069 Now complete the sentences from their conversation with the words in the box. Listen again and check.**

branches	bushes	caves	cliff	glacier
iceberg	leaves	rainforest	riverbank	
sand dunes	shore	stones	waterfall	waves

1 ***Liz:*** It looks freezing! Is that an [1] ________ ?
Paul: No, it's a [2] ________ . I've always wanted to see one. You can go into [3] ________ of ice.

2 ***Paul:*** I like being on the water, but I want to be near a beach or a [4] ________ . We can't see any [5] ________ at all here. And the big [6] ________ would make me feel sick.

3 ***Liz:*** Don't you see those beautiful [7] ________ ?
Paul: Yeah, but I don't see any trees with [8] ________ and [9] ________ that could give us some shade. Those little [10] ________ wouldn't help.

4 ***Liz:*** OK, how about a race through the [11] ________ , then? If it gets too hot, we could have a shower under this [12] ________ .
Paul: Yeah or we could fall down that [13] ________ or break a leg on those [14] ________ .

4 **Put the adjectives in the box into three pairs of opposites. Then, with a partner, say which of them could describe the places in the photos.**

dense	dry	empty	humid	noisy	quiet

READING

1 **Read the introduction and scan the four texts opposite. They describe the sports challenges that Liz and Paul discussed. Find where in the world each one takes place.**

2 **Read the texts again. Which race do the sentences describe?**

1. This is the longest of the four races.
2. Competitors in this race will get very hot and very wet.
3. Speed is not the most important thing in this event.
4. This race lasts for one week.

3 **Underline sentences in the text that give you this information.**

1. Jungle Ultra runners may have breathing problems.
2. Some animals in the Gobi desert may soon disappear.
3. You have to understand the dangers of the natural world if you want to finish the Alaska race.
4. The Volvo Ocean Challenge can also be dangerous for the competitors.

4 **Work in small groups and discuss one of the four events. What would be the hardest thing about it? What would be good about it? Would anyone in your group really like to do it?**

5 **Do you know about any challenging races in your country? Tell the class.**

FOUR SPORTS CHALLENGES THAT COULD CHANGE YOUR LIFE

So you think you're sporty, but have you ever pushed yourself to the limit? Have you ever wondered just how far you can go? Here are four ideas for people who want a real challenge.

A The Jungle Ultra run takes you through 230 kilometres of some of the world's most exciting landscapes, and some of the most extreme climates! It's a five-day race through the Manu National Park in Peru. You'll see parrots, monkeys and beautiful butterflies. You'll push past the leaves, branches and huge flowers of the rainforests, run through rivers, and climb up and down mountain paths. The humid air of the dense jungle, and the thin air of the mountains will be a new challenge. Are you ready for it?

B The Gobi March is held in the Gobi desert in Mongolia, and it is one of the '4 Deserts' series. There is sand in the Gobi desert, but there are also rocky paths, and huge areas of grass. The temperatures can be extremely cold as well as extremely hot. This seven-day, 250-kilometre race takes you through many different landscapes and temperatures. You will see camels and wild horses. (You probably won't see a Gobi bear as, like some other animals here, this is an endangered species.) You will need to be determined, and *very* fit. If that describes you, go for it!

C You don't have to be especially fast for the Alaska Mountain Wilderness Classic – an adventure challenge. All you have to do is complete the course … but only the fittest people will manage that! You have to climb mountains, cross glaciers and travel down icy rivers. You can carry anything you want, but how many heavy things do you want to carry over 300 or 400 kilometres? One thing that everyone *must* carry is a satellite phone. This is a truly dangerous trip and people sometimes have to be rescued. You won't meet many people on the course, but you may see a moose or even a bear. Respect nature! That's the key to completing this amazing challenge.

D You should be an experienced sailor if you want to take part in the Volvo Ocean Challenge. And you need to have quite a lot of time: it takes about nine months to sail around the whole world. What will you see on the way? Four different oceans, storms, waves, whales, sharks, dolphins, endless water and endless skies. This race tests competitors in so many ways. Your family may be very worried about you, and there are good reasons for this. However, you will later be able to tell them that this was the best experience of your life.

LISTENING

1 **Read this description of a radio programme. In pairs, write three questions that you would like to ask Lisa about herself and her Jungle Ultra experience.**

RUN THE RAINFOREST

A crazy decision, a jaguar and a call to save one of the Earth's most important environments: adventure sportswoman Lisa Basra tells Ian Watkins about running in this year's Jungle Ultra marathon.

2 070 **Now listen to the interview. Were your questions answered?**

3 **Match these words from the interview (1–4) with the definitions (a–d).**

1	marathon	**a**	very difficult and challenging
2	tough	**b**	spoke very quietly
3	feared	**c**	a very long running race
4	whispered	**d**	was frightened or worried

4 070 **Listen again. Answer these questions in your own words.**

1. What kind of race had Lisa run before the Jungle Ultra?
2. How did she feel after she registered to take part in the race?
3. How did she feel after each day of running in the Jungle Ultra?
4. What animal frightened her when she saw it in the jungle?
5. How does Lisa feel about the rainforest now?

5 **Work in groups and discuss the questions.**

1. Why did Ian say 'you must be a very brave person'?
2. Why did Lisa say 'I think I'm lucky to be alive'?
3. Do you think an event like the Jungle Ultra is too dangerous for the competitors?

VOCABULARY

ADJECTIVES WITH *-ED* AND *-ING*

1 **Read the sentences below and choose the correct options to complete the rules.**

*You soon feel exhaust**ed**.* *I was terrifi**ed**.*
*The race is exhaust**ing**.* *It was a terrify**ing** experience.*

We use adjectives ending in [1]*-ed/-ing* to describe how we feel.
We use adjectives ending in [2]*-ed/-ing* to describe the thing that makes us feel like that.
When we add ***-ed*** to a verb that ends in a **consonant** + ***-y***, the *y* changes to *i*.
worry ➜ *worried*
When we add ***-ed*** or ***-ing*** to a verb that ends in a **consonant** + ***-e***, the *e* of the verb is dropped.
challenge ➜ *challenged* ➜ *challenging*

2 **Conor wrote a blog entry about his holiday in the desert. Complete the sentences with an *-ed* or *-ing* adjective based on the verb in brackets.**

So I've just come back from my week in the desert. Was it as good as I had hoped? Well, to be honest, I found the trip quite [1] .... (challenge).

We had enough food and water, but I still felt [2] .... (worry). What if we got lost? There are no roads but luckily our guides never got [3] .... (confuse) about where we were. They saw that I was a bit scared and they were very [4] .... (encourage), which helped me to feel more [5] .... (relax).

But despite all my fears, I had a very good time. Some things were great. The desert sky is [6] .... (amaze). You can see some very [7] .... (surprise) colours that I had never seen before.

In the end, I was [8] .... (satisfy) with my desert holiday. It was hard but wonderful.

3 **Write one or two sentences about these situations. Use adjectives with *-ing* or *-ed*.**

You buy the new book by your favourite author. You read it, and it's bad.
I'm disappointed. / That's disappointing. I had hoped to enjoy the book.

1. The news today is all about environmental problems.
2. You are on a bus. The person next to you is singing.
3. It's not your birthday, but your friend gives you a present.
4. It's Sunday morning and you have nothing to do.

GRAMMAR

MODALS OF SPECULATION

GRAMMAR ON THE MOVE
Watch the video

1 **Read the sentences and then complete the rules with a modal verb.**

You weren't scared. You ***must*** *be a very brave person!*
A snake ***might*** *bite me!*
I ***might not*** *be fit enough.*
I ***may*** *have problems with the temperature.*
You ***may not*** *be strong enough to keep going.*
In a few years, it ***could*** *be too late.*
It ***can't*** *be a tiger. There aren't any tigers here.*

> When we feel sure that something is true, we use [1] ....
> When we think something is possible but we aren't sure, we use [2] .... , [3] .... or [4] ....
> If we feel sure that something isn't true, we use [5] ....
> We don't use *mustn't*, *can* or *couldn't* when we are speculating.

➔ **GRAMMAR REFERENCE** / *page 214.*

2 **Choose the correct verbs to complete the sentences.**

A: Where's Tim? I've tried to call him, but I just got his voicemail.
B: I don't know. He [1]*might/must* be at college.
A: Don't be silly. It's Sunday so he [2]*can't/might* be at college.
B: Yes, but sometimes they have special weekend projects that they do in the library, so he [3]*can't/could* be there.
A: I really don't think it's open on a Sunday. But he [4]*may/must* have football training. I think he plays football. He [5]*can't/could* be at the sports centre.
B: Yes, but he told me he [6]*can't/might* stop playing football because he's tired and he needs to sleep more at weekends.
A: OK, if he's sleeping, he [7]*may not/must* want me to phone him. I'll send him a message. Oh, look, he's online. He [8]*must/could* be awake now!

DID YOU KNOW?

British English speakers say that someone is **at** college *or* **at** school. *They only say* in the school *if they are talking about the school building, e.g.* There was a fire in the school.
In the USA you can say, she's **in** school/**in** college *to mean she is attending school.*

3 **Say the sentences in a different way. Use a modal verb. Sometimes more than one modal is possible.**

Maybe I'm ready for an adventure alone.
I could/may/might be ready for an adventure alone.

1. I feel sure that Peru is an exciting country.
2. Maybe I will go there next summer.
3. But I'm sure that the flights are not cheap.
4. It's possible that I don't have enough money.
5. Maybe I'll ask my parents to pay for the flights.
6. But then it's possible they'll want to come with me.

4 **P ELISION** 071
Listen to these sentences below. Do you hear the *t* in *must*, *might* and *can't*?

It must be true.
It might be true.
It can't be true.

> **The /t/ sound often disappears between two consonants. This is called *elision*. A /d/ sound also often disappears between two other consonants:**
> ***You and me.***

5 **P** 072 **Listen and repeat these sentences. Cross out the /t/ or /d/ sounds that disappear.**

1. You're the first person to arrive.
2. I don't want eggs.
3. See you next week.
4. You could be a star!
5. He bought a used car.

VOCABULARY

ANIMALS AND THEIR HABITATS

Grasslands

Tropical forests

Temperate forests

Polar regions

1 **Match the photos (A–J) with the words in the box.**

arctic wolf	giraffe	green iguana	hedgehog	kangaroo
orangutan	penguin	polar bear	red deer	red squirrel

A

B

C

D

E

F

G

H

2 **Work in pairs and discuss in which habitats and countries or continents the animals are found.**

> Giraffes and kangaroos are both grassland animals but you find giraffes in Africa and kangaroos in Australia.

> Yes, and in African grasslands you also find …

3 **Work in groups and talk about animals and their habitats in your country.**

> In Germany we have a lot of forests, so we have animals like deer and squirrels …

PUSH YOURSELF B2

VOCABULARY: ANIMALS' BODIES

1 073 **Listen to five people talking about their favourite animal. Which of these animals (A–F) is each person describing?**

1 ....

2 ....

3 ....

4 ....

5 ....

6 ....

7 ....

8 ....

10 ....

9 ....

11 ....

12 ....

2 073 **Listen again and write the body parts for each animal. Use the words in the box.**

antlers	beak	claws	feathers	fur	hoof	mane	paw	tail	trunk	tusks	whiskers

3 **Look at the animal parts and their names. Answer the questions.**

1 What animals in the photos have hooves?
2 What types of animal generally have a beak?
3 How many of the animals in the photos have a tail?
4 What covers the skin of a tiger and a deer?
5 What other animals do you know with paws and claws?

SPEAKING PART 2 TRAINING

1 **Here is a photograph. It shows a man and a yak. Work with a partner and discuss where you think the photograph was taken.**

2 **074 Listen to an exam candidate describing the photo. Tick what the candidate does.**

say what things and people are in the photo ....
say where things are ....
use a conversation filler while she's thinking of what to say ....
describe something when she doesn't know the word ....

3 **074 When you look at a photo, some things are facts and some are your opinons. Match sentences (1–6) with sentences (a–f). Listen again and check.**

1 There is a beautiful lake, with a yak resting beside it.
2 We can see a man with a backpack. He looks European.
3 He's wearing comfortable walking shoes.
4 There is snow on the mountains in the background.
5 The man is wearing a T-shirt and no jacket.
6 The yak is wearing something colourful on its back.

a It could be a cold country, or the mountains may be very high.
b He must be a tourist.
c It must be warm today, or it might always be warmer away from the mountains.
d He could be on a hiking holiday.
e This can't be a lake in Europe.
f It might be waiting to carry the man or his bags.

4 **Work in pairs. Student A, describe one thing in this photo. Student B, speculate about it. Use *must*, *could*, *may*, *might* and *can't*. Then swap and respond to your partner's statement.**

Before you start talking, make some notes about these things:

- the place
- the temperature
- the person
- the animal's 'job'

5 **Work in pairs. Pick one of the photos on page 194 each and talk to your partner for one minute about what you can see in the photo. Look again at Unit 3, pages 47 and 49 to review the language for describing photographs.**

WRITING PART 2 TRAINING

AN ARTICLE

1 **Work in pairs and answer the questions. Use the words in the box for ideas.**

1. What kind of articles do you like to read?
2. Where do you like to read them?

magazines	newspapers	online

2 **To write an article you have to think about content and structure. Look at this task.**

> **Articles wanted!**
>
> **A beautiful part of my country**
>
> *What part of your country do you really love?*
>
> *What are the things that make this place special?*
>
> *What can people do in this beautiful place?*

3 **A student from Italy has brainstormed these ideas about Sardinia. With a partner, decide which words describe Sardinia and which describe things you can do there.**

beaches	camping	cliffs	coast	eating fish	island
look at moon and stars	sailing	swimming	wildlife		

4 **Read the article and underline the parts where the student has answered the three questions in exercise 2.**

A BEAUTIFUL PART OF MY COUNTRY

My favourite part of Italy is Sardinia.

Sardinia is an island, so it has a long coast. You can find [1] .... cliffs as well as [2] .... , sandy beaches. The landscapes are [3] .... and you can see [4] .... wildlife. Although it's popular, Sardinia is not as full of tourists as many parts of Italy.

For me, the best thing to do in Sardinia is swimming in the [5] .... sea. Then, when you're really hungry from the exercise, you can eat [6] .... fish. What's more, there are excellent campsites on the coast. At night, you can look at the moon and stars over the water and feel very happy!

5 **The article needs some adjectives to make it more interesting. With your partner, choose adjectives for the gaps. You can use these words or your own ideas.**

amazing	clear	cool	delicious
exciting	fantastic	fresh	high
interesting	long	relaxing	rocky

6 **There are several linking words and phrases in the article about Sardinia. Underline them.**

7 **Look again at the exam task in exercise 2. Write an article about a beautiful part of your country.**

Follow these steps:

- brainstorm ideas (you don't have to use all of them!)
- organise the ideas in a plan and write the text
- make sure you answer the three questions in the task
- use some adjectives to make the article more interesting
- use linking words
- make sure to give your personal opinion
- check your spelling and punctuation

EXAM FOCUS

WRITING PART 2

AN ARTICLE

EXAM FACTS

- *In Question 2, you read a notice from an English-language magazine or website which is asking students to write articles on a particular topic.*
- *There are usually about three questions on this topic in the notice.*
- *You write approximately 100 words.*

EXAM TIPS

- *Remember to answer all the questions in the notice.*
- *You can answer the questions in any order, but make sure that the content of your article is presented in a logical order: begin with a general comment or introduction and end with some kind of conclusion.*
- *Include linking words and phrases to connect your ideas.*
- *Include adjectives and adverbs to make your writing interesting.*
- *When you have written your article, read it again to check that grammar, spelling and punctuation are correct.*

Do the task.

You see this notice in an English-language magazine.
Write your **article** in about **100** words.

Articles wanted!

Wildlife

Tell us about a time when you saw some interesting wildlife!

Would you rather see animals in the wild in their natural environment, on a TV documentary, or in a zoo? Why?

The best article will win a prize.

➜ **WRITING BANK** / *pages 230–231.*

SPEAKING PART 2

EXAM CHECK

1 Answer the questions.

1. In Part 2 of the Speaking test, you have to
   - *a* describe what is in a photograph.
   - *b* discuss a photograph with your partner.
2. You talk about a photograph which
   - *a* the examiner has given to you.
   - *b* you have chosen yourself.
3. You must talk about the photograph
   - *a* for as long as possible.
   - *b* for about a minute.
4. If you don't know how to say something, you should
   - *a* try to describe it using other words.
   - *b* ask the examiner for the right words.
5. If you have finished saying what you are sure you can see, you can
   - *a* start to talk about a topic which is related to the photograph.
   - *b* talk about things which you think might be true about the photograph.

2 The examiner gives you this photograph and says, 'Here is a photograph. It shows people doing an activity. Please tell us what you can see in the photograph.' Talk for about one minute.

➜ ***SPEAKING BANK** / pages 236–240.*

HOW WAS IT?

- Gave it a go ☐
- Getting there ☐
- Aced it! ☐

REAL WORLD

VISITING A NATIONAL PARK IN ... WYOMING

1 Look at the photos of Yellowstone National Park, in the US. What can you see? What activities do you think are popular in the park? What do you think tourists need to be careful of?

YELLOWSTONE NATIONAL PARK

Keep yourself safe, keep the park safe
Yellowstone Park is sure to amaze you: don't let it kill you. Protect yourself by following a few simple rules:

Never park in the road
If you're driving, pull off the road to watch wildlife and leave enough space for other cars to pass. Stay with your vehicle if you see wildlife on the road.

Stay on boardwalks
The hot water in Yellowstone's geysers and hot springs has injured more people than any other natural feature in the park. Stay on the boardwalks so you don't get too close to the hot water.

Keep your distance from animals
The safest way to watch wildlife is from inside your car. Always stand at least 100 yards (91 metres) away from bears and wolves, and at least 25 yards (23 metres) away from bison and deer.

Never feed wildlife
Animals that get used to receiving food from humans may become dangerous. This is bad for people, and also for the animals, as they have to be killed to keep visitors safe. Keep all food and garbage packed away.

When hiking:
Keep an eye on the weather. Calm, sunny mornings in Yellowstone can quickly turn into stormy days. If you see a storm approaching, move away from mountain tops and open places. Forests offer the best protection from lightning.

Take a map
The trails in Yellowstone can be hard to follow. We strongly recommend that if you are hiking, you take a map with you, and make sure you know how to use it.

Learn about bears
Ask at the visitor center about any recent bear activity. Always carry bear spray, which is safe and works well. Read the information on bears, or ask a park ranger for advice.

Don't drink the water
We recommend that you boil or chemically treat all drinking water. Although water may look fresh, it may not be safe to drink.

Be aware of ticks and mosquitoes
Ticks can attach themselves to your skin and cause infections. Wear tick repellent on your boots, socks and pant legs. Tuck your pant legs into your socks and your shirt into your pants. Mosquitoes in Yellowstone do not carry diseases, but they can be annoying, so carry insect repellent.

2 **Read part of a website about Yellowstone National Park. Join the beginnings and endings of these sentences about things you should do to stay safe.**

1 Never leave your car
2 Stay on the paths
3 Never go near
4 Don't leave food
5 Move into a forest area
6 Take a map
7 Have a bear

a when you go hiking.
b if there is lightning.
c spray with you.
d wild animals.
e lying around.
f on the road.
g when you are close to hot springs.

3 **Find the words and expressions (1–6) in the text and match them with the meanings (a–f).**

1 boardwalks
2 natural feature
3 trails
4 visitor center
5 park ranger
6 tick/insect repellent

a paths through forest or the countryside
b a place where tourists can find information about a national park
c wooden paths that are lifted off the ground a little bit
d a liquid or cream that stops a particular animal from coming near you
e someone who works for a national park and helps protect the park and visitors
f something that you see in the countryside, for example a mountain or lake

4 **075 Listen to three conversations in Yellowstone National Park. What are the travellers doing in each conversation? There is one answer you don't need.**

a asking about a trail
b asking for information about how to avoid ticks and mosquitoes
c asking for advice on which parts of the park to visit
d asking if a particular area is safe

5 **075 Complete the sentences and questions you can use when you visit a national park with the phrases in the box. Listen and check.**

a problem	any tips	easy to follow
find a tick	go hiking	need to take

PHRASES YOU MIGHT USE

1 We want to ________ near Clear Creek.
2 Can you give us ________ about bears?
3 Will it be ________ the trail?
4 Do we ________ a map with us?
5 Are mosquitoes ________ ?
6 What do we do if we ________ on our body?

6 **Choose the correct meaning for each sentence.**

PHRASES YOU MIGHT HEAR

1 With any luck, they'll go off in the opposite direction.
  a They will probably move away from you.
  b If you're lucky, they will follow you.
2 Gradually back off.
  a Move backwards slowly.
  b Quickly run away.
3 Better safe than sorry.
  a I'm sorry that you might not be safe.
  b It's better to be careful and avoid an accident.
4 It's a bit tricky in places.
  a Some parts of the trail are difficult.
  b Some parts of the trail are beautiful.
5 Stick to the high ground.
  a Avoid going up into the mountains.
  b Stay high up in the mountains.
6 Don't expose any skin.
  a Keep your skin covered by clothes.
  b Don't put repellent on your skin.

7 **Watch the video about Yellowstone National Park. What do you learn about these things? Make notes.**

- camping
- hot springs
- park rangers
- bears
- streams and rivers

8 **Compare your notes. Then watch again to check your ideas.**

LIFE COMPETENCIES

CREATIVE THINKING, UNDERSTANDING GLOBAL ISSUES

9 **Work in groups to make a poster about how to respect the environment and stay safe in a national park.**

Choose a national park and think about:

- the wildlife
- dangerous animals
- hiking
- driving

Make the poster and present it to the class.

PROGRESS CHECK 3

SOCIAL MEDIA

1 Complete the text with the words in the box.

block comments posts request tag update

Home Advice About Search

What should you do when you get a friend [1] ________ from a person that you don't like? Maybe it's not important but sometimes it's a problem. People can write rude [2] ________ under your [3] ________ , or they can [4] ________ you in photos that you don't like. It's best to [5] ________ people if they are unfriendly online. You don't need *everybody* to see it when you post an [6] ________ .

FUTURE FORMS

2 Choose the correct forms to complete the mini-dialogues.

1 **A:** *I'll spend/I'm going to spend* my holidays in England next summer.
B: Cool! You know I love postcards. Please send me one!
A: OK, *I'll send/I'm going to send* you lots of postcards!

2 **A:** *Are you going to/Do you* visit your Uncle Peter in Edinburgh soon?
B: Yes! The flight is booked. *I'm flying/I'll fly* on 15th July.

3 **A:** David *will see/is seeing* the doctor at 5 p.m.
B: Then he should hurry. There's only one bus in the afternoon and *it's leaving/it leaves* at half past three.

4 **A:** Oh no, this traffic is terrible. *We're going to be/We're being* late!
B: I hope they invent flying cars soon. Then we *don't/won't* have to sit in traffic jams.

CLOTHES AND SHOPPING ADJECTIVES – OPPOSITES

3 Complete the words in the second sentences.

1 This T-shirt is not loose enough. It's much too t________ !
2 This dress is too expensive. It's not g________ v________ .
3 This shirt doesn't have a pattern. It's p________ .
4 This shop isn't tidy at all. It's really m________ .

SHOPPING

4 Complete the text with the words in the box. There are two words you don't need.

bargain complain damaged deliver exchange goods receipt refund

Sometimes customers at our shop are not happy with the [1] ________ that they have bought. They say that the products are [2] ________ , or that they simply don't want them after all. Customers often want a [3] ________ , but unfortunately we can't give people their money back without a [4] ________ . Some people [5] ________ about this, but I think we are flexible enough. If you don't have a receipt, it is possible to [6] ________ things. You can give one thing back and take a completely different thing.

REPORTED SPEECH

5 Yesterday, Diana told her flatmate about a shop. Now Diana's flatmate is telling her friend about the conversation. Finish her flatmate's sentences.

1 'There is a new clothes shop in town.'
Diana said that ________ .
2 'Have you been there yet?'
She asked me ________ .
3 'It has a lot of nice things.'
She told me ________ .
4 'Do you like my dress?'
She asked ________ .
5 'I bought it at the new clothes shop.'
She said ________ .
6 'When will you go shopping with me?'
She asked ________ .
7 'Can you lend me some money?'
She asked ________ .
8 'I've spent all my money on new clothes!'
She told ________ .

THE NATURAL WORLD

6 Complete the sentences with the words in the box. There are two words you don't need.

branches	caves	cliff	glacier	icebergs
leaves	sand	waterfall	waves	

1 Most trees have _______ and _______ .
2 You can find _______ dunes in some deserts and on some beaches.
3 When a river flows over a _______ , there is a _______ .
4 It's not always safe to swim in the sea. There are sometimes dangerous _______ .
5 In really cold oceans you can see _______ in the water.

ANIMALS

7 Decide if the sentences are true or false. If a sentence is false, replace the animal with one of the animals in the box.

giraffes hedgehogs penguins

1 Squirrels live in forests and can jump from tree to tree.
2 Wolves can eat leaves from tall trees.
3 Orangutans are birds, but they can't fly.
4 Polar bears need ice, so climate change is a disaster for them.
5 Deer protect themselves by rolling into a dangerous little ball.

ADJECTIVES WITH *-ING* AND *-ED*

8 Match sentences 1–6 with sentences a–f. In sentences a–f make the verb in brackets into an adjective with *-ing* or *-ed*.

1 I once went to the jungle for two weeks.
2 On the first night I heard a lot of strange noises.
3 The next day we saw huge jungle flowers.
4 We wanted to see a tiger but we didn't see one.
5 You can't go far into the jungle without a guide.
6 The jungle holiday was better than I had expected.

a I felt a bit _______ . (worry)
b That was _______ . (disappoint)
c I had 14 exciting days but it wasn't a _______ holiday. (relax)
d I was _______ that I loved it so much. (surprise)
e Their colours were _______ . (amaze)
f It's dangerous and finding your way is _______ . (challenge)

MODALS OF SPECULATION

9 Choose the correct words to complete the text.

I can't find my glasses. They [1]*must/may* be here in the house because I had them yesterday and I haven't been out. They [2]*must/might* be in the living room … let's see. No, they're not here. They [3]*can't/may not* be in the bedroom because I never wear them there. Maybe my husband took them. They [4]*could/can't* be in his bag. I'll phone him. He [5]*might/might not* answer his phone because he's at work, but then I'll send a message. Where's my phone? Oh no, now I've lost my phone, too. It [6]*may/can't* be true!

COMMON MISTAKES

10 Find one mistake in each sentence and rewrite the sentences.

1 I will go to visit my grandmother tomorrow.
2 We going to see a film this evening.
3 Are you going to ate with us?
4 We meet our friends later this evening.
5 Noel say me that he liked fish.
6 She said that she is reading a good book.
7 My dad asked me if I have enough money.
8 You can think this is easy, but I think it's difficult.

EXPENSIVE HOLIDAYS

11 Think of the word which best fits each gap.

My friends post so many holiday photos on [1] _______ media. They always seem to do really exciting things. One friend has gone to the rainforest to help save an endangered [2] _______ . Another is shopping in New York. She posted a photo of herself in a new pink and green blouse. Pink and green! Personally, I think she's definitely not on [3] _______ , but she [4] _______ be happy with the blouse because she's smiling in the photo. I didn't write a negative comment about the colours because I don't want to [5] _______ out with her. She's a nice person and I get [6] _______ with her. I'm surprised that my friends have enough money for these holidays. I'm [7] _______ to spend my next holiday on the beach. It's cheap, and I know that I'll enjoy it. I might post some funny selfies with a face [8] _______ , but you'll never see photos of me shopping or saving animals. On holiday, I just want to relax!

9 ALWAYS LEARNING

READING PART 3 TRAINING

1 **Look at these two photos and describe what is happening in each photo.**

2 **076 Listen to people talking about the photos and write *A* or *B* next to the words you hear.**

formal	informal	lively
relaxed	strict	traditional

3 **Is or was your school more like photo A or B?**

4 **You're going to read an article about a school where 'children are free to be themselves'. What do you think this means? What kind of school do you think it is? Read this first paragraph and find out.**

THE SCHOOL WHERE CHILDREN ARE FREE TO BE THEMSELVES

I'm Hannah Liu, I'm 17, and I go to a Free School in New York City. It's a school where nobody has to attend lessons, write an essay or do any homework! We can study anything from ancient history to hip-hop music, or the school can hire instructors to help us learn skills like movie-making. If we want, we can take classes with teachers, or study on our own, or work in groups helping each other. We *are encouraged* to develop our own interests, and everyone chooses their own curriculum and decides what qualifications they want to get. Everyone here takes notice of my views and respects my choices, and that's what I think is really awesome.

5 **Look at the question below and choose the correct answer.**

Options A, B, C and D all contain true information about the school, but Hannah only mentions one of these things as a reason why she likes the school. Find the information which means the same as each of the four options and underline the phrase which shows Hannah's opinion.

Remember that an opinion can come before or after the thing which the writer is talking about.

1 Hannah says she likes the Free School because
- **A** people listen to her ideas.
- **B** pupils help each other learn.
- **C** she doesn't have to go to lessons.
- **D** there are lots of activities she can do there.

I used to go to an ordinary school where the pupils *were told* what to do. The teachers were pretty nice, but their lessons just focused on getting us ready to take exams. I couldn't stand that. Even though I got high grades in all my subjects, I still hated that kind of education. So, I moved to a Free School. It was the best decision I've ever made.

When I arrived on my first day, I thought, 'Wow. I've never seen a school like this before!' Like all schools, it was noisy, but, amazingly, it was full of kids having a good time and doing stuff they actually enjoyed. Nobody tells you what to do, but I soon discovered that there are rules about how to behave: for example, we *aren't allowed* to hurt anyone or take their things. I was also surprised to find there were only around 70 pupils, which meant that I soon felt at home.

Everyone is involved with everything that happens at the school. We're preparing to put on a show at the moment, and I'm designing the costumes and baking cookies to raise money to buy the materials. And every Wednesday we have a meeting where we talk about how the school *is run*. Everyone has to go, but you don't have to take part in the discussion or even pay attention: you just have to be there. If we need to make a decision, we all vote by raising our hands to say 'yes' or 'no'. What's more, everyone, both children and teachers, has an equal vote. My school is a really cool school!

6 **Now read the rest of the article. For each question, choose the correct answer.**

2 Hannah left her previous school because she
- **A** wasn't doing well in her exams.
- **B** didn't get on well with her teachers.
- **C** didn't like the way that the classes were taught.
- **D** wasn't interested in the subjects she was studying.

3 How did Hannah feel on her first day at the Free School?
- **A** She was surprised by how noisy the school was.
- **B** She was impressed by how happy everyone was.
- **C** She was shocked by how many rules there were.
- **D** She was disappointed by how few pupils there were.

7 **Now answer Question 4.**

Only one option is completely correct: the other three options contain some things which Hannah would write, but they also contain some things which she wouldn't write.

4 What would Hannah write in her blog on a Wednesday evening?
- **A** I like Wednesdays! We discussed things at the meeting, and then, as usual, just us kids were allowed to vote. Cool, isn't it?
- **B** As usual, I decided not to go to the meeting. Instead, I baked cookies to raise money for our show. Mmm, they're delicious!
- **C** My new book about hip-hop music was stolen while I was in the meeting! But I couldn't complain because it's OK to take people's stuff here. It's not fair.
- **D** Another good day! I went to the meeting, but I didn't listen. I just sat there drawing pictures of costumes for our show. Nobody minded, though!

8 **What do you think about the Free School? Here are some things that you can say:**

USEFUL LANGUAGE

I'd like to go there. I think it sounds/looks …
interesting, fun, exciting, incredible, amazing

I wouldn't like to go there. I think it would be …
strange, weird, awful, dreadful

DID YOU KNOW?

In Britain, people go to ***university*** *to study for a degree.*
In the United States, people go to ***college*** *to study for a degree.*

VOCABULARY

EDUCATION

1 **Match these words from the article with the meanings.**

attend curriculum education essay grades qualifications rules skills

1. the process of teaching and learning
2. the group of subjects which schools teach
3. what we do when we go to an event, for example, a lesson or a concert
4. the numbers or letters which show how good our work or performance is
5. a piece of writing in which students write about a particular subject
6. what you have if you've learned and practised how to do something well
7. a set of instructions which tell people what they must and mustn't do
8. things you receive when you are successful in exams or a course of study

2 **Complete these questions using the words from the box in exercise 1.**

1. What do you think are the most important subjects on a school's .... ?
2. Do you think it is necessary for students to .... every lesson?
3. What is the best .... that you have ever written?
4. Why is it important for students to take exams to get .... ?
5. What useful .... would you like to learn in your life?
6. Do you think that schools need to have a lot of .... for students to follow?
7. Do you get upset when you get bad .... ?
8. Do you think that .... should be the same for boys and girls?

3 **Work in pairs. Ask and answer some of the questions in exercise 2.**

GRAMMAR

PASSIVE

GRAMMAR ON THE MOVE
Watch the video

1 **Look at these sentences from the article. They are all <u>passive</u>. Which sentence is in the past tense? Which ones are in the present tense? Which one is negative?**

*We **are encouraged** to develop our own interests.*
*The pupils **were told** what to do.*
*We **aren't allowed** to hurt anyone.*
*We talk about how the school **is run**.*

2 **Compare these two sentences and answer the questions.**

a *My new phone was stolen.* = passive
b *Somebody stole my new phone.* = active

1. Do we know who stole the phone? Why is it better to use a passive sentence here?
2. What is the subject of sentence a? What is the subject of sentence b?

- When we change a sentence from active to passive, the **object** of the active sentence becomes the **subject** of the passive one.
  *Someone stole **my book**. ➜ **My book** was stolen.*
- We use **be** followed by the past participle of the main verb.
- The verb **be** must be in the same tense as the active sentence:
  *Someone **stole** my book. ➜ My book **was** stolen.*
  (main verb: past simple) (***be***: past simple)
  and it must agree with the subject of the passive sentence.
- If we want to say who did the action, we can add this person or thing to the passive sentence, connected with the word ***by***.
  *My book was stolen **by** another student.*

➜ **GRAMMAR REFERENCE** / *page 215.*

3 **Read the rule and complete these passive sentences with the correct form of *be*.**

1. We use English in all our classes.
English ________ used in all our classes.
2. You need these books for tomorrow's lesson.
These books ________ needed for tomorrow's lesson.
3. Our school holds a big sports day every summer.
A big sports day ________ held every summer.
4. Our teacher gives us a test on Friday afternoons.
We ________ given a test on Friday afternoons.
5. Someone wrote our textbook in 2018.
Our textbook ________ written in 2018.

4 **Complete this text about a first day at school using the passive form of the verbs in brackets.**

I remember my first day at primary school. I was five years old. I [1] ________ (take) to school by my mum, and then I [2] ________ (show) into a classroom by one of the teachers. There were lots of other children there, and we [3] ________ (tell) to sit down and say 'Yes!' when our names [4] ________ (call). We [5] ________ (not/allow) to speak unless the teacher spoke to us first. I [6] ________ (show) a puzzle and I [7] ________ (ask) to fit coloured shapes into spaces in a picture. At breaktime, we [8] ________ (give) a glass of milk and we [9] ________ (send) outside to play in the playground. I was so tired at the end of the day!

5 **Do you remember your first day at a school or in a new job? Make some notes about it using passive sentences, then tell your partner.**

I was taken … We were given …

PUSH YOURSELF B2

GRAMMAR: PASSIVE IN OTHER TENSES

1 **Match the active sentences (1–10) with the passive sentences (a–j).**

Present simple:
1. People **speak** English.

Present continuous:
2. People **are speaking** English.

Past simple:
3. People **spoke** English.

Past continuous:
4. People **were speaking** English.

Present perfect:
5. People **have spoken** English.

Past perfect:
6. People **had spoken** English.

Modal verbs:
7. People **will speak** English.
8. People **can speak** English.
9. People **must speak** English.
10. People **should speak** English.

a English was spoken.
b English has been spoken.
c English must be spoken.
d English is spoken.
e English had been spoken.
f English can be spoken.
g English is being spoken.
h English should be spoken.
i English was being spoken.
j English will be spoken.

2 **Complete the passive sentences by putting one word in each gap.**

1. They are building a new secondary school.
A new secondary school ________ ________ ________ .
2. Ms Lopez will teach today's science lesson.
Today's science lesson ________ ________ ________ by Ms Lopez.
3. Someone was painting our classrooms last week.
Our classrooms ________ ________ ________ last week.
4. They have already published the exam results.
The exam results ________ already ________ ________ .
5. Somebody should give the students new notebooks.
The students ________ ________ ________ new notebooks.
6. You can find more details on the school website.
More details ________ ________ ________ on the school website.

VOCABULARY

HIGHER EDUCATION

1 Discuss the questions in pairs.

1. What differences are there between school education and higher education?
2. What problems do you think young people have when they leave school and start studying at college or university?

2 Look at these comments written by students at university and complete the meanings using the words in blue.

In my first few **terms**, the hardest thing for me was going to **lectures**. I found it a challenge to listen to someone speaking about a **topic** for a full hour, and I also found it difficult to take notes in lectures.

2 12 16

I'm studying law, and I have to work on my own a lot and do **research** in the library, which isn't always easy. But fortunately I have a really helpful **tutor** who always gives me good advice about my studies. And I know that when I **graduate** at the end of my university course, I'll have a useful **degree** that will help me find a good job.

1 5 9

You've got to take a lot of exams at uni, and they're harder than at school. If you don't **revise** enough before an exam, you're going to **fail**. I've managed to **pass** all my exams so far, but it was hard work!

0 3 18

1. Students .... when they've successfully completed their university course of three or more years.
2. A .... is a qualification you study for at university and which you receive at the end of your course.
3. The school and university year is divided into three .... which are each usually 10–15 weeks long.
4. Students who do badly in an exam will .... the exam and may need to take it again.
5. Students who do well in an exam will get good marks and will .... the exam.
6. A .... is a particular subject that you write about or talk about.
7. When you do ...., you try to find out a lot of information about a subject from books or the internet.
8. When you .... for an exam, you look at the work you have done and try to remember the information.
9. Students at university need to listen to ...., which are formal talks about a subject.
10. A .... is a university teacher who teaches students in small groups.

LISTENING PART 2 TRAINING

1 **Read this conversation between two university students talking about a lecture. Look at the question below and the parts of the conversation where the students mention the three ideas in options A, B and C.**

M: So, what did you think of that lecture?
W: Hmm, I didn't learn much.
M: Me neither. I wanted to know about the subject, but the guy who was giving the lecture made no effort to help us understand what it was about. I couldn't follow what he was saying at all.
W: I thought he made things pretty clear, actually, but I just found the subject a bit dull and boring. And it went on for about two and a half hours, didn't it? Nobody can concentrate for that amount of time.
M: Well, I certainly can't! It was awful.

You will hear two university students talking about a lecture which they attended.
They agree that
A the person giving the lecture didn't explain things well.
B the topic of the lecture was uninteresting.
C the lecture was too long.

2 **077 Now listen to the conversation. For each option A, B or C, write *M* (man), *W* (woman) or *B* (both) if the person gives that opinion. What did both the man and the woman agree on?**

3 **078 Listen to three more conversations. For each question, choose the correct answer.**

Before you hear each conversation, look at the questions below and underline the important vocabulary. Listen carefully for words and phrases which have the same meaning as the words you have underlined.

1 You will hear two university students talking about a book.
They agree that the book
A is easy to understand.
B contains all the information they need.
C is organised in a helpful way.

2 You will hear a student telling his friend about an exam.
He thinks that he failed his exam because he
A didn't spend enough time revising.
B revised the wrong topics.
C answered the wrong question.

3 You will hear a sixth-form student talking about her future plans to a classmate.
What is she unsure about?
A whether to do a degree or not
B which university to apply to
C what subject to study

VOCABULARY

EDUCATION COLLOCATIONS

1 **Look at these sentences from this unit. Then choose the correct endings for sentences 1–4.**

Nobody has to ***do*** *any* ***homework****.*
I ***got*** *high* ***grades*** *in all my subjects.*
I have to ***do research****.*
You don't have to ***pay attention****.*
We need to ***make*** *a* ***decision****.*
We all ***make mistakes****.*
I'll ***get*** *a useful* ***degree****.*
You've got to ***take*** *a lot of* ***exams****.*
I also found it difficult to ***take notes*** *in lectures.*

1 Do you think this student will do
a many mistakes in his test?
b notes during the lesson?
c his homework on time?

2 It's important to get
a attention when you're listening to lectures.
b a degree from a good university.
c exams during the course.

3 My course involves doing
a a lot of research.
b decisions about what to study.
c good grades in my exams.

4 You don't have to make
a any decisions about your degree yet.
b your homework until next week.
c an exam at the end of term.

2 **Complete the questions with the correct form of one of the verbs in the box. One verb is used twice.**

do	get	make	pay	take

1 What kind of mistakes do you .... when you're speaking English?
2 What do you think is the best way to .... research when you're studying?
3 What's the most difficult exam that you have ever .... ?
4 Why is it important for students to .... attention when they're in class?
5 Do you prefer to .... notes by hand or on a computer?
6 What do you think is the best way to .... good grades in exams?

3 **Work in pairs. Ask and answer the questions in exercise 2.**

SPEAKING

LIKES AND DISLIKES

1 079 **Listen to five people talking about school subjects. Write the number of the speaker next to the correct subject.**

art biology chemistry economics English geography history IT maths physics

2 079 **Listen again and tick the phrases you hear.**

🙂	😐	😣
I liked … I was interested in … I loved … I enjoyed … I was fascinated by … I was … good at … great at … brilliant at … I thought … was (fairly/pretty/really/extremely/incredibly) interesting (absolutely) fascinating	I didn't mind … I was OK at … I wasn't bad at …	I wasn't keen on … I was bored by … I hated … I couldn't stand … I couldn't bear … I was … useless at … terrible at … I thought … was (fairly/pretty/really/extremely/incredibly) dull boring

3 Choose the correct words to complete these sentences.

1 I'm OK at maths, but I'm often fairly .... during the lessons. I just don't find maths interesting.
 a fascinated b interested c bored
2 I'm .... at IT. I never pass any of my exams.
 a terrible b great c brilliant
3 I can't stand physics. I find it extremely ....
 a fascinating b dull c bored

4 Work in pairs. Ask and answer the questions. Then write two more questions to ask your partner.

1 What's/What was your favourite subject?
2 Why do/did you like it?
3 What subjects are/were you good at?

5 Report back to the class about what your partner told you.

6 Work in pairs and discuss the questions.

1 Do you think that everybody should learn a foreign language? Why? / Why not?
2 What do you think are the most important school subjects?
3 Are there any new subjects which schools should teach?

7 **P** **WORD STRESS** 080
Listen to these words, and decide which syllable has the main stress in each word.

biology	o O o o	o o O o
economics	o O o o	o o O o
education	o O o o	o o O o

8 **P** **Complete the rules.**

1 In words that end in 'ology', the main stress is on
 a 'ol' b 'og' c 'y'
2 In words that end in 'ics', the main stress is on
 a the first syllable
 b the last syllable
 c the syllable before 'ics'
3 In words that end in 'tion', the main stress is on
 a the first syllable
 b the last syllable
 c the syllable before 'tion'

9 **P** 081 **Read these words and underline the syllable that has the main stress. Then listen and check your answers.**

archaeology imagination
correction mathematics
geology translation

WRITING

A FORMAL EMAIL

1 **Lots of schools and colleges offer evening and weekend courses to the public. Have you ever done a course in your free time? What did you study? What would you like to learn: a sport, a musical skill or an art or craft?**

2 **Look at this advertisement and email and tick the things that Anna wants to know.**

1. how much the course costs ......
2. if the next course is fully booked ......
3. if she needs to bring her own camera ......
4. when the course will take place ......
5. if you need to have experience to do the course ......

Dear Ms Bolton,

I am writing to enquire about the photography courses at Queenswood Hall.

Please could you tell me if all the equipment is provided? I'd also like to know if the courses are suitable for beginners.

Finally, please could you let me know if there are still places available on next weekend's course?

I look forward to hearing from you.

Yours sincerely,

Anna Rossi

3 **Look at Anna's email again and find the phrases which she uses to:**

1. start the email with a formal greeting
2. explain her reason for writing
3. ask for information
4. ask for additional information
5. end the email

4 **Look at these pairs of sentences. Decide which sentence in each pair sounds more polite and is more suitable for formal conversations, letters and emails.**

1. a Is all the equipment provided?
   b I'd like to know if all the equipment is provided.
2. a How much does the course cost?
   b Please tell me how much the course costs.
3. a When will the course take place?
   b Please could you let me know when the course takes place?

5 **Change these direct questions into indirect questions.**

1. When does the course start?
   I'd like to ....
2. Is accommodation provided?
   Please could you tell ...... ?
3. Can under-18s do the course?
   I'd also like to ....
4. How should I pay for the course?
   Please let me ....

6 **Look at this advert and notes. Write an email to Mr Collins asking him for the information in the notes.**

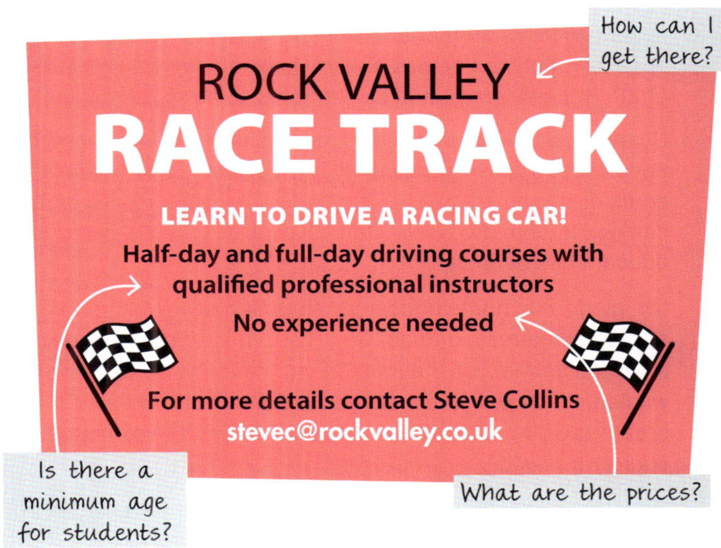

EXAM FOCUS

READING PART 3

EXAM CHECK

1 Complete these sentences about Reading Part 3 by choosing some words in the box.

280	360	articles	attitudes	five	four	notices	whole

In this part of the test, you read a text that is a maximum of [1] .... words long. Part 3 texts are usually [2] .... and they include information about people's [3] .... and opinions. There are [4] .... questions in total. Most of the questions focus on a specific part of the text, while the last question has longer options and tests the [5] .... text. Each question has [6] .... options.

2 For each question, choose the correct answer.

Sanjeev Kanwar

When you meet Sanjeev Kanwar, he seems like any other 15-year-old. Sanjeev, from Birmingham in the centre of England, loves football, hates tidying his bedroom, and is always fighting with his brother and sister for the family's TV remote control. But there is something special about him: he has already finished university. While most students get degrees at 21 or 22, Sanjeev graduated just after his 15th birthday.

By the time he was three, Sanjeev could already read and do maths. When he started school aged five, there was nothing for him to do in class while the other children were learning to count or copy the alphabet. School bored him, and his parents were afraid he would start causing trouble. So, when Sanjeev was six, they decided to take him out of school and educate him at home.

'I'm glad I was home educated,' says Sanjeev. 'Mum and Dad developed a curriculum that suited my interests and abilities. They're the people who know me best, so they were the ideal teachers for me. But the main reason learning at home works well is because not a moment is wasted. At school, hours are spent getting kids to behave well, stand in line, go in and out for breaks, and so on. Meanwhile, at home, you concentrate 100% on your studies and learn at your own speed.'

Nobody was surprised when, at the age of 12, Sanjeev was offered a place studying physics at Sheffield University. He realised that studying in a city 100 miles from home would mean a lot of changes. He was looking forward to spending term times with his aunt in Sheffield, and knew he'd be glad to come home during the holidays and hang out with friends his own age. He felt confident about managing the course work, but anxious about how his classmates would act towards him. Maybe they'd laugh at him or ignore him? In fact, he loved his three years at university, and made good friends there.

Sanjeev hasn't decided what to do next in his life, though. For the moment, he's just relaxing and enjoying being a teenager.

1 What is the writer doing in the first paragraph?
- **A** comparing Sanjeev to other members of his family
- **B** showing that Sanjeev is a normal teenager in many ways
- **C** explaining how Sanjeev managed to graduate from university at only 15
- **D** giving details of several things that make Sanjeev an unusual 15-year-old

2 Why did Sanjeev's parents take him out of school when he was six?
- **A** He behaved badly when he was in class.
- **B** He didn't get on well with the other children.
- **C** He asked to be educated at home.
- **D** He didn't find the work challenging enough.

3 What does Sanjeev think is the biggest advantage of home education?
- **A** It is a very efficient use of students' time.
- **B** It encourages students to enjoy their work.
- **C** Students can study the subjects that interest them.
- **D** Students are taught by someone who knows them well.

4 What did Sanjeev feel nervous about before he started university?
- **A** going to live in another city
- **B** dealing with the course work
- **C** being accepted by the other students
- **D** being able to keep in touch with friends of his own age

5 What would be a good introduction to this article?
- **A** Sanjeev Kanwar had been an ordinary schoolboy until the age of 12, when he amazed his family by getting a place at university.
- **B** Thanks to his parents, who educated him at home and then moved to Sheffield so that he could attend university, Sanjeev Kanwar got his degree when he was only 15.
- **C** In order to concentrate on studying for his degree, teenager Sanjeev Kanwar had to give up his social life during his time at Sheffield University.
- **D** After a successful three years at university, 15-year-old physics graduate Sanjeev Kanwar is in no hurry to make plans for his future.

LISTENING PART 2

EXAM CHECK

1 **Find five mistakes in these sentences about Listening Part 2 and correct them.**

In this part, you have to answer five questions. For each question, you listen to one person talking, and look at some pictures to find the correct answer. Each question has four possible answers. You hear the recording three times.

2 082 **For each question, choose the correct answer.**

1 You will hear a girl talking to a classmate. Why does she want to talk to him?
- **A** to remind him to do tonight's homework
- **B** to ask for advice about tonight's homework
- **C** to check the topic of tonight's homework

2 You will hear two university students talking about a lecture. What did the man think about it?
- **A** It was not well organised.
- **B** It dealt with too many different topics.
- **C** It didn't include the right kind of information.

3 You will hear two students talking about a visit to a college. What did the young man like best about the college?
- **A** the location
- **B** the atmosphere
- **C** the range of subjects

4 You will hear a woman talking to a friend about a problem with her studies. What does her friend suggest that she should do?
- **A** change to another course
- **B** give up one of her subjects
- **C** have a break from her studies

5 You will hear two students talking about an IT exam. They agree that
- **A** the questions were too similar.
- **B** there were too many questions.
- **C** the questions were too difficult.

6 You will hear a boy talking to a friend about a teacher. What does the boy like best about the teacher?
- **A** how strict she is
- **B** how patient she is
- **C** how amusing she is

HOW WAS IT?
- Gave it a go
- Getting there
- Aced it!

REAL WORLD

BOOKING ONTO A LANGUAGE COURSE IN ... OXFORD

1 **Look at the photos of students on an English course. Why do you think this is a popular course?**

ENGLISH PLUS

Want more than just an English course? Then try English Plus. Our English Plus courses provide engaging language classes in the morning and a range of fun activities in the afternoon.
All the afternoon activities are taught by professional teachers or coaches, and help students develop their skills while they are learning about something they are interested in, having fun and making new friends.

This course is great for students who want to:

- expand their vocabulary
- develop their speaking skills
- improve their exam technique
- start a university course in the UK or another country

Activities that students can choose from include art, cookery, dance, drama, history, photography and tennis. The activities are all suitable for students of all levels. Students can choose to improve on a skill they already have, or learn a new skill. If students are staying for more than one week, they can continue with the same activity or change each week. Groups are small, so students get plenty of one-to-one attention. Students also enjoy one excursion per week to a place of interest. There are shopping trips into Oxford, trips to exciting cities such as London and Birmingham, and a visit to the beautiful countryside around Oxford.

What's included in the price?

- All tuition and course materials
- Accommodation close to the school
- 24-hour supervision (for under-18s only)
- Full-board, including breakfast, lunch and dinner, plus snacks and drinks
- Educational trips
- Transfers to and from airports

What's not included?

- Spending money for souvenirs and shopping

Click here to see details of dates and prices, and to enrol on a course.

2 **Read part of the language school's website. Decide if the sentences are true or false.**

1. Students have language classes all day.
2. The course is not suitable for students who are preparing for exams.
3. Students can choose activities that they haven't done before.
4. Students go on more than one trip each week.
5. All meals are included in the price.

3 **Find the words in the text (1–6) and match them with the meanings (a–f).**

1 coaches
2 excursion
3 tuition
4 supervision
5 full-board
6 enrol

a to become a student on a course
b when all meals are included in a price
c people who teach students sports or other skills
d a trip to a place
e teaching
f looking after someone and making sure they stay safe

4 083 **Listen to three conversations at a language school. What are the students doing in each conversation? There is one answer you don't need.**

a discussing the activity they are doing
b complaining about a course
c arriving at the school
d asking for information about a course

5 083 **Complete the sentences and questions with words and phrases in the box. Then listen and check.**

are you staying	can't eat	possible
some information	the course	where is

PHRASES YOU MIGHT USE

1 I'd like ________ about the English Plus course.
2 One of my friends ________ any gluten.
3 Are you enjoying ________ ?
4 How long ________ here?
5 This afternoon I'm doing art. ________ this class?
6 My friend wants to change her course and do art with me. Is that ________ ?

6 **Choose the correct meaning for each sentence.**

PHRASES YOU MIGHT HEAR

1 Is this for an individual booking or a group booking?
a Are you coming alone, or with a big group?
b Would you like to be part of a group?
2 Let me just check the availability.
a Which weeks are you able to come?
b I will find out if/when there are spaces on the course.
3 The week beginning 6 August is looking pretty full.
a This week might soon be full.
b This week probably won't be full.
4 Do you have any special dietary requirements?
a information about food that you like
b information about food that you can't eat
5 Here we go.
a I have found the information I need.
b This is where you should go.
6 Have a word with the art teacher.
a Speak to the art teacher.
b Show this note to the art teacher.

7 **Watch the video about studying English in Oxford. What do you learn about these things? Make notes.**

- the city and university
- language schools and courses
- things to do in and around Oxford

8 **Compare your notes. Then watch again to check your ideas.**

WATCH

LIFE COMPETENCIES

CREATIVE THINKING, TAKING CONTROL OF LEARNING

9 **Work in groups to design your own language course for learning English. Think about:**

- where it is
- the teachers
- the lessons
- extra-curricular activities

Tell the class about what you chose and why.

10 TRAVELLING WELL

VOCABULARY

TRANSPORT WORDS

1 **Work in pairs. Look at the photos and say how you feel about them.**

That looks like the start of an exciting journey!

2 084 **Listen to four people talking about different types of transport. Match the people with the photos (A–D).**

3 084 **Complete the sentences with the words below. Then listen again and check.**

boarding pass	delays	ferry	flight
petrol stations	platform	port	traffic jam

1 Sometimes they want to see my ………… and sometimes they want to see my passport.
2 When I'm in my seat in the cabin, I start to enjoy the ………… .
3 The ………… on motorways are expensive and I always forget to fill up before I start my journey.
4 In a ………… , a car isn't any faster than a bus.
5 You often have to wait for your train because there are ………… .
6 Sometimes there's no waiting room so you have to stand for a long time on a cold ………… .
7 We went on an overnight car ………… from Ireland to France.
8 It was lovely to arrive at a busy ………… early in the morning.

4 **Do you prefer to travel by road, by air, by rail or by sea? Work in groups and discuss the advantages and disadvantages.**

If the journey is not too long, I prefer to travel by road. I drive my car.

DID YOU KNOW?

For some words related to transport, there are differences between British and American English.

American English		British English
railroad	=	*railway*
truck	=	*lorry*
gas station	=	*petrol station*
freeway	=	*motorway*

READING PART 4 TRAINING

In Reading Part 4, you need to understand the gist of a whole article. Look back at Unit 3, page 48 to review the exam tips for this part of the exam.

1 **Have you ever especially enjoyed a trip on a plane or other transport?**

2 **Read the article and complete the summary below in your own words.**

A FABULOUS FLIGHT

Unless you are one of the super-rich, you'll be unlikely to ever travel on a private jet. But lucky passengers Tony Nolan and Marie Headon were treated like stars when they were the only passengers on flight 391 from Manchester to Dublin last week.

'My girlfriend and I have never enjoyed flying, but we do a lot of it,' Tony told us. 'We live in Manchester but our parents are in Ireland. *1* .... Crowded airports, delays and full planes are tiring and stressful, but we have no choice: if we want to see our families, we take a flight.'

While the couple was travelling to the airport last Friday evening, Marie received a text message from the airline. Their flight was delayed, so Tony and Marie decided to get off their train to the airport and do some shopping. They had completed the online check-in, so when they got to the airport later, they went straight to the departure lounge. *2* .... At the gate, staff told them that all the others had been given seats on other planes. They were the only ones left on their flight. 'They won't take us if we're the only passengers,' thought Marie. *3* ....

'As soon as we got on the plane, they started to treat us like stars!' says Tony. He and Marie were given business-class seats and served a three-course meal. The pilot and cabin staff were cheerful as they were going home for the weekend. *4* .... Tony and Marie could have as much food as they wanted and the flight attendants took photos of them acting like film stars. 'We decided to make them feel really special,' says flight attendant Sean Collins. 'It was fun for all of us.' The pilot showed them the cockpit, too, which they found really interesting.

'If flying was always that good, we'd do it every day,' say Tony and Marie. Unfortunately, the 'private plane' was probably a once-in-a-lifetime experience for them.
5 ....

A man and woman were the only two …
They were treated …
Normally, they don't like flying but this experience …

3 **Five sentences have been removed from the article. Look at gap number 1. Which of these sentences fits into the gap? How do you know?**

1 She wants to go home sometimes.
2 If we go to visit them, it's always by plane.
3 Luckily, the people at the airports are nice.

4 **For each question in the text (2–5), choose the correct answer. There are two extra sentences which you do not need to use.**

A That's why they missed the flight.
B They were surprised to see that no other passengers were waiting there.
C Luckily, she was wrong.
D Their flight back to Manchester was full, late and no fun at all.
E However, she didn't have a good experience this time.
F Everybody on the plane was feeling happy.

5 **Find these words in the text and match them with the meanings.**

airline	business-class seat	cabin staff	check-in
cockpit	departure lounge	flight attendant	gate

1 The team of people on a plane who serve food and help passengers.
2 One member of the team described in sentence 1.
3 The place where people leave the airport and get on the plane.
4 A company that provides flights.
5 You get your boarding pass when you do this.
6 The area where you wait for your flight.
7 The place where the pilot sits.
8 A more comfortable and expensive place to sit on a plane.

6 **Work in groups and discuss the questions. Should airlines fly a big plane for only two passengers? Think about the environment and also about good customer service.**

VOCABULARY

PHRASAL VERBS WITH *GET*

1 Read the sentences (1–7) and then match the phrasal verbs with their meanings (a–g).

1 *Tony and Marie decided to **get off** their train and do some shopping.*
2 *As soon as we **got on** the plane, they started to treat us like stars!*
3 *Kenny parked in front of the shop and **got out of** his car.*
4 *I **got into** a taxi and asked the driver to take me to the airport.*
5 *I left home at six and **got to** work early.*
6 *I didn't **get back** home until late in the evening.*
7 *It's easy to **get around** a city that has good public transport.*

a arrive at a place
b arrive home after a journey
c enter a small vehicle like a car or taxi
d board a large vehicle like a bus, plane or ship
e leave a small vehicle
f leave a large vehicle
g go to different places

2 Complete the text using phrasal verbs with *get* in the correct tense.

We're on holiday on La Palma. It's beautiful, but the journey here was terrible! First, when we [1] ________ the car it didn't start. After we had tried everything to start the engine, we called a taxi to take us to the station. The driver was horribly slow! When we [2] ________ the taxi we had only one minute to buy our tickets. We [3] ________ the train just in time. Then, after about 10 minutes, we stopped in a tunnel and had to wait for ages. I started to panic. I wanted to [4] ________ the train, but of course that would be too dangerous. Well, in the end we started moving again. We [5] ________ the airport 30 minutes before our flight. That's much too late, of course, but we were lucky: the flight was delayed. So now we're having a fantastic holiday. We've rented a car to [6] ________ the island. I just hope we can [7] ________ more easily than we got here!

3 Have you ever had a very stressful journey? Tell your partner.

GRAMMAR

ZERO AND FIRST CONDITIONALS

GRAMMAR ON THE MOVE
Watch the video

1 Read the sentences and choose the correct option to complete the rule.

***If** we **go** to visit them, it**'s** always by plane.*
***If** we **want** to see our families, we **take** a flight.*

Zero conditional
The zero conditional is used to talk about something which *is generally true/will possibly be true*. We form it like this:
***If/When* + present + present**
***If** a city **has** good public transport, it **makes** life easier.*
***When** the weather **is** good, it**'s** fun to go by bike.*
present + *if/when* + present
*You **don't need** a car **if** public transport **is** good.*
*It**'s** fun to go by bike **when** the weather **is** good.*

➔ **GRAMMAR REFERENCE** / *page 216.*

2 Complete this blog entry with the correct form of one of the verbs in the box.

be	feel	get	go	rain

Home Blog About Search

It's spring! It's time to start riding my bike to work. Cycling has so many advantages. You get really fit if you [1] ________ everywhere by bike. Moreover, it doesn't hurt the environment and it's fun! When the weather [2] ________ right, I love cycling. But what is the right weather? If it's icy or snowy, I [3] ________ safe on a bicycle. And of course, I don't cycle to work when it [4] ________ . I can't arrive at the office with wet hair and clothes. If I cycle when it's too warm, I [5] ________ a red face. That's why I can't go to work by bike on warm days. So you see, it's not so easy.

3 Write sentences with the zero conditional using these ideas. You can put the *if* clause or the main clause first.

bus / full – people / uncomfortable
If the bus is full, people feel uncomfortable. / People feel uncomfortable if the bus is full.

1 train / late – people / angry
2 you fly / business class – food / better
3 people travel by bike – they / fitter
4 I travel by ferry – I / seasick

First conditional

We use the first conditional to describe possibilities in the future. We form it like this:

If* + present + *will/won't

*If my car **doesn't start**, I'**ll take** the bus.*

***will/won't* + *if* + present**

*I'**ll** take a taxi **if** I **miss** the bus.*

We can also use ***unless*** in conditional sentences. It means ***if not***.

***Unless** there's a traffic jam, we'll arrive on time.*

*I won't take a taxi **unless** I'm in a hurry.*

➜ **GRAMMAR REFERENCE** / pages 216–217.

4 **Read the rules and complete the sentences with the correct form of the verbs in brackets.**

1. Take a taxi! If you .... (take) the bus, you .... (arrive late).
2. I .... (buy) a car unless somebody .... (lend) me some money.
3. No parking here today! If you .... (park) here, the police .... (give) you a ticket.
4. Here's the bus. If it .... (be) very full, I .... (not get) on it.
5. .... your parents .... (pay) for your ticket if you .... (fly) home for Christmas?
6. What .... you .... (do) if your flight .... (be) delayed?

5 **Think about next weekend. Answer the questions with your own ideas.**

1. Where will you go if you want to meet your friends?
2. What will you do if your friends aren't free?
3. What will you do if the weather is bad?
4. What will you do if you feel sick?

6 **Choose the correct verb forms to make sentences in the zero or first conditional.**

1. *We go/We'll go* to the beach this afternoon if it *doesn't rain/won't rain*.
2. Unless I *have/will have* too much work, *I visit/I'll visit* you tomorrow.
3. Susie usually *goes/will go* to school by bike unless the weather *is/will be* bad.
4. Shawn likes walking to work, but he *takes/will take* the bus when he *feels/will feel* tired.
5. *I go/I'll go* to the cinema tonight unless our teacher *gives/will give* us a lot of homework.
6. I don't know how long the journey home will be, but *I call/I'll call* you when I *get/will get* there.

PUSH YOURSELF B2

LISTENING: OPINIONS

1 **How do you get around your home town? What do you think about public transport in your area? What problems are there? How could the public transport be better?**

2 **085 You will hear four people talking about public transport in their city. For each speaker, choose the sentence that best fits their opinion. There is one extra sentence which you do not need.**

Speaker one ....
Speaker two ....
Speaker three ....
Speaker four ....

1. It's good but it's too expensive.
2. It's not bad but it's too slow.
3. Nothing about it is good.
4. The underground is fast but the rest is too slow.
5. It's the best way to get around town.

3 **Match the phrases the speakers use (1–5) with the meanings (a–e).**

1. I find it annoying.
2. It's just a dream.
3. It's the best option.
4. It's useless.
5. They cost much too much.

a. They are too expensive.
b. It's better than the other possibilities.
c. It doesn't work well at all.
d. It won't happen in real life.
e. It makes me feel a bit angry.

LISTENING

1 **How often do you go to watch bands? What kind of environmental impact can bands on tour have?**

2 **086 Listen to this introduction to a radio show. Tick the phrases that you hear.**

be green ....
turn off the lights ....
use a bike, not a car ....
stop eating meat ....
paper bags only ....
use less water ....

3 **086 Now read and listen again. Match the words and phrases in pink with the meanings.**

It's not too hard to be green at home. We can make sure to turn off the lights and the TV when we're not using them. All of our **rubbish** can go to the right **recycling bin**. We can try to buy things that don't have too much **packaging**, and we can get food from **local producers**.
However, when we're out and about, things change. We buy drinks in plastic bottles and eat meals in plastic packaging, which we throw away. And of course, the fuel that we use when we travel is so bad for our air. Transport causes air **pollution**, and that pollution is causing **global warming** and climate change.
So what about people who are hardly ever at home? Bands on tour can be a disaster for the environment. Max Carver of the band *Yellow Ducks* tells us what they can do about it.

1 things that we don't need and that we throw away
2 the way that temperatures in the world are going up
3 farms that sell food to people who live nearby
4 a container for rubbish, especially for glass, paper, etc.
5 paper, plastic or a box around a product
6 dirt and gases in our air or water

4 **087 What do you think Max Carver will say about what his band does to protect the environment? Listen and check.**

5 **087 Listen again and decide if the sentences are true or false.**

1 Max and his band *Yellow Ducks* use biofuels in their tour buses.
2 Reusing bottles is not a big thing.
3 *Yellow Ducks* could produce a mountain of waste every day, but they don't.
4 They don't want everyone to go to their concerts in a car.
5 Fans at their concerts can't easily recycle their waste.
6 The food at concerts is always produced by local farms.

6 **Match the words and phrases below in the interview with Max with the meanings. Which word was not in the interview?**

bottle bank	car sharing	environmentally friendly	gas	reuse

1 a way to make sure one vehicle is used by many people
2 good for the world around us
3 a place where you can leave used glass
4 use something again
5 the American word for petrol

7 **What do you think of Max Carver's ideas? Should more bands do things to protect the environment?**

GRAMMAR

SECOND CONDITIONAL

GRAMMAR ON THE MOVE
Watch the video

We use the second conditional to talk about things that we can imagine but would probably not happen in reality. We form it like this:

If* + past + *would

*If everybody **went** to festivals in cars, we **would have** terrible traffic jams.*

***would* + *if* + past**

*Fans **would come** to concerts on public transport **if** we always **performed** in cities.*

In the second conditional, we sometimes use **were** instead of **was**:

*If I **were** the boss, I'd drive a big car. / If I **was** the boss, I'd drive a big car.*

The meaning stays the same. In formal language we usually use **were**. In informal language both are possible.

➡ **GRAMMAR REFERENCE** / *pages 216–217.*

1 **Read the rules and join the beginnings and endings of these sentences.**

1. If fewer people drove cars,
2. It would be much better for the environment
3. Maybe more people would travel by rail
4. If petrol were really expensive,
5. But personally, I wouldn't stop using my car

a. unless I had excellent public transport near my home.
b. the air would be cleaner.
c. if everyone travelled by train.
d. people wouldn't use their cars so much.
e. if it were cheaper.

2 **Choose the correct form of the verbs to complete the text.**

I don't have a car. If I [1]*had/would have* a car, my life [2]*was/would be* easier. I [3]*didn't/wouldn't* wait here every morning for a bus that always comes late. My friends [4]*were/would be* very happy if I [5]*drove/would drive* them to school. [6]*Did/Would* I have more friends then? Yes, probably! I'm dreaming of course. If I [7]*bought/would buy* a car it really [8]*didn't/wouldn't* help me. I'm only 15 and I can't drive!

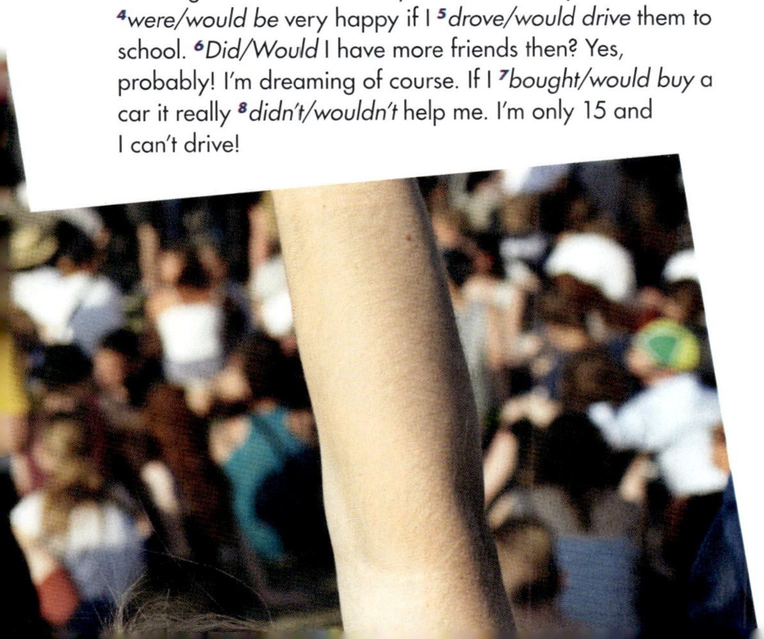

3 **Complete the sentences with the verb in brackets in the correct form. Use the second conditional.**

1. If we .... (buy) fewer products from other countries, there .... (be) fewer ships at sea.
2. If there .... (be) fewer ships, it .... (reduce) pollution in the water.
3. Also, it .... (help) our oceans if we .... (use) less plastic.
4. Maybe people .... (stop) using so much plastic if they .... (know) about the islands of rubbish in the sea.
5. If the price of plastic bottles .... (increase), maybe people .... (not use) so many of them.

4 **Choose the correct verb forms to make sentences with the zero, first or second conditional.**

There [1]*are/were* often environmental problems when too many tourists [2]*go/will go* to one place. In my town, the airport is too small for all the people who arrive for holidays here. The government says we [3]*solve/will solve* the problem if we [4]*make/would make* the airport bigger. However, I don't agree. I think if the airport [5]*were/would be* bigger, even more tourists [6]*will/would* arrive. I know most tourists are nice and they spend a lot of money here, but I still think it [7]*is/would be* better if we [8]*can/could* have a maximum number of people who arrive at our airport on one day.

5 **Read the sentences. Are they real possibilities, or things that will probably not happen? Write sentences about the situations. Use the first or second conditional.**

Buses are free in your city.
There would be less traffic in my city if buses were free.

1. More people fly to other countries on holiday.
2. City streets become safer for people on bikes.
3. Global warming gets worse.

6 **P 'LL AND 'D** 088
Listen to six phrases and decide if you hear a shortened *will* or *would*.

In spoken conditional sentences, we almost always shorten *will* to *'ll* and *would* to *'d*. Sometimes it is hard to hear these contractions.

7 **P** 088 **Listen again and repeat each phrase.**

WRITING PART 2 TRAINING

A STORY

- *In Part 2 of the Writing exam, you will write a story or an article of about 100 words.*
- *For all stories and for some articles you will need narrative tenses.*
- *Look again at Unit 4, pages 54–56 to review narrative tenses and page 61 to review exam tips.*

1 **Match the verbs in bold in the example sentences with the name of the tense and the use of the tense.**

EXAMPLE	*NAME OF TENSE*	*WE USE IT TO TALK ABOUT …*
I **went** to the cinema yesterday.	Past continuous	things that happened *before* other actions in the past
While I **was walking** down the street, my friend phoned me.	Past simple	finished past actions and actions that were repeated in the past
After I **had seen** the film, I went to my friend's house.	Past perfect	things in progress at a certain time in the past, or while another action took place

2 **Choose the correct narrative tenses to complete this story.**

An old friend

I [1]*waited/was waiting* at the railway station when I saw an old friend. I [2]*didn't see/hadn't seen* him for a long time, but he looked just as cheerful and lively as ever.

'Hey, Conor!' I called excitedly, and he [3]*saw/had seen* me. We started to chat on the platform. Then I saw that an inspector [4]*was waving/had waved* angrily at us. 'What are you two doing?' he asked. 'Board the train!' Conor looked up at the station clock. 'Oh no!' he cried, and he suddenly [5]*ran/was running* away. I was confused, but I quickly got on the train. While I [6]*looked/was looking* for my seat, the train driver made an announcement. 'Ladies and gentlemen, we apologise for the late departure,' he said. Finally, I understood. Conor was the driver.

3 **Answer these questions about the story.**

1. How many paragraphs are there?
2. What is the function of each paragraph?
3. What time linkers can you find in the story?
4. What adjectives can you find?
5. What adverbs can you find which describe people's actions?

4 **Direct speech can make your story or article more lively. Find examples of direct speech in the story and answer these questions.**

1. What punctuation is used in the story after the direct speech?
2. Find verbs you can sometimes use after direct speech.

5 **Complete these examples of direct speech with the verbs in the box.**

asked shouted told whispered

1. 'Hey! Stop!' the policeman ....
2. 'This is an example of a simple motor,' the guide .... us.
3. 'What are you doing?' my mum ....
4. 'Ssssh, be quiet or my father will hear us,' .... the little boy.

6 **Write a story in about 100 words. Before you begin, write a plan of your story. Your story must begin with this sentence:**

The journey had started well.

Don't forget to use …

- narrative tenses
- paragraphs
- time linkers
- direct speech
- adjectives and adverbs

SPEAKING

SPECULATING

1 **Work in pairs. Look at the photo and brainstorm words for what you can see. Then describe the photo.**

2 **Where do you think the photo was taken? Use the modals of speculation in the box.**

can't be	could be	may (not) be	might be	must be

It can't be Britain because they are driving on the right …

3 **Read the information and then work in groups and discuss the questions.**

The photo above was taken in a country where the economy has grown very quickly. In the past, most people lived in the countryside and very few people had a car. Now, most people live in huge cities and millions of people have a car.

1 What are the advantages of living in a very big modern city?
2 What negative effects can this lifestyle have on the environment?

4 **089 Listen to a student talking about her country. What would she do to solve the biggest environmental problem in her country?**

5 **Work in groups and decide what you would do to protect the environment if you were the leaders of your country. Think of three things you would do. Then tell the class.**

First, we would make public transport free. This is because …

EXAM FOCUS

READING PART 4

EXAM CHECK

1 Put these instructions in the correct order.

A Look at the eight options and find the sentence which fits in the gap.
B Read the sentences on either side of the gap and decide what information is missing.
C Read the completed text to check that it makes sense.
D Go back to the beginning of the text and look at the first gap.
E Look at the three unused sentences and check that they don't fit in any of the gaps.
F Put the sentence into the gap and check it fits in terms of meaning and grammar.
G Do the same thing for the other four gaps.
H Read the text. *1*

2 You are going to read an article about a man who went on an unexpected trip.

Five sentences have been removed from the article below. For each question, choose the correct answer. There are three extra sentences which you do not need to use.

Joe's surprise holiday

Most people go on holiday with friends or family, so would you invite a complete stranger to go on holiday with you? **1** ______ The group, from Bristol in the UK, had planned a weekend away together to celebrate one of their birthdays. Everything was arranged, including plane tickets to the sunny island of Mallorca in the Mediterranean, and three days' accommodation on the island. **2** ______ It was too late to cancel his reservation or change the name on the ticket. But what could they do with a plane ticket in the name of Joe McGrath?

3 ______ This involved going onto Facebook and looking for people with that name. They messaged 15 men and offered a free holiday to anyone who wanted it – the only requirement was that you had to be called Joe McGrath! **4** ______ At first, this Joe thought that the message was a joke. But then he spoke to the people from Bristol and he realised that their offer was real. He considered the idea for a couple of days, and then he thought 'Why not?' So he packed his bags, and drove down to Bristol. **5** ______ But they still all had a great weekend together. Joe is even planning to invite his new friends for a weekend in Manchester soon.

A Then the friends had a brilliant idea.
B Unfortunately, just a week before they were due to travel, one of the friends found out that he couldn't go on the trip.
C But the airline refused to give Joe a refund on the ticket.
D The friends didn't need to wait long to get a reply.
E Well, that's exactly what 10 good friends did recently.
F The next day, Joe flew to Mallorca with 10 people he had only just met.
G Not many people would want to do that.
H Only one person answered – 21-year-old Joe McGrath from Manchester.

WRITING PART 2

A STORY

EXAM CHECK

1 **Complete this information about Writing Part 2 using some of the words in the box.**

adjectives	advertisement	around	article	capital
exactly	linkers	past	present	spelling

In this part, you have the choice of writing either an [1] ________ or a story that is [2] ________ 100 words long. Your story should be written using [3] ________ tenses. Remember to use [4] ________ to make your story flow well and to use [5] ________ and adverbs to make your story interesting. It is important to use correct [6] ________ , punctuation and grammar in your story. You should also remember to use [7] ________ letters at the beginning of sentences and names, and for the pronoun 'I'.

2 **Do the task.**

Your English teacher has asked you to write a story.
Your story must begin with this sentence:
By the time I got on the bus with my luggage, there were very few seats left.
Write your **story** in about 100 words.

➔ **WRITING BANK** / *pages 232–233.*

HOW WAS IT?

Gave it a go ☐

Getting there ☐

Aced it! ☐

REAL WORLD

GETTING THROUGH THE AIRPORT IN ... LONDON

1 **How often do you fly? Do you like airports? What is fun or boring about being at the airport?**

2 **Look at the photos and match them with the words below.**

check-in desk departure lounge passport control security

3 **Read the tips for getting through Heathrow Airport quickly. Answer the questions.**

1 What should you do before you travel?
2 What do you need to check when you pack your bags?
3 What should you do with liquids?
4 What should you take off when you go through security?
5 Where can you wait after the security check?
6 What do you need to have ready when you arrive, after your flight?

GETTING THROUGH HEATHROW AIRPORT QUICKLY AND WITHOUT PROBLEMS

- If you can print out your boarding pass in advance, this is a good idea, especially if you are not checking in bags.
- Pack your bags carefully and check the size and weight. Check what your baggage allowance is.
- If you pack any liquids in your hand luggage, make sure they are under 100 ml. Keep them together in a clear plastic bag.
- Arrive at the airport two to three hours before your flight time. It might take longer than you think to get to the airport or get through security.
- If you didn't check in online, or if you need to check in a bag, find the check-in desk for your airline. Have your passport or ID ready.
- Go to the security area for your terminal, and get ready to go through security. Remove liquids and electronic equipment from your luggage, as they have to go through on their own. Take off your coat and shoes. Remove coins and keys from your pockets. Put all your bags, shoes and anything made of metal in a tray to go through the machine.
- A security officer will call you through the security check. When you get through, don't forget to collect your luggage, shoes, etc.
- Watch the departure board and find the gate number for your flight when it is shown. Go to the gate, and wait in the waiting area. Airline staff will give you instructions when it is time to board.
- When you get on the plane, find your seat and put your luggage in the overhead locker.
- Relax and enjoy your flight!
- When you arrive at your destination, remember to have your passport ready to go through passport control.

4 **Find these words in the text (1–6) and match them with the meanings (a–f).**

1	boarding pass	**4**	tray
2	baggage allowance	**5**	departure board
3	terminal	**6**	overhead locker

a a board with a list of flights and where they are going to
b a document that allows you to get on the plane
c the amount of luggage that you are allowed to take on your flight
d the part above your head on the plane, where you can put bags
e a flat container with sides, which you put your luggage in to go through the security machine
f the part of the airport where planes arrive and depart from

5 090 **Listen to three conversations at an airport. Where are the people? There is one answer you don't need.**

a at a check-in desk
b going through security
c on the plane, ready to leave
d arriving at Heathrow and going through passport control

6 090 **Complete the sentences and questions with the words in the box. Then listen and check.**

check in	here's	home
OK	passport	understand

PHRASES YOU MIGHT USE

1 Shall I put my .... in here, too?
2 Sorry, I don't .... the question.
3 I'm going .... in three weeks.
4 .... my ticket.
5 I have one bag to ....
6 Is that .... now?

7 **Match the sentences (1–6) with the meanings (a–f).**

PHRASES YOU MIGHT HEAR

1 I'm afraid I'll have to take it off you.
2 Any loose change?
3 Just pop it in there.
4 If you could step this way, please.
5 What's the purpose of your visit?
6 That's under the limit now.

a Come over here, please.
b It isn't too heavy now.
c Put it here.
d I'm sorry, but I will remove this and keep it.
e Why are you in this country?
f Do you have any coins?

8 **Watch the video about Heathrow Airport. What facts do you learn about these things? Make notes.**

- the airport
- flights
- passengers
- baggage
- security
- shops and restaurants

9 **Compare your notes. Then watch again and check your facts.**

WATCH

LIFE COMPETENCIES

SYNTHESISING INFORMATION, EVALUATING IDEAS

10 **Work in groups. Choose another airport and read some customer reviews. Make notes on typical problems that travellers have with facilities. Compare notes with other groups and decide which airport sounds the easiest to travel through.**

11 A GREAT LOCATION

VOCABULARY

HOMES

1 **Look at the homes in the photos. What differences can you see? Where do you think they are?**

2 **091 Listen to a conversation in which Jessica talks about staying in each of the three homes. Write *A*, *B* or *C* next to the phrases you hear.**

block of flats	brand new	business district
convenient	cosy	old-fashioned	suburbs
terraced	top floor	two-storey house

3 **092 Work in pairs and discuss which place you think Jessica liked best. Then listen and check.**

4 **Complete the sentences with some of the words and phrases in exercise 2.**

1. A .... is a tall building with lots of homes, one above the other.
2. A small place which is warm and comfortable can be described as ....
3. If you're on the ...., you're at the highest level of a building.
4. A .... house is one of a line of houses which are all connected.
5. The .... is the part of a city where big companies have their offices.
6. A .... is a home that has one floor downstairs and one upstairs.
7. A .... location for a home is one that is near everything that you need.
8. If you live in the ...., your home is in an area on the edge of a large town or city.

5 **Work in pairs and discuss which of the three homes you like best.**

READING

1 **What do you think life is like for the people who live in the three homes on page 140?**

2 **Read these texts about the homes and answer the questions.**

Which writer says that they …

1. have a good relationship with their neighbours?
2. like the view from their home?
3. have lived in their home for many years?
4. moved into their home a short time ago?
5. don't know their neighbours?
6. employed someone to repair part of their home?

DID YOU KNOW?

For some words related to housing, there are differences between British and American English.

American English		British English
apartment	=	*flat*
apartment block	=	*block of flats*

A I live and work in London. Home for me is in a modern block of flats in the city, so I don't have to travel far to get to my office, and my flat is smart, comfortable and very easy to look after. I have the flat cleaned once a week while I'm at work. Mine is the only flat on the top floor, and there's a lift which takes me all the way from the ground floor to my home. This means that I don't really have any contact with my neighbours, which is perhaps a shame. But, on the other hand, it's quiet and relaxing up here. I wouldn't want to move.

8 2 30

B Our house, which was built more than 300 years ago, is a pretty cottage in the countryside. We've only lived here for a few months, but it really feels like home. Before we moved in, we got the roof mended. Our home has a 'thatched roof', which is very traditional. There was a period when many English country houses had these roofs, but now they're not so common because it's difficult to make them. Luckily, we managed to hire a man whose father and grandfather taught him how to do this very skilled work. He did a brilliant job for us. There's also a nice woman who comes and helps with the garden. My favourite thing about living in our cottage is the fact that I can see for miles over beautiful woods, fields and hills. It's so peaceful here.

0 2 8

C We've both grown up in this terraced house in the suburbs of London. Our parents moved here before we were born, but now that we're teenagers the house is starting to seem quite small for us. So, Mum and Dad are thinking of having another room put in the roof. If that happens, it'll be our first major change: we've had our doors painted every few years, but we haven't had much else done to our house in all the time we've been here. Our neighbours, who are all families like us, are really nice. In fact, most of the kids that live in our street are friends of ours. We love living here because we get on well with everyone who lives in the area.

3 8 12

GRAMMAR

RELATIVE CLAUSES

GRAMMAR ON THE MOVE

Watch the video

1 Read the sentences and complete the rules with the words in bold.

the part of a city ***where*** *lots of big companies have their offices*
a period ***when*** *many English country houses had these roofs*
a lift ***which*** *takes me all the way from the ground floor*
a home ***that*** *has one floor downstairs and one upstairs*
a nice woman ***who*** *comes and helps with the garden*
a man ***whose*** *father and grandfather taught him*
most of the kids ***that*** *live in our street*

> In relative clauses we use:
> 1 .... or 2 .... for things
> 3 .... or 4 .... for people
> 5 .... for times
> 6 .... for places
> 7 .... to say who something belongs to or someone is connected to

➜ **GRAMMAR REFERENCE** / *pages 217–218.*

2 Complete these questions using the words in bold from exercise 1.

What do you call …

1. the building or part of the building .... you park your car?
2. the piece of electrical equipment .... gets our clothes clean?
3. a person .... comes to look after children for a short time while their parents aren't at home?
4. the time of day .... people usually relax and watch TV in their living room?
5. a person .... job it is to look after flowers, plants and grass for you?

3 Can you answer the questions above?

4 Look at the relative clauses in bold in these sentences and complete the rules.

a *We get on well with everyone* ***who lives in the area****.*
b *In fact, most of the kids* ***that live in our street*** *are friends of ours.*
c *I don't really have any contact with my neighbours,* ***which is perhaps a shame****.*
d *Our neighbours,* ***who are all families like us****, are really nice.*

> Relative clauses which are essential for the meaning of the sentence are called 'defining relative clauses'.
> Sentences: 1 .... and 2 ....
> Relative clauses which just add extra information, and can be removed without changing the meaning of the sentence are called 'non-defining relative clauses'.
> Sentences 3 .... and 4 ....
> Non-defining relative clauses must use **which** for things and **who** for people.

➜ **GRAMMAR REFERENCE** / *pages 217–218.*

5 Which of these sentences contain defining relative clauses, and which ones contain non-defining relative clauses?

1. My house is close to the station, ... **is very convenient**.
2. The man .... **bought the house next door** seems very nice.
3. Do you want to see the flat .... **I'm going to rent?**
4. My grandparents, ... **are both 85**, have lived in the same house for 60 years.

6 Now complete the sentences in exercise 5.

7 Look at these sentences and answer the questions. Then complete the rule.

a *She's the woman* ***that*** *lives in the cottage by the river.*
b *This is the house* ***that*** *I lived in when I was a child.* or *This is the house I lived in when I was a child.*

1. Is **that** the subject or the object of sentence a?
2. Is **that** the subject or the object of sentence b?

> You can leave out ***that***, ***which*** or ***who*** if it is the .... of the sentence.

8 Look at exercise 5 again. Which sentence has a relative pronoun which you could miss out?

9 Only one of these sentences is correct. Find the mistakes in the other sentences, and correct them.

1. How long have you lived in the flat which you live now?
2. Have you ever met anyone who home is a boat?
3. Do you get on well with the people live next door to you?
4. What is the most beautiful home you have ever seen?

10 Check your answers to exercise 9, then ask and answer the questions with a partner.

VOCABULARY

FURNITURE AND FURNISHINGS

1 **Have you or your friends or family ever rented somewhere to live for a short time? What problems can people have when they rent places to live?**

2 **Here are some photos of Josh's holiday apartment. Match the items (A–J) with the descriptions from the holiday apartment website (1–10).**

1. Plenty of **wardrobe** space to hang your clothes.
2. Wooden floors throughout with attractive handmade **rugs**.
3. Stylish kitchen with floor to ceiling cupboards and wall **cabinets**.
4. Egyptian cotton sheets and **duvet** covers.
5. **Chest of drawers** provide additional storage for clothes.
6. Fully equipped kitchen with **kettle**, toaster and ovens.
7. **Bin** for all your laundry needs.
8. Two steel **sinks** with flexible **taps** for easy food preparation.
9. Cosy seating area with lamp and **cushions**.
10. Underfloor **heating** for cold days.

3 **Look at the picture and complete the email using the bold words from exercise 2.**

Dear Mr Rackham,

I have just moved into student accommodation which I am renting from you. Unfortunately, there are some differences between the room as I found it and the way that it was advertised on your website.

There is a hole in the wall behind the [1]w............, and the [2]c............ above the [3]s............ is cracked. The [4]k............ is broken, and the [5]r............ on the floor is worn out. There is also no hot water from the [6]t............ . The [7]d............ on the bed is torn, and there is no [8]c............ on the armchair. There's [9]h............, but it isn't working, so the room is cold. In the picture on the website, there is a [10]c............ for my clothes and a [11]b............ underneath the desk. However, these items are missing.

I'd be grateful if you could come to the room as soon as possible to sort out these issues.

Yours sincerely,

Jake Moss

4 **Look at the picture of Jake's room again. Decide if the sentences are true or false. Correct the false statements.**

1. The cabinet is over the bed.
2. The bin is underneath the desk.
3. The kettle is beside the sink.
4. The bed is opposite the desk.
5. The hole in the wall is above the armchair.

5 **Work in pairs. Student A turn to page 192, choose a photo, and describe it to Student B. Student B turn to page 192 and guess which photo Student A has described. Then repeat the activity with Student B describing a room.**

6 **P** **/ʌ/ AND /æ/** 093

Look at and listen to these words which all contain the vowel sound /ʌ/.

rug cup cut

7 **P** 094 **Listen to these pairs of words. Can you hear the difference?**

rug rag   cup cap   cut cat

8 **P** 095 **Decide if the words are the same or different.**

1	same / different	**3**	same / different
2	same / different	**4**	same / different

> **To pronounce /ʌ/ try saying the sound /ɔː/ (as in *cause*), but with your mouth half-closed and your lips loose and relaxed.**

LISTENING PART 1 TRAINING

1 **Look at these three pictures. What are the differences? Complete the sentences below.**

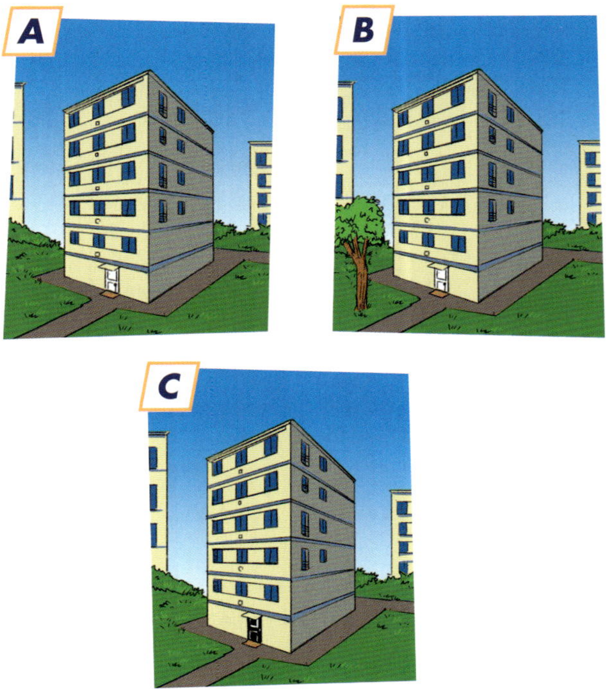

1 The building in picture C has a .... door.

2 The buildings in pictures A and B both have a .... door.

3 In picture B, there's a .... in front of the building.

2 096 **Listen to a phone conversation in which a woman describes her house to a friend. Choose picture A, B or C in exercise 1 to answer this question:**

What does the woman's block of flats look like now?

> - *Before you listen to each recording, look at the differences between the pictures and think about the words you might hear.*
> - *Listen carefully to both speakers – the information you need to answer the question can come from one or both speakers. One person may mention something, then another person may give more information about it.*

What does the woman say about the door and the tree? What is the correct answer?

3 097 **Read the exam tip above. Then listen, and for each question, choose the correct answer.**

1 Where is the woman's purse?

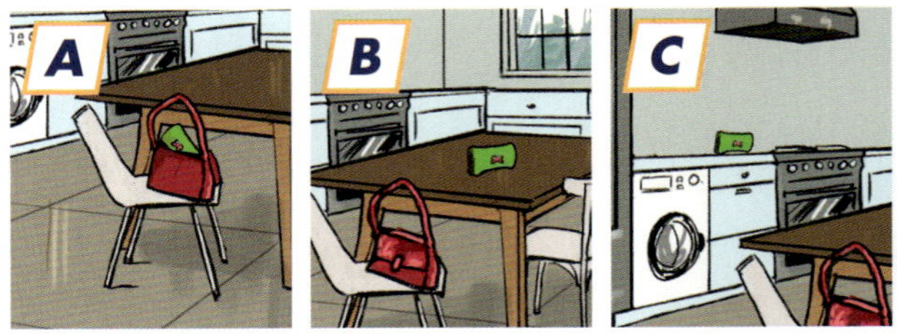

2 Which cushions do the friends decide to buy?

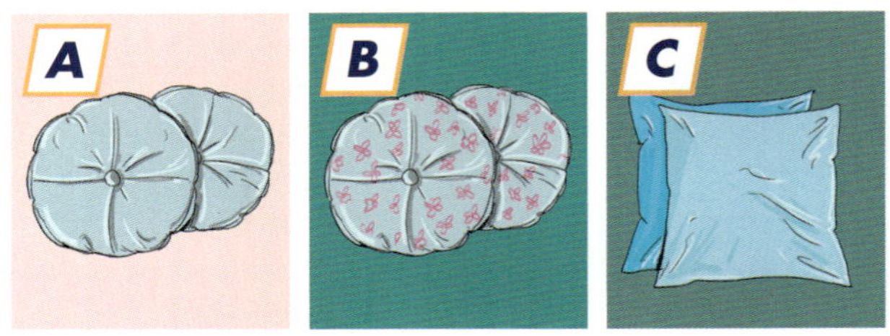

3 Which product costs less than usual at the moment?

4 What does the study in the man's flat look like?

GRAMMAR

HAVE/GET SOMETHING DONE

GRAMMAR ON THE MOVE
Watch the video

1 Read the sentence. What does the woman mean?

'I have the flat cleaned once a week while I'm at work.'

a She cleans her flat.
b She pays *another person* to clean her flat for her.

When we talk about arranging for another person to do a job for us, we can use these constructions:
***have/get* + object + past participle**
*I **had/got a photo taken** when I graduated from university.*
Have is more formal than ***get***.

➜ **GRAMMAR REFERENCE** / *page 218.*

2 Read the rule and then look at text C on page 141. Find the phrases which mean these things.

1. We've paid people to paint our doors.
   We've ....
2. Nobody has done much else to our house.
   We haven't ....

3 Complete these questions. Use the noun and the correct form of the verb in brackets.

1. Have you ever .... ? (your eyes/test)
2. When did you last .... ? (your hair/cut)
3. How often do you .... ? (your teeth/check)
4. Have you ever .... for you? (clothes/make)
5. When your phone stops working, do you usually .... or buy a new one? (it/fix)
6. Which do you prefer, eating pizza in a restaurant or .... to your home? (it/deliver)

4 Work in pairs and ask and answer the questions in exercise 3.

PUSH YOURSELF B2

VOCABULARY: ADJECTIVES FOR HOMES

1 Look at this photo of a flat and the advertisement below. What kind of people might want to live there?

Excelsior Court

How would you like to rent a **stunning** modern flat by the sea, with **picturesque** views of a traditional fishing harbour?
Set in **delightful** gardens, Excelsior Court is a brand new block in a **residential** area only a short walk from the sea. The flats are not only light and **spacious**, but also **luxurious**. What's more, each one is **unique**, individually designed by a top architect and **furnished** to the highest standard.
So what are you waiting for? Book an appointment to see a flat today!

2 Match the words in red in exercise 1 with the meanings below.

1. extremely impressive and beautiful
2. special and original
3. pretty and attractive in an old-fashioned way
4. very pleasant
5. a place which just has homes in it
6. having plenty of room inside
7. very comfortable and expensive
8. containing equipment and furniture

3 Choose the correct words to complete these sentences.

1. I like staying in five-star hotels because they're so *furnished/luxurious*.
2. We spent the summer in a *delightful/residential* little cottage by a lake.
3. The house is in a *spacious/stunning* position on the top of a hill.
4. This is a typical 19th century seaside village, so it's very *picturesque/unique*.

4 Would you like to live in the flat in exercise 1? Why? / Why not?

WRITING PART 1 TRAINING

1 **Look at this photo of a couple called Joanna and Nick. Do you think that they have lived in their flat for a long time? Why?**

2 **Read this email. Why are Joanna and Nick writing to Melissa? What do you think a 'housewarming party' is?**

To: Melissa
From: Joanna and Nick
Subject: Housewarming party

Reply Forward

Dear Melissa,

Do you remember that we told you we were planning to move house?

Well, we've done it! We finally moved out of our old flat and we've bought a new one. We moved in here last week. — *Congratulations!*

Here's a photo of our flat. It's nice, isn't it? — *Yes! It looks …*

We're having a housewarming party next Saturday evening. Can you come? — *No, because …*

Our address is Flat 3, Bennett House, King Street, Bridgeford.

It would be so nice to see you.

Love,

Joanna and Nick

3 **Which two of these things are Joanna and Nick doing in their email?**

1 saying where they live now
2 asking Melissa for her address
3 inviting Melissa to a celebration at their home
4 describing what their new flat looks like
5 explaining why they left their old flat

4 **Now look at the notes Melissa made when she received Joanna and Nick's email. What does she think about their new flat? Is she able to go to their party?**

5 **Look at Melissa's reply below. Find the phrases which Melissa uses to …**

1 say thanks
2 offer congratulations
3 say what she thinks about the flat
4 refuse the party invitation politely
5 give a reason why she can't go to the party
6 make a suggestion for another arrangement
7 end the email in a positive way

To: Joanna and Nick
From: Melissa
Subject: Housewarming party

Reply Forward

Dear Joanna and Nick,

Thank you for your email, and congratulations on your new home!

Your flat looks beautiful!

Thank you also for inviting me to your housewarming party. I'd love to come to the party, but unfortunately I can't. I'm afraid I'll be away next weekend on a sailing course.

Perhaps I could come and visit you another evening soon? I'm really looking forward to seeing your flat.

Love,

Melissa

6 **Read this email from your English-speaking friend Chris, and the notes you have made. Write your email to Chris using all the notes. Write your answer in about 100 words.**

From: Chris
Subject: Staying at our country cottage
Reply Forward

Hi!

It's great that you can come to our cottage in the countryside next Saturday! I'm really looking forward to it. — *Me too!*

On Saturday afternoon, we can go swimming in the lake, or hiking in the hills. Which would you prefer? — *Tell Chris*

We've just had an extra bedroom put under the roof of our cottage, so there's lots of room now. Would you like to stay there on Saturday night? It'd be great if you could spend the whole weekend. — *Thanks, but …*

Write back soon.

All the best

Chris

SPEAKING

INFORMAL REACTIONS

1 **Work in pairs and discuss the questions.**

1. How big is your home?
2. How many rooms has it got?
3. Do you think that your home is too big, or too small, or just the right size?

2 **098 You're going to listen to two friends talking about someone who lives in a flat which is very small. Listen to the conversation. What do the friends think about this flat?**

3 **098 Listen again. Who says these phrases, the man (*M*) or the woman (*W*)?**

1. You're joking! *M*
2. No way!
3. How incredible!
4. There's a kind of shelf.
5. Wow. That's unbelievable.
6. There's, like, a big door.
7. Really?
8. There's a sort of chest of drawers …
9. He's got music, books, games and stuff like that.
10. There's even a type of cupboard in the floor.
11. … brushes and those kinds of things.
12. That's amazing.

4 **Choose the correct option to complete these sentences about the conversation.**

1. The words which the man uses tell us that he is
   a annoyed. **b** surprised. **c** amused.
2. The words which the woman uses tell us that she
   a doesn't know exactly how to describe the objects.
   b wants to be accurate when she describes the objects.

5 **Complete this conversation with words from the conversation in exercise 3. Some questions have more than one possible answer.**

A: My friend's granddad lives in a house that's got 50 rooms.
B: You're [1] .... !
A: He does! It's a [2] .... castle.
B: No [3] .... !
A: It's true. There's even, [4] .... , a zoo in the garden, with camels and giraffes and things [5] .... !
B: Wow. [6] .... incredible.

6 **Think of some things that a very large home might have: a full-size cinema, an Olympic swimming pool, etc. Then take turns telling your partner about this very large house. Talk about the house and respond to the information using the expressions from the conversation in exercise 3.**

EXAM FOCUS

LISTENING PART 1

EXAM CHECK

1 **Choose the correct words to complete these sentences about Part 1 of the test.**

In this part of the test, you have to answer [1]*six/seven* questions. For each question, you hear either [2]*one/three* or two people speaking. To answer each question, you listen to the recording and look at some [3]*sentences/pictures*. There are [4]*three/four* possible answers for each question. Each recording is played [5]*once/twice*.

2 099 **For each question, choose the correct answer.**

1 Where is the poster now?

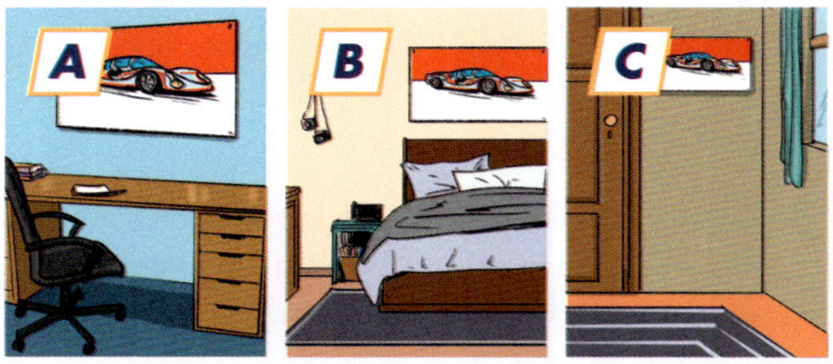

2 What do the man and woman need to buy soon?

3 Where did the man put the key?

4 What are the girl's parents going to bring her?

5 What does the woman's home look like?

6 Which piece of furniture belonged to the first owner of the house?

7 Which flat will the man and woman rent?

WRITING PART 1

EXAM CHECK

1 Are these sentences true or false?

1. You read an email and some notes.
2. You have to write a reply to this email.
3. You only need to use two or three of the notes.
4. You must put the information in your email in the same order as the notes.
5. You have to write some ideas of your own in your email.
6. You should use suitable phrases to start and finish your email.

2 Read this email from your English-speaking friend Alex, and the notes you have made.

From: Alex
Subject: Housewarming party
Reply Forward

Hi

Thank you so much for inviting me to your housewarming party. I'd love to come! — *Great!*

I'm looking forward to seeing your new home. Please could you tell me how to get there? — *Explain to Alex.*

Shall I bring something to eat or drink to the party? I could make a cake or some pizza if you like. — *No, because …*

And finally, what should I wear? Is everyone going to wear smart or casual clothes? Please let me know! — *Tell Alex.*

See you soon

Alex

Write your email to Alex using all the notes. Write your answer in about 100 words.

➡ ***WRITING BANK*** / *pages 227–229.*

HOW WAS IT?

- Gave it a go ☐
- Getting there ☐
- Aced it! ☐

REAL WORLD

FINDING STUDENT ACCOMMODATION IN ... GRENOBLE

1 **Look at the photos of student rooms. What differences can you see? Which room would you prefer? Why?**

2 **Read the text about student accommodation in Grenoble. Decide if the sentences are true or false.**

1. You should start looking for accommodation as soon as you get to Grenoble.
2. University accommodation is normally cheaper than private accommodation.
3. A studio flat is the most expensive kind of university accommodation.
4. In a shared flat, there are some extra costs, as well as your rent.
5. An estate agent will usually find people you can share your flat with.

STUDENT ACCOMMODATION IN GRENOBLE

Grenoble is a popular place to study, and students come here from all over the world. There is plenty of student accommodation available, but our advice is to start looking two months before you arrive in the city.

There are two main kinds of accommodation: university halls of residence and private rented accommodation. Student halls of residence are usually less expensive than private flats. There are three main kinds:

- a traditional furnished room. Toilets, shower and kitchen are shared, usually with between 6 and 10 other students. Average cost: 150€ per month.
- a furnished room with an en-suite bathroom, but a shared kitchen. Average cost: 300€ per month.
- a furnished studio flat, with its own toilet, shower and small kitchen. Average cost: 380€ per month.

Most university halls of residence are close to the university, so it is easy to get to classes. You will also have to pay a deposit, which is usually the same amount as one month's rent. You get this money back when you leave the flat, if you leave it clean, and nothing is broken.

Private accommodation is also available in a shared flat. You will share the rent with your flatmates, and you will have to pay bills, such as electricity, as well as your rent.

Private accommodation is usually in the city, and may be quite a distance from the university. To find a private rented flat, you will probably need to go to an estate agent. They will take you to see some flats, and you will pay your rent to them. It's up to you to find your flatmates. You can choose to share with friends you already know, or look at flatsharing websites to find flatmates.

3 **Read the text again. Match the words and phrases (1–8) with the meanings (a–h).**

1	halls of residence	**5**	shared flat
2	furnished	**6**	deposit
3	studio flat	**7**	estate agent
4	rent	**8**	flatmates

a an apartment that you live in with other people
b a large building with a lot of student rooms
c with a bed, chair, desk, etc.
d people that you share an apartment with
e an amount of money that you pay before you move into a room or flat, and get back when you leave
f someone who organises flats and houses for people to rent or buy
g money that you pay each month to live in a flat or house
h a room with its own kitchen and bathroom

4 **100 Listen to three conversations about accommodation. Who is each student talking to? There is one answer you don't need.**

a someone at the university accommodation service
b a student who lives in halls of residence
c an estate agent
d another student in a shared flat

5 **100 Complete the sentences and questions with the words in the box. Then listen and check.**

expensive	happy	looking for
rent	room	share	take

PHRASES YOU MIGHT USE

1 I'm ________ a flat.
2 I have two friends and we want to ________ a flat.
3 How much is the ________ ?
4 I'm here to see the ________ in your flat.
5 I'm ________ to share.
6 That's quite ________ .
7 OK, I'll ________ a room there.

6 **Choose the correct meaning for each sentence.**

PHRASES YOU MIGHT HEAR

1 There's electricity on top of that.
  a You have to pay extra for electricity.
  b You don't have to pay extra for electricity.
2 You might be looking at a total of 550 euros.
  a It might cost more than 550 euros.
  b It might cost 550 euros altogether.
3 Would you like to arrange a viewing?
  a Do you want to go and see the flat?
  b Shall I show you some photos of the flat?
4 We try to keep on top of the cleaning.
  a We don't keep the flat very clean.
  b We clean the flat regularly.
5 It's a bit on the small side.
  a It's quite small.
  b It isn't too small.
6 There are no additional costs.
  a You have to pay some other bills.
  b You don't have to pay any other bills.

7 **Watch the video about Grenoble. What do you learn about these things?**

- the city
- the university
- accommodation for students
- places to eat

WATCH

LIFE COMPETENCIES

EVALUATING OPTIONS, MANAGING CONVERSATIONS

8 **In groups, choose a city where you might like to study one day. Find out about the university and the accommodation. Compare with another group. Discuss which city is best for students.**

PROGRESS CHECK 4

EDUCATION

1 Join the beginnings and endings of these sentences.

1. I want to study medicine so I have to get
2. At university you need to take
3. Daniel thinks he might fail
4. Please pay
5. I really enjoy doing
6. At college I have to attend

a his exams.
b research in the library.
c high grades at school.
d notes in lectures.
e lectures every day.
f attention to the teacher!

PASSIVES

2 Rewrite these sentences about the first day in a new job. Use the passive.

1. They gave me a desk and a computer. *I was …*
2. They asked my new colleagues to introduce themselves.
3. They showed me around the office.
4. They took me to a nice café at lunchtime.
5. They pay the employees well at this company.
6. However, they expect us to work very hard.

TRAVEL AND THE ENVIRONMENT

3 Complete the text with the words in the box. There are two words you don't need.

air pollution	boarding pass	check-in	delays	departure lounge	fuel	get into	get on	platform	port

I don't like flying. There are always [1] ________ when I fly and I have to sit in the [2] ________ for hours. I know that's better than sitting on a cold [3] ________ when a train is delayed, but it's still annoying. Of course, you can get your [4] ________ online and print it at home, but if you have big bags, you still have to wait in a queue at [5] ________ . However, I think the worst thing about flights is the [6] ________ that they cause. A lot of [7] ________ is used for every flight and we really hurt our environment every time we [8] ________ a plane.

CONDITIONALS

4 Choose the correct options to complete the sentences.

1. If the bus *is/will be* full, it's not very comfortable.
2. I go to work on foot when the weather *isn't/wasn't* too bad.
3. If you want to buy a bike, *I'll give/give* you some money.
4. You'll be late for work *if/unless* your bus is delayed.
5. *If/Unless* we stop flying and driving so much, we'll destroy our environment.
6. *I'll/'d* recycle more waste if there were recycling bins near my home.
7. There *wouldn't be/weren't* so many traffic jams if people shared cars.
8. I wouldn't buy a car unless I *lived/would live* in a place with no public transport.

FLATS AND FURNITURE

5 Complete the text with the words and phrases in the box. There are three words you don't need.

accommodation	block of flats	cushion	drawers	sink	rug	top floor	wardrobe

A room in my flat could be perfect [1] ________ for your holiday! The flat is in a great location near the city centre. It's on the [2] ________ of a three-storey [3] ________ . The bedroom is big, with a double bed, a sofa and a chest of [4] ________ . You will share a bathroom with me but there is also a [5] ________ in your room. You can check your appearance in a full-length mirror and I can give you a hairdryer, or anything else you need during your stay.

HAVE/GET SOMETHING DONE

6 **Complete the sentences using the correct form of *have* and *get* plus the past participles of the verbs in brackets.**

1 We .... our house .... every 10 years. (have/paint)
2 I .... the windows .... once a month. (get/wash)
3 We can't go out now because we're .... a pizza .... (have/deliver)
4 I .... the carpet .... last month and now it's dirty again! (have/clean)
5 If you can't read this, you should .... your eyes .... (get/check)
6 I've never .... the grass .... I can do it myself! (have/cut)

RELATIVE CLAUSES

7 **Choose the correct options to complete the text.**

When I go on holiday, I want to stay in a flat [1]*that/where/who* I can cook big meals. I'm a person [2]*who/whose/which* loves shopping at markets and cooking, so a flat is better than a hotel room, and it has to be a flat [3]*where/whose/that* has a good kitchen.

I usually go on holiday with my best friend, Ina, [4]*which/who/whose* father is a famous chef, and with other friends. It's really fun to spend a day preparing a meal with Ina. First we go to a market, [5]*that/which/where* we look for the best and freshest meat, fish and vegetables. Then we often call Ina's dad, [6]*whose/who/that* can give us ideas for interesting ways to cook them.

Our friends usually go to the beach, but we are happy to spend a whole afternoon in the kitchen preparing the dinner, [7]*which/that/who* does not feel like hard work.

For me, a perfect holiday evening is one [8]*who/-/where* I share with relaxed people at a big table with a fantastic meal.

And a perfect day is spent preparing for that evening.

8 **Find one mistake in each sentence and rewrite the sentences.**

1 Sally's favourite film called *Avatar*.
2 A lot of clothes made in Asia.
3 My best friend it is called Gerry.
4 This house is built 100 years ago.
5 When I have any questions, I'll ask you.
6 He'll visit me later if he'll have time.
7 I like people which have a sense of humour.
8 We played tennis, that is a sport we really enjoy.

HOMES AND THE ENVIRONMENT

9 **Choose the correct word for each gap.**

School Blog About Search

Our teacher asked us to write an [1]............ on homes and the environment. I'm learning a lot. I would love to live in a [2]............ in the country, but you use a lot of energy in this type of home. You need less energy in a flat or a [3]............ house where you have neighbours on both sides. Flats are the best because [4]............ you have another home under you, you don't need to heat your home so much. Moreover, if you live in the middle of a city, it's easier to get [5]............ , and you don't need a car. So generally, you use less [6]............ if you live in a city.

1	a	story	b	email	c	essay	d	lecture
2	a	cottage	b	boat	c	palace	d	tent
3	a	suburb	b	holiday	c	block	d	terraced
4	a	whether	b	if	c	as	d	unless
5	a	into	b	by	c	out of	d	around
6	a	fuel	b	climate	c	packaging	d	time

12 THE PERFECT JOB

VOCABULARY

JOBS AND OCCUPATIONS

1 **Which photo looks like a good workplace to you? Why? Tell your classmates.**

2 **Match the jobs below with the meanings.**

accountant architect astronaut
electrician lawyer lecturer pharmacist
plumber politician programmer

A person who …

1 writes computer programs
2 goes into space
3 installs or repairs water pipes and sinks, showers, etc.
4 deals with bills and other financial documents
5 designs buildings
6 gives advice about the law
7 teaches at a university
8 sells medicines
9 installs or repairs electrical wires
10 works in politics and might be part of the government

3 101 **Listen to five people talking about their dream jobs when they were children, and about what they do now. Write the job they wanted to do and the job they do now beside each name.**

Nora: ………… …………
Mia: ………… …………
Rory: ………… …………
Fiona: ………… …………
Patrick: ………… …………

4 101 **Why does each person have the occupation that they have now? Listen again and match the motivations with the people.**

1 He/She wants to change things in the world. — Nora
2 He/She likes building work and helping to create new houses. — Mia
3 He/She decided to choose an occupation that is well paid. — Rory
4 He/She decided to do what people in the family usually do. — Fiona
5 He/She took a job that was easy to find. — Patrick

5 **Work in groups and discuss the questions.**

1 Can you remember what your dream job was when you were a small child?
2 Do you do that job now or do you think you will ever do that job? Why? / Why not?

LISTENING PART 3 TRAINING

1 102 **Barry is talking about his job. Read and listen to the beginning of his speech, and match the words in orange in the article with these meanings.**

1. a university qualification
2. chances to get a job
3. money paid for the work that you do
4. the hours that a person works in a day, or a night

I'm from a very small town in an area full of rivers and lakes. It's beautiful, but there are few **employment opportunities**, except in tourism. When I finished school, I tried to get a job in a tourist office but that wasn't possible. So, I started to work in a hotel. I had to work long **shifts** and the employers made me work every weekend because I didn't have children. It was awful. I decided to get a **degree** in Business, moved to the city and started studying. I didn't really enjoy it, but I knew someday I would have a good **salary**.

2 Complete the sentence below with a word from the text. First think about what kind of word you will need. Will it be a person, place, thing or number?

Barry's first job after school was in a ....

3 Before you listen to the rest of Barry's speech, work in groups and discuss the questions.

1. Should Barry continue studying a subject he does not enjoy?
2. How important is it to have a high salary?

4 103 **Listen to the rest of Barry's speech. For each question, write the correct answer in the gap. Write one or two words, or a number or a date or a time.**

Barry saw the job advertisement on [1].................. .
He had learned some skills for office work at [2].................. .
He lived in the city for one [3].................. .
Barry now has a nice [4].................. .

GRAMMAR

MODALS OF PERMISSION

GRAMMAR ON THE MOVE
Watch the video

1 **Annie has some questions for her new boss. Read the conversation and then complete the rules.**

May I ask you some questions?

Yes, of course you **may**.

Can I use my work mobile for private calls?

Yes, you **can**. You**'re allowed to** take the phone home, but you **mustn't** make personal calls when you are at work.

Of course. And one more thing: **could** I put a lamp on my desk? It's a bit dark.

Oh yes, you're right. I'll buy a lamp. You **can** choose it if you like.

- We use the modal verbs 1 .... and 2 .... to ask for and give permission.
- We use the modal verb 3 .... to ask for permission but *not* to give permission.
- If we want to say that something is not permitted, we can use the modal verbs ***can't***, ***may not*** or 4 ....
- We can also use *be* 5 .... *to* to ask for and give permission.

➜ ***GRAMMAR REFERENCE*** / *page 219.*

2 **Choose the correct options to complete the sentences.**

1. Students *may/can't* take their mobile phones to school but they *can/mustn't* use them in lessons.
2. **A:** Mum, *can/can't* I go out with Tina tonight?
   B: No, you *can't/couldn't*. It's a school night!
3. **A:** In my office, we *must/can't* listen to music while we're working. What's it like in your office?
   B: Well, there's a sign that says 'Employees *couldn't/may not* listen to music', so we don't.

3 ***May*** **and** ***may not*** **are more formal than** ***can*** **and** ***can't***. **Choose the correct options for these sentences.**

1. 'Customers may not smoke here.'
   a a sign in a restaurant
   b a waiter chatting to a customer
2. 'Can I have some chocolate?'
   a a customer in an expensive café
   b a child talking to his mother
3. 'May I sit down here?'
   a a person at a job interview
   b a girl at her friend's house

Modal verbs are often used when we talk about the present, but we can't always use the same verbs to talk about the past.
*I **must** clean my room today.* ➜ *I **had to** clean my room when I was a child.*
*I **can** use my mum's tablet.* ➜ *I **was allowed to** use my mum's tablet when I was younger.*

➜ ***GRAMMAR REFERENCE*** / *page 219.*

4 **Read the rule and complete the text with (*not*) *allowed to* and a present or past form of the verb *be*.**

My parents are far more laid-back with my sister than they were with me at her age. My sister is only 15 and she 1 .... do what she wants. My parents were much stricter when I was her age. When I was 15, I 2 .... stay out late. I had to be home at nine, even at the weekend. All my friends 3 .... stay out longer so it was embarrassing when I had to go home. Dad says I shouldn't complain. When he was 15 he 4 .... go out on school nights at all. So why does he let my sister do it?

5 **Work in pairs and ask and answer questions about what you were allowed to do when you were younger. Think about these things.**

- going out/coming home
- using a phone/tablet/other technology
- choosing your clothes

Were you allowed to go out in the evenings when you were 12?

No, I wasn't. I had to go to bed very early.

VOCABULARY

PEOPLE IN THE WORKPLACE

1 **Read what these people say about their jobs. How happy are they at work? Rank them from 1 (very happy) to 4 (very unhappy).**

Mark

I love working for a small business. My **co-workers** and I work very hard, but we really enjoy it and we all have a good salary. Our **director** is nice and he really respects us, which creates a very good atmosphere.

Cathy

I'm a **freelancer**, so I work for a lot of different companies. The work is interesting, but sometimes I have too much to do and sometimes I don't have enough. I think it would be easier to work for just one **employer**.

Martha

It's a stressful job – I'm often in the office very early and don't leave until very late. I'm not complaining, though. My **personal assistant** is wonderful and in fact all of my **employees** are good. I just need a bit more free time!

George

There's a lot of competition when you work with other sales **staff**. Who's the best, who sells the most … ? We are always arguing with each other! I'm never the best, and my **line manager** doesn't like me. It's awful!

2 **Complete the sentences with the words in purple from exercise 1.**

1. The person who is responsible for managing your work is your ....
2. A person who manages a whole company or part of a company is a ....
3. .... are paid to work at one company or organisation.
4. A .... works for different organisations, not just for one company.
5. .... are people who work with you in the same organisation.
6. The person or company that someone works for is their ....
7. A .... organises things like meetings, appointments and travel for a manager.
8. The group of people that work for an organisation is called the ....

3 **Work in groups and discuss the reasons why people like or don't like their jobs. What do you think is important in a job? Use the ideas in exercise 1 and your own ideas.**

4 **P LEAVING OUT SYLLABLES 104**
Listen to these three words and say how many syllables you hear. Then say the words yourself.

1. business
2. different
3. interesting

> **In spoken English, we leave out syllables in many words. It means that you may not hear as many syllables as you expect to hear if you read a word.**

5 **P 105 Here are some more words in which speakers leave out syllables. Say the words out loud and cross out the letters that you think are not pronounced. Then listen and check.**

1. camera
2. chocolate
3. factory
4. favourite
5. restaurant
6. temperature
7. vegetables

GRAMMAR

MAKE/LET

GRAMMAR ON THE MOVE
Watch the video

1 **Read the sentences and complete the rules.**

*They **made** me work every weekend.*
*She **lets** me take a boat out whenever I want to.*

- To say that someone allows something, we can use **subject** + [1] .... + **object** + **infinitive without *to***.
- To say that someone has to do something, even if they don't want to, we can use **subject** + [2] .... + **object** + **infinitive without *to***.

➔ ***GRAMMAR REFERENCE** / page 219.*

2 **Choose the correct verbs to complete the sentences.**

1. When I was a child my parents *made/let* me tidy my room every weekend.
2. Marco's mother *makes/lets* him do whatever he wants.
3. My boss *makes/lets* me work until very late in the evening.
4. My last boss was better. She *let/made* me have enough free time.
5. Susie didn't *let/make* her brother borrow her car. She thinks he's a bad driver.

3 **Complete the conversation with the correct form of *make* or *let* and one of these verbs.**

borrow	feel	pay	promise	walk

Lou: Why are you so late?
Karen: Sorry. My sister usually [1] .... me .... the car, but this evening she needed it herself. I asked her to drive me but she said no! She [2] .... me ....
Lou: OK, but why didn't you tell me? I've been waiting for you for ages.
Karen: Sorry again! But do you want to [3] .... me .... bad? Why didn't *you* text *me*?
Lou: I don't know. Never mind. Let's go and have dinner.
Karen: OK, but I won't [4] .... you .... for me this time! It's my turn.
Lou: But you never have any money …
Karen: My granny gave me some money and she [5] .... me .... to go somewhere nice, so let's go!

4 **Write a paragraph about rules in your life when you were younger. Write about a school you went to or a job you had. Use *make*, *let* and (*not*) *allowed to*.**

SPEAKING

AGREEING AND DISAGREEING

1 **Work in groups of three and describe what you see in the photos. Talk about:**

- where the things and people are
- what the people look like
- what you think the people are doing

Remember, you can use modal verbs of speculation when you can't be 100% sure about things.

He might be a chef.

She must be a doctor.

A

B

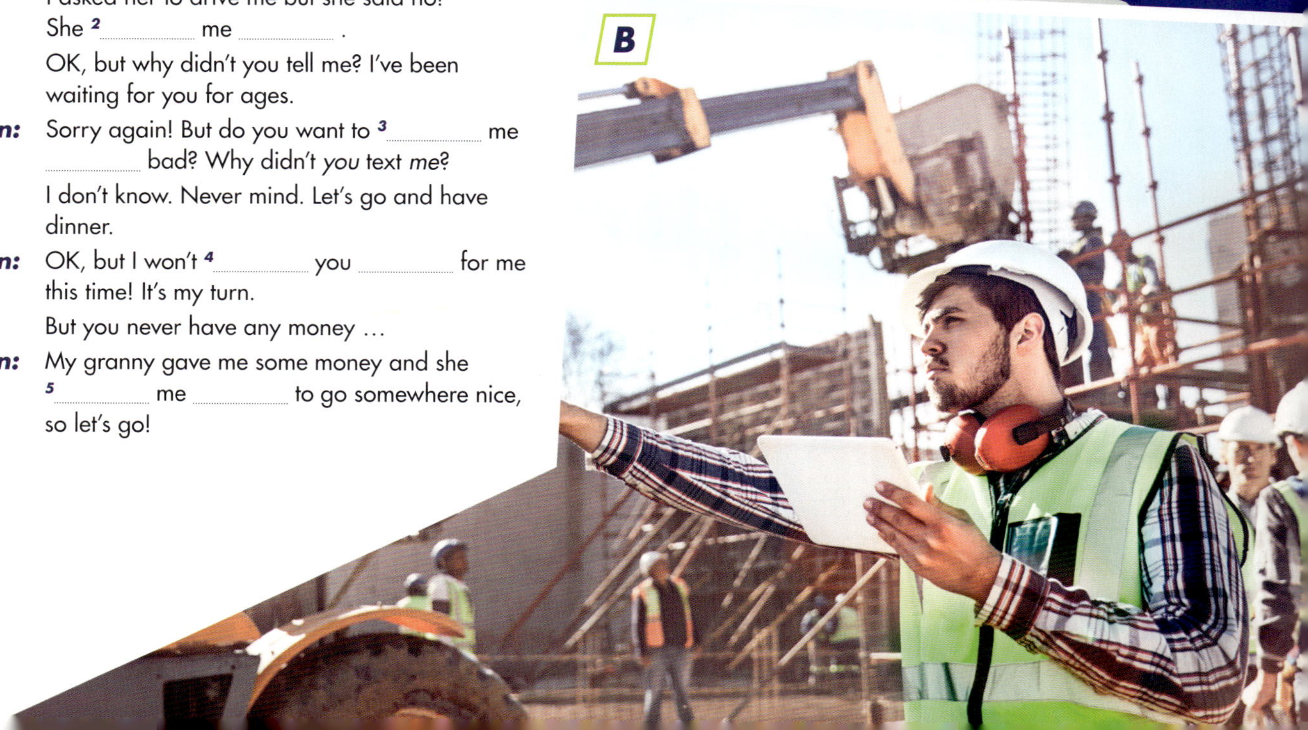

2 106 **Listen to a man trying to convince others that his job is the best in the world. Tick the phrases that you hear for agreeing and disagreeing.**

AGREEING	*DISAGREEING*
I agree with you.	Sorry, but I don't agree.
Yes, you're right.	I'm afraid I disagree.
You're absolutely right!	Perhaps, but …
I'd agree with that.	I don't think that's true.
Exactly!	I take your point, but …

3 **Choose one of the jobs in the photos. Make a note of all of the good things about the job.**

good salary, work outside …

4 **Work in groups of three and discuss the jobs you have chosen. Each of you should try to convince the others that the job you have chosen is the best.**

> I think being a doctor is the best job that anyone can have because …

DID YOU KNOW?

If you are sick, in the USA you can go to the ***doctor's office****. In the UK, this is called the* ***doctor's surgery****. In the UK people go to their local* ***GP*** *(general practitioner) if they are feeling ill. GP is also used in the USA, but most people talk about their* ***family doctor****.*

PUSH YOURSELF B2

GRAMMAR: *BE ABLE TO*

We can use ***be able to*** with modal verbs.
I ***might be able to*** *go to your party. I'm not sure yet.*

1 **Join the beginnings and endings of these sentences.**

1. You must be able to speak at least two languages
2. Danny might be able to work as a Danish–English translator
3. He must be able to speak Danish very well
4. He should be able to speak German, too,
5. He'd be able to learn it quickly
6. He'll be able to find a good job, anyway,

a. as his mother comes from Denmark.
b. if he can find customers who need those languages.
c. because he has a lot of skills.
d. if you want to be a translator.
e. if he wanted to.
f. but in fact he can't speak it at all.

2 **Work in pairs and discuss the questions. Use modal verbs +** ***be able to*****.**

1. Will you be able to get your perfect job?

> I may be able to get my perfect job, but I'll need to study hard!

2. Will you be able to have the holiday of your dreams?
3. Will you be able to speak English perfectly one day?

➜ **GRAMMAR REFERENCE** / *page 219.*

C

D

READING PART 5 TRAINING

1 **What professions do these photos represent? How old do you think you should be to have these jobs?**

2 **Read the paragraph below and choose the correct word for the gap.**

When we board a plane, we don't always see the captain, but when we are in the air, a person will .... an announcement: 'Good afternoon ladies and gentlemen, this is your captain speaking …' Traditionally, the person is a man, and he is not young. However, things are changing.

A say **B** make **C** send **D** tell

3 **The verbs (A–D) in exercise 2 can all be used with a noun to talk about communication, but only one of them goes with *announcement*. Match these verbs in the box with the nouns.**

make	say	send	tell

1 an announcement
2 a message
3 a word
4 a lie

4 **Read the rest of the article and for each question choose the correct answer. Look at page 94 to review the exam tips.**

When Captain Kate McWilliams and pilot Luke Elsworth flew from London to Malaga in 2016, they were possibly the youngest team that had ever [1] .... responsible for a commercial flight. At 26, Kate was believed to be the world's youngest captain, and 19-year-old Luke was the UK's youngest commercial pilot.
Young pilots are still a surprise for passengers, and they are often asked about their age. Kate and Luke have both had that [2] .... However, they feel that if you have completed all the training and passed the tests, age doesn't [3] .... It is possible to begin training as a commercial pilot at 18, and more and more people – male and female – are doing that.
Lots of pilots are keen to [4] .... young people to think about a career as a pilot. It's an interesting job and you can fly to really exciting places.

1 **A** had **B** given
C taken **D** been
2 **A** practice **B** experience
C reality **D** event
3 **A** matter **B** mean
C care **D** mind
4 **A** confirm **B** excite
C support **D** encourage

5 **Would you like to be a pilot? Why? / Why not? Work in groups and discuss the advantages and disadvantages of the job.**

VOCABULARY

QUALITIES AND QUALIFICATIONS FOR A JOB

1 **107** **You will hear four people talking about their jobs. Match the adjectives with the speaker who uses them.**

calm	creative	flexible	friendly
intelligent	organised	patient	reliable

the programmer
the lecturer
the wedding planner
the yoga teacher

2 **107** **Listen again and match a skill and a qualification with each person in exercise 1.**

Skills	**Qualifications**
be good at presenting information	a high-school diploma
be good with people	a certificate
have good communication skills	a bachelor's/master's degree
have problem-solving skills	a PhD/doctorate

3 **Read the sentences and complete the rule with *at* or *with*.**

*Zoe is **good with** children, but she's not very **good at** dealing with adults.*

> To talk about somebody's talent or skills we use ***good*** [1] .... + **verb** + **-*ing*** or ***good*** [2] .... + a noun.

4 **Complete the text with the educational qualifications from exercise 2.**

Most people complete at least 10 years of school and get a [1] .... Some people then start working or start some kind of job training. Others go to university and get a [2] .... after about three years, and then maybe a [3] .... if they study for another year. If they decide to stay at university, maybe because they want to work there, they can get a [4] .... When you learn new skills for a job, you can often get a [5] .... which shows what training you have done and what skills you now have.

5 **Look at these jobs and say what kind of person you need to be and/or what qualifications you need to have the jobs.**

astronaut   dentist   journalist   plumber

> Dentists need to be calm and good with people because sometimes the patients are scared. They need to have a degree. I think there are special dentistry schools for that.

WRITING

A JOB ADVERTISEMENT

1 **Say whether each of these words is a noun or a verb.**

1 apply   **2** applicant   **3** application

2 **Complete the sentences with the words in exercise 1.**

1 I saw an interesting job advertisement, so I decided to write an .... for it.
2 If you want to .... for a job, you should read the advertisement very carefully.
3 If a job is good, there will be a lot of .... who want it.

A

3 **Look at this job advertisement and answer the questions. Use the phrases in green to help you.**

PANDA NANNIES

Become a panda nanny at The Panda Research Centre. This is a **great opportunity for** animal lovers who want to protect this endangered species. You will live at our research centre and care for a family of pandas. This is a **full-time job** for one year.

Applicants should be at least 20 years old and **must be able to** drive a car and to take high-quality photographs. **You should be good with** animals and be a calm and patient person. **You must also be a team player** as you will live and **work in a team** with other panda nannies. **As a minimum qualification, you must** have a high-school diploma.

Please send your application to: **infojobs@pandarc.org**

1 What qualification(s) do you need for the job?
2 What skill(s) do you need?
3 What type of person do you need to be?

4 **Here are three unusual jobs that really exist. Match the photos with the jobs. Work in groups and discuss what you think is involved in each job.**

1 fortune-cookie writers
2 dog surfing instructors
3 line standers

B

C

5 **Pick one of the jobs and write a job advertisement for it. Include information on:**

- qualifications
- skills
- the type of person an applicant should be

EXAM FOCUS

READING PART 5

EXAM CHECK

1 Choose the correct options to complete this text.

The main purpose of this part of the exam is to test your [1]*grammar/vocabulary*. There are [2]*five/six* questions in this task. You have to read [3]*a text/a set of sentences* with gaps where words are missing. For each gap, you are given [4]*three/four* words to choose from. The options may be adverbs, verbs, adjectives or [5]*nouns/pronouns*.

2 For each question, choose the correct answer.

Dream Jobs

Do today's children have the same ambitions as children of previous generations? It seems that they do.

An American employment agency recently **(1)** .... out some research with 5–10-year-olds and found that most kids still want to become sports champions and movie stars, just like their parents did.

The smallest children often want to be wizards or superheroes and will soon be disappointed when they **(2)** .... that these jobs don't really exist. There are also a **(3)** .... of jobs – such as being an astronaut – which many children dream of, but which few people are **(4)** .... to do. Not all children want to be celebrities, however. Some want the **(5)** .... to help others by becoming doctors or firefighters, and these are the ones who will most probably succeed in **(6)** .... their goals according to career experts.

1	**A**	took	**B**	gave	**C**	got	**D**	carried
2	**A**	realise	**B**	imagine	**C**	explain	**D**	agree
3	**A**	total	**B**	sum	**C**	number	**D**	figure
4	**A**	possible	**B**	likely	**C**	hopeful	**D**	reasonable
5	**A**	event	**B**	chance	**C**	turn	**D**	moment
6	**A**	touching	**B**	arriving	**C**	achieving	**D**	gaining

LISTENING PART 3

EXAM CHECK

1 Decide if the sentences about Listening Part 3 are true or false. Correct the false statements.

1 You listen to two people giving information.
2 You have to fill in seven gaps in some notes or sentences.
3 You always have to write a word in the gaps.
4 You must write down exactly what you hear.
5 You must spell words correctly.
6 You hear some words which fit in the gaps but which are incorrect answers.

2 108 For each question, write the correct answer in the gap. Write one or two words, or a number or a date or a time. You will hear a woman called Lara McGee talking to a group of students about her job.

Lara McGee – digital artist

When she was a child, Lara wanted to be a **(1)** ....

Lara decided to become a video game artist following a suggestion from her **(2)** ....

Lara studied **(3)** .... at university.

Lara got her first job from an advertisement on the **(4)** ....

Lara thinks that the best thing she has done is a **(5)** .... game.

Lara would like a job in the **(6)** .... business next.

HOW WAS IT?

Gave it a go ☐

Getting there ☐

Aced it! ☐

REAL WORLD

GETTING A SUMMER JOB IN ... FLORIDA

1 **Have you ever been to a summer camp? What did you do? Would you like to go one day? What kinds of activities do you think people do at summer camp?**

2 **Look at the photos of young people working at summer camps. Read the text quickly and decide what job each person is doing.**

SUMMER CAMP

A

B

C

Summer camp is a great fun place for both kids and adults. Most camps offer a wide range of activities, including traditional sports and also more exciting activities such as kayaking, archery and mountain biking. Working at a summer camp in North America is one of the best summer jobs you can get.

There are different roles you can do, depending on what kind of person you are and what you enjoy doing.

CAMP COUNSELLOR

As a camp counsellor, you'll spend most of your time with the kids. You help get them up in the mornings, organise their activities and make sure they get to meals on time. Because you stay with the same group, you'll get to know the kids really well. And the best thing is that you can have a go at all the activities. You'll be on the go from the moment you get up to when you go to bed at night, so apply for this job if you've got lots of energy, and want a really active summer.

ACTIVITY LEADER

One of the things kids most enjoy about summer camp is learning new skills, or improving skills they already have. As an activity leader, you will work as a coach, teaching your special skill, which could be a sport or an activity such as painting. The advantage of this role is that you get to meet lots of different kids, rather than staying with one group. And you'll spend five or six hours a day doing something you love, and getting better, of course!

SUPPORT STAFF

Support staff are people like office staff or kitchen staff, who do all the necessary jobs that keep the camp working well. Roles include answering the phone and doing paperwork, doing general housework, cooking, shopping, cleaning equipment and mending bikes. You'll be part of the team, but working in the background. Apply for these roles if you want the experience of summer camp but don't fancy dealing with a load of excited kids.

3 **Read the text again. Match each sentence (1–6) with a role. Write *CC* (Camp Counsellor), *AL* (Activity Leader) or *SS* (Support Staff).**

1. You will teach the children something you know.
2. Your job might be to repair things.
3. You will be very busy all day.
4. You won't work with the children.
5. You will spend a lot of time with the same children.
6. You can improve your own skills.

4 **Find the words in the text (1–6) and match them with the definitions (a–f).**

1 training
2 role
3 coach
4 office staff
5 paperwork
6 housework

a work that helps to keep a building clean and tidy
b teaching someone how to do a job
c people who work in an office
d a particular job that someone does, often as part of a team
e someone who teaches other people a skill such as a sport
f work in an office, for example completing forms

5 109 **Listen to three conversations at a summer camp. What is happening in each one? There is one answer you don't need.**

a a training event for new staff
b a conversation between a new member of staff and a guest
c an informal conversation between two new members of staff
d a welcome event for new members of staff

6 109 **Complete the questions you can use when you ask for information about a job with words and phrases in the box. Listen and check.**

are there many	do we get	possible
should we do	what's your	will there be

PHRASES YOU MIGHT USE

1 Is it .... to try a different role?
2 .... any days off?
3 How many kids .... in my group?
4 .... accidents?
5 What .... if a child becomes ill?
6 .... activity?

7 **Choose the correct meaning for each sentence.**

PHRASES YOU MIGHT HEAR

1 She's the go-to person for any problems.
  a She has a lot of problems.
  b She's the person you should talk to if you have any problems.
2 It's all in your terms and conditions.
  a It is written in the documents about your job.
  b It depends on the situation.
3 You can call her and fix up an appointment.
  a You can call her and agree a time to meet.
  b You can call her if you have an appointment.
4 If you follow the guidelines, …
  a If you decide the best way to behave, …
  b If you follow the rules we give you, …
5 We'll go into all that on day three.
  a We will discuss that on day three.
  b We will visit that place on day three.

8 **Watch the video about summer camps. What do you learn about these things? Make notes.**

- the activities at summer camp
- the advantages of working at a summer camp

9 **Compare your notes. Then watch again to check your ideas.**

WATCH

LIFE COMPETENCIES

COLLABORATION, EMOTIONAL SKILLS, SOCIAL RESPONSIBILITY

10 **Work in pairs to write an email to a friend about a summer job abroad. Think about:**

- what the job is
- where it is
- what you have to do
- the problems

Write the email describing your experiences.

13 GET INVOLVED!

VOCABULARY

SPORTS VERBS

1 **Work in pairs and discuss the questions.**

1. What do you enjoy doing in your free time?
2. How often do you play sports?

2 **Look at the photos of Dan, Lizzie and Neil. What do you think they enjoy doing in their free time?**

3 **110 Read the sentences below. Who do you think said these things? Write *D* (Dan), *L* (Lizzie) or *N* (Neil). Then listen and check your answers.**

1. My friends come and **support** me at every game I play. ....
2. It's something that the whole family can **take part in**. ....
3. My team **represented** our city in a national tournament. ....
4. A local radio station was **holding** a competition, so I decided to enter. ....
5. So I went along with him and I **joined**. ....
6. It's great to **hang out with** friends while I'm doing something I love. ....
7. It's always a fantastic feeling when you **score** a point. ....
8. I **took** it **up** because I really enjoy discovering new places. ....
9. I love **going out** in the evenings and having fun. ....
10. I try not to feel upset when another team **beats** us. ....

4 **Complete the sentences with the correct form of the words in bold from exercise 3.**

1. I wanted to get fitter, so I decided to .... running.
2. Our team played really well and we .... the other team 3 – 0.
3. Who do you think will .... the most goals in tomorrow's game?
4. It's fun to .... the other players on our team before and after our matches.
5. I .... my local baseball team, so I try to watch all their games.
6. I can't often .... in the evenings because I have to train after school every day.
7. The sports centre is going to .... a volleyball tournament in the summer.
8. If you want to make new friends, why don't you .... a sports team?
9. I'm training hard because I'm going to .... a tennis match next week.
10. My dream is to .... my country in the Olympic Games.

5 **Work in pairs and discuss the questions.**

1. Do you support a sports team?
2. If you had the chance to take up any new hobby, what would you choose?
3. Have you ever won a sports competition?

LISTENING

1 111 **Listen to Dan talking some more about his hobby. Which of these things does he talk about?**

his family	his fitness	his friends	his studies

2 111 **Now listen again and decide if these sentences are true or false.**

1. Dan is looking forward to playing international matches.
2. Dan thinks that keeping fit is the main benefit of basketball.
3. Dan enjoys playing matches where the crowds make a lot of noise.
4. Dan always does his basketball training together with other players.
5. Dan gets annoyed if he has to miss social events because of his basketball.
6. Dan's college work has improved since he's been a basketball player.

VOCABULARY

PEOPLE IN SPORT

1 **Join the beginnings and endings of these sentences.**

1. Most of the best players on our team were missing that day, so
2. Nobody was surprised when Louise was chosen to become our **captain** because
3. George injured his shoulder last week, so
4. Our **supporters** can find out our news any time they want now that
5. There's space for more **spectators** to watch us play since
6. Two football players started kicking each other during the match, so
7. Amy sprained her ankle during a match, so
8. The athletics contest was cancelled because of bad weather, so

a. the **referee** gave them a red card and sent them off.
b. her **teammates** stopped playing and carried her to the side of the court.
c. our **opponents** beat us easily.
d. our volleyball team has its own website.
e. all the **competitors** had to come back on another day.
f. we've started playing matches in a larger stadium.
g. the **coach** told him that he couldn't play for the next few games.
h. she is the most experienced player on our team.

2 **Work in pairs and discuss the questions.**

1. When you go to a sports game, would you rather be a spectator or a competitor? Why?
2. Which do you think is the harder job – being a coach or a referee?

DID YOU KNOW?

*In British English people use the word **pitch** to talk about where sports like football are played, but in American English people use the word **field**.*

GRAMMAR

GERUNDS

GRAMMAR ON THE MOVE
Watch the video

1 **Read the sentences (a–f) and match them with the rules below (1–6).**

a *Do you **fancy joining** a basketball club?*
b *What's the best thing **about taking** part in a basketball match?*
c ***Playing** music has always been a hobby of mine.*
d *I've always been keen **on doing** different sports.*
e *I don't **mind spending** so much time training.*
f *It's **worth missing** a few parties.*

We use the gerund (***-ing***) form of the verb:

- after certain verbs — [1] .... [2] ....
- after prepositions — [3] .... [4] ....
- when the verb is a subject or object — [5] ....
- after certain adjectives — [6] ....

➡ **GRAMMAR REFERENCE** / *pages 220–221.*

2 **Make sentences that are true for you by putting the gerund form of verbs into the sentences below.**

1 I think I'd be good at ....
2 I have never tried ....
3 .... looks dangerous to me.
4 I don't know much about ....
5 I get tired ....

3 **Match your sentences in exercise 2 with a rule from exercise 1.**

4 **Read this article about scuba diving and complete the gaps with these verbs that are followed by the gerund form.**

imagine	involve	love	practise	recommend

Can you [1] .... feeling like you are weightless, floating gently in a silent and peaceful world under the sea? Well, that's what scuba diving is like. It's my favourite hobby, because I really [2] .... being underwater and seeing the amazing colourful universe down there. If you think that diving might be for you, I'd [3] .... doing an introductory course at an official diving school. This will [4] .... spending time in a classroom and in a pool, as well as in open water. When you're on the course, you'll [5] .... using the equipment and breathing underwater. Why not have a go? There's a beautiful world of adventure waiting for you down there!

5 **Work in pairs. Ask and answer questions using the verbs and activities in the box and the phrases below. Remember to use gerunds.**

board games	card games	computer games		
concerts	cycle	draw	films	golf	go out
photos	play	skateboard	take	team sports
the cinema	the gym	volleyball	watch	work out

USEFUL LANGUAGE

Have you ever tried … ? Would you enjoy … ?
Would you fancy … ?
I think I'd enjoy … I wouldn't mind …
I wouldn't enjoy … because …
I hate … I can't stand … I don't like …
I'm afraid of … I'm not keen on …
I don't mind … I enjoy … I like … I love …

SPEAKING PART 1 TRAINING

WHAT YOU DO IN YOUR FREE TIME AND WHY

1 **Do you think you have enough free time? Do you have enough time to do the sports and hobbies that you like to do?**

2 **112 Listen to a student called Elena telling an examiner about her free time in Part 1 of the Speaking test. Does she prefer indoor or outdoor sports? Does she give reasons?**

3 112 **Join the beginnings and endings of the sentences and find the words that Elena uses to give reasons. Then listen again and check.**

1 As I live in the mountains,
2 I like keeping fit,
3 Because I work in an office all day,
4 I can't stand being in crowded places,
5 I'm going to a large festival this summer, though
6 I enjoy playing the piano because

a I'm crazy about mountain biking.
b which is why I never go to clubs.
c I find it relaxing after a busy day at work.
d since my favourite band is playing there.
e so I play tennis two or three times a week.
f I'm not keen on spending time indoors at weekends.

4 What questions did the examiner ask? Put these words into the correct order to form questions.

1 What / your / doing / time / you / do / in / enjoy / free / ?
2 How / skiing / go / you / often / do / ?
3 Do / hobbies / other / have / any / you / ?
4 How / playing / have / long / tennis / been / you / ?
5 Why / you / playing / do / like / tennis / ?
6 What / doing / the / like / you / evenings / do / in / ?
7 Can / instrument / play / a / you / musical / ?

5 Work in pairs. Ask and answer the questions in exercise 4. Use the language from exercise 3 to explain why you do or don't do these things.

WRITING

AN ARTICLE

1 Do you enjoy playing board games? Which ones do you play, and why?

2 Look at the photo of a board game called *Go*. What kind of game do you think it is: a word game, a strategy game, a fantasy game? Scan the magazine article and find out.

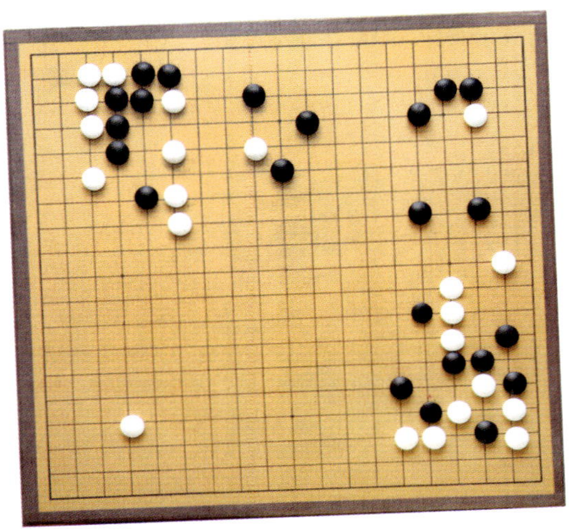

Let's *Go* and have fun!

My favourite hobby is an ancient board game called *Go*. It was invented in China more than 2,500 years ago. To play this game, you need two players, a board with squares on it, and black and white counters which are known as 'stones'. Players take turns to place their stones on the board in order to win space and capture their opponent's stones.

I've been playing *Go* for about 10 years. My uncle taught me to play it one day when I was ill and I couldn't go to school. Since then, I've taken part in *Go* competitions all over the country. In fact, next year I'm going to enter an online tournament with competitors from around the world.

In my view, playing *Go* is an excellent way to develop thinking skills. Although it looks like a simple game, it's actually quite complicated, and also very interesting. This is because you have to think carefully about your moves and plan your strategy in advance. It's fun to play, too. Why don't you try it?

3 Read the article again. Which paragraph contains information about ...

1 when the writer first learned to play *Go*?
2 what kind of game *Go* is?
3 the writer's opinion about *Go*?

4 Have you ever played *Go*? Would you like to try it? Why? / Why not?

5 Read the article again and find examples of (1–4) below. The first examples have already been highlighted for you.

1 topic sentences that tell us what each paragraph is about
2 adjectives and adverbs
3 different verb tenses
4 phrases which link ideas

6 You are going to write a magazine article about your favourite hobby. Before you write, plan your article. Decide on a topic sentence for each paragraph and think about the adjectives and adverbs you could use to make your writing more interesting. Now write your article.

7 Use the checklist to check your article.

- ☐ **Have you organised the information into paragraphs, each with a topic sentence?**
- ☐ **Are the ideas linked using linkers?**
- ☐ **Have you used different verb tenses?**
- ☐ **Have you used adjectives and adverbs to make your writing interesting?**
- ☐ **Have you checked your spelling and punctuation?**

READING PART 2 TRAINING

1 **Have you ever taken a sports course in your free time? What kind of sports did you do? Indoor or outdoor sports? Team or individual sports?**

2 **Look at the sentences below. These people all want to take a weekend sports course. Look at the phrases in pink in question 1. These are Samira's three requirements for a course. Now read the sentences 2–4, and find three requirements for the other people.**

1 Samira is looking for an opportunity to practise a **team sport** that's played **out of doors**. She'd also like some **advice from experts** about how to play better.

ANSWER: ......

2 Joe and Erica want to do an outdoor activity together with their 14-year-old son Max, and would also like to take home some kind of souvenir of their weekend.

ANSWER: ......

3 Cathy wants to get fitter, so she would like to join a class in order to learn an indoor fitness activity which she can also do on her own.

ANSWER: ......

4 Ivan is keen to learn a few watersports. He has never done any activities like this before, so he'd like to try several different sports. He is only free on Saturdays and Sundays.

ANSWER: ......

3 **Look at the tips for Reading Part 2 on page 22. Read the descriptions of six courses (A–F), and find the ideas that match the requirements you identified in exercise 2. For each person, find the course which meets all three of that person's requirements.**

4 **Work in pairs. Which of these courses would you like to do? Why?**

WEEKEND SPORTS COURSES

A Premier Sports

There's fun for the whole family here on our weekend courses. All our activities take place under one roof in modern air-conditioned rooms. How about taking part in a table-tennis tournament? All competitors get a free souvenir video of their game to take home. There are also basketball, volleyball and badminton courts for anyone who prefers team sports.

B The Brightway Club

If you want to get fit and have fun in the fresh air, this is the place for you. Would you like to go diving, sailing, windsurfing or surfboarding? Or all of them, if you prefer! Two-day weekend courses are available at beginner, intermediate and advanced levels. Separate groups for adults and under-16s.

C Viva Centre

This is the place to come to work out or do aerobics, gymnastics or yoga in our studios. If you feel that your body needs more exercise, sign up for one of our weekend courses. These activities are taught in groups of 10 to 15 people but can be practised at home. Then afterwards, why not go for a swim in our heated pool?

D Oakwood College

Do you fancy spending a weekend playing baseball? Then come along to Oakwood College. We have a full-size baseball field, as well as qualified instructors who can give you tips on improving your technique and beating your opponents! Anyone aged 14 or older can attend. Or if you'd rather do an indoor activity, we also have a squash court in the college.

E Lakeside Sports Centre

If you need an expert opinion, we have professional trainers available on our sports track to help you with activities such as running and long jump. Or if you prefer watersports, why not come and join us on the lake for a special weekend of waterskiing? The course is suitable for anyone with some experience of doing this exciting sport.

F Leisure Unlimited

After a class on the basics of horseriding on Saturday morning, you'll be ready to enjoy a weekend of riding along country paths through forests and farmland. The price includes a framed professional photo to remind you of the experience. Suitable for anyone over 12.

VOCABULARY

DO/GO/PLAY + SPORTS AND HOBBIES

1 113 **Listen to a person telling a group of students about sports and fitness facilities. Tick the activities below that you hear.**

athletics basketball football golf
hockey ice skating skateboarding
swimming tennis a workout yoga

2 Complete the rules with *do*, *go* and *play* and then write *do*, *go* or *play* in columns A–C of the table below.

For games, we use [1] ________ .
For sports ending in *-ing* involving movement from one place to another, we use [2] ________ .
For all other activities, we use [3] ________ .

A ________	B ________	C ________
running	*basketball*	*yoga*

3 Add the other activities from exercise 1 to the table in exercise 2.

4 113 **Can you guess what people do at these places? Complete the names of these places in bold using some of the words in exercise 1. Listen and check.**

1. My friends and I play a game at the local *football* **pitch** every weekend.
2. Is it OK to leave my clothes and towel at the side of the ________ **pool**?
3. You can hire rackets and balls at the ________ **court**.
4. It takes me just over a minute to run round the ________ **track**.
5. Local teenagers practise their moves at the ________ **ramp** at the park.
6. Every winter they build a temporary outdoor ________ **rink** in the town square.
7. You'll see some lovely views of the sea as you walk across the grass of the ________ **course**.

5 Work in pairs. Look at the places in exercise 4 again. Which ones have you been to? Do you go there often? What do you do there? When did you last go there?

PUSH YOURSELF B2

VOCABULARY: PHRASAL VERBS

1 Look at the woman in the photo. What is she doing?

2 Read this article about the woman's hobby quickly and find out whether she found it easy or not.

HAVE A GO AT GO-KARTING!

Have you ever tried go-karting? I first **got into** it a few years ago. I knew I needed something to help me to **chill out**, and a friend suggested go-karting. I didn't know much about it but I decided to **have a go**.
At first, it seemed simple. I went along to my local track and signed up for a beginner's session. We learned how to control the go-kart, and I soon **picked** that **up**. Then the next week, I took part in my first race. But the problem was, I was too slow and I kept coming last. I didn't give up, though. I **stuck at** it and little by little, I started to **get the hang of** racing. After six weeks, I won my first race!
I now go to the track as often as I can and I've even entered a league. I find it's the ideal way to **wind down** after a long day at work. However stressed I feel, racing **cheers** me **up**. And it's even better if I win the race!

3 Match the phrases in green with the meanings below.

1. learnt a new skill without being taught
2. to relax completely
3. gradually relax after a period of hard work
4. became very interested or involved in something
5. make an attempt to do something
6. learn how to do something
7. makes someone happier than before
8. kept on trying to do something

4 Choose the correct form of the phrase in green in exercise 2 to complete these sentences.

1. I'd played cricket for years, so I was able to ________ baseball quite easily.
2. I was the only one of my friends who had never been diving, so they persuaded me to ________ .
3. Playing the violin was hard at first, but I ________ it, and learned to play quite well in the end.
4. I grew up in the mountains, so I ________ snowboarding when I was quite young.
5. When I get home in the evenings, I like to ________ by painting or drawing.
6. I go to the beach to swim and ________ at the weekends.

GRAMMAR

VERB + *TO* INFINITIVE

GRAMMAR ON THE MOVE
Watch the video

1 **Look at these sentences. What form of the verb in brackets should follow the phrases in bold?**

a I can't **wait** ______ that. (do)
b It's **important** ______ your muscles. (warm up)
c We **travel all over the country** ______ to matches. (go)
d Our coach **advises us** ______ for 20 minutes. (exercise)

2 **Look again at the sentences above and think about why we use *to* and the infinitive. Read the rules and write the letters (a–d) in the gaps.**

We use ***to* + the infinitive** of the verb:

- after certain verbs, e.g. *learn, want, hope, decide*, e.g. *She learned **to dive**.* [1] ______
- after certain verbs + noun or pronoun, e.g. *He invited me **to play** my music.* [2] ______
- after some adjectives, e.g. *It's nice **to meet** you.* [3] ______
- to say why we do something, e.g. *People came to the concert **to listen** to me.* [4] ______

There are some verbs – ***love***, ***like***, ***hate***, ***start*** and ***begin*** – which can be followed by either the infinite or the gerund, e.g. *I started **singing** = I started **to sing**.*

➡ **GRAMMAR REFERENCE** / *pages 220–221.*

3 **Complete these sentences with *to* and a suitable verb.**

1 I wanted to get fitter, so I decided ______ a sports club.
2 I've arranged ______ basketball with friends tomorrow afternoon.
3 It was a tough match, but we finally managed ______ the other team.
4 After a long day at work, I was too tired ______ running.
5 I learned ______ judo when I was at college.
6 I'm hoping ______ a prize in the dance competition next week.

4 **Complete these sentences using the correct form of the verb in brackets. Use either the gerund or *to* + the infinitive.**

I'm a student, and [1] ______ (swim) is my favourite hobby. It's good exercise, so I do it [2] ______ (keep) fit. It's usually quite cheap [3] ______ (go) to a pool, and so I can get exercise without [4] ______ (spend) too much money. I've even persuaded some of my friends [5] ______ (come) along to the pool with me. And as well as [6] ______ (be) healthy, it's also fun. I particularly enjoy [7] ______ (relax) in the water when I've finished [8] ______ (study) at the end of a long day.

5 **Complete these sentences about your free time.**

My favourite hobby is [1] ______ . I do it to [2] ______ , and also because I enjoy [3] ______ . If possible, I'd like to be able [4] ______ in the future. If I had more free time, I'd learn [5] ______ because I've always dreamed of [6] ______ .

ASKING FOR OPINIONS

1 **Is there a public park near your home? What do people do there?**

2 **Look at the pictures and the Part 3 Speaking task below. What are the different things which the council could build?**

> A town council has some money to spend on the local park. Here are some things which they could build.
> Talk together about the different things which they could build and say which one would be the best.

3 **114 Listen to two students talking. What do they think that the council should build? Tick the phrases you hear in the box.**

USEFUL LANGUAGE

a What's your opinion?
b I think they should …
c Really?
d I don't agree with you.
e What do you think?
f I'm not sure that's the best idea.
g How about … ?
h I agree with you.
i You're right.
j That's a good idea.

4 **Which of the phrases above can we use to …**

1 ask what another person thinks?
2 make a suggestion?
3 agree?
4 disagree?

Look at page 20 to find more expressions.

5 **Look at the Part 3 Speaking task in exercise 2 again, and discuss the question with your partner.**

6 **P STRESS IN QUESTIONS 115**
Listen to this question.

What do you think?

Which words in the question are stressed? Which are unstressed?

7 **P 116 Now listen to some more questions and mark the stressed syllables. What do you notice about the stress pattern in these questions?**

Where did they meet? What does it mean?
How do you know? When will they go?

8 **117 Now listen to a student answering questions in Part 4 of the Speaking test. Do you think he likes sports? Does he give good answers? How could the answers be improved?**

9 **Look at these questions. Choose the better answers, a or b.**

1 Are there many sports facilities near your home?
a There aren't many. I live in quite a small town, so there's just a swimming pool and a football pitch.
b A sports centre, a golf course, a tennis court, an ice skating rink, a basketball court.

2 Do a lot of people use the sports facilities?
a Yes. The leisure centre is very popular, especially at weekends.
b Yes. A lot of people use the sports facilities.

3 What about you? Do you use the sports facilities near where you live?
a Yes, I do. The swimming pool is two kilometres from the city centre and the football pitch is just one kilometre.
b Not really. They're quite expensive, so I just go jogging, instead. It's good exercise and it doesn't cost me anything.

4 Are there any other sports facilities that you'd like to have?
a I like many sports facilities. I love football, baseball and basketball. Football is my favourite sport.
b Oh, I'm not sure. But a skateboard ramp might be nice! Young people could meet there and have fun.

10 **118 Now listen to another student answering the questions. Why are this student's answers better than the answers in exercise 8?**

11 **Work in pairs. Ask and answer the questions from exercise 9.**

EXAM FOCUS

READING PART 2

EXAM CHECK

1 Put these sentences into the correct order.

a Re-read all the other descriptions quickly to check that you've chosen the correct one.
b As you're reading, underline things which match with what the different people want.
c Then read the eight descriptions of, for example, places, courses or websites.
d For each one, identify and underline the three things which this person is looking for.
e Read the five questions carefully.
f Match each question with the description where you've underlined all three of that person's requirements.

2 For each question, choose the correct answer. The people below (left) are all looking for a winter sports holiday. Below (right) are eight descriptions of skiing destinations. Decide which destination would be most suitable for the people.

1 Julia and Karen have never been skiing before. They'd like to stay in modern accommodation and eat out in various different places in the evenings.

2 Mario, Daniella and their two children are looking for a winter holiday in a resort which isn't too crowded. Mario doesn't ski, so he wants activities to do while the rest of the family are skiing.

3 Andreas and Oliver are both serious expert skiers and are keen not to waste time waiting to get up onto the ski slopes. They'd also like to stay in comfortable, stylish accommodation.

4 Vera and Sergei want to take part in a few different winter sports. They'd like accommodation where they can make their own meals, but are also looking forward to enjoying some entertainment in the evenings.

5 Gerry and Teresa are interested in skiing in less common locations away from busy ski areas, and would also like to photograph some attractive views. They don't want to spend much on their accommodation.

A **MONTEBELLO** You can find a wide variety of sports on offer at this resort, from ice hockey to snowboarding, ice climbing to snowmobiling. The skiing facilities are excellent as well, but the slopes are too challenging for beginners. If you enjoy eating out in the evenings, there are a number of quiet restaurants serving delicious local dishes.

B **EAGLE CREEK** Although this area is famous for its beautiful mountain scenery, you can still find hotel rooms that don't cost too much. It's also a good place for anyone who wants to avoid the popular ski slopes and go off skiing in quiet forests and hidden valleys.

C **VAL DU NORD** This is a popular location with skiers of all levels, from beginners to advanced. It's a busy resort, but there are plenty of ski lifts, so you don't need to wait too long to get onto the slopes. Accommodation is basic, but reasonably priced. There's even children's entertainment during the school holidays.

D **SAN BERNARDO** The gentle slopes in this region are ideal for families with children and for new or less experienced skiers. The resort is also well known for its wide range of fine restaurants and cosy cafés. There are several smart, newly built hotels here, as well as many comfortable apartments with their own kitchens.

E **JEFFERSON RIDGE** This is the place to come if you like lively bars and clubs, many of which have live music and singing late into the night. It's also an ideal location for people who want to try snowboarding, ski-jumping and kite-skiing. Most visitors stay in apartments with cooking facilities, but there are some reasonably priced hotels here, too.

F **LES BRUNELLES** Visitors to this region love the pretty views and excellent skiing opportunities. You can even get away from the crowds and ski in quieter areas that most tourists don't know about. There's also plenty to do in the evenings, with live music and dancing. Accommodation here is comfortable but expensive.

G **STEINDORF** There's a wide choice of places to stay here, from simple basic apartments to luxury hotels designed by top architects. It's also a great destination if your skiing is at intermediate or advanced level. And if you prefer a quieter resort where you never have to queue for a ski lift, this could be the place for you.

H **REDWOOD PEAK** This destination is rarely busy, even in high season, and is ideal for skiers of all abilities and ages. There's a range of hotels to suit all tastes, as well as a leisure centre with a well-equipped gym, fitness facilities and a large ice-skating rink.

SPEAKING PART 3

EXAM CHECK

1 Complete these sentences using phrases a–g below.

1. In Part 3 of the Speaking test, you have to ....
2. In Part 3 of the Speaking test, you don't have to ....

a agree with all your partner's opinions
b compare options shown in the pictures
c respond to what your partner says
d give reasons why you think an option is good or bad
e tell the truth about your <u>real</u> opinions
f agree on a final decision at the end
g discuss every option in the pictures

2 A small town wants to hold a sports event for local people to take part in.
Here are some events which they could hold.
Talk together about the different events which they could hold and say which one would be the best.

➡ ***SPEAKING BANK*** / *pages 241–242.*

SPEAKING PART 4

EXAM CHECK

1 Choose the correct options to complete this paragraph.

Speaking Part 4 lasts about [1]*one minute/three minutes*. In this part of the test, you will answer questions about [2]*the same topic as/a different topic from* Part 3. Remember that [3]*all/not all* of the questions will be directed at you. You [4]*will/won't* have to ask the other candidate questions. It is important for you to use [5]*a variety of structures and tenses/perfect grammar* in the answers that you give.

2 Work in pairs and ask and answer the questions.

1. What do you do to keep fit in your free time?
2. Do you prefer indoor or outdoor sports?
3. What kind of sports events do you like watching?
4. What was the best sports event that you have ever seen?
5. Do you think it's better to go to a live event or to watch it on TV?

➡ ***SPEAKING BANK*** / *page 243.*

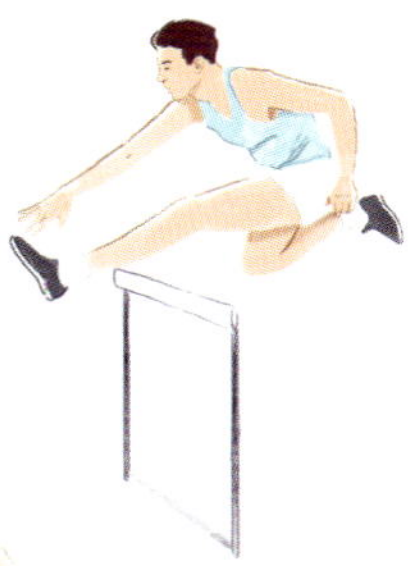

HOW WAS IT?

Gave it a go	☐
Getting there	☐
Aced it!	☐

USING SPORTS FACILITIES ON HOLIDAY IN ... GREECE

1 **What do you like doing when you are on holiday? Look at the photos. Which of these holiday activities have you done? Which ones would you like to try?**

2 **Match the notices (1–4) to the activities (A–D).**

1

All watersports equipment is free for guests to use.
Children under 12 **must be accompanied** by an adult if using paddle boards or kayaks.
Life jackets are available and recommended for all guests.
Please ask a member of staff to **help with fitting**.

2

Guests must wear **appropriate footwear** on the tennis courts.
Courts can be booked in advance at Reception.
Group coaching sessions from 2–3 p.m. each day. **There is no charge**, and booking is not necessary.
Individual tuition is available **on demand**.
Pre-book at Reception.
Ball and racket hire is also available.

3

Hire prices
Daily: 10 euros
Weekly: 50 euros
Hire of helmets: 1 euro per day
A 30 euro **deposit** is required for each bike.
Maps and suggested routes are available inside.

4

Please note, the opening hours for the pool are 8 a.m. to 6 p.m.
Use of the pool is **not permitted** outside these times.
Diving is only allowed in the diving pool, not the main pool.
Parents are advised to **supervise** young children at all times.

3 **Read the notices again. Decide if the sentences are true or false.**

1. You have to pay to use paddle boards.
2. Everyone must wear a life jacket if they are using a paddle board.
3. You don't have to book to take part in a group tennis lesson.
4. You can get ideas about where to go in the bike-hire shop.
5. You can't use the pool after 6 p.m.
6. You can't dive in any pool.

4 **Look at the blue words and phrases in the texts. Match them with the meanings.**

- **a** not allowed
- **b** an amount of money that you get back if you return something with no damage
- **c** to look after or take care of someone
- **d** to find the correct size for you
- **e** suitable shoes for the place or activity
- **f** should have with them and looking after them
- **g** you don't have to pay
- **h** if you want something and ask for it

5 119 **Listen to three conversations at a holiday resort. What is the tourist doing in each one? There is one answer you don't need.**

- **a** asking for information about hiring a bike
- **b** booking a tennis court
- **c** asking about individual tuition
- **d** asking to use a paddle board

6 119 **Complete the sentences and questions with the words and phrases below. Listen and check.**

any rules	have to wear	how long
rackets	some bikes	to book / try

PHRASES YOU MIGHT USE

1. I'd like .... a tennis court.
2. We need four ....
3. I'd like to .... a paddle board.
4. Do I .... a life jacket?
5. Are there .... about where I can go?
6. We'd like to hire ....
7. .... is half a day?

7 **Choose the correct meaning for each sentence.**

PHRASES YOU MIGHT HEAR

1 Let's have a look.
- **a** I will check the bookings.
- **b** Go and see if the courts are free.

2 That's all sorted for you.
- **a** I'm sorry, but you can't play.
- **b** I have booked a court for you.

3 Are you familiar with the courts?
- **a** Do you know where the courts are?
- **b** Are other people in your family playing?

4 If you take that for me.
- **a** Please remove that.
- **b** Please hold that.

5 It's good to have the life jacket as a backup.
- **a** It's good to have one to protect your back.
- **b** It's good to have one if there's a problem.

6 Can you just pop that on for me?
- **a** Please hold that.
- **b** Please put that on.

7 I'll just sort out your bikes.
- **a** I'll find some bikes for you.
- **b** I'll mend your bikes.

8 If you just hop on this bike, …
- **a** Please hold this bike.
- **b** Please get on this bike.

8 **Watch the video about holiday resorts in Greece. What do you learn about these things? Make notes.**

- beaches in Greece
- the sea around Greece
- holiday resorts
- watersports
- biking

9 **Compare your notes. Then watch again to check your ideas.**

10 **Which of the activities in the video have you tried? Which would you like to try?**

WATCH

LIFE COMPETENCIES

CREATIVITY AND INNOVATION, COLLABORATION

11 **Work in groups to plan your ideal activity holiday. Think about:**

- the types of sports facilities and activities
- the times you can do the activities
- the prices

Present your activity holiday to the class.

14 ON TOP OF THE WORLD

READING PART 1 TRAINING

1 **Work in pairs and discuss one of the photos. Think about these things:**

- the people's relationship (friends/family …)
- how they are feeling (happy/excited/sad/worried …)
- what they might be talking about

2 **Look at the messages in exercises 3 and 4 and say which emotion goes with which text.**

disappointed	excited	worried

3 **Look at text 1 and the exam tips on page 72 again. With a partner, decide what the text says and choose the correct letter, A, B or C. Underline the words that show you which answer is correct.**

1

Hey Toni, do you have time to meet me and Sue this evening at Carla's Café at 7? Something fantastic has happened at work and I can't wait to tell you about it!
Alicia

What does Alicia want to share with Toni?

A some news about Sue
B some news about her job
C some news about a café

4 **Work alone. For each question, choose the correct answer.**

2

From: Pete
Subject: party
Reply Forward

Sarah, I'm sorry but I can't go to your party. I was really looking forward to it, but I'm sick and I need to go to bed. You have a great evening!
Pete

What does Pete tell Sarah?

A He is too sick to go to a party.
B Sarah can't go to a party.
C He'll meet Sarah in the evening.

3

Dad, I'm at Ian's house. He invited me to share an evening meal with his family, and I said yes. I hope you're not angry! I'll be back at ten.
Lou xxx

Lou is saying that

A he would like to go to his friend's house.
B his friend is coming to his house for a meal.
C he will spend the evening at his friend's house.

5 **Do you think these could be phone messages instead of written text? Why? / Why not?**

READING PART 6 TRAINING

1 **What are emojis? Tell the class when you use them and which ones you use.**

2 **In Part 6 of the Reading test you have to think of words to fit gaps in a text. For each type of word, write at least four examples.**

1. subject, object and possessive pronouns
2. relative pronouns
3. prepositions of time, place or movement
4. linkers

3 **Look at the exam tips on page 73 again and read the first paragraph of this article. Think of the word which best fits each gap. It will be a type of word in exercise 7.**

CALL A FRIEND AND TALK

Day and night, my phone shows me messages from [1] ________ boss, colleagues, friends and relatives. Why don't people call me? Maybe they don't want to disturb me when I'm with my family or in my office, [2] ________ I am always very busy. It's kind of them to respect my time. However, when my best friend texted me to tell me that she was getting married, I nearly cried. Just a text message? I sent her a short 'congratulations' message with lots of emojis and I tried to feel happy [3] ________ I felt bad. For me, words and symbols [4] ________ a screen are not enough. If it's important, we should talk.

What type of word is this?

Am I an old-fashioned person? On the phone, you can hear whether a person is happy or sad, excited or **disappointed** by what you are saying. You can hear emotions – how they feel. But maybe that's exactly the problem. Maybe we are scared of people's emotional reactions when we call them. Or perhaps we don't want them to hear *our* true emotions.

In the social media world, we seem to be **cheerful** all the time. Or we are **delighted**, or **shocked**, or some other extreme emotion that makes us use lots (yes, lots!!!!!!) of exclamation marks. That's not real life. Some days are boring. Sometimes we might feel just a little **depressed** but a chat with a good friend would cheer us up. Try it! You don't have to talk about how **miserable** you've been feeling. Just talk. If your friend takes the time for you, you'll feel so much better after talking to him or her. And friendship is about sharing your true emotions, the negative ones and the positive ones.

4 **Now read the rest of the article. Decide if the sentences are true or false, and correct the false sentences.**

The writer thinks …

1. speaking on the phone is better than writing and reading messages.
2. it's hard to judge how a person is feeling during a phone call.
3. using social media makes us feel cheerful.
4. even if you don't talk about your feelings, a talk on the phone can make you feel better.
5. friends should share both their good and their bad feelings.

5 **Work in groups and discuss these questions. Do you call friends just to chat? Why? / Why not?**

VOCABULARY

EMOTIONS

1 **Look at the words in purple in the article. Match each word with one of the meanings.**

1. very happy about something that has happened
2. unhappy because something was not as good as you had hoped
3. very surprised and upset by something
4. in a good mood, lively and positive
5. feeling negative and without much hope
6. very unhappy

2 **Read these messages and match each emotion in bold with one of the emojis.**

Oh no, exams! I'm so **nervous**!

Maria is laughing with my boyfriend and it's making me **jealous**.

We're all feeling **satisfied** after a wonderful meal.

Wow, did you make that cake yourself? I'm **impressed**!

That's a funny photo. Everyone who sees it is **amused**.

I'm so **embarrassed** because Jenny told Mark that I really like him. It's not true!

I feel so **guilty** because I forgot your birthday.

3 **Choose one of the emotions from exercise 1 or 2. Write a short text about a time you felt that emotion. Read it to your partner for them to guess the emotion.**

Once, when I was younger, my grandmother made me a pink sweater with hearts on it. My mum made me wear it when we went to visit Granny. Unfortunately, some friends saw me on the street and they all laughed!

You were embarrassed!

GRAMMAR REVIEW

CONDITIONALS

1 Which kinds of conditional sentences are these: zero, first or second conditional? Match the sentences (1–3) with the explanations (a–c).

1 If I feel unhappy, I phone a friend.
2 He would feel better if he talked to his friends more often.
3 If you phone me this evening, I'll tell you all my news.

a a possibility in the future
b something that is unlikely or improbable
c something that is generally true

2 Complete the email with the correct conditional forms of the verbs in brackets.

Hi Sam

I've tried to call you a few times but you never answer your phone. I know you prefer texting, but if I [1] .... (have) important news I always want to talk about it. Texting isn't enough. So please don't ignore my calls. If you [2] .... (not answer) your phone, I won't be able to tell you about my new job. And if you don't know about my new job, you [3] .... (not know) why I'm leaving town, and where I'm going. If you [4] .... (know) about it, I'm sure you'd make plans to visit me.

So come on, Sam, answer your phone. I'm going away, but it [5] .... (be) a pity if our friendship ended here. I'd be really unhappy if I never [6] .... (see) you again. Let's make sure that can't happen.

Talk to you soon (I hope!)

Jules

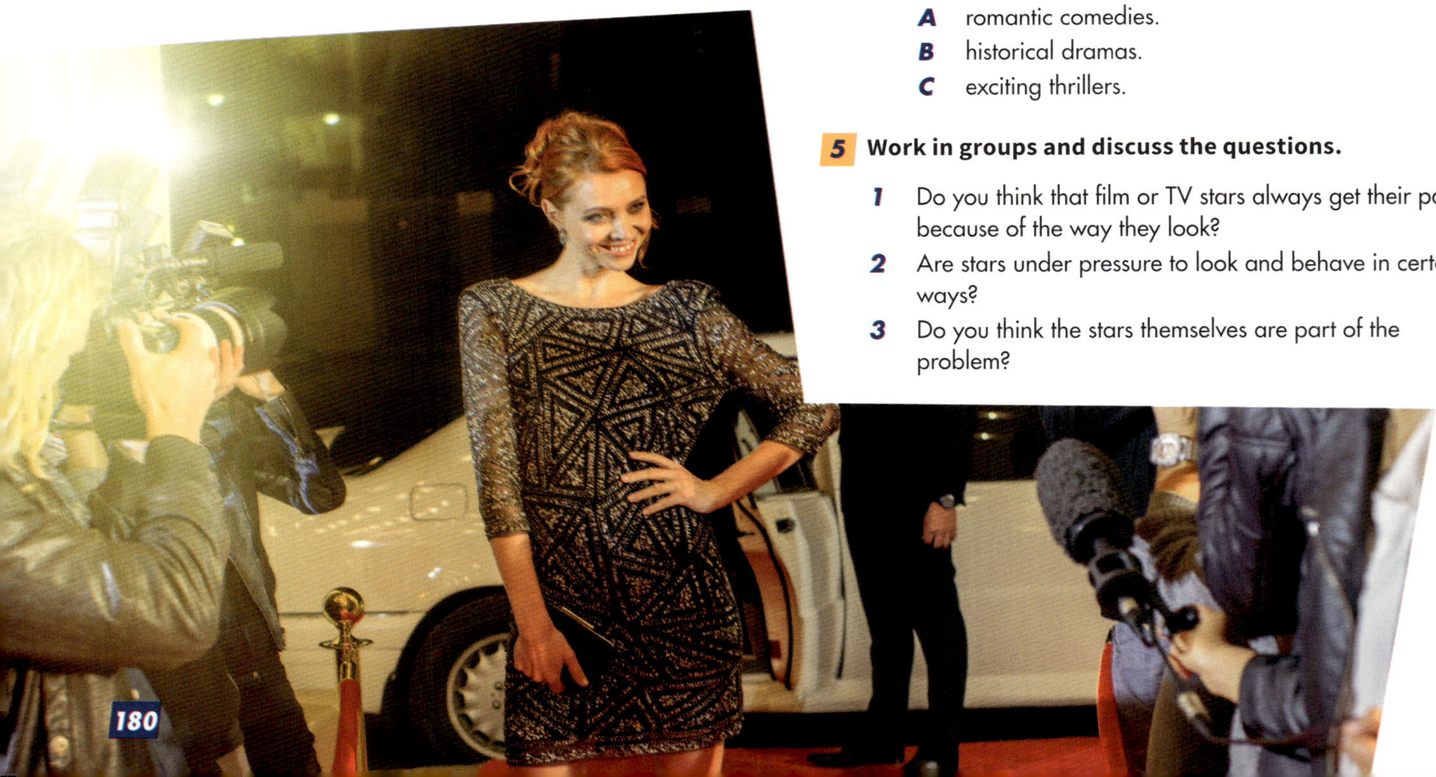

LISTENING PART 4 TRAINING

1 Tell the class about an actor or actress that you like. Why is he or she good?

2 You are going to listen to the start of an interview with an actress. Before you listen, look at the exam tips on page 99 again, then work with a partner and underline key words in this question and options A, B and C.

How did Mara feel about playing Lady Georgina Bentley?
A worried because Georgina was not a nice person
B excited because this was Mara's first big part
C nervous because Georgina was a complicated person

3 120 Listen and choose the correct answer for exercise 2. Work in pairs and discuss why the answer is correct and the others are wrong.

4 121 Listen to all of the interview and for each question, choose the correct answer.

1 How does Mara feel when people talk about her appearance?
   A disappointed because her acting is more important
   B happy because her hair looks so good
   C satisfied because beauty is so important

2 Mara says one special thing that good actors need is
   A an ability to work very hard.
   B an interest in other people.
   C a strong interest in themselves.

3 What does Mara say about having a private life?
   A Everyone should leave famous people alone.
   B Famous actors' lives can't be completely private.
   C It's fun to share your life with your fans.

4 Mara's favourite films are
   A romantic comedies.
   B historical dramas.
   C exciting thrillers.

5 Work in groups and discuss the questions.

1 Do you think that film or TV stars always get their parts because of the way they look?
2 Are stars under pressure to look and behave in certain ways?
3 Do you think the stars themselves are part of the problem?

VOCABULARY

APPEARANCE AND PERSONALITY

What ever happened to ...

TYLER JONES?

Your favourite child star talks to us about life then and now.

I starred in my first film when I was five. It was fun. Everybody said I looked so **cute** and I was going to be a star. Of course I believed them, so I never worked hard at school. I starred in three more films and my adult colleagues were always kind to me even though I was often **rude** to them. I think I was **cruel** to other children. I said terrible things to them because, unfortunately, I thought I was better than them. Now I know how **stupid** my behaviour was.

Remember how sweet he was? Tyler in his first film, *Tobi's Holiday*.

When I was 15, I didn't get a part that I wanted in a teen film. The film director told me I wasn't fit enough. I said, 'No problem, I'll do more sports.' However, the director still didn't want me. He needed someone with **clear** skin and I had begun to get spots. And he thought my **curly** hair wasn't **fashionable** or cool. Everything he said was about my appearance and nothing was about my talent as an actor. It was a real shock.
In the end, I stopped acting and started to work harder at school. I met friendly and **generous** people who helped me. They said that I was **brave** because I had decided to change my life. Now I'm a teacher and my life is great.

1 **The words in pink describe appearance and personality. Which four describe appearance?**

2 **Complete the sentences with the words in pink from the article.**

1. She knows what people are wearing this year. Her clothes are always ....
2. He uses cream to stop spots. He wants .... skin.
3. I don't think it's intelligent to worry about your appearance all day. In fact, I think it's .... !
4. She sometimes kicks her cat. That's .... !
5. Look at that lovely baby. He's so ....
6. Diana is moving to another country on her own and she's not worried at all. I think she's ....
7. He takes what he wants and never says 'thank you'. He's a really .... man.
8. Straight hair can be beautiful but I like my hair, too. It's very ....
9. He always gives people lovely presents. He's ....

3 **Work in groups and discuss the question. Do you think it is good for children to become famous? Why? / Why not?**

4 **P SPELLINGS AND THE /ʃ/ SOUND 122**
Listen to these words. What happens to the *t* in the words?

essential patient relations

> **When you see *ti* followed by *a*/*e*/*o*, it is often pronounced /ʃ/ like *sh*: *relation*. The same thing often happens when a word has *ci* followed by *a*/*e*/*o* in it: *musician*.**

5 **P 123 Say these words. Then listen, check and repeat.**

education	emotion	special
information	efficient	delicious
station	social	

GRAMMAR REVIEW

REPORTED SPEECH

1 Complete the sentences. Use reported speech. Then write how the tenses change.

1 'I love films.' Mara said that she ___*loved*___ films.
present simple → ___*past simple*___

2 'Everyone is saying how amazing you look.' Mike told Mara that everyone __________ how amazing she looked.
present continuous → __________

3 'I've played in a lot of romantic comedies.' She said she __________ in a lot of romantic comedies.
present perfect → __________

4 'Georgina helped a lot of people.' She said that Georgina __________ a lot of people.
past simple → __________

5 'I hope people will talk about my performance.' She told us that she hoped people __________ about her performance.
will → __________

2 Complete the text reporting this conversation.

Kiera: Where's Owen?
Maria: I don't know. I haven't seen him since breakfast time.
Kiera: Oh. I hope he's OK.
Maria: Why are you worried about him?
Kiera: Because Mark posted an embarrassing photo of him. He was furious about it yesterday.
Maria: I see. But to be honest I think he's feeling good today. I'm sure he'll be home soon.

Kiera asked [1] __________ . Maria said she [2] __________ and that she [3] __________ since breakfast time. Kiera said she [4] __________ and Maria asked [5] __________ about him. Kiera told her that Mark [6] __________ of him and that he [7] __________ about it the day before. Maria wasn't too worried. She said she thought [8] __________ and that he [9] __________ .

PUSH YOURSELF B2

VOCABULARY: COMPOUND ADJECTIVES

1 Read the examples and complete the rules.

*She's a woman with **short hair**. → She's a **short-haired** woman.*
*He's a boy with **blue eyes**. → He's a **blue-eyed** boy.*
*He's a doctor who they **pay well**. → He's a **well-paid** doctor.*
*This is a restaurant that people **recommend highly**. → This is a **highly recommended** restaurant.*

- If we make a compound adjective from an adjective + a noun, we often add **-ed** to the [1] __________ which changes it into an adjective.
  In **adjective + noun** compound adjectives, the words stay in the same order:
  with short hair → short-haired
- If we make a compound adjective from a verb + an adverb, the [2] __________ changes to a past participle.
  In **verb + adverb** compound adjectives, the order is reversed:
  pay well → well-paid

→ **GRAMMAR REFERENCE** / *page 222.*

2 Rewrite the sentences using a compound adjective. Don't forget to use hyphens where they are needed.

1 She's a teacher with a kind heart.
2 She's an actress that people know well.
3 He's an author that people respect highly.
4 She's a girl with brown eyes.
5 He's a child who behaves badly.
6 He's a person with an open mind.

WRITING

A PROFILE OF A PERSON YOU LIKE

1 **Read a profile of a person called Emilio and answer the questions.**

1 Emilio is my cousin but he was born far away from me, in Mexico. My Aunt Maria went to live there when she got married. When we were children, we used to visit Emilio and his family in Mexico every summer. Now he's studying in Spain and he lives near me, so I can see him much more often.

2 Although Emilio and I are cousins, we don't look like each other at all. He is tall and has short, dark hair. I'm not into clothes but Emilio always looks fashionable and wears well-made clothes that cost quite a lot of money.

3 However, Emilio does not just think of himself and his appearance. He's a very generous and kind-hearted person. He's also ambitious and he's studying political science because he wants to get a job where he can really make a difference. I don't like many politicians, but I think that Emilio would be a very good one.

4 When we meet up, we always have fun. Sometimes we go to a concert or meet some other friends and have a meal together. Whatever we do, we usually have an extremely interesting conversation. I like it when people are really clever, but they also know how to relax and have a good time. That's Emilio!

Which paragraph …

1 tells us about Emilio's appearance?
2 says what the writer and Emilio do together?
3 introduces some facts about Emilio's life?
4 tells us about his personality?

2 **Find the following things in the profile.**

1 five adjectives describing Emilio's appearance, including one compound adjective
2 four adjectives describing Emilio's personality, including one compound adjective
3 two reasons why the writer likes spending time with him

3 **Write a profile of a person that you like. Use four paragraphs and include this information:**

- facts about his/her life
- his/her appearance
- his/her personality
- your relationship and why you like the person

GRAMMAR REVIEW

MODAL VERBS

1 Look at the modal verbs in bold in the sentences (1–10) and match them with their functions (a–j).

1. Little Jodie **can** already walk!
2. You **have to** wear sports shoes in the gym.
3. Sorry but you **can't** eat or drink in this theatre.
4. **Can** I sit down here?
5. You **should** eat more fish. It's good for you!
6. You **don't have to** pay if you are under 18.
7. Where is your coat? You **must** be freezing!
8. I don't know where Jill is but she **might** be at home.
9. Fred **may not** be at work today.
10. Stefan had a big dinner so he **can't** be hungry.

a. give advice
b. talk about ability
c. talk about obligation
d. say that something is not allowed
e. ask for permission
f. say that you feel sure something is true
g. say that you feel sure something is not true
h. speculate that something is possibly true
i. speculate that something is probably not true
j. say that something is not necessary

2 Work in pairs. Where it is possible, rewrite the sentences in exercise 1 with other modal verbs in the box below.

can	can't	could	couldn't	don't have to	have to	may	might	mightn't	must	mustn't	ought to

3 Rewrite the sentences with (*not*) *allowed to* or (*not*) *able to*.

I could ride a horse when I was seven.
I was able to ride a horse when I was seven.
You can't use your phone in class.
You're not allowed to use your phone in class.

1. She couldn't talk when she was a year old.
2. We can use the school computers during our lunch break.
3. We can't eat in the classroom.
4. Did your parents let you play computer games when you were five?
5. My father can speak six languages.

RELATIVE CLAUSES

1 Can you remember? Answer the questions with the relative pronouns in the box.

that	where	which	who	whose

1. Which relative pronouns can you use to introduce a clause about a person?
2. Which relative pronouns can you use to introduce a clause about a thing?
3. Which relative pronoun is usually used to introduce a clause about a place?
4. Which relative pronoun is usually used to introduce a clause about something that belongs to someone?

2 Add relative pronouns to the text. If you don't need the pronoun, leave the gap empty. Sometimes more than one pronoun is possible.

My friend Lea is a life coach. She works with people [1] ______ want to change their life in some way. Some of her customers have a problem [2] ______ they want to solve, and others are just hoping to become even more successful. Lea works in a room [3] ______ is really sunny. She says it's important to have a space [4] ______ people can feel positive. There are many things [5] ______ you can change with a positive attitude, she thinks, but it's not always easy to change your attitude. I'm sure Lea is good at her job. She's always been the first person [6] ______ advice I ask for when I have a problem.

SPEAKING

FINDING OUT INFORMATION

1 124 **Carmen is a student who has been given the task below. Listen to Carmen talking to Martin and Ben, the others in her group, and answer the questions.**

Find the person in your group who …

- has been to the biggest city.
- has the most pairs of shoes.
- is having a holiday the soonest.
- is the bravest.

1. Who has been to the biggest city?
2. Who has the most pairs of shoes?
3. Who is having a holiday the soonest?
4. Who does Carmen say is the bravest?
5. What question has Carmen thought of to find out who the bravest is?

2 **Work in groups of three. Each of you takes one task. Write questions to find the information you need.**

Task A

Find the person in your group who …

1. has been to the most different countries.
2. does the most sports.
3. is going to get up the latest tomorrow.
4. is the kindest.

Task B

Find the person in your group who …

1. has been camping the most often.
2. has the most T-shirts in their wardrobe.
3. is going to see the most people this weekend.
4. is the most patient.

Task C

Find the person in your group who …

1. has had the most unusual meal.
2. spends the most time using his/her phone.
3. is going to do the most housework this weekend.
4. is the most generous.

3 **Now take it in turns to ask all of your questions and get the information you need.**

4 **These are some topics you have discussed in preparation for the Speaking exam. In pairs, write eight questions, one for each topic. Use some of the ideas below to form your questions.**

friends and family holidays other hobbies
school and college shopping sports
transport your home

How do you … ?
How often do you … ?
How long have you … ?
What do you think is the best … ?
Can you … ?
Is it important to … ?
Do you prefer to … or … ?
Which would you prefer, … ?
Which is more interesting, … ?
Why do you … ?

5 **Work in pairs and ask and answer the questions you have written for exercise 4.**

6 **Work in groups and discuss the questions.**

What should you do in the exam if …

1. you don't understand a question?
2. you need time to think of what to say?
3. you can't think of a word that you need?

DID YOU KNOW?

We often talk about the differences between American English and British English but there are many more varieties of the language. We can also talk about Australian English, South African English, Indian English … Don't worry, though, we usually all understand each other. So, keep learning English and you'll be able to speak to people all over the world!

EXAM FOCUS

READING PART 1

EXAM CHECK

1 Match the questions (1–5) with the answers (a–g). There are two answers which you don't need.

1. How many questions are there in this part?
2. How many options are there for each question?
3. How do you answer the questions?
4. Does each question have the same type of text?
5. Are the texts of different lengths?

a There are three.
b Yes, but the maximum is 35 words.
c There are four.
d You choose the best option which has the same meaning as the text.
e No, some are messages and others are notices or advertisements.
f There are five.
g You write words in gaps.

2 For each question, choose the correct answer.

Hi James
Just to let you know, I'm planning a surprise birthday party for Grandma on 20th April. Make sure you're free that day, but don't tell anyone!
Love
Sally

1 What does Sally want James to do?
A keep something a secret
B help to organise a celebration
C tell her which day he'll be free

To: Jake
From: Charlie
Reply Forward

I'm really looking forward to the concert tonight, only my car's broken down and I was wondering if you have a spare seat in yours? Call me!

2 What does Charlie want to know?
A how Jake is going to the concert
B whether Jake can take him to the concert
C if Jake wants to come to the concert with him

Hi Pedro
Here's the number of the piano teacher you asked me about: Martina: 07796 34643.
Don't worry – she's really kind and patient. You'll soon learn how to play!
Yolanda

3 What is Yolanda doing in her message?
A recommending a teacher
B asking for help in finding a teacher
C checking some information about a teacher

Today's
Special Offer
Dr Bob Schwarz's bestseller
Be Happy, Be Successful
Buy two copies – get a third one free!

4 What can customers do today?
A get one extra book at a lower price
B buy two books but only pay for one of them
C have three books for the cost of two

Hi Dasha
As you know, Rita is leaving our hockey team, and I thought I'd ask Jess to take her place. She's a great player and very friendly. Let me know if you approve.
Ellie

5 Why is Ellie texting Dasha?
A to find out her opinion
B to ask for a suggestion
C to give her some advice

READING PART 6

EXAM CHECK

1 **Complete this information using the correct words in the box. There are four words you don't need.**

five	grammar	options	questions
sentence	six	text	vocabulary

Reading Part 6 tests your [1] .... In this part, you have to complete a [2] .... by filling in gaps. You have to put one word in each of the [3] .... gaps. As there are no [4] .... to choose from in this part, you have to think of the word yourself.

2 **For each question, write the correct answer. Write one word for each gap.**

What is happiness?

What is happiness? This question has interested writers and thinkers for thousands of years. Most people agree that happiness is more **(1)** .... just a temporary good feeling or positive mood. According to experts, we are happiest when **(2)** .... lives have purpose and meaning.

It seems that money can **(3)** .... people happier, but only up to a certain point. Research shows that people **(4)** .... already have enough money to buy food, clothes and accommodation don't become any happier when they become richer. **(5)** .... fact, studies suggest that the happiest people have interests and challenges, as well **(6)** .... goals which they set and achieve. But the most important thing of all, it seems, is to have close relationships with family and friends.

LISTENING PART 4

EXAM CHECK

1 **Join the beginnings and endings of these sentences about Listening Part 4.**

1 You have to listen to
2 You have to answer
3 You have to choose the correct answer
4 You should answer all the questions
5 You will hear the recording

a from three possible options.
b six questions about what you hear.
c a person interviewing someone.
d two times.
e as you're listening to the interview.

2 125 **For each question, choose the correct answer. You will hear an interview with a woman called Alisha Bennett, who teaches yoga.**

1 What does Alisha say about yoga?
A It's not as difficult as it looks.
B It's suitable for a wide range of people.
C It's become more popular in recent years.

2 Alisha took up yoga because she thought it would help her
A learn to relax.
B make new friends.
C recover from an injury.

3 Why did Alisha decide to become a full-time yoga teacher?
A She wanted to work for herself.
B She needed a career change.
C She had to earn some more money.

4 Alisha says her students are often surprised when
A their fitness improves.
B their energy levels increase.
C their attitude towards life changes.

5 What benefit of yoga teaching does Alisha mention?
A She has become more confident.
B She is now a more cheerful person.
C She has developed a good sense of humour.

6 What does Alisha intend to do in the near future?
A write a book
B post videos online
C set up another school

HOW WAS IT?

Gave it a go [ ]
Getting there [ ]
Aced it! [ ]

HAVING A JOB INTERVIEW IN ... TENERIFE

1 **What kinds of jobs can students and young people do in other countries? Look at the photos. What advantages do you think there are to working abroad? Read Part A of the text to compare your ideas.**

A

Home About Careers Search

Getting a job abroad is a great way to get some work experience before you go to university or start a full-time job. You can also improve your language skills and have fun. The most common jobs are working as a waiter, in a café or restaurant, or working as a holiday rep, looking after guests for a holiday company. Tenerife is a very popular place for holiday jobs because there are plenty of tourists, and also plenty of sun all year!

B

Home About Careers Search

Once you've applied for a job and got an interview, it's important to prepare well for your interview.

Look for examples of the questions that interviewers often ask and 1 .... them.

Dress nicely. Be smart, but make sure you 2 .... with what you are wearing.

Be 3 .... during your interview.

Be positive about yourself, but don't say 4 ....

C

Home About Careers Search

Typical job interview questions

Why are you interested in this job?
What **academic qualifications** do you have?
When are you **available** to start?
What are your **strengths** and **weaknesses**?
Do you have any **relevant** work experience?
If I asked your teachers to describe you, what would they say?
Can you give me the name of two **referees**?
Give an example of your ability to work in a team.
Explain why it's important to be **punctual** and **reliable**.
Why should we **hire** you?

2 **Read Part B of the text. Complete the tips on how to prepare for a job interview with the phrases below. Which tip do you think is the most important? Why?**

anything that isn't true	feel comfortable
interested and enthusiastic	practise answering

3 **Read the typical interview questions in Part C of the text. Match the blue words with the meanings.**

1. to give someone a job
2. arriving on time, not late
3. related to the job you are applying for
4. people who can give information about you and say what kind of person you are
5. free and able to do something
6. exams that you have passed
7. good things about you and your character
8. bad things about you and your character
9. can be trusted to behave well and work hard

4 **Read the interview questions again. Which three would be the most difficult to answer? Why? Compare with your classmates.**

5 126 **Listen to two interviews for holiday jobs. What kind of job is each person applying for?**

6 126 **Complete the things you can say about yourself in a job interview with the words and phrases in the box. Listen and check.**

get on	hard	my best	pay attention
quickly	would enjoy		

PHRASES YOU MIGHT USE

1. I think I ________ working here.
2. I always do ________ .
3. I can ________ to detail.
4. I work very ________ .
5. I learn ________ .
6. I ________ well with everyone.

7 **Choose the correct meaning for each sentence.**

PHRASES YOU MIGHT HEAR

1. Take a seat.
   - a Please bring a chair from outside.
   - b Please sit down.
2. Did you find the office OK?
   - a Did you find the office easily?
   - b Do you like our office?
3. We'll be in touch.
   - a We will contact you.
   - b Please contact us.
4. How flexible can you be on dates?
   - a Can you repeat those dates?
   - b Can you start earlier or later than this?
5. We'll let you know.
   - a We will contact you.
   - b Please contact us.
6. We'll need to follow up your references.
   - a We need to check the references you gave us.
   - b You need to give us more references.

8 **Watch the video about job interviews. What tips do you learn? Write a list of things you should and shouldn't do.**

9 **Compare your lists. Then watch again and check your ideas.**

WATCH

LIFE COMPETENCIES

CREATIVITY AND INNOVATION, COLLABORATION

10 **Imagine you want to apply for a job as a waiter in Tenerife. Work in pairs.**

- write typical interview questions
- prepare your answers

Work with a new partner.

- ask four of your questions
- decide if you would give your partner the job

Tell your class about your interview.

PROGRESS CHECK 5

WORKING AND SKILLS

1 Complete the sentences with these words.

at	calm	co-workers	freelancer
organised	patient	salary	with

1 It's good to work in a team if you have nice ________ .
2 Some people want to be an employee at one company but others prefer working as a ________ .
3 Accountants usually earn a high ________ .
4 A teacher should be ________ because some people learn very slowly.
5 A doctor should be good ________ people.
6 You have to be ________ if you want to be a personal assistant.
7 A mechanic needs to be good ________ repairing things.
8 A chef needs to stay ________ when the restaurant gets very busy.

MODALS OF PERMISSION

2 Choose the correct options to complete the conversation.

A: Mum, [1]*could/must* I have a smartwatch for my birthday?
B: Oh, why do you want one of those?
A: Because we [2]*can't/aren't allowed* to use our smartphones at school …
B: So you want to use a smartwatch instead! No, sorry, but if you [3]*can't/couldn't* use a smartphone then they shouldn't allow smartwatches either. Isn't there a rule about it?
A: Not yet. The rules say students [4]*may not/not allowed to* use a smartphone in class but there's nothing about watches. So [5]*can I/am I able to* have one?
B: You can have one for your birthday but you [6]*couldn't/mustn't* use it in class.

SPORTS AND HOBBIES

3 Join the beginnings and endings of these sentences.

1 I love reading so I've joined
2 It's fun to take part
3 Julie wants to take up
4 Everybody in my town supports
5 We were so excited when our team scored
6 The local school is planning to hold
7 It would be amazing to represent
8 Ian just wants to hang

a volleyball because her best friend plays it.
b a singing competition.
c out with his friends.
d the first goal of the match.
e a book club.
f my country at an international event.
g in sports events.
h the local football team.

GERUNDS AND VERB + *TO* INFINITIVE

4 Complete the conversation using the correct form of the verbs in the box. Use either the gerund (*-ing*) or verb + *to* infinitive.

be	do	find	go	join	keep	take up	talk

A: What can I do [1] ________ fit? [2] ________ a fitness club is expensive. I don't have much money, and I don't have much time, either.
B: I advise you [3] ________ running. It's free and you can do it any time. You could do it in the evenings after work.
A: Oh, I'm much too tired [4] ________ out and do sports after work. And anyway, I don't enjoy [5] ________ things alone. I need a teacher, or maybe teammates.
B: Do you fancy [6] ________ in a football team? I play with my team every Saturday.
A: That sounds good but I usually go to my parents' town at the weekend …
B: But when will you manage [7] ________ time if you are too tired after work and you aren't at home at the weekends? [8] ________ about fitness won't make you fit. You have to make the time and *do* something!

PEOPLE AND EMOTIONS

5 **Decide if the sentences are true or false. In the false sentences, replace the word in italics with one of the words in the box.**

amused	brave	depressed
generous	guilty	satisfied

1. If you've done something and you know it was wrong, you feel *jealous*.
2. People often feel *miserable* if they don't have any friends.
3. If the winter is long and dark, many people start to feel *delighted*.
4. A *nervous* person is happy to give time or things to others.
5. A *cruel* person does things that hurt other people or animals.
6. A *lazy* person does things that other people might not do because they are afraid.
7. If you see a funny film, you'll feel *embarrassed*.
8. If you get high grades in your exams, you'll feel *kind* with yourself.

GRAMMAR REVIEW

6 **Choose the correct options to complete the text.**

It's important to know what makes you feel good. For example, if I feel a bit sad, I [1]*do/would do* some sport. That always makes me feel better. People [2]*which/who* are fit and healthy usually feel better than unfit people. However, I told my cousin Bart that he [3]*should/might* do more sports and he said that he just [4]*didn't/won't* enjoy any sport. If he [5]*goes/went* running, he would feel tired for the rest of the day. It's not his thing.
Bart thinks that having nice people in your life is the key to happiness. He told me that he has always [6]*have/had* very good friends, [7]*which/that* is the most important thing for him. Bart is never alone and he's cheerful all the time so he [8]*must/can't* be very satisfied with his life.

7 **Find one mistake in each sentence and rewrite the sentences.**

1. She asked her dad let her go to the party.
2. We're going to arrive late tomorrow night, but I'm sure we can find a taxi.
3. I love swim in the sea.
4. Would you like go to the cinema with me?
5. Tim enjoys to help his co-workers.

A CAREERS ADVISER

8 **Complete the text with words which best fit each gap.**

Home About Search

I'm a careers adviser. I help young people when they are learning about careers and also older people [1] .... want to change careers. A lot of young people feel that they have to go to university and get a [2] .... , but this type of qualification is not the best for everybody. Some people are not [3] .... to find a job after university, or they realise that they studied the wrong [4] .... You won't do well at university [5] .... you study something that interests you. And remember, you don't [6] .... to study. There are other paths to a satisfying job. I know that some young people feel [7] .... if their parents spend a lot of money on their school education and then they don't go to university, but it's important for everybody to find his or her own path.
If you've started a career but you don't like it, you really should make a change. Last week a man [8] .... me that I had completely changed his life. We had found out that he was good [9] .... children. He stopped working for a bank and now he's a sports teacher. He's so happy! Things like that [10] .... me love my own job.

COMMUNICATION ACTIVITIES

UNIT 1: VOCABULARY – EXERCISE 4, PAGE 14

Quiz: What kind of holidaymaker are you?

Mainly As?	You're the kind of person who goes on holiday to RELAX
Mainly Bs?	You're the kind of person who goes on holiday to have FUN
Mainly Cs?	You're the kind of person who goes on holiday to have ADVENTURES

UNIT 3: SPEAKING – EXERCISE 4, PAGE 47

Photo A

UNIT 3: SPEAKING – EXERCISE 4, PAGE 47

Photo B

UNIT 4: READING – EXERCISE 2, PAGE 52

Quiz results

Mostly a: You're a city person. You want people, shops and entertainment around you.
Mostly b: You're a country person. You love nature and open spaces.

UNIT 7: VOCABULARY – EXERCISE 3, PAGE 90

Quiz: On trend or stuck in a fashion rut?

Give yourself a score (0, 1 or 2 points) for each of your answers, then add up your points.

1	***a***	1	***2***	***a***	1	***3***	***a***	1	***4***	***a***	0
	b	0		***b***	2		***b***	2		***b***	2
	c	2		***c***	0		***c***	0		***c***	1

What's your total score?

0–2 Fashion means very little to you. You want to be comfortable and you're not interested in the latest styles.
3–6 You care about your appearance, but there are things that matter more to you than wearing the latest fashion.
7–8 You're right on trend! You know what the latest styles are and you want to wear them!

UNIT 8: SPEAKING – EXERCISE 5, PAGE 108

Photo A

Photo B

UNIT 11: VOCABULARY – EXERCISE 5, PAGE 143

Photo A

Photo B

Photo C

Photo D

GRAMMAR REFERENCE

STARTER

PRESENT SIMPLE AND PRESENT CONTINUOUS

PRESENT SIMPLE

POSITIVE/NEGATIVE FORMS		
I/You/We/They	**take**	photos.
	don't take	
He/She/It	**takes**	
	doesn't take	

QUESTION FORMS			
Do	I/you/we/they	**take**	photos?
Does	he/she/it		

SHORT ANSWERS		
Yes,	I/you/we/they	**do**.
	he/she/it	**does**.
No,	I/you/we/they	**don't**.
	he/she/it	**doesn't**.

We can use the present simple to talk about something that:

- happens regularly (and habits and routines).
  *I **play** tennis every Tuesday.*
- is generally true and permanent at the present time.
  *My brother **lives** in France.*
- is a fact or always true.
  *The sun **rises** in the east.*

PRESENT CONTINUOUS

POSITIVE/NEGATIVE FORMS		
I	**am/'m**	**working** at the moment.
	am/'m not	
You/We/They	**are/'re**	
	are not/aren't/'re not	
He/She/It	**is/'s**	
	is not/isn't/'s not	

QUESTION FORMS AND SHORT ANSWERS		
Am	I	**working** at the moment?
Are	you/we/they	
Is	he/she/it	
Yes,	I	**am**.
	you/we/they	**are**.
	he/she/it	**is**.
No,	I	**am/'m not**.
	you/we/they	**are not/aren't**.
	he/she/it	**is not/isn't**.

We can use the present continuous to talk about:

- something happening now.
  *They**'re living** with friends while their house **is being decorated**.*
- a temporary situation which is true now.
  *He**'s** doi**ng** his homework in his bedroom.*
- a temporary situation in the present but not necessarily at the moment.
  *My sister**'s studying** art.*

PRACTICE

1 Choose the correct options to complete the text. Sometimes there may be more than one possible answer.

Many people [1]*take up/are taking up* cycling these days. Cycling is great because it [2]*helps/is helping* our general fitness. When we cycle, we [3]*use up/are using up* more energy than when we [4]*walk/are walking*. I [5]*go/am going* cycling regularly, but only on small roads where there aren't many cars. At the moment, I [6]*train/'m training* for a race, so I [7]*spend/'m spending* a lot of time on my bike.

ADVERBS OF FREQUENCY

always (100%)
usually
often
sometimes
occasionally
hardly ever
rarely
never (0%)

We usually put frequency adverbs before the main verb.
*I **usually/sometimes/rarely/never** go to college in the evening.*
*I don't **often** go to college at the weekend.*

We don't use *never, rarely, hardly ever* and *always* at the beginning or end of sentences, but we can sometimes use *sometimes* and *occasionally* at the beginning or end of sentences.
***Sometimes**, it snows in April.*

We put frequency adverbs after the verb *be*.
*I am **often** ill in the winter.*
*She is **usually** at college at eight o'clock.*

There are other expressions that we can use to talk about frequency. These expressions are used at the beginning or end of sentences, not in the middle:

- *every day, every week, every month, every year …*
- *once a day, twice a week, three times a month, four times a year …*
- *on Fridays, at weekends …*
- *most days, most nights, most weeks …*

***On Fridays**, I go to college by bike.*
*I see my best friend **once a week**.*

PRACTICE

1 Put the words in order to make sentences.

1 a / go / gym / I / the / to / twice / week.

....

2 an / hour / I / more / hardly ever / spend / than / there.

....

3 an / for / half / hour. / I / run / sometimes

....

4 I / I'm / listen / music / running. / to / usually / while

....

5 always / exhausted. / gets / home, / he's / when / he

....

6 every / Friday. / friends / go / we / our / out / with

....

7 rarely / watch / TV / you / the / week. / during

....

PRESENT CONTINUOUS WITH ALWAYS

We usually use adverbs of frequency (see opposite) with the present simple. But we can use *always* with the present continuous to say that something we don't like happens repeatedly or frequently.
We put *always* between *be* and the verb with *-ing*.
*John is **always** complaining about work.*
*My parents are **always** telling me I shouldn't drink too much coffee.*

1 Write sentences with the present continuous. Put *always* in the correct part of the sentence.

1 He / forget / my birthday.

....

2 My friends / ring / me late at night.

....

3 Our tennis trainer / tell / us to train hard.

....

4 She / talk / about her job.

....

5 They / eat / crisps.

....

WH- QUESTION WORDS

We use question words to ask certain types of questions.

We call these words *Wh-* words because they contain the letters *w* and *h* (*Why, What, How*).

QUESTION WORD	USE	EXAMPLE
What	asking for information	*What is your name?*
What … for	asking why	*What did you do that for?*
When	asking about time	*When did she arrive?*
Where	asking what place	*Where do you live?*
Which	asking about choice	*Which size do you want?*
Who	asking which person	*Who opened the door?*
Whose	asking about ownership	*Whose is this bag?*
Why	asking for a reason	*Why did you do that?*
How	asking about manner or quality	*How is the cake?*
How far	asking about distance	*How far is your college from here?*
How long	asking about length	*How long is the journey?*
How many	asking about quantity (countable)	*How many people are there?*
How much	asking about quantity (uncountable)	*How much sugar do you like in your tea?*
How old	asking about age	*How old is she?*

PRACTICE

1 Complete the questions with the correct question words.

1. .... do you live?
   I live in New York.
2. .... is that man?
   He's my father.
3. .... do you go to work?
   By car.
4. .... does the supermarket open?
   At eight o'clock.
5. .... are you wearing that coat?
   Because it's cold!

2 Complete the questions about the words in bold.

1. He drank **water**.
   .... did he drink?
2. They went to **London**.
   .... did they go?
3. She writes **computer programs**.
   .... does she write?
4. The town hall is **next to the theatre**.
   .... is the town hall?
5. My new bike was **very expensive**.
   .... did it cost?
6. She's only **22 years** old.
   .... old is she?

YES/NO QUESTIONS

We call questions that need either a *yes* or a *no* answer *yes/no* questions.
Do you like milk in your coffee? (answer: *yes* or *no*)
Have you ever been to Dubai? (answer: *yes* or *no*)

***Is** she Polish?*	***Were** you in London last week?*
***Does** that taste good?*	***Did** you eat out at the weekend?*
***Has** he seen that film?*	***Had** they visited New York before?*
*Modal: **Could** you help me move the sofa?*	***Should** I start work now?*

SHORT ANSWERS TO *YES/NO* QUESTIONS

It is more polite to answer a *yes/no* question with more than just *Yes* or *No*! That's why short answers are often used.
To form a short answer, we use the first word from the question, which is either an auxiliary verb or part of the verb *be*.

QUESTION	POSITIVE	NEGATIVE
Do we know them?	Yes, we do.	No, we don't.
Can he see us?	Yes, he can.	No, he can't.
Have they seen the film?	Yes, they have.	No, they haven't.
Is she here?	Yes, she is.	No, she isn't.

Note: If the question starts with *Are you*, we answer *I am* if *you* refers to one person, or *we are* if it refers to two.

QUESTION	POSITIVE	NEGATIVE
Do you know them?	Yes, I/we do.	No, I/we don't.
Are you thirsty?	Yes, I am.	No, I'm not.
	Yes, we are.	No, we aren't.

PRACTICE

1 Put the words in order to make *yes/no* questions.

1. at / living / she / moment? / England / is / in / the
2. a / he / bank / now? / does / work / in
3. project? / could / help / you / me / with / my
4. they / moment? / holiday / are / on / at / the
5. the / do / soup? / like / of / you / taste / the

2 Complete the possible short answers.

1. Are you from Italy, Franco?
   Yes, ... No, ...
2. Are Jack and Peter your friends?
   Yes, ... No, ...
3. Has your brother got a flat in town?
   Yes, ... No, ...
4. Can he play chess?
   Yes, ... No, ...
5. Is she coming by train?
   Yes, ... No, ...
6. Did you see him at the party?
   Yes, ... No, ...

UNIT 1

COMPARATIVE AND SUPERLATIVE ADJECTIVES

We use comparative adjectives (e.g. *bigger than*) to compare two people or things and to say if one has more of a quality (e.g. size, height, etc.) than the other.

Comparative adjectives are usually followed by *than*.
We use superlative adjectives (e.g. *the fastest, the most important*) to say that in a particular group, something has the most of a quality.

REGULAR ADJECTIVES

	COMPARATIVE	SUPERLATIVE
For most adjectives, add *-er or -est.*	***small*** → *smaller* *Italy is **smaller** than Spain.*	***small*** → *the smallest* *Vatican City is **the smallest** country in the world.*
For short adjectives ending in *-e*, add *-r* or *-st.*	***large*** → *larger* *Canada is **larger** than China.*	***large*** → *the largest* *Russia is **the largest** country in the world.*
For short adjectives with a vowel + a consonant, double the consonant and add *-er* or *-est.*	***hot*** → *hotter* *Algeria is **hotter** than Mexico.*	***hot*** → *the hottest* *Libya is **the hottest** country in the world.*
For two-syllable adjectives ending in *-y*, change the *y* to *i* and add *-er* or *-est.*	***heavy*** → *heavier* *Elephants are **heavier** than crocodiles.*	***heavy*** → *the heaviest* *Blue whales are **the heaviest** animals in the world.*
For some two-syllable adjectives, we can either add *-er, -est* or use *more, the most.* These are adjectives ending in *-ow, -le, -er* plus *polite, quiet, common* and *stupid.*	***polite*** → *politer* *Mia is **more polite** than me. (Mia is **politer** than me.)*	***polite*** → *the politest* *Mia is **the most polite** girl in the class. (Mia is **the politest** girl in the class.)*
For longer adjectives, or two-syllable adjectives ending in *-ful*, put *more/less* or *the most/least* in front of the adjective.	***difficult*** → ***more/less difficult*** *Some people think it's **more difficult** to make friends when you are older.*	***difficult*** → ***the most/least difficult*** *Is it true that Japanese is **the most difficult** language for English speakers to learn?*

IRREGULAR ADJECTIVES

There are three irregular adjectives: *good, bad, far*:
good → *better* → *the best*
bad → *worse* → *the worst*
far → *farther/further** → *the farthest/furthest**
*There is no difference in meaning, but *further/the furthest* is more common.

PRACTICE

1 Complete the comparative and superlative adjectives.

		Comparative	Superlative
1	thin	thinner than	....
2	nice	.... than	the nicest
3	....	lazier than	the laziest
4	comfortable	.... than	the most comfortable
5	good	better than	....
6	bad	.... than	the worst
7	....	farther/further than	the farthest/furthest

2 Complete the sentences with the comparative or superlative form of the adjectives in brackets.

1 It rained every day in December 2015 in Portland, USA. It was .... (wet) December for 75 years.
2 Some people think that the Sydney Opera House is .... (beautiful) modern building in the world.
3 A blue whale is .... (heavy) than an elephant.
4 I felt ill all weekend, but I'm much .... (good) now.
5 This writer's new book is .... (bad) than her others.
6 We've moved house. Now, we live .... (far) from my school than we used to.

A BIT, A LITTLE, (NOT) MUCH, FAR, (NOT) A LOT

We can use these words with comparative adjectives.

We use *a bit, a little, not much* or *not a lot* to describe a small difference.
My brother is ***a little*** *younger than me.*
I'm ***a bit*** *older than him.*

We use *much, a lot* or *far* to describe a large difference.
I'm ***much*** *fitter than my brother, but he's* ***a lot*** *faster than me.*
He's ***much*** *more polite than his cousin.*

(NOT) AS … AS

We use **not as** + **adjective/adverb** + **as** to say that one thing is less than another.
*My brother is**n't as fit as** me. = I am fitter than my brother.*
I'm ***not as fast as*** *my brother. = My brother is faster than me.*

We use **as** + **adjective/adverb** + **as** to say that two things are the same.
Hannah is ***as tall as*** *Jess.*
Today is ***as warm as*** *yesterday.*

PRACTICE

1 Rewrite the sentences so that they mean the same thing as the original sentence. Use the words in brackets.

1. Roman is taller than Josh.
   Josh .... (not as)
2. My old phone was cheap. My new phone is very expensive.
   My new phone .... (much)
3. Burgers aren't as healthy as fruit.
   Fruit is .... (a lot)
4. Spain is a big country in Europe. It's 505,370 km^2. France is a little bigger, at 643,801 km^2.
   Spain is .... (a bit)
5. The old shopping centre was good, but the new one is much nicer.
   The new shopping centre is .... (far)

COMPARATIVE AND SUPERLATIVE ADVERBS

	COMPARATIVE	SUPERLATIVE
Adverbs with two or more syllables: *carefully*	add **more** **more carefully**	add **the most** **the most carefully**
Adverbs with one syllable: *fast* *late*	add -**er** **faster** **later**	add -**est** **the fastest** **the latest**
Irregular adverbs: *well* *badly*	 **better** **worse**	 **the best** **the worst**

As with comparative adjectives, we often use **than** with comparative adverbs.
Although *early* has two syllables, the comparative and superlative forms are *earlier* and *the earliest.*

We use comparative adverbs to say how things are done or happen at different times.
Today it's raining ***more heavily*** *than it did yesterday.*

We use superlative adverbs to say how things are done by someone or something else.
Everyone in my class works hard, but Jon works ***the hardest****.*

PRACTICE

1 Complete the sentences with the comparative or superlative form of the adverbs in brackets.

1. Your writing is hard to read. Please write .... (clearly).
2. Our football team played .... (well) in our group.
3. Motorbikes can travel much .... (fast) than bicycles.
4. My brother works .... (hard) than I do.
5. When you revise .... (serious), you do .... (well) in your exams.
6. My brother drives .... (carefully) of everyone in my family.

2 **Underline and correct the mistakes in these sentences.**

1. Jan dances most beautifully than Lucy.
2. We all write well, but Jon writes the better of all.
3. Peter waited the more patiently to see the doctor.
4. You need to work more hardly, especially at exam time.
5. You must go to bed more earlier than you did last night.
6. My sister runs more faster than me.

TOO … TO … / TOO … FOR …

The words *too … to* make a sentence negative. They mean 'more than is necessary or desirable'.
*He was **too** nervous **to** do well in the exam.*
*I was **too** tired **to** go out.*
*The text was **too** difficult **to** read without using a dictionary.*
*It was **too** cold **to** go for a walk.*

We use *too* to say something is more than is needed, wanted or allowed.

too **+ adjective/adverb**
*I didn't go out because I was **too tired**.*
*Slow down! You're walking **too quickly**.*

too **+ adjective/adverb + infinitive**
*Anna's **too young to drive**.*
*It was **too cold to go** for a walk.*

too **+ adjective/adverb +** ***for*** **someone + infinitive**
*The trainers were **too expensive for me to buy**.*
*There were **too many books for him to read**.*

PRACTICE

1 **Join the sentences using *too … to* or *too … for …* .**

1. The room was very dark. I couldn't see anything.
2. He is very unfit. He can't play football.
3. The project was very difficult. The students couldn't do it.
4. I arrived very late. I didn't catch my flight.
5. Jane's not going to school today. She's ill.
6. This book is hard. My child can't read it.

ENOUGH, SO, SUCH

We use **enough** to show that we have what we need.
*We have **enough** water for everyone.* = Everyone has some water.
We don't have enough glasses for everyone. = Some people don't have a glass.
Note: We write *enough* in front of a noun.
*We have **enough books** for everybody.*
Write *enough* after an adjective or verb.
*Are you **comfortable enough**?*
*You don't **work hard enough**.*
Sentences with *enough* are sometimes followed by *to* + verb infinitive.
*He isn't tall **enough to be** a police officer.*

SO

So means 'very'.
*It's **so** cold this morning.*
We generally use *so* before an adjective or an adverb.
*She's **so clever**! He plays chess **so well**!*
We use *so* with a *that* clause to show a result of the first part of a sentence.
*I was **so** cold **that** I couldn't fall asleep.*

SUCH

Such also means 'very'. We use *such* before an adjective or a noun.
*They are **such nice neighbours**.*
A/An, go **after** *such*, not in front.
~~*That's a such fast car.*~~ ➜ *That's **such a** fast car!*
Like *so*, we use *such* with a *that* clause to show a result.
*It was **such** a cold day **that** we decided to stay at home.*

PRACTICE

1 **Underline and correct the mistakes in these sentences.**

1. Are you enough warm?
2. We have books enough for all the students.
3. They aren't enough strong or fit to be firefighters.
4. It was such hot that I couldn't concentrate on my work.
5. She's a such good teacher.

UNIT 2

USED TO

POSITIVE/NEGATIVE FORMS		
I/You/He/She/It/ We/They	**used to**	enjoy watching football.
	didn't use to	

QUESTION FORMS AND SHORT ANSWERS			
Did	I/you/he/she/it/we/they	**use to**	play football?
Yes,	I/you/he/she/it/we/they	did.	
No,	I/you/he/she/it/we/they	didn't.	

We use *used to* to talk about the past. There is no present form of *used to*.

Note: In negative and question forms, the spelling is *use* not *used*.

We use ***used to*** + **infinitive** to talk about:

- things that happened regularly in the past but don't happen now.
  *I **used to drink** milk for breakfast, but now I always drink orange juice.*
- actions that didn't happen in the past but happen now.
  *I **didn't use to drink** orange juice, but now I have three glasses a day.*
- past states or conditions that are different now.
  *I **used to have** long, dark hair.* (I don't any more.)

PRACTICE

1 Rewrite the sentences so that they mean the same as the original sentence. Use the correct form of *used to*.

1 I like hot weather now, but I didn't in the past.

....

2 My brother played football regularly until he broke his leg.

....

3 My hair was blond, now it's brown.

....

4 Did you go on holiday with your friends when you were a child?

....

5 When I was younger, I didn't get up late.

....

PRESENT PERFECT

We use the present perfect to connect the present with the past.

POSITIVE/NEGATIVE FORMS		
I/You/We/They	**have/'ve**	**finished** work.
I/You/We/They	**have not/ haven't**	**finished** work.
He/She/It	**has/'s**	**finished** work.
He/She/It	**has not/hasn't**	**finished** work.

QUESTION FORMS AND SHORT ANSWERS		
Have	I/you/we/they	**finished** work?
Has	he/she/it	**finished** work?
Yes,	I/you/we/they	**have**.
	he/she/it	**has**.
No,	I/you/we/they	**haven't**.
	he/she/it	**hasn't**.

The present perfect is formed with the correct form of *have* in the present and the past participle of the main verb. The past participle of regular verbs and some irregular verbs is the same as the past simple. The past participle is underlined in the examples below.

PAST SIMPLE	PRESENT PERFECT
*I **finished** work.*	*I **have <u>finished</u>** work.*
*He **read** some novels by Dickens.*	*He **has <u>read</u>** some novels by Dickens.*

Some irregular verbs have past participles which are not the same as the past simple form.

PAST SIMPLE	PRESENT PERFECT
*She **ate** her lunch.*	*She **has <u>eaten</u>** her lunch.*
*She **wrote** a letter.*	*She **has <u>written</u>** a letter.*

We use the present perfect to talk about:

- past experiences which refer to an unstated time in the past, often with *ever* and *never*.
  *Anna **has been** to a concert, but she **has never been** to a pop festival.*
- recent past actions.
  ***Have** you **seen** that new musical yet?*
- something which started in the past and is connected with the present.
  *Ed **has broken** his leg, so he can't play football this weekend.*
- something which started in the past and is still true.
  *Ben and Karen **have lived** in London for seven years.*

PRESENT PERFECT OR PAST SIMPLE?

We use the present perfect to talk about a past experience without saying when it happened.
*I've **been** to the top of the Eiffel Tower.*

To say when something happened, use the past simple.
*I **went** to the top of the Eiffel Tower last summer.*

We use the present perfect to talk about the continuing effect of a past event or action on the present.
*There **has been** an accident on the motorway. Now there are long queues of traffic into the city centre.*

We use the present perfect to talk about the time period up to the present.
*I've **been** to town this morning.* (It is still the morning.)
*My brother **has written** a short story.* (He may write more stories.)

If the time period is now over, we use the past simple.
*I **went** into town this morning.* (It is now afternoon or evening.)
*Prince **wrote** over 150 songs.* (He died in 2016, so can't write any more.)

PRACTICE

1 Complete the conversations with the past simple or present perfect form of the verbs in brackets. Make any other changes necessary.

1 **A:** You look terrible. Are you OK?
B: I'm all right. I .... (go) to bed late last night and I .... (just wake up).

2 **A:** Where's Chloe?
B: I don't know. Her train .... (arrive) half an hour ago, but I .... (not see her yet).

3 **A:** Shall we go and see the new Star Wars film tonight?
B: No, I .... (already see) it.
A: Really?
B: Yes, I .... (see) it last week.

4 **A:** What's the most expensive thing you .... (ever buy)?
B: My racing bike. It .... (cost) 500 euros.
A: I .... (never spend) as much money as that on anything!

5 **A:** .... you .... (ever do) gymnastics?
B: Yes, but I .... (never do) karate.

6 **A:** Where .... you .... (go) on holiday last year?
B: We .... (go) to New Zealand.
A: Really? I've got relatives there, but I .... (never visit) them.

2 Underline and correct the mistakes in the conversation.

A: Have you heard? My oldest sister's getting married to a guy called Elliot.
B: Really! How long did she know him?
A: Only six months. Apparently they've met at work.
B: Have you met Elliot already?
A: No, not yet, but my sister's told me a lot about him.
B: When have you seen her?
A: I've seen her last week. She drove me to school one day.

SINCE AND FOR

We can use *since* and *for* with the present perfect to talk about a time that started in the past and continues to the present.
Since is followed by a point in time.
*We've lived here **since** December 2017.*

For is followed by a period of time.
*She's lived there **for** six and a half years.*

PRACTICE

1 Complete the sentences with *for* or *since*.

1 My father has worked for the same company .... 20 years.
2 Megan has played football .... she was six years old.
3 I haven't eaten anything .... seven o'clock this morning.
4 Sofia can't still be tired. She's slept .... 11 hours!
5 I've made lots of new friends .... I've been at this school.

YET AND ALREADY

already = before now, often sooner than expected
*He's **already** written his essay, so he can go and see that Bollywood film.*

Already is placed between *have/has* and the past participle.

yet = until now
We use *yet* in negative sentences and questions to talk about things we plan to do in the future, but which are not done. *Yet* is placed at the end of a sentence.
*I haven't finished my project **yet**.*
*Have you finished your project **yet**?*

PRACTICE

1 Complete the sentences with *already* or *yet*.

1 I've .... finished my homework, so I might go out now.
2 **A:** Let's tell our friends the news.
B: I've .... told them. I told them last week.
3 I'm not hungry because I've .... had lunch. I ate earlier.
4 Have you met Benoit .... ?
5 I haven't got dressed .... because I've just woken up.

UNIT 3

COUNTABLE AND UNCOUNTABLE NOUNS

COUNTABLE NOUNS

Countable nouns refer to nouns which can be counted.
They have singular and plural forms.
tree* → *trees*; *knife* → *knives*; *child* → *children*; *man* → *men
Singular countable nouns can be used with *a/an*.
***a** book, **an** elephant*
Plural countable nouns can be used with numbers, *some* and *any*.
*Our family has **some** animals – a dog and **three** cats.*

UNCOUNTABLE NOUNS

Uncountable nouns refer to nouns which <u>cannot</u> be counted.
They have no plural form.
advice ~~advices~~, ***furniture*** ~~furnitures~~, ***information*** ~~informations~~, ***homework*** ~~homeworks~~, etc.

BOTH COUNTABLE AND UNCOUNTABLE

Some nouns can be countable and uncountable.
*I love **lambs** but I don't eat **lamb**.*
lamb (countable) = animal
lamb (uncountable) = meat from a lamb

To make uncountable nouns countable, we use countable nouns like *piece, slice, spoonful, box*, etc.
*a **piece** of advice*
*three **slices** of bread*
*two **spoonfuls** of sugar*
*a **bowl** of rice*

PRACTICE

1 Underline the countable nouns and circle the uncountable nouns in this short text.

As well as giving us energy, sugar in our diet makes our food taste better. Sometimes we add sugar to our breakfast cereals. Sugar is also used in biscuits, ice cream, chocolate and many other things we eat. It is also in fruit and vegetables and even in a glass of milk!

SOME AND *ANY* WITH COUNTABLE AND UNCOUNTABLE NOUNS

We use *some* and *any* when we can't or don't want to specify a number or an exact amount.
I saw six cars without parking permits in the car park. (It is important that you know how many cars I saw.)
*I saw **some** cars without parking permits in the car park.*
(I don't know exactly how many cars I saw.)

In general, we use *some* in positive sentences.
*I got **some** nice presents for my birthday this year.*
*This job in the garden will take **some** time.*

In general, we use *any* in negative sentences and questions.
*I didn't get **any** nice presents for my birthday this year.*
*I looked in my desk, but I couldn't find **any** pens.*
*I don't need **any** advice.*

Note: We can use *some* in questions when we offer or request something.
*Would you like **some** coffee?*
*Could I have **some** juice, please?*

PRACTICE

1 Complete the sentences with *some* or *any*.

1. There are .... big birds in the garden.
2. You have .... ketchup on your shirt.
3. If you are hungry, there is .... ice cream in the freezer.
4. She's always aggressive. That's why she doesn't have .... friends.
5. Has he got .... brothers or sisters?
6. Have you read .... good books recently?
7. Would you like .... milk in your tea?
8. Can I have .... water, please?

MUCH, MANY, A LOT OF AND *LOTS OF*

These words and phrases are quantifiers. They tell us how much of something there is.
For large quantities, use *many* with plural countable nouns.
*There aren't **many** trains at night.*
*How **many** times have you been to London?*

Use *much* with uncountable nouns in questions and negative sentences.
*How **much** money do you need?*
*We don't have **much** time.*

Use *a lot of* or *lots of* with plural countable nouns or uncountable nouns.
***A lot of/Lots of** students ride bikes to college.*
*You can save **a lot of/lots of** money if you cycle or walk.*

PRACTICE

1 Underline and correct the mistakes in these sentences.

1. We haven't got many time.
2. I drink much water when I wake up.
3. There are lot of things we need to talk about.
4. How much friends do you have online?
5. We have driven a lots of miles today.

FEW, A FEW

We use *few* when we want to talk about very small quantities with plural countable nouns.

***Few** people in my class speak Russian.* (hardly any)

We use the phrase *a few* when we mean *some*.

***A few** people in my class speak Russian.* (a small number)

LITTLE, A LITTLE

Little and *a little* follow the same pattern as *few* and *a few*. The only difference is that we use *few* and *a few* with countable nouns in the plural form, and we use *little* and *a little* with uncountable nouns.

*We had **little** time to prepare before the exam started.* (hardly any)

*We had **a little** time to prepare before the exam started.* (a small amount)

In the first example, we didn't have a lot of time before the exam started. In the second one, we had some time (but not a lot).

ALL/ALMOST ALL/MOST

The words *all*, *almost* and *most* cause some confusion. Here are the most important differences between them.

All means 100%.

Almost is an adverb, which means 'nearly'.

*I **almost** failed my driving test.* (but I didn't fail)

*He's **almost** a hundred years old.* (He'll be 100 next month.)

Almost all means 'nearly all'.

*I know **almost all** the people here.* (nearly all the people)

Most means the majority or 60+%.

***Most** young people would like to be rich and famous.*

*I have visited **most** countries in Africa.* (but not all)

We can also use *most* as a pronoun.

***Most** of my friends are aged 20 to 30.*

PRACTICE

1 Underline and correct the mistakes in these sentences.

1. I'd like little advice about going to university, please.
2. They only gave us few information about the trip.
3. Little people in my class are hard-working.
4. We only had a few water left at the end of the day.
5. Almost cars have four doors.
6. She's most 20 years old.

VERBS + ADJECTIVES

Verbs, such as *look, seem, appear, taste, sound, feel* and *smell* can be followed by an adjective.

*The biscuits **taste great**!*

*That dress **looks fantastic** on you!*

PRACTICE

1 Write sentences.

1. That car / look / expensive

   ....

2. He / appear / sad

   ....

3. The engine / sound / loud

   ....

4. This room / feel / cold

   ....

5. Your socks / smell / bad

   ....

ARTICLES

INDEFINITE ARTICLES

We use *a* or *an*:

- with singular, countable nouns mentioned for the first time.
  ***A** new **car** loses 10% of its value, as soon as you buy it.*
- to talk about jobs.
  *My ambition is to become **a doctor**.*

We do not use *a* or *an* with uncountable nouns or plural countable nouns.

*If you have **information**, you have **power**.*

*More **women** than **men** go to university.*

We use *an* before words which begin with a vowel sound.

*I've just downloaded **an app**.*

*Let's meet in **an hour**.*

THE DEFINITE ARTICLE WITH COUNTABLE AND UNCOUNTABLE NOUNS

We use *the*:

- with things we have mentioned before or when it's clear who or what we are referring to from the context.
  *Two new teachers have just joined **the school**.*
  ***The tennis coach** is from Spain.*
  *Could you get me some milk from **the shop**, please?*
  (i.e. the shop we always go to)
- when referring to particular things.
  *I love most musicals, but I don't like **the new version of** Mamma Mia.*
- with things which are unique.
  *I spend hours studying **the sky** at night with my new telescope. I love watching **the moon** and **the stars**.*
- with adjectives to express groups.
  *In New York, **the poor** mainly live in this part of town.*
- with nationalities.
  ***The English** usually spend their summer holidays abroad.*
- with superlative adjectives.
  *The ferry from Staten Island to New York is **the cheapest** service in the world. It's free!*

Ø (ZERO ARTICLE)

It is possible to have a noun phrase with no article (the zero article, ø).

We use the zero article (ø) in the following cases with plural and uncountable nouns:

- general nouns: *bikes, people, life, milk*
  Motorbikes can be dangerous.
- abstract nouns: *education, courage*
  Happiness is important.
- names of people and places: *Bill, England, Oxford Street*
  I gave the book to Mary.
- languages: *Spanish*
  Do you speak English?
- days and months: *Monday, December*
  He arrived in London on Monday.
- games and sports: *football, chess*
  He is good at football.
- meals: *breakfast, lunch, dinner*
  Lunch is at midday.
- noun + number: *platform 6, room 10, page 50*
  They are in room 45.
- routine places: *in bed, at home, to school*
  He's in bed.
- movement or transport: *on foot, by car*
  I go to school by bus.

PRACTICE

1 Complete the sentences with the definite article, an indefinite article or ø (no article).

1 I heard .... noise in .... street.
2 I think that .... man riding .... bicycle is .... member of .... British Olympic team.
3 I'm looking for .... flat in .... centre of .... town.
4 What's .... longest river in Europe?
5 .... dog next door chases .... cats.
6 He's .... doctor from one of .... best hospitals in England.

2 Choose the correct option: the definite article, an indefinite article or ø (no article).

1 Could you go to *the/a/ø* bank and get some money out?
2 *The/A* company has bought two cars. *The/A* three-litre Jaguar is for *the/a* manager and *the/a* Mini is for her assistant.
3 *The/A* French and *the/a* Spanish don't often speak German.
4 *The/A* window in *the/a/ø* kitchen is *the/a* biggest in *the/a* house.
5 She's got *a/an/ø* university degree in biology.
6 They've just bought *the/a/ø* furniture for their holiday home in *the/a/ø* France.

UNIT 4

PAST SIMPLE

BE

POSITIVE/NEGATIVE FORMS		
I/He/She/It	**was**	here yesterday.
	wasn't	
You/We/They	**were**	
	weren't	

QUESTION FORMS AND SHORT ANSWERS		
Was	I/he/she/it	here yesterday?
Were	you/we/they	
Yes,	I/he/she/it	**was**.
	you/we/they	**were**.
No,	I/he/she/it	**wasn't**.
	you/we/they	**weren't**.

OTHER VERBS

play (regular)
go (irregular)

POSITIVE/NEGATIVE FORMS		
I/You/We/They/ He/She/It	**played**	tennis yesterday.
	didn't play	
	went	to school yesterday.
	didn't go	

QUESTION FORMS AND SHORT ANSWERS			
Did	I/you/we/they/he/she/it	**play**	tennis yesterday?
		go	to school yesterday?
Yes,	I/you/we/they/he/she/it	**did**.	
No,	I/you/we/they/he/she/it	**didn't**.	

SPELLING OF REGULAR PAST SIMPLE VERBS

For regular verbs, we add *-ed* to the base form of the verb, or *-d* if the verb already ends in *-e*.

FOR VERBS:	PRESENT SIMPLE	PAST SIMPLE
ending in a consonant + *-y*, remove *-y* and add *-ied*	*study* *carry*	*stud**ied*** *carr**ied***
ending in a vowel + a consonant (with stress on last syllable), double the final consonant and add *-ed*	*plan* *prefer* *drop*	*pla**nned*** *prefe**rred*** *dro**pped***
ending in a vowel + *-l*, double the *l* and add *-ed*	*travel* *control*	*trave**lled*** *contro**lled***
ending in a vowel + a consonant (with no stress on the last syllable), add *-ed*	*happen* *visit*	*happen**ed*** *visit**ed***

We use the past simple to talk about:

- past actions/events/states which have finished.
  *Jenny **was** tired after she **went** ice skating.*
- repeated past actions.
  *I **cycled** to school every day when I was a student.*
- a sequence of past actions.
  *We **left** home, **walked** to the station and **caught** the train.*

PAST CONTINUOUS

POSITIVE/NEGATIVE FORMS		
I/He/She/It	**was**	**studying** all evening.
	wasn't	
You/We/They	**were**	
	weren't	

QUESTION FORMS AND SHORT ANSWERS		
Was	I/he/she/it	**studying** all evening?
Were	you/we/they	
Yes,	I/he/she/it	**was**.
	you/we/they	**were**.
No,	I/he/she/it	**wasn't**.
	you/we/they	**weren't**.

We use the past continuous to talk about:

- a particular moment in the past.
  *Emily **was walking** the dog at 5 p.m.*
- temporary actions which give extra (less important) information.
  *It **was raining**, so I decided not to go out.*
- two or more actions happening at the same time.
  *While I **was doing** my homework, my brother **was playing** the guitar.*
- an action happening when another action happened.
  *He **was cleaning** his bike when he hurt his hand.*

WHEN, WHILE AND AS

We can use *when*, *while* and *as* with the past continuous and the past simple to introduce an action happening at the same time as another. The past continuous is used for the background activity and the past simple is the shorter activity that suddenly occurs while the longer activity is happening.

***When** Joe was walking home, it started to rain.*
*The phone rang **while** I was having breakfast.*
*They arrived **as** we were leaving.*

PRACTICE

1 Choose the correct options to complete the sentences.

1 While I *watched/was watching* TV, my sister was doing her homework.
2 My friends *often phoned/were often phoning* me when my parents were out.
3 While I was talking to my friend, I *realised/was realising* that something was wrong.
4 It was a lovely day. The sun *shone/was shining* and the birds *sang/were singing*.
5 Lionel Messi *won/was winning* a gold medal for Argentina in the Beijing Olympics.

2 Complete the sentences with the past simple or past continuous form of the verbs in brackets.

1 While I .... (tidy) my room, I .... (find) some old photographs.
2 As I .... (leave) the cinema, I .... (realise) that I'd left my phone behind.
3 While Simon .... (watch) television, his brother .... (cook) dinner.
4 When we .... (hear) the fire alarm, we all .... (stop) what we .... (do) and .... (walk) out of the building.
5 My computer .... (crash) while I .... (update) my web page.

PAST PERFECT

POSITIVE/NEGATIVE FORMS		
I/You/He/She/It/ We/They	**had/'d**	**finished** school by five o'clock.
	had not/hadn't	

QUESTION FORMS AND SHORT ANSWERS		
Had	I/you/he/she/it/ we/they	**finished** school by five o'clock?
Yes,	I/you/he/she/it/ we/they	**had**.
No,	I/you/he/she/it/ we/they	**hadn't**.

PAST PERFECT AND PAST SIMPLE

We use the past perfect and the past simple to:

- make the order of past events clear. The past perfect describes something that happened before an action/event in the past.
  *My parents **had left** when I **arrived** home.* (My parents were not there when I arrived home.)
- say what was completed before a specific past time.
  *By nine o'clock, I**'d phoned** three people and **had sent** five emails.*
- explain past events or situations, or give background information.
  *He**'d drunk** nothing all day, so he was really thirsty.*
  *I**'d got** up at five o'clock, so by midday I was very tired.*
- talk about situations that have changed.
  *I**'d planned** to finish writing my essay this morning, but I've got a terrible headache.*

PRACTICE

1 Complete the sentences with the past simple or past perfect form of the verbs in brackets.

1. It .... (rain) all night and, although it .... (stop), the ground .... (be) still very wet.
2. We .... (plan) to have a picnic, but then it started raining, so we .... (have to) think of something else to do.
3. It .... (be) sunny every day for two weeks, but then it .... (start) to snow.
4. We .... (cannot) go for a walk in the forest yesterday because the snow and ice .... (make) the paths too dangerous.
5. Yesterday, we .... (go) to the cinema because there was a new film that none of us .... (see).

UNIT 5

ABILITY AND ADVICE

TALKING ABOUT ABILITY AND INABILITY

We use *can/can't* and *could/couldn't* to talk about ability or inability. They are followed by the infinitive without *to.*
*Anna **can speak** French, but she **can't speak** Chinese.*
*Max **could walk** when he was a year old, but he **couldn't talk** until he was two.*

***Can** Anna speak French?*	*Yes, she **can**.*
***Can** she speak Chinese?*	*No, she **can't**.*
***Could** Max walk when he was one?*	*Yes, he **could**.*
***Could** he talk when he was one?*	*No, he **couldn't**.*

BE ABLE TO

Be able to is like *can*. We use it to talk about abilities. We often use it in places where it is not possible to use *can*, for example, after another modal verb.
*She **won't be able to** walk that far.*

Be able to is more formal than *can*.
*I am very sorry, but I **am not able to** attend the meeting.*

We use *was/were able to* to talk about past achievements.
*Only one student **was able to** pass the exam.*

We use *wasn't/weren't able to* in negative sentences.
*We **weren't able to** complete the project in time.*

PRACTICE

1 Complete the sentences with *can*, *can't*, *could*, *couldn't* or *be able to*. Sometimes more than one answer is possible.

1. I've looked everywhere for my phone, but I .... find it.
2. My brother .... swim when he was four years old. He learned very quickly.
3. Although my ankle was sprained, I .... finish the race.
4. I .... play the piano, but I don't play very often.
5. Kieran .... ride a bike until he was nearly 12.

2 Join the beginnings and endings of these sentences. Then choose the correct modal verb in italics.

1 Luis spent a year in Paris so he *could/can*
2 I have an exam tomorrow, so I *can't/couldn't*
3 I had a great driving instructor so I *was able to/could*
4 My little sister is very clever. She *can/could*
5 I missed the start of the film because I *can't/couldn't*

a pass my test the first time.
b find the cinema.
c go to Sara's party tonight.
d speak French really well now.
e play the piano when she was five.

SHOULD/SHOULDN'T

We use *should/shouldn't* to give or ask for advice. *Should/Shouldn't* is followed by the infinitive without *to*.
*You **should join** a gym if you want to keep fit.*
*You **shouldn't eat** too much chocolate.*
*What **should** I **do**?*

An alternative to *should* is *ought to* + infinitive. This is more formal.
*You **ought to eat** more fruit and vegetables.*

OTHER WAYS OF GIVING ADVICE

Here are some other ways to give advice or make recommendations:
Why don't you go on a diet?
How about eating less fast food?
I suggest you stop smoking.
I recommend (that) you go to bed earlier.

For stronger advice we can use *have to* or *must*.
*You **must** see a doctor.*
*You **have to** take her to see a doctor!*

We can use the **imperative** + **-ing** to give advice.
***Start** doing some exercise.*
***Stop** drinking so much.*
***Consider** eating more salads.*
***Try** walking to work.*

PRACTICE

1 Put the words in order to make sentences and questions.

1 you / fruit / eat / vegetables. / lots / should / of / and

....

2 eat / you / too / chips. / many / shouldn't / burgers / and

....

3 you / why / don't / jogging? / start

....

4 doing / about / exercise? / more / how

....

5 for / you / start / recommend / exam. / I / revising / your

....

6 I / you / suggest / getting / late. / up / stop / so

....

7 more / eating / salads. / consider

....

OBLIGATION

MUST, HAVE TO

We use *must* and *have to* to express obligation.
*You **must** take your passport with you when you travel abroad.*
*We **have to** show our passports when we cross the border.*

We often use *must* to talk about rules or laws which we agree with or believe in.
*We **must** wear a seat belt in the car, even for short journeys.*

We often use *have to* to talk about rules or laws which were made by someone else or which we may not agree with.
*My teacher says that I **have to** finish the homework tonight or I'll be in trouble.*

DON'T HAVE TO

We use *don't have to* or *needn't* (but not *mustn't*) when it's not necessary to do something.
*We **didn't have to** show our passports when we crossed into Scotland.*
*We **don't need to** wear a uniform at our school.*

MUSTN'T

We use *mustn't* to express prohibition, to say that something is not allowed.
*You **mustn't use** your phone in the cinema.*
We can also use *can't* instead of *mustn't*.
*You **can't talk** during the exam.*
There is no past tense form of *mustn't*. Use *not allowed to*.
*We **weren't allowed to go** into the concert without a ticket.*

PRACTICE

1 **Look at the photos and complete the sentences with *can*, *can't*, *must* or *mustn't*. Sometimes there may be more than one possible answer.**

1. We .... bring a dog in here.
2. We .... pay in cash. We .... pay by credit card.
3. We .... use wifi here.
4. We .... use our phones here.
5. We .... sit at this table. It's reserved.

1

2

3

4

5

2 **Choose the correct options to complete the text.**

When my grandfather was young, children [1]*must not/didn't have to* stay at school until the age of 18 or even 16. They [2]*could/couldn't* leave when they were 14. My grandfather for example had no choice. He [3]*had to/didn't have to* go out and work to earn money for his family. At the end of every week, he [4]*could/had to* give his wages to his mother. She gave him a small amount of pocket money which he [5]*had to/could* spend as he liked. When he was 18, he wanted to join the army, but unfortunately, he failed the medical examination, so he [6]*had to/couldn't* do military service. This meant he couldn't fight for his country. Instead of being a soldier like all his friends, he drove an ambulance.

UNIT 6

PLANS AND INTENTIONS

BE GOING TO

POSITIVE/NEGATIVE FORMS		
I	**am/'m** **am not/'m not**	**going to** study tonight.
You/We/They	**are/'re** **are not/aren't**	
He/She	**is/'s** **is not/isn't**	

QUESTION FORMS AND SHORT ANSWERS		
Am	I	**going to** study hard?
Are	you/we/they	
Is	he/she	
Yes,	I	**am**.
	you/we/they	**are**.
	he/she	**is**.
No,	I	**am/'m not**.
	you/we/they	**aren't**.
	he/she	**isn't**.

We use *going to* to talk about:

- future plans and things we intend to do.
  *I'**m going to** watch the match on TV.*
- things we predict based on what we can see, or something that we think is certain to happen.
  *I'**m going to** sneeze.*

PRESENT CONTINUOUS FORMS FOR THE FUTURE

We use the present continuous to talk about arrangements or plans which have already been made.
*I'**m starting** a new course tomorrow.*

PRESENT SIMPLE FORMS FOR THE FUTURE

We use the present simple to talk about:

- events in the future that are certain because they are facts.
  *The match **starts** at 3.30 p.m. Don't miss it!*
- fixed or planned events.
  *The lesson **ends** at 7.30 this evening.*

WILL

We use *will* to:

- talk about quick decisions about what to do next.
  A: *I am going to go to Paris next Friday morning.*
  B: *OK, I'**ll** come too. I can get leave from work.*
- for spontaneous offers.
  *There's someone at the door. I'**ll** open it.*
- to talk about things we expect to happen or things we predict will happen.
  *More people **will** buy electric cars in the future.*

PRACTICE

1 Choose the correct options to complete the sentences.

1 We *see/'re going to see* the new *Spider-Man* film tomorrow. I bought the tickets online.
2 I don't think *I'll be/am* late home. The lesson usually finishes at three o'clock.
3 I've got an important exam tomorrow, so I *go/'m going to go* to bed early this evening.
4 Our train *leaves/is leaving* at 10.45 a.m. tomorrow morning.
5 **A:** We've run out of bread.
  B: OK, *I'll go/'m going to go* and get some more.

PROBABLY, DEFINITELY, THERE'S A GOOD/ NOT MUCH CHANCE THAT ... , I DOUBT

We can use adverbs and expressions such as *probably* and *I doubt* with *will* to express future certainty and uncertainty:
***I'll probably** have my hair cut this weekend.*
***He'll definitely** pass the exam.*
***There's a good chance he'll** win the race.*
***I doubt she'll** come.*

PRACTICE

1 Choose the correct alternative, a or b.

1 You can come with us but we're leaving early in the morning.
  a That's OK. I'll come too. **b** I will leave then.
2 The phone's ringing.
  a I'll get it. **b** I get it.
3 There's no bread in the kitchen.
  a I look in the cupboard. **b** I'll go and buy some.
4 More people .... electric cars in the future.
  a will buy **b** are buying
5 .... have my hair cut this weekend.
  a I'm going **b** I'll probably
6 There's a good chance .... win the race.
  a he'll **b** he's going

UNIT 7

REPORTED SPEECH

REPORTED SPEECH WITH MIXED TENSES

Direct speech is what we call the words people say when they speak.
He said, 'I haven't seen you for a long time.'

Indirect or reported speech is how we report (tell someone) what another person says.
He said he hadn't seen me for a long time.

Verb tenses often change when we report what people said.

DIRECT SPEECH	REPORTED SPEECH
present simple *'I **go** to a school in the city centre.'*	past simple *She said she **went** to a school in the city centre.*
present continuous *'I'**m waiting** for a bus.'*	past continuous *He said he **was waiting** for a bus.*
present perfect *'I **have** already **had** lunch.'*	past perfect *He said he **had** already **had** lunch.*
past simple *'I **enjoyed** my dinner.'*	past perfect *She said she **had enjoyed** her dinner.*
will future *'I'**ll** call you later.'*	*would* *She said she **would** call me later.*
can *'I **can** speak four languages.'*	*could* *She said she **could** speak four languages.*

We also make other changes when we report what people said, as follows:

- subject and object pronouns
  *'**I** have already told **you**.' → **She** said **she** had already told **me**.*
  *'**We** live in Paris.' → **They** said **they** lived in Paris.*
- possessive adjectives
  *'**I**'ve mended **my** bike.' → **He** said **he**'d mended **his** bike.*
  *'**We** love **our** new flat.' → **They** said **they** loved **their** new flat.*
- time references
  *'We're going on holiday **tomorrow**.' → They said they were going on holiday **the next day**.*
- place references
  *'I want to stay **here**.' → He said he wanted to stay **there**.*

CHANGING TIME AND PLACE REFERENCES IN REPORTED SPEECH

PHRASE IN DIRECT SPEECH	PHRASE IN REPORTED SPEECH
*'I met him **today**,' he said.*	*He said that he had met him **that day**.*
*'I saw him **yesterday**,' she said.*	*She said that she had seen him **the day before**.*
*'I met her **the day before yesterday**,' he said.*	*He said that he had met her **two days before**.*
*'I'll see you **tomorrow**,' he said.*	*He said that he would see me **the next day**.*
*'We'll come **the day after tomorrow**,' they said.*	*They said that they would come **in two days time**.*
*'I have an appointment **next week**,' she said.*	*She said that she had an appointment **the following week**.*
*'I was on holiday **last week**,' he told us.*	*He told us that he had been on holiday **the previous week**.*
*'I saw her **a week ago**,' he said.*	*He said he had seen her **a week before**.*
this (for time)	***that***
*'I'm getting a new car **this week**,' she said.*	*She said she was getting a new car **that week**.*
*'Do you like **this shirt**?' he asked.*	*He asked if I liked **that shirt**.*
*He said, 'I live **here**.'*	*He told me he lived **there**.*

In general, personal pronouns change to the third person singular or plural, except when the speaker reports his or her own words:

I/me → my/mine

I said: *'I'm going to **my** friend's house.' → I said that I was going to **my** friend's house.*

you/your/yours → him/his/her/hers

He said: *'I like **your** new car.' He told her that he liked **her** new car.*

we/us, our/ours, you/your/yours → they/their/theirs

She said: *'**We** had a great holiday last year.' → She told him that **they** had a great holiday last year.*

REPORTED COMMANDS

We can use *tell* to report commands. We need to include the object (the person who needs to listen to the command) + infinitive after *tell*.

DIRECT COMMANDS	REPORTED COMMANDS
'Stop talking!'	*The teacher **told them to stop** talking.*
'Don't be late!'	*The father **told his daughter not to be** late.*

PRACTICE

1 Write the reported speech as direct speech.

1 She said she was living in Moscow.
'I'm living in Moscow.'

2 I said I was sorry, but I couldn't lend her any more money.
....

3 He says he still feels ill.
....

4 She says she's older than me.
....

5 They said they'd come and see me later.
....

6 Max said he'd left the day before.
....

7 She told him to stop worrying.
....

2 Write the statements and commands as reported speech.

1 'I'm leaving school at the end of next year.'
He said ....

2 'I've got a surprise for you.'
She said ....

3 'Shut the door!'
She told him ....

4 'We've all passed our English exam.'
They said ....

5 'It's my birthday tomorrow.'
He said ....

6 'You're the only person I know who likes classical music.'
She said ....

7 'We went to Italy for our holiday last year.'
They said ....

8 'Don't drink any more coffee!'
He told Max ....

REPORTED QUESTIONS

The word order in reported questions is the same as for positive phrases.

POSITIVE PHRASE	DIRECT QUESTION	REPORTED QUESTION
*I **was smiling**.*	*'Why are you smiling?'*	*He asked me why I **was smiling**.*

We use *ask* when we report questions. We need to make changes to tenses, pronouns, times and places. We don't use question marks.

DIRECT QUESTION	REPORTED QUESTION
*'**Why** are you smiling?'*	*He **asked** me **why** I was smiling.*
*'**What** are you doing tomorrow?'*	*She **asked** us **what** we were doing the next day.*
*'**When** do you finish football practice?'*	*He **asked** me **when** I finished football practice.*
*'**Why** did you come here?'*	*She **asked** me **why** I had gone there.*

With *yes/no* questions, we need to use *if* or *whether* after *ask*.

DIRECT QUESTION	REPORTED QUESTION
*'**Are** you feeling OK?'*	*She **asked if/whether** I was feeling OK.*
*'**Do** you need a break?'*	*He **asked if/whether** I needed a break.*

PRACTICE

1 Rewrite the reported sentences as direct questions.

1. They asked me why I was there.
   'Why are you here?'
2. Helen asked me if I was enjoying my new course.
   ....
3. Alex asked if anyone had found his keys.
   ....
4. Sasha wanted to know what we'd done the day before.
   ....
5. I asked Veronika if she could come to my party that evening.
   ....
6. We asked a policeman if he could tell us where the station was.
   ....
7. Jan wanted to know who my favourite actor was.
   ....
8. I asked my brother if he had tried to phone me.
   ....

2 Write the direct questions as reported questions.

1. 'Why are you wearing your best clothes?'
   My mum asked ....
2. 'Where are you going?'
   My dad asked ....
3. 'What are you going to do there?'
   My brother asked ....
4. 'Are you going with anyone?'
   My sister asked ....
5. 'Do I know who you're going with?'
   My dad asked ....
6. 'What time will you be back?'
   My mum asked ....
7. 'How will you get home?'
   My brother asked ....
8. 'What will you do if you miss the last bus?'
   My sister asked ....

INDIRECT QUESTIONS

Indirect questions are a polite way of asking for information. We use expressions like *Could you tell me … ?* or *I was wondering …* to introduce the question.

DIRECT QUESTIONS	INDIRECT QUESTIONS
Are you busy later?	***Could you tell me if*** *you're busy later?*
Do you know the time?	***I was wondering if*** *you know the time.*
Where do you work?	***I'd like to know where*** *you work.*

The word order in indirect questions is the same as for statements.

*'How long **have you lived** here?'*

*'I would like to know how long **you have lived** here.'*

We do not use the auxiliary verbs *do*, *does* and *did* in indirect questions. However, we sometimes need to change the tense of the verb.

*'When **does** the train **leave**?'*

✓ *Could you tell me **when the train leaves**?*

✗ ~~*Could you tell me when does the train leave?*~~

*'When **did** you **get** home?'*

✓ *Could you tell me **when** you **got** home?*

✗ ~~*Could you tell me when did you get home?*~~

If there is no question word (*What*, *When*, etc.), use *if* or *whether*.

'Is the train late?'

*'Could you tell me **if** the train is late?'*

PRACTICE

1 Write the direct questions as indirect questions.

1. 'Where do you live?'
   Could you tell me .... ?
2. 'Are you doing anything at the weekend?'
   I was wondering ....
3. 'What did they do last weekend?'
   Can you tell me .... ?
4. 'What did you think of the film?'
   I'd like to know ....

UNIT 8

MODALS OF SPECULATION

We use modal verbs to say how sure we are about something.

MUST

We use *must* when we feel sure that something is true because there's lots of evidence.

*He **must** live near here because he walks to work.*

*You're a nurse? That **must** be hard work.*

Note: *Must* is followed by an infinitive without *to*.

MIGHT, MAY, COULD

We use *might*, *may* or *could* to say that we think something is possible but we're not sure.

*Did you hear the noise? I think there **might** be a bird in the bedroom.* (I'm not sure there's a bird, but I think it's possible.)

*'Where's John?' 'He's coming from London, so he **may** be in a traffic jam.'*

*'Where's my phone?' 'You were using it in the kitchen, so it **could** be there.'*

We can use *might not* and *may not* to talk about negative possibilities.

*She **may not** be awake yet.*

Note: We don't use *could* in the negative.

CAN'T

We use *can't* when we feel sure something is not true.

*It **can't** be a bird. None of the windows are open.* (I don't know it's not a bird but I feel sure it's not.)

*Our hotel **can't** be far away now, because we've been travelling for hours.*

PRACTICE

1 Choose the correct alternative, a or b.

1. He wasn't at all frightened. He .... be very brave.
   a must **b** might
2. It .... be a tiger. There aren't any tigers here.
   a could **b** can't
3. He .... live near his office, because he walks to work.
   a must **b** may
4. She lives on a cruise ship. She .... have a life of luxury.
   a might **b** must
5. I've phoned her several times but got no reply. I'm sure she .... be asleep. It's midday!
   a must **b** can't
6. They .... be at college, because it's Sunday.
   a can't **b** might

UNIT 9

PASSIVE

PAST AND PRESENT TENSES AND WITH MODALS

We form the passive by using the correct form of *be* followed by the past participle.

ACTIVE	PASSIVE
We **feed** *our cat twice a day.* (present simple)	*Our cat* **is fed** *twice a day.*
They **built** *our school in 2012.* (past simple)	*Our school* **was built** *in 2012.*
Someone **has cut** *the grass.* (past perfect)	*The grass* **has been cut**.
They **are serving** *lunch now.* (present continuous)	*Lunch* **is being served** *now.*
Someone **had attacked** *them.* (past perfect)	*They* **had been attacked**.
Somebody **might have invited** *her to the party.* (modal)	*She might* **have been invited** *to the party.*

We use passive verbs rather than active verbs when:

- we are more interested in who or what is affected by the action of the verb than who or what does the action.
  My car **was made** *in France.* (The focus is on *my car* rather than the workers or the company that made it.)
  We **have been given** *a lot of homework to do in the holidays.* (The focus is on *we*, not the homework or the teachers who gave the homework.)
- we don't know who did the action.
  My bike **was stolen** *yesterday.* (I don't know who stole it.)
- who or what did something is obvious.
  The driver of the car **is being arrested** *as I speak.* (We know that the police arrest people so we don't need to mention them).

To say who or what did the action in a passive sentence, we can add a *by* phrase.

This opera **was composed by** *Mozart.* (Mozart is the person who did the action).

The concert **was being conducted by** *a famous German conductor.*

PRACTICE

1 Complete the sentences with the passive form of the verbs in brackets. Use the present simple or the past simple.

1. Last year's final, which .... (play) in the newly built stadium, ... (watch) by over 2 million people.
2. In the past, most children walked to school, but now many .... (take) by their parents. Most of them .... (drive) by car.
3. I've just finished reading a science-fiction novel that .... (write) in 1980. Many of the things that .... (predict) by the author have come true.

2 Change the active sentences into passive ones.

1. A vet is seeing our cat this morning.
   ....
2. Last night, the police closed the roads because of the storm.
   ....
3. A famous author wrote the book.
   ....
4. Six women cooked all this fantastic food.
   ....
5. My grandfather had taught me how to sing.
   ....

FUTURE PASSIVE: *WILL*

AFFIRMATIVE FORM	Object + *will* + *be* + verb (past participle)
QUESTION FORM	*Will* + object + *be* + verb (past participle)

Active: *People will buy several million new computers this year.*
Passive: *Several million new computers will be bought this year.*
Active: *Will the heavy rain destroy the crops?*
Passive: *Will the crops be destroyed by heavy rain?*

PRACTICE

1 Put the following sentences into the future passive voice.

1. Will her husband pick up the kids from school tomorrow?
2. The birds will eat all the food on the table in the garden.
3. Millions of people will watch the race.
4. The next heavy rain will flood the town because the river is so high.
5. Will the council's workmen repair the road?

UNIT 10

CONDITIONALS

We use conditional sentences to talk about possible situations or actions and their results. Conditional sentences usually have two clauses: a conditional (*if*) clause and a main clause (usually a result).

CONDITIONAL CLAUSE	MAIN CLAUSE/RESULT
If I see Matt,	*I'll tell him to call you.*

There are three types of conditional sentences which can refer to the present or the future.

ZERO CONDITIONAL

We use the zero conditional to talk about things which are always true.

CONDITIONAL CLAUSE	MAIN CLAUSE/RESULT
If/When + present simple	**Present simple**
If/When *the sun* ***is*** *too hot,*	*it* ***burns*** *you.*

FIRST CONDITIONAL

We use the first conditional to talk about likely situations/actions.

CONDITIONAL CLAUSE	MAIN CLAUSE/RESULT
If + present simple	**Will* + infinitive**
If *we* ***go*** *by bus,*	*we**'ll** get there on time.*
If *we* ***win*** *the basketball match this afternoon,*	*we**'ll** be so happy.*

*We can also use modal verbs with future meanings (*shall, should, can, could, may, might*) in first conditional sentences.
If we collect enough money, we ***can*** *buy our teacher a good present.*

SECOND CONDITIONAL

We use the second conditional to talk about unlikely situations/actions. We can also use it to imagine situations in the present or future.

CONDITIONAL CLAUSE	MAIN CLAUSE/RESULT
If + past simple	**Would* + infinitive**
If *we* ***went*** *by bike,*	*we**'d get** there very late.*
If *I* ***had*** *a lot of money,*	*I**'d** buy a new smartphone.*

*We can also use other modal verbs (*should, might, could*) in second conditional sentences.
If I knew how to snowboard, I ***could*** *enter the competition.*

We can use *were* instead of *was* in the conditional clause.
If I ***were/was*** *you, I'd look for a new hobby.*
If my sister ***were/was*** *a nurse, all her patients would love her.*

Note: Conditional (*if*) clauses can come before or after the main clause in the first and second conditional. When the conditional clause comes before the main clause, it is followed by a comma.

I'll tell Matt to call you	*if I see him.*
If I see Matt,	*I'll tell him to call you.*
We'd go for a bike ride	*if it was sunny.*
If it was sunny,	*we'd go for a bike ride.*

PRACTICE

1 Join the beginnings and endings of these sentences to make zero, first and second conditional sentences.

1 If I have time,
2 If I had more time
3 If you mix blue and yellow
4 You wouldn't fall asleep in class
5 She would be really angry
6 If he phones her,
7 If my computer breaks down again
8 If I had enough money

a you get green.
b she refuses to speak to him.
c if she knew the truth.
d I'll phone you.
e I'll have to buy a new one.
f I'd buy a new car.
g I'd cycle to college every morning.
h if you went to bed earlier.

2 Make second conditional sentences.

1 I'd like to do the high jump, but I'm not very tall.
If I were/was taller, I'd do the high jump.
2 She can't study in Canada because she doesn't speak English.
If ....
3 I haven't got enough free time to learn to play a musical instrument.
If ....
4 I'd like to buy a laptop, but I haven't got enough money.
If ....
5 We all want to watch the new comedy programme on TV, but we aren't at home this evening.
If ....

WHEN

We use *when* to talk about things that will happen at a particular time.
***When** I get home this evening, I'll have a shower.*

IF

We use *if* for things that may or may not happen, or to say what happens if something else happens.
***If** I finish work early, I'll go swimming.*

UNLESS

Unless means the same as 'if not'.
***Unless** I get home early, I won't go swimming.* (If I do not get home early, I won't go swimming.)
***Unless** I won a lot of money, I wouldn't be able to go on that expensive cruise.*

PRACTICE

1 Complete these sentences with *if*, *when* or *unless*.

1. .... you take me to the station, I'll have to walk.
2. We'll fail the exam .... we revise.
3. .... we hurry, we'll get there in time.
4. Let's watch the late film .... you are not too tired.
5. In some countries, you can't drive .... you are over 18.
6. .... I'm sad, I usually talk to my friends.
7. .... you're not feeling better tomorrow, you should go to the doctor.
8. I'll watch some TV .... I get home tonight.

UNIT 11

RELATIVE CLAUSES

Relative clauses are used to link different pieces of information in one sentence.
The film Titanic, ***which made Leonardo di Caprio famous**, was made in 1997.*

We use relative clauses to avoid short, simple sentences like this:
The film Titanic *was made in 1997. It made Leonardo di Caprio famous.*

We use these relative pronouns to introduce relative clauses:

- *who* refers to people
- *which* refers to things
- *that* can refer to people or things
- *whose* refers to possession or relationships
  *The student **whose** brother was on TV is in my class.*
- *where* refers to places
  *The village **where** I live is on the outskirts of the city.*
- *when* refers to times
  *The time **when** I was my happiest was my years at school.*
- *why* refers to reasons or explanations
  *The reason **why** I got up so early is that I couldn't sleep.*

DEFINING RELATIVE CLAUSES

These clauses give us essential information which tells us exactly which person or thing we are referring to.
*The actor **who plays Luke Skywalker** is Mark Hamill.*

Without the information in the relative clause, we would not know which actor we are talking about.
✗ ~~*The actor is Mark Hamill.*~~

NON-DEFINING RELATIVE CLAUSES

These clauses give us extra, non-essential information. The sentence still makes sense without this relative clause.
*The first Star Wars film, **which was directed by George Lucas**, came out in 1977.*
✓ *The first Star Wars film came out in 1977.*

DEFINING CLAUSES	NON-DEFINING CLAUSES
Do not have commas.	Have commas – they are like pauses in spoken English.
We use these relative pronouns: *who, which, whose, where, when, why, that.*	We use these relative pronouns: *who, which, whose, where, when, why.*
That can be used instead of *who* or *which*.	Don't use *that*.
Who, which or *that* can be left out if they are the object of the clause.	Relative pronouns cannot be left out.

PRACTICE

1 **Complete the sentences with a relative pronoun. Sometimes there may be more than one possible answer.**

1 Ben's the person .... bike was stolen last week.
2 That's the dog .... tried to bite me.
3 She doesn't like people .... are unfriendly.
4 That's the house .... they want to live.
5 Where are the keys .... were on the kitchen table?
6 We're moving to a quiet place .... we can't hear the traffic.
7 The company .... David works for makes computers.
8 I read a lot of books .... I was ill at home.

2 **Choose the sentence in exercise 1 where it is possible to leave out the relative pronoun.**

3 **Rewrite each pair of sentences as one sentence using relative clauses.**

1 The music was by Mozart. Gisela was playing the music last night.
The music which ....
2 The violin was not hers. Gisela was playing the violin in the concert.
The violin that ....
3 James is Gisela's music teacher. Gisela borrowed James' violin.
James, ...
4 We've just listened to Gisela's latest recording. Gisela's recording is number 1 in the classical charts.
We've just listened ....
5 Gisela's mother is very proud of her. Gisela's mother was in the audience tonight.
Gisela's mother, ...
6 Tomorrow, Gisela is going back to Vienna. Gisela goes to music school in Vienna.
Tomorrow, Gisela is ....

HAVE/GET SOMETHING DONE

We use *have something done* to talk about things we ask other people to do for us; things that we do not want to or cannot do ourselves.
I'm ***having my teeth checked*** *tomorrow.*

We can also use *get something done*. It has the same meaning but is more informal.
I'm ***getting my hair cut*** *tomorrow.*

Notice the order of words: *have + object + past participle*.
A different word order changes the meaning.
She ***has her hair cut****.* (Someone does it for her.)
She has cut her hair. (She did it herself recently.)

We can use *have something done* in any tense.
I ***(don't) have my hair cut*** *every week.*
*We****'re (not) having our flat decorated****.*
We ***had (didn't have) our computer repaired*** *yesterday.*
*We****'ll have our car washed*** *tomorrow.*

PRACTICE

1 **Put the words in order to make sentences.**

1 you / your / had / cut? / ~~have~~ / hair
Have ....
2 bedroom / have / painted / ~~I~~ / might / my / blue.
I ....
3 fixed / had / Michael / yet? / bike / his / ~~has~~
Has ....
4 get / teeth / ~~I~~ / every / my / months. / polished / six
I ....
5 checked / your / have / computer / viruses. / should / ~~you~~ / for
You ....

2 **Write sentences with *have something done*. Use the words given and the tense in brackets.**

1 he / his computer / repair (present perfect simple)
....
2 she / her car / wash / yesterday (past simple)
....
3 he / his shoes / clean (present perfect simple)
....
4 they / their house / paint (present continuous)
....
5 he / his tooth / take out / this morning (past simple)
....
6 she / her eyes / test / tomorrow (*will*)
....

UNIT 12

MODALS OF PERMISSION

We use *can* and *could* to ask for and give permission.
***Can** I sit here?*
*You **can** borrow my motorbike.*
***Can** I give you some advice?*
***Could** I open the window?*

We also use *may* and *could* to ask for and give permission, but *can* is more common.

CAN/CAN'T

We can also use *can/can't* to express permission or lack of permission.
*You **can leave** any time you like.*
*You **can't bring** animals in here.*
***Can** I **use** your phone, please?*
Note: We can also use *can't* for prohibition.
*You **can't do** that now!*

PRACTICE

1 Choose the correct options to complete the sentences.

1 Why *may/can't* we use our iPads in the library?
2 Students *can/mustn't* use their mobile phones in the lunch break, but they must talk quietly.
3 Dad, why *can/can't* we watch the football match on TV tonight?
4 We *must/can't* surf the internet in the office during working hours.
5 The sign over there says, 'Customers *may not/couldn't* smoke in the restaurant.'
6 *Could/Must* I have another piece of chocolate cake?

MAKE/LET

We use *let* to mean 'allow' or 'give permission'.
*I **let** my best friend use my car.*
*The office manager **let** us leave early.*

Let can also mean 'make something possible'.
*You can buy a travel card which **lets** you buy cheaper tickets.*

However, *Let's* + infinitive is often used to make a suggestion.
***Let's go** out tonight.*

We use *make* to force someone to do something that he or she doesn't want to do.
*His teacher **made** him finish his project.*

We can also use *make* with the meaning 'cause something to happen'.
*That film **made** me laugh so much!*
*The delayed flight **made** us late.*

PRACTICE

1 Complete the sentences with *make* or *let* in the correct form.

1 My mother used to ________ me tidy my bedroom.
2 The teacher doesn't ________ the students use their mobile phones in lessons.
3 Tom's father doesn't ________ him borrow his car.
4 The police officer ________ the teenagers pick up the rubbish they had left on the beach.
5 My parents never ________ me stay out late when I was a teenager.
6 I might ________ you borrow my laptop if you ask me nicely.

MIGHT BE ABLE TO, WILL BE ABLE TO

Be able to is not a modal verb, but we often use it like *can* and *could*, which are modal auxiliary verbs, to express ability.
*I **have been able to** read and write since I was five.* (present perfect)
*You **will be able to** speak very good English very soon.* (future simple)
*I **might be able to** learn Japanese next year.* (There is a possibility.)

COULD/WAS ABLE TO

We use *could* or *was/were able to* to talk about a general ability in the past.
*I **could/was able to** run long distances.*
*I **could/was able to** swim quite fast.*

We only use *was/were able to* when we talk about a specific success in the past.
*The test to become a fighter pilot was so difficult that only a few airmen **were able to** pass it.* (NOT ~~*could pass it*~~)

PRACTICE

1 Choose the correct words to complete the sentences. More than one answer may be possible.

1 That famous composer ________ write little pieces of music when she was four. (general ability)
   a can b could
   c was able to d is able to
2 We ________ reach the top of the mountain before lunch yesterday. (specific success in the past)
   a can b could
   c were able to d aren't able to
3 He ________ swim when he was five. (inability in the past)
   a can't b couldn't
   c wasn't able to d isn't able to

UNIT 13

GERUNDS VS INFINITIVES

VERBS FOLLOWED BY THE INFINITIVE WITH *TO* OR THE GERUND (-ING)

Some verbs are always followed by an infinitive (*to* + verb).
When I was 15, I ***decided to become*** *a professional musician.*

Others are always followed by the gerund (*-ing*) form of the verb.
Mike ***kept falling*** *asleep during the lesson.*

There are some verbs which can be followed by either an infinitive with *to* or the *-ing* form.

Unfortunately, there are no rules to help you work out whether verbs are followed by the infinitive with *to* or the *-ing* form, or either, so you need to learn them.

Verbs followed by the infinitive with *to*

afford agree arrange attempt choose decide
expect help hope intend learn manage offer
plan promise refuse seem want would like

Verbs followed by the gerund (*-ing*)

admit avoid can't stand* consider dislike*
don't mind* enjoy* fancy* feel like finish
give up imagine mind miss postpone practise
prevent put off suggest

Note: The verbs marked * all express likes or dislikes.

Verbs followed by the infinitive with *to* or *-ing* with no difference in meaning

begin continue intend start

Verbs followed by the infinitive with *to* or *-ing* with little difference in meaning

hate like love prefer

There is a small difference in meaning between the two forms.

- *-ing* form: the action or experience is more important.
  He ***likes baking*** *cakes.*
- infinitive form with *to*: result of the action is more important, or to describe a habit/something we prefer.
  He ***likes to bake*** *cakes for special occasions.*

The *-ing* form is more common after *hate* and *love*.
I ***hate playing*** *ball sports. I* ***love doing*** *gymnastics.*

VERBS FOLLOWED BY THE INFINITIVE WITH *TO* OR *-ING* WHERE THERE IS A CLEAR DIFFERENCE IN MEANING

	INFINITIVE WITH TO	-ING
forget	*I* ***forgot to say*** *thank you.* (I didn't say thank you.)	*I* ***forgot saying*** *that.* (I have no memory of this.)
go on	*He* ***went on to talk*** *about his childhood.* (This was the next thing he talked about.)	*He* ***went on talking***. (He continued talking.)
remember	*I* ***remembered to lock*** *the door.* (I did something I had to do.)	*I* ***remember locking*** *the door.* (I have a memory of this.)
stop	*Let's* ***stop to buy*** *flowers.* (in order to do something)	*Let's* ***stop buying*** *flowers.* (not continue)
try	*I* ***tried to learn*** *Japanese, but it was too difficult, so I stopped.* (try something and not succeed)	*I* ***tried eating*** *spinach, but I didn't like it.* (try something and find out what it's like)

In negative sentences, we put *not* after the first verb.
He's ***decided not to go*** *to university next year.*
She ***considered not going*** *away for the weekend.* (But now she is going.)

In sentences which include an object, we put the object after the first verb.
I ***helped my friend to do*** *his homework.*
We should ***stop people using*** *their phones while they're driving.*

PRACTICE

1 **Complete the conversation with the correct form of the verbs in brackets.**

A: It's really hot here, isn't it? Do you fancy [1] .... (go) for a swim?
B: Yes, I'd love [2] .... (have) a swim.
A: Can I suggest [3] .... (go) this afternoon?
B: I'd planned [4] .... (go) to the cinema this afternoon, but I don't mind [5] .... (do) that tomorrow instead.
A: I can't imagine [6] .... (live) in a hot country all the time.
B: I'm sure you'd manage [7] .... (have) a nice time.
A: Maybe I'd get used to it. I certainly enjoy [8] .... (spend) my summer holidays here.

2 **Choose the pairs of sentences which have the same meanings.**

1 **a** The teacher continued to talk even though the bell had rung for the end of class.
b The teacher continued talking even though the bell had rung for the end of class.
2 **a** I began to learn German two years ago.
b I began learning German two years ago.
3 **a** Ben stopped to phone his parents.
b Ben stopped phoning his parents.
4 **a** I prefer to watch football than to play it.
b I prefer watching football to playing it.
5 **a** I like to watch the sunrise.
b I like watching the sunrise.
6 **a** They went on to tell us about their holiday.
b They went on telling us about their holiday.

GERUNDS AFTER PREPOSITIONS

We use the gerund when a verb comes after a preposition.
Can you eat ***without opening*** *your mouth?*
She is not very good ***at drawing****.*
We arrived in Athens ***after travelling*** *all day.*
There's no point ***in waiting*** *any longer.*
Do you think you will ***give up smoking****?*
She keeps ***on asking*** *me for help.*

GERUNDS WHEN THE VERB IS THE SUBJECT

We use the gerund when the verb is the subject of a sentence.
Eating *too much sugar is bad for you.*
Flying *makes me very nervous.*

GERUNDS OR INFINITIVES WITH *TO* AFTER CERTAIN ADJECTIVES

We use the gerund or the infinitive with *to* after certain adjectives.
It's ***good to meet*** *you.*
It's ***great seeing*** *you again.*

PRACTICE

1 **Complete the sentences with the correct form of the verbs in brackets.**

1 It's really nice .... (be) with you.
2 .... (swim) in the sea can be dangerous.
3 .... (smoke) kills lots of people.
4 Can you run for hours without .... (stop)?
5 He went to bed after .... (watch) the film.

UNIT 14

COMPOUND ADJECTIVES

We can join two or more words to form a new adjective (compound adjective). These words can be nouns, adjectives, past participles or adverbs. Compound adjectives are usually joined by a hyphen (-).

She has a ***part-time*** *job.* (adjective + noun)

That criminal was really ***cold-blooded****.* (adjective + noun)

The room was ***brightly lit****.* (adverb + participle)

I think you are very ***open-minded*** *about things.* (adjective + adjective)

PRACTICE

1 Put the words in order to make sentences.

1. stuck / vehicle. / behind / were / a / slow-moving / we

   ....

2. made / last-minute / trains. / we / a / change / to / decision

   ....

3. he / managed / finally / a / to / full-time / get / job.

   ....

4. very / the / badly behaved. / were / teenagers

   ....

5. was / middle-aged / thief / with / black / a / man / hair. / short / the

   ....

IRREGULAR VERB LIST

VERB	PAST SIMPLE	PAST PARTICIPLE
be	was/were	been
beat	beat	beaten
become	became	become
begin	began	begun
bend	bent	bent
bite	bit	bitten
bleed	bled	bled
blow	blew	blown
break	broke	broken
bring	brought	brought
build	built	built
burn	burnt/burned	burnt/burned
buy	bought	bought
catch	caught	caught
choose	chose	chosen
come	came	come
cost	cost	cost
cut	cut	cut
deal	dealt	dealt
dig	dug	dug
do	did	done
draw	drew	drawn
dream	dreamt/dreamed	dreamt/dreamed
drink	drank	drunk
drive	drove	driven
eat	ate	eaten
fall	fell	fallen
feed	fed	fed
feel	felt	felt
fight	fought	fought
find	found	found
fly	flew	flown
forbid	forbade	forbidden
forget	forgot	forgotten
forgive	forgave	forgiven
freeze	froze	frozen
get	got	got
give	gave	given
go	went	gone
grow	grew	grown
hang	hung	hung
have	had	had
hear	heard	heard
hide	hid	hidden
hit	hit	hit
hold	held	held
hurt	hurt	hurt
keep	kept	kept
kneel	knelt	knelt
know	knew	known
lay	laid	laid
lead	led	led
learn	learnt/learned	learnt/learned
leave	left	left

VERB	PAST SIMPLE	PAST PARTICIPLE
lend	lent	lent
let	let	let
lie	lay	lain
light	lit	lit
lose	lost	lost
make	made	made
mean	meant	meant
meet	met	met
pay	paid	paid
put	put	put
read	read	read
ride	rode	ridden
ring	rang	rung
rise	rose	risen
run	ran	run
say	said	said
see	saw	seen
sell	sold	sold
send	sent	sent
set	set	set
sew	sewed	sewn
shake	shook	shaken
shine	shone	shone
shoot	shot	shot
show	showed	shown
shut	shut	shut
sing	sang	sung
sink	sank	sunk
sit	sat	sat
sleep	slept	slept
smell	smelt/smelled	smelt/smelled
speak	spoke	spoken
spell	spelt/spelled	spelt/spelled
spend	spent	spent
spill	spilt/spilled	spilt/spilled
spoil	spoilt/spoiled	spoilt/spoiled
stand	stood	stood
steal	stole	stolen
stick	stuck	stuck
strike	struck	struck
sweep	swept	swept
swim	swam	swum
swing	swung	swung
take	took	taken
teach	taught	taught
tear	tore	torn
tell	told	told
think	thought	thought
throw	threw	thrown
understand	understood	understood
wake	woke	woken
wear	wore	worn
win	won	won
write	wrote	written

PHRASAL VERB BANK

A phrasal verb is a verb with two or three parts. The meaning of the verb is sometimes different from the meaning of its separate parts. Phrasal verbs can combine verbs with prepositions or adverbs.
This section focuses on phrasal verbs related to four topics:
relationships, **travel**, **communication** and **daily routines**.

RELATIONSHIPS

1 Match the phrasal verbs with the definitions below.

bring up	get on with	get together
go out with	look after	split up

1 .... = take care of someone
2 .... = have a friendly relationship with someone
3 .... = look after children until they are adults
4 .... = end a relationship
5 .... = meet
6 .... = have a romantic relationship with someone

2 Choose the correct option to complete the sentences.

1 I *get on/get together* with my friends every weekend to play football.
2 I *split up/get on* with everyone in my family. Everyone's very friendly.
3 My grandparents *brought up/went out* four children in a very small house.
4 I need to *look after/bring up* my flatmate's dog when she goes on holiday.
5 The band *got together/split up* because they didn't enjoy playing together any more.

3 Write a sentence using each of the phrasal verbs.

TRAVEL

1 Match the phrasal verbs with the definitions below.

break down	check in	get back
set off	take off	turn up

1 .... = when a plane leaves the ground
2 .... = return
3 .... = leave on a journey
4 .... = when something (e.g. a car or computer) stops working
5 .... = arrive, come
6 .... = arrive at an airport as a passenger, or a hotel as a guest

2 Complete the sentences with the past simple form of the phrasal verbs in the box in exercise 1.

1 We .... for the airport at seven o'clock in the morning.
2 After we had been driving for 10 minutes, our car ...., so my friend called a garage. Five minutes later, a mechanic .... and fixed the problem.
3 When we got to the airport, we parked the car and .... at the departures desk.
4 Half an hour later, our plane .... and our holiday began!
5 When we .... home a week later, we felt very relaxed.

3 Write a sentence using each of the phrasal verbs.

COMMUNICATION

1 **Match the phrasal verbs with the definitions below.**

call (someone) back fill in something hang up ring up (someone) switch (something) off

1 .... = end a phone conversation
2 .... = turn off something (e.g. computer)
3 .... = return a phone call
4 .... = complete a form
5 .... = make a phone call

2 **Choose the correct option to complete the sentences.**

My internet stopped working yesterday, so I [1]*switched off/switched it off* and [2]*called back/rang up* a help line. But the line was busy so I [3]*filled in/hung up*. I waited 10 minutes and then [4]*rang up/called back*. The person who answered the phone asked me to [5]*ring up/fill in* an online form, and gave me another number to call. In 10 minutes, my internet was working again!

3 **Write a sentence using each of the phrasal verbs.**

DAILY ROUTINES

1 **Match the phrasal verbs with the definitions below.**

get up pick (someone) up put (something) on tidy up wake (someone) up

1 .... = stop (someone) sleeping
2 .... = get out of bed
3 .... = collect someone in a car
4 .... = make a place look clean
5 .... = put clothes on your body

2 **Complete the sentences with the correct form of the phrasal verbs in the box in exercise 1. Add any other words you need.**

My flatmate and I have very different routines. Every morning, I [1] .... at seven o'clock as I need to be at the office at eight and my colleague [2] .... in her car at 7.30. James works in a restaurant and usually doesn't [3] .... until nine o'clock and sometimes doesn't [4] .... his clothes until midday! He likes the flat to be clean, so he always [5] .... the living room and kitchen before he goes to work.

3 **Write a sentence using each of the phrasal verbs.**

WRITING BANK

MAKING YOUR WRITING MORE INTERESTING

To make a sentence more interesting, we can add more details.

1 **Look at how the underlined words add information. Match the new information (1–8) with the descriptions (a–h).**

- *I went to Spain.*
  [1]Last year, I went to Spain, [2]which is my favourite country.
- *I like warm weather.*
  I like warm weather, [3]but I don't like cold weather.
- *I've got an exam tomorrow.*
  I've got an [4]important exam tomorrow, [5]so I have to wake up early.
- *George was happy.*
  George was [6]really happy [7]because it was his birthday.
- *I read the letter.*
- I read the letter [8]slowly and carefully.

a adding a contrasting idea ___3___
b giving a reason ______
c saying when something happened ______
d giving the result of an action ______
e using a relative clause to give extra information ______
f using an adjective to describe something ______
g using an adverb to make an adjective stronger ______
h using adverbs to describe how something happens ______

2 **Complete the table with the words and phrases from the box.**

and beautiful because but completely delicious easily later that day loudly modern quickly so the next day this morning wonderful yesterday

ADJECTIVES	ADVERBS	LINKING WORDS	TIME EXPRESSIONS

3 **Make the sentences more interesting. Use the word and phrases in the box. Can you think of any other words to use?**

but early the next morning large really suddenly

1 It ______ started to rain.
2 I called Max, ______ he didn't answer his phone.
3 We set out for London ______ .
4 I ordered a cup of coffee and a ______ slice of cake.
5 The film was ______ boring!

4 **Join the two parts of the sentences with *and*, *but*, *so* or *because*.**

we didn't play tennis – the weather was bad
We didn't play tennis because the weather was bad.

1 I was very tired – I went straight to bed
______

2 we all went to the party – everyone had a great time
______

3 Paul wanted to come with us – he couldn't
______

4 we all laughed – it was so funny
______

WRITING PART 1: AN EMAIL

1 **Read the exam task. What information should you include in the email?**

Read this email from your English-speaking friend Sam, and the notes you have made.

From: Sam
Subject: Sports tickets!

Reply Forward

Hi,

Guess what? Do you remember the sports competition I entered last month? They announced the results yesterday, and I've won two tickets to go and watch an international sports event! — *Amazing!*

Would you like to come to the event with me? We can choose to go in July or August. — *Yes – tell Sam when you can make it.*

We have to book which sport we want to see in advance. There are football and basketball matches. Which sport do you prefer to watch? — *Tell Sam.*

They sell lots of souvenirs at the stadium. What do you think we should buy? — *Suggest …*

Bye for now,

Sam

Write your **email** to Sam, using **all** the **notes**.

MODEL ANSWER

Use an informal phrase to start the email.

Hi Sam,

Remember you are replying to Sam's email.

Thanks for your email. That's amazing news about the competition! Well done!

Yes, I love sport, so it would be incredible to go to a big sports event with you. I can go with you in July, but I can't go in August because I'm on holiday then.

This answers the question about when you can or can't make it, and gives a reason.

I'm a big football fan, so I'd love to see an international football match. It would be brilliant to see some of my favourite heroes in action.

This answers the question 'Which sport do you prefer to watch?'

Why don't we buy football shirts as souvenirs? We can wear them at the match!

See you soon,

Tom

Use an informal phrase at the end.

This is a suggestion.

KEY LANGUAGE AND IDEAS FOR EMAILS

Opening an email:
Hi Hi, Tom Hi, there Hello

Closing an email:
Love, See you soon, Take care, Bye

Responding to an email:
Thanks for your email. It's good to hear from you.

Responding to good news:
That's amazing news! I'm so happy for you! Wow! How exciting! Well done!

Responding to bad news:
I'm sorry to hear about …

Making a suggestion:
Why don't you/we … ? You/We could … If I were you, I'd … Make sure you …

Making an offer or promise:
I could … if you like. Would you like me to … ? I can … if you want.

Making a request:
Could you … ? Can you … ? Would you mind … -ing?

Giving good or bad news:
You'll be pleased to hear that … I'm afraid … Guess what … ? I'm sorry, but …

Linking words and phrases:
and but so because also as well

Informal language:
- contractions: *I'm you're he's*
- informal words and phrases: *awesome great keep in touch take care I guess …*
- exclamation marks to show emotion: *That's great news! Wow!*

2 **Join the beginnings and endings of these sentences. Then decide if each sentence is a suggestion (*S*), an offer (*O*), a promise (*P*) or a request (*R*).**

1	Could you	**a**	I'd definitely accept the job.
2	If I were you,	**b**	some useful addresses if you want.
3	I can send you	**c**	be there to help on the day.
4	Don't worry, I'll	**d**	let me know what time you're arriving?

3 **Correct the underlined mistakes in the sentences giving good or bad news. Use the *Key language and ideas* box to check your answers.**

1 <u>I afraid</u> I won't be able to come to your party.
2 <u>Guess that where</u> I'm going next week.
3 <u>I'm sorry</u>, and Dan won't be here when you visit.
4 <u>You'll be pleased hear</u> that I've now finished all my exams!

4 **Choose the correct linking words to complete the sentences.**

1 I finish work at six o'clock, *because/so* I can meet you at 6.30.
2 My sister Martha is *also/as well* coming home next weekend.
3 I'm not very good at singing, *because/but* I still enjoy it.
4 I'm a bit disappointed *because/so* my exam results weren't brilliant.
5 I'll find the document *also/and* send it to you in an email.

5 **Read the exam task. What information must you include in your email?**

Great idea!

From: Logan
Subject: Summer barbecue

Reply Forward

Hi,

The weather forecast looks good next weekend, so my flatmates and I are having a barbecue to celebrate the beginning of summer. Would you like to come? — *Yes – say which day.*

I'd like to invite everyone in our English class. What kind of food do you think our classmates would like to eat at a barbecue? — *Tell Logan.*

I'd also like everyone to play a sport after we eat. What sport do you think would be best for our classmates? — *Suggest …*

See you soon,

Logan

6 **Before you write your email, complete the table with ideas.**

Paragraph 1 (respond to the invitation)	
Paragraph 2 (suggest some food)	
Paragraph 3 (suggest a sport and explain why)	
Useful phrases I can use	

7 **Write your email using your notes from exercise 6. Write about 100 words.**

8 **Check your email and make changes if necessary.**

- ☐ Have you answered all the questions and included all the necessary information?
- ☐ Have you used a suitable phrase to open and close your email?
- ☐ Have you tried to make your writing more interesting by adding details?
- ☐ Have you used informal language?
- ☐ Have you used linking words and phrases?
- ☐ Have you used the correct number of words?

WRITING PART 2: AN ARTICLE

1 **Read the exam task. What should your article be about? What information should it include?**

Articles wanted!

My favourite city

What's your favourite city?

What's so special about this city?

What city would you love to travel to in the future?

Tell us what you think!

Write an article answering these questions and we will publish the most interesting ones on our website.

2 **Choose the best introductory sentence in italics for each opening paragraph.**

1 *There are many benefits to keeping fit./I don't really do enough exercise.* Doing regular exercise is good for your heart, and it helps you to lose weight. It can also improve your mood, especially if you are feeling tired or unhappy.

2 *Some older people are not used to the internet./The internet has changed people's lives in many ways.* People can now go online to do their shopping and book restaurants and holidays. Students also have access to lots of information that was difficult to find before the internet.

3 *Teaching is a very difficult job./I would like to become a teacher.* Students are not always interested in learning, and teachers have to work hard to encourage their students to study. Also, there are sometimes problems with bad behaviour from students.

MODEL ANSWER

The first paragraph answers the first question and gives a reason.

My favourite city is Paris because it is so lively and interesting. It is also full of surprises.

Adjectives make the article more interesting to read.

The second paragraph gives more details and answers the second question in the task.

Paris is a city of variety. It has many beautiful old buildings, but it also feels modern. You can visit expensive designer shops or small, traditional markets. There are hundreds of restaurants which serve French food, or different food from around the world. You can meet all kinds of people, too. There is something for everyone.

The third paragraph is about a city the writer would like to go to in the future.

I would love to travel to New York in the future because I've seen the city in so many films, and I would love to visit it in real life.

KEY LANGUAGE AND IDEAS FOR ARTICLES

Use adjectives for describing people and things:
attractive brave calm cheerful convenient

Use linking words and phrases:
although and as well because but so

Use an introductory sentence for each paragraph:
Paris is a city of variety. A good job should be creative. Photography is a great hobby.

Give your opinion:
I think … It seems to me that … I would say that …

3 Complete the table with the adjectives in the box. Can you add any more adjectives?

amusing delicious freezing frightening old-fashioned peaceful quiet stormy tasty tight

CLOTHES	FILMS	FOOD	COUNTRYSIDE	WEATHER

4 Read the exam task. What should your article be about? What should it include?

Articles wanted!

My perfect job

What makes the perfect job?

Is it being creative, travelling, meeting people, or something else?

How important is it to earn a lot of money?

Tell us what you think!

Write an article answering these questions and we will publish the most interesting articles on our website.

5 Before you write your article, complete the table with ideas.

Paragraph 1 (answer the first question)	
Paragraph 2 (give more details)	
Paragraph 3 (give your opinion about money)	
Useful phrases I can use	

6 Write your article using your notes from exercise 5. Write about 100 words.

7 Check your article and make changes if necessary.

- ☐ Have you answered all the questions and included all the necessary information?
- ☐ Have you used adjectives to make your article interesting to read?
- ☐ Have you expressed a personal opinion?
- ☐ Have you used linking words and phrases?
- ☐ Have you used the correct number of words?

WRITING PART 2: A STORY

1 **Read the exam task. Which is the best way to continue the story (1, 2 or 3)? Why?**

- Your English teacher has asked you to write a story.
- Your story must begin with this sentence:
  I opened the letter from my cousins in Brazil.

1 I have three cousins who live in Brazil, and I get on very well with them. They are all very keen on football.

2 They said they were coming to visit me, and they were arriving on the 15th – today!

3 I think Brazil is a really interesting country, and I would love to go there one day. There are lots of amazing wild animals there.

MODEL ANSWER

The first paragraph gives background to the story.

I opened the letter from my cousins in Brazil. They said they were coming to visit me, and they were arriving on the 15th – today!

I was really excited. First, I cleaned everything in the flat. Then I went to the supermarket to buy food. After that, I made a cake to make them feel welcome. By evening, I was completely exhausted. I picked up the letter again to check the time of their flight, and that's when I noticed the date. They were arriving on 15th July, but today was 15th June!

We had a wonderful time together in July, and all laughed about the mistake I had made!

The second paragraph gives the main events of the story.

Time expressions make the order of events clear.

Adjectives and adverbs make the story more interesting.

The last paragraph ends the story.

KEY LANGUAGE AND IDEAS FOR STORIES

Use past simple verbs for the main events:
I went to a restaurant. *I found a letter.*

Use past continuous verbs for longer actions in the past:
I was waiting for the bus. *The sun was shining.*

Use past perfect verbs for background events:
Unfortunately, I had forgotten my purse.

Time expressions:
First *then* *later* *the next day* *finally …*

Adjectives to describe people:
friendly *kind* *tall*

Adjectives to describe places:
busy *quiet* *modern*

Adjectives to describe feelings:
excited *angry* *delighted*

Adverbs to describe how someone does something:
quickly *slowly* *carefully*

Adverbs to comment on what happened:
luckily *fortunately* *unfortunately*

2 **Complete the sentences with the correct form of the verbs in brackets. Use the past simple, past continuous or past perfect.**

1 I packed my bags and then .... (call) a taxi to take me to the airport.
2 Sara .... (wait) for me when I got to the restaurant.
3 I could finally relax because I .... (pass) all my exams!
4 I found an old key while I .... (walk) along the beach.
5 James was late because he .... (forget) to set his alarm.
6 I opened the door and then quickly .... (close) it again.

3 **Choose the correct time expressions to complete the sentences.**

I was really scared when my car broke down near the forest. [1]*Then/First,* I tried starting the car, but that didn't work. [2]*Finally/Then,* I tried to call a friend, but I had no signal on my phone. [3]*Next/After,* I decided to wait for another car so I could ask for help. [4]*An hour later/Before an hour,* I was still sitting there! Suddenly, I heard the sound of another car. [5]*Finally/After,* someone came to help me and I got home safely.

4 **Complete the sentences with adjectives in the box.**

curly	disappointed	entertaining
messy	smart	spicy

1 She introduced me to a tall young man with .... hair.
2 She was wearing a very nice, ... jacket and skirt.
3 He cooked some delicious, ... food for us.
4 The show was fun and very ....
5 The room was .... and not very clean.
6 I was very .... when she didn't call me.

5 **Read the exam task. Before you write your story, complete the table with ideas.**

- Your English teacher has asked you to write a story.
- Your story must begin with this sentence:
  We had decided to spend the day at the zoo.
- Write your **story** in about **100** words.

Paragraph 1 (the background to the story)
Paragraph 2 (the main events)
Paragraph 3 (the ending)
Language I can use

6 **Write your story using your notes from exercise 5.**

7 **Check your story and make changes if necessary.**

☐ Does your story have a clear beginning, middle and ending?
☐ Have you used verbs in the past simple, past continuous and past perfect?
☐ Have you used time expressions to order the events?
☐ Have you used adjectives and adverbs to make your story interesting?
☐ Have you used the correct number of words?

SPEAKING BANK

SPEAKING PART 1

1 127 **Listen to Maria answering the questions. Does she use full sentences in her answers?**

1. What's your name?
2. What's your surname?
3. Where do you come from?
4. Do you work, or are you a student?

2 128 **Listen to Maria answering more questions. Notice how she adds extra information.**

1. What did you do yesterday evening?
2. Do you think that English will be useful to you in the future?
3. Tell us about a place you would like to visit in the future.
4. Can you describe your house or flat?
5. What do you enjoy doing in your free time?

KEY LANGUAGE AND IDEAS FOR PERSONAL QUESTIONS

Use frequency adverbs to talk about habits and routines:
I usually have breakfast …
I often watch TV …
Use the past simple and time expressions to talk about the past:
Yesterday, I watched …
Last weekend, I visited …
Use *be going to* and time expressions to talk about
future plans:
Next summer, I'm going to travel to …
Talk about future hopes:
I'd like to visit …
I want to get a job …
I hope I'll work …
Add extra information: *Actually and Also*
Add contrasting information: *but …*
Add reasons and results: *because so That's why …*
Add examples: *For example, … For instance, …*

3 128 **Complete Maria's answers with the words in the box. Listen again and check.**

also and because but for example often so

1. I .... watch films with my friends.
2. I hope I'll travel to different countries with my job, ... I'm sure I will need English.
3. I'd love to go to New York one day .... it looks like such an exciting city.
4. The kitchen is very small, ... the living room is quite big.
5. ...., it's got a balcony.
6. I'm quite into sport, ... I do quite a lot of sport in my free time.
7. ...., I sometimes go running in the evenings.

4 **Complete the table with the time expressions in the box.**

always last night last weekend next weekend sometimes tomorrow tonight usually when I was younger

PRESENT SIMPLE	PAST SIMPLE	BE GOING TO

5 129 **Match the questions (1–5) with the answers (a–e). Then choose one extra piece of information (f–j) to add to each answer. Listen and check.**

1 Tell us about your English teacher.
2 Would you like to live in a different country?
3 Can you tell us about your hometown?
4 How do you usually travel to university or work?
5 What did you do last weekend?

a My hometown is Barcelona. …
b His name's Mr Adams. …
c On Saturday I played football. …
d I wouldn't like to for long. …
e I usually catch the bus. …

f It's on the coast.
g We usually have a match every Saturday.
h I'd miss my family and friends at home.
i He's really funny.
j I prefer to walk.

6 129 **How does the student introduce extra information? Complete the sentences. Listen again and check.**

1 I like him .... he always makes our lessons interesting.
2 I'd like to visit different countries, ... the United States or maybe Australia.
3 There are lots of beautiful buildings .... are very famous.
4 I'd prefer to walk, ... it's too far for me.
5 We usually have a match every Saturday. .... , we didn't win last week.

7 **Practise answering the questions. Use a range of tenses, and add extra information.**

- What's your name?
- What's your surname?
- Where do you come from?
- Do you work, or are you a student?

- What did you do yesterday evening?
- Do you think that English will be useful to you in the future?
- Tell us about a place you would like to visit in the future.
- Can you describe your house or flat?

- What do you enjoy doing in your free time?
- Tell us about your English teacher.
- Would you like to live in a different country?
- Can you tell us about your hometown?
- How do you usually travel to school or work?
- What did you do last weekend?

SPEAKING PART 2

1 130 **Listen to Pablo describing a photo. What guesses does he make about the people?**

KEY LANGUAGE AND IDEAS FOR DESCRIBING A PHOTO

Say what you can see:
The picture shows … *I can see …* *There's a …*
There are some … *but you can't see …* *She's got …* *He has …*

Describe where things are in the picture:
at the front *in the background* *on the left* *on the right* *in the middle*
behind *in front of* *next to*

Use the present continuous:
He's wearing … *She's running …*

Talk about the people:
tall *long / short hair* *young* *old*

Talk about the place:
indoors *outdoors* *attractive* *comfortable* *safe*

Talk about the weather:
sunny *cloudy* *wet*

When you don't know the word for something:
It's a kind of … *It looks like a …*

Make guesses:
He looks like … *He seems to be …* *I guess he's probably …* *I think maybe …*
It might be …

2 **Look at the photo. Choose the correct words in italics to describe where the people are.**

1. There are two young women *at the front/in the background* of the photo.
2. There's an old man with a beard on the *right/left*.
3. There's a young couple on the *left/right*, further back in the bus.
4. You can see someone's legs *behind/next to* the old man, but you can't see their face.
5. *In the background/At the front*, you can see a man standing up.

3 131 **Look at the photo again. Complete the sentences with the correct present continuous form of the verbs in brackets. Listen and check.**

1. The photo shows some people who .... (travel) by bus.
2. The two women at the front of the photo .... (smile).
3. One woman .... (show) the other one something on her phone.
4. The older man on the right .... (look) forwards. Maybe he .... (think) about where to get off the bus.
5. In the background, there's a man .... (stand) up. He .... (talk) to another passenger.

4 **Look at the photo. Complete the sentences with words in the box.**

guess	looks	might	probably	seem

1 I think the people are .... father and son.
2 They .... be watching TV.
3 They're eating something from a box. It .... like pizza.
4 They .... to be quite relaxed.
5 I .... they're probably having a relaxing evening at home.

5 132 **Look at the photo in exercise 4 again. Practise describing it. Then listen and compare your ideas.**

6 Practise describing the photos on these pages.

SPEAKING PART 3

1 133 **Listen to two students doing the task below. Do they talk about all the options? Which present do they agree on?**

It is your friend's birthday soon, and you would like to buy her a present.
Here are some ideas.
Talk together about the different presents you could buy, and say which would be the most suitable.

KEY LANGUAGE AND IDEAS FOR DISCUSSING OPTIONS

Making suggestions:
What about … ? *What do you think about … ?* *Would … be a good idea?*

Responding to suggestions:
That's a great idea. *Yes, good idea.* *I'm not sure.*

Giving your opinion:
I think … *In my opinion, …*

Asking someone's opinion:
What do you think? *Do you agree?*

Agreeing:
That's true. *I agree (with you).* *Yes, I think you're right.* *OK, so …*

Disagreeing:
I don't agree with you because … *I'm not sure about that because …*

Considering alternatives:
… might be a better choice. *What if we … ?*

Reaching agreement:
It's time to decide. *Are you OK with that?* *We'll go for that one, then.*

2 133 **Complete the discussion with words in the box. Then listen again and check.**

agree	go	idea	OK	opinion	so	sure	think

A: What do you [1] .... about that idea?

B: I'm not [2] ....

A: It's difficult to choose a book for someone else.

B: I [3] .... with you. And I don't think flowers are a good idea, because they're a bit boring in my [4] ....

A: Would a T-shirt be a good [5] .... ? Most people wear T-shirts.

B: Well, I don't really like it when people buy me clothes, because I prefer to choose them myself.

A: OK, [6] .... not a T-shirt.

A: Maybe we should choose the cinema tickets. Are you [7] .... with that?

B: Yes, good idea. We'll [8] .... for that one, then.

3 **Join the beginnings and endings of these sentences.**

1	That's a	**a**	agree with you.
2	Do you	**b**	be a better choice.
3	I don't	**c**	to decide.
4	Flowers might	**d**	great idea.
5	It's time	**e**	you're right.
6	Yes, I think	**f**	agree?

4 134 **Work in pairs. Do the task below. Then listen and compare your ideas.**

Two friends are discussing how their class should celebrate the end of exams. Here are some ideas.
Talk together about the different ideas and say which would be the most fun.

SPEAKING PART 4

1 135 **Listen to two students answering the questions. Which things do they do?**

give reasons for their answers ......
interrupt each other ......
ask for each other's opinions ......
disagree with each other ......
use an expression to allow time to think about the answer ......

1 Who do you most enjoy buying presents for?
2 Which people in your family are the most difficult to choose presents for?
3 Do you like receiving money instead of presents?

KEY LANGUAGE AND IDEAS FOR DISCUSSING IDEAS

Talking about likes/dislikes/preferences:
I like/love + -ing *I prefer to …* *I enjoy …*

Talking about habits:
I sometimes/usually/always …

Giving your opinion:
I think … *In my opinion, …*

Asking someone's opinion:
What do you think? *Do you agree?*

Agreeing:
That's true. *I agree with you.* *Yes, I think you're right.*

Disagreeing:
I don't agree with you because …
I'm not sure about that because …

Giving yourself time to think:
That's an interesting question.
That's a difficult question. *Let me see.*

2 Choose the correct words to complete the sentences.

1 I enjoy *to buy/buying* things for my nephew.
2 It *sometimes is/is sometimes* nice to receive money.
3 I *usually get/get usually* money from three or four relatives.
4 I prefer *get/to get* money from people who don't know me very well.
5 I love *get/getting* presents.

3 Complete the dialogues with phrases in the box.

Do you agree?	That's an interesting question.	That's true.	What do you think?

A: I think surprise presents are the best presents. [1] ......
B: Yes, I do. I love opening presents when I have no idea what they are!
A: I think money is sometimes the most useful present to get.
B: [2] ...... Because then you can use it to buy something you really need.
A: In my opinion, men are the most difficult people to buy presents for. [3] ......
B: Yes, I think you're right. I never know what to buy for my dad or my uncle.
A: Do you think that some people spend too much money on presents?
B: Hmm. [4] ...... I think most people spend as much as they can afford.

4 Work in pairs. Discuss these questions together.

1 Would you like to have more social events with your English class?
2 Do you think watching sports events can be more fun than taking part?
3 Do you prefer cooking a meal for friends or eating out in a restaurant?

5 136 **Listen and compare your ideas.**

B1 PRELIMINARY EXAM INFORMATION

PART/TIMING	CONTENT	EXAM FOCUS
1 **Reading** 45 minutes	**Part 1** Five very short texts: signs and messages, postcards, notes, emails, labels, etc. followed by five three-option multiple choice questions. **Part 2** Five descriptions of people to match to eight short texts. **Part 3** Longer text with five four-option multiple choice questions. **Part 4** Gapped text where five sentences have been removed. Candidates must select the five correct sentences from a list of eight. **Part 5** Four-option multiple choice cloze text with six gaps. Candidates select the word which best fits each gap. **Part 6** An open cloze text consisting of a text with six gaps. Candidates think of a word which best suits each gap.	**Parts 1–4** and **Part 6**: Candidates are expected to read for the main message, global meaning, specific information, detailed comprehension, understanding of attitude, opinion and writer purpose and inference. **Part 5**: Candidates are expected to show understanding of vocabulary and grammar in a short text, and the lexico-structural patterns in the text.
2 **Writing** 45 minutes	**Part 1** An informal email. Candidates write an email of about 100 words in response to a text. **Part 2** An article or story. There is a choice of two questions. Candidates are provided with a clear context and topic. Candidates write about 100 words.	Candidates are mainly assessed on their ability to use and control a range of Preliminary-level language. Coherent organisation, spelling and punctuation are also assessed.
3 **Listening** approximately 30 minutes	**Part 1** Short monologues or dialogues with seven three-option multiple choice questions with pictures. **Part 2** Six short unrelated dialogues with six three-option multiple choice questions. **Part 3** Longer monologue. Candidates complete six sentences with information from the recording. **Part 4** Longer interview. Six three-option multiple choice questions.	Candidates are expected to identify the attitudes and opinions of speakers, and listen to identify gist, key information, specific information and detailed meaning, and to identify, understand and interpret meaning.
4 **Speaking** 12 minutes	**Part 1** A short conversation with the interlocutor. The interlocutor asks the candidates questions in turn, using standardised questions. **Part 2** An individual long turn for each candidate. A colour photograph is given to each candidate in turn and they talk about it for about a minute. Each photo has a different topic. **Part 3** A two-way conversation between candidates (visual stimulus with spoken instructions). The interlocutor sets up the activity. **Part 4** A discussion on topics related to the collaborative task in Part 3. The interlocutor asks the candidates the questions.	Candidates are expected to be able to ask and understand questions and make appropriate responses, and to talk freely on topics of personal interest.

STARTER

Page 8

VOCABULARY

Exercise 1

Suggested answers

A sport; snorkelling
B travel; trekking; holidays; walking
C art and crafts; pottery
D shopping; fashion

Exercise 2

A sports
B travel
C arts and crafts
D fashion

Exercise 3

Students' own answers.

Exercise 4

-ing

Exercise 5

Students' own answers.

Page 9

READING

Exercise 1

1 with
2 of
3 in
4 every
5 to
6 my

Exercise 2

Students' own answers.

VOCABULARY

Exercise 1

Students' own answers.

Exercise 2

1 eats out
2 get up
3 hangs out with
4 meet up
5 work out

Exercise 3

Students' own answers.

Page 10

GRAMMAR

Exercise 1

1 c
2 b
3 a

1 simple
2 continuous
3 continuous

Exercise 2

Present simple: Why do I get up so early?
Present continuous: So what am I writing?
1 do
2 does
3 be

Exercise 3

1 do; do
2 does; work
3 is; working
4 is; having

Exercise 4

Present simple: I don't go to bed late.
Present continuous: It's the autumn term now, and I'm not travelling.
1 doesn't
2 isn't

Exercise 5

1 write
2 do you earn
3 'm not earning
4 'm working
5 Do you interview
6 don't understand
7 is getting

Exercise 6

Students' own answers.

Page 11

VOCABULARY

Exercise 1

A chef; 3
B mechanic; 5
C gardener; 4
D police officer; 1
E sales assistant; 6
F hairdresser; 2

Exercise 2

He's a waiter.

Track 002

I get up at about eight or nine o'clock. Then, I have a shower and a cup of coffee. I leave my flat at half past eleven. At work, we get a small lunch from the restaurant before we start, and at twelve thirty the first customers arrive. I finish serving lunch at about four o'clock, and I have a break of two hours. I often go to the gym and work out, or I hang out with friends. Then I go back to work at six in the evening and serve dinner for the next three or four hours. Sometimes, I can go home at about ten o'clock, but it's often much later: eleven p.m., or even after midnight on Saturdays if big groups of people have eaten in the restaurant. But that's OK. I like working with the relaxed customers in the evenings.

Exercise 3

Students' own answers.

LISTENING

Exercise 1

A
1 Simone
2 Biles
B
1 Tom
2 Holland

Exercise 2

Students' own answers.

Track 003

Successful, famous and still very young. Today, we are announcing this year's Young Celebrity of the Year. We asked which young celebrities our listeners like and respect the most. Hundreds of you wrote to us. Thank you for all your tweets and messages. We now have the two most popular young celebrities, successful in very different ways. From the world of film, our listeners really love Tom Holland and sports fans have chosen gymnast Simone Biles. And today we want listeners to vote for one winner.

Exercise 3

A
3 (gymnast)
4 14th March 1997
5 Ohio
6 (Belizean and) American
7 one sister and two brothers
8 reading, history and spending time with friends
B
3 actor
4 English
5 1st June 1996
6 London
7 three brothers
8 watching football

Track 004

OK, let's start with sport now. Simone Biles is a gymnast. She was born on the 14th of March 1997 in Ohio in the USA, but she grew up in Texas, where she still lives today. She's American, but she also has Belizean nationality, as her mother was born in Belize. Simone has a sister and two brothers. Simone's teachers saw her talent for gymnastics when she was six years old, and she quickly started winning competitions. She has won in the World Championships many times, and in 2016, she won gold four times at the Olympic Games. Simone's successful because she does a lot of training, but she also likes to sit down with a good book. She enjoys reading and is very interested in history. We love Simone because you have to work really, really hard to be a world-class gymnast, but she finds time for friends, hobbies and fun, too.

Our second young celebrity is the English actor Tom Holland and he was born on the first of June 1996 in London, where he grew up with his three brothers. Tom started acting, and also dancing, when he was very young. He started working in theatre and then went on to having parts on TV and in films. Tom Holland is most famous for playing *Spider-Man* in several hugely successful films. He still lives in London. In his free time, he likes watching football – he supports Arsenal – but we don't think he has a lot of free time at the moment! We love Tom because although he's very rich and very famous, he's also such a normal, nice guy. So now it's time for you to vote. Who is your Young Celebrity of the Year? You can message us …

Exercise 4

Model answer

This person is an actor from my country, Mexico. He was born in 1978 so he's a bit older then the celebrities in the listening. I don't know if he has siblings but he has two children. He started acting when he was a child. He's had roles in the theatre, on television and in films. Most of his films are Mexican but some of them are famous all over the world. One famous film that he starred in was *Babel*.

(Answer: Gael García Bernal)

Page 12

GRAMMAR

Exercise 1

1 between the subject and the main verb
2 it comes after the verb

Exercise 2

1 rarely
2 often
3 hardly ever
4 usually

Exercise 3

Students' own answers.

Exercise 4

Students' own answers.

Exercise 5

1 continuous
2 verb

Exercise 6

1 I'm always forgetting my telephone number.
2 My sister is always taking my phone.
3 Our teacher is always giving us extra homework.
4 He's always complaining about my work.

Exercise 7

Students' own answers.

WRITING

Exercise 1

Model answer

A personal profile

Hello! My name is Ricardo. Welcome to my blog.

I'm 20 years old, Spanish and a student at the University of Valencia. I study political science and I share a flat with three other students. My room is tiny but life in our little flat is fun.

I have a typical student life. From Monday to Friday I work very hard. I get up early every day and go to lectures or to the university library. We have a lot of exams and essays so I'm always busy. I usually meet up with my friends at lunchtime but only for one hour. I hardly ever go out in the evening.

However, at the weekend, everything changes! I never get up early on Saturday or Sunday. On Saturday afternoon I work out at the gym or in summer I often go swimming at the beach. In the evening I eat out with friends or go to a party. I'm usually very lazy on Sundays. I hang out with the others in my flat and we sometimes cook together. We all need our energy for the next week at university.

Page 13

SPEAKING

Exercises 1 & 2

Students' own answers.

Exercise 3

Nice to meet you.
Really?
Me too.
What do you do?
That sounds interesting.

Track 005

Zoe: Hi, I'm Zoe. What's your name?
Anne: I'm Anne.
Zoe: Nice to meet you! Anne … are you Karl's friend from the film club?
Anne: No, that's Anne McDonald. I'm Anne Dumont. I was at school with Karl. How do *you* know him?
Zoe: He's my cousin, so I've known him all my life. And we sometimes play tennis together.
Anne: Really? You play tennis? Me too. I go to the new club in Green Park. Where do you play?
Zoe: Oh, we just play in the park near the swimming pool. It's not great, but it's cheap. I'm a student, so I don't have much money. What do you do?
Anne: I'm a journalist.
Zoe: Oh, that sounds interesting. Is it hard to be a journalist nowadays, with all the bloggers …

Exercise 4

1 b
2 a
3 a

Track 006

1 A
Karen: I go swimming every morning.
Sam: [flat intonation] Really?
1 B
Karen: I go swimming every morning.
Sam: [interested, rise-fall intonation] Really?
2 A
Karen: I think everyone should have a hobby.
Sam: [interested, rise-fall intonation] I agree.
2 B
Karen: I think everyone should have a hobby.
Sam: [flat intonation] I agree.
3 A
Karen: I love watching winter sports on TV.
Sam: [interested, rise-fall intonation] Me too.
3 B
Karen: I love watching winter sports on TV.
Sam: [flat intonation] Me too.

Exercise 5

Students' own answers.

UNIT 1

Page 14

VOCABULARY

Exercise 1

A hiking
B buying souvenirs
C sunbathing
D sightseeing; taking photos

Exercise 2

1 B
2 C
3 A

Track 007

1
Woman: It's what I always do on the last day of my holidays. I like having something to take home with me. It reminds me of my holiday, and I get presents for my friends and family, too.

2

Man: No, I never do that. It looks so boring – just lying there doing nothing. I prefer being active when I'm on holiday, doing sports and things.

3

Man: That's my favourite thing! I really like spending time outdoors when I'm on holiday. I love fresh air, doing some exercise and seeing the countryside.

Exercises 3, 4 & 5

Students' own answers.

Page 15

READING PART 2 TRAINING

Exercise 1

1 E
2 A
3 D
4 C

Exercise 2

Students' own answers.

Page 16

GRAMMAR

Exercise 1

By train.

Exercise 2

1 plane
2 car
3 car
4 plane
5 train

Track 008

Emma: Hey, Tim. Let's talk about our weekend trip to Edinburgh next month. I'm so excited about going to Scotland.

Tim: Me too.

Emma: I really want to take a tour of Edinburgh castle.

Tim: So do I. It looks great.

Emma: So, what about transport? How shall we go?

Tim: Do you want to go by car? It's much easier than taking a bus or a train.

Emma: Hmm, I'm not sure about that. Edinburgh is such a long way from London! It's 650 kilometres, you know. The journey will take us at least seven hours. We're only going for three days, so that'll only leave us one full day in Edinburgh.

Tim: I see what you mean. It's too far to drive for the weekend. So, how do you think we should go?

Emma: Maybe by plane? It's fast. The flight is just over an hour.

Tim: Yes, but the tickets are often so expensive. If we fly, we won't have enough money to have fun in Edinburgh.

Emma: Mmm, that's true. Air travel costs a lot.

Tim: You know, if we want to save money, we could drive. Driving is cheaper than buying two air tickets. In fact, it's even cheaper than buying two train tickets.

Emma: Yes, but going by train is much faster than by going by car – it only takes four hours by train.

Tim: Does it? That's not too bad.

Emma: And what's more, the train's much greener than either driving or flying.

Tim: Yeah, you're right. Let's do that.

Exercise 3

1 easier
2 more
3 quickly
4 better

Exercise 4

1 bigger
2 the largest
3 more slowly
4 the worst
5 more comfortable
6 better
7 more quietly
8 better

Exercise 5

1 a smaller amount
2 a different amount
3 the same

Page 17

WRITING

Exercise 1

Yes, the reviewer enjoyed the trip.

Exercise 2

Adds more information: and; too; also; what's more; as well as
Contrast: although; but; though

Exercise 3

1 but
2 Although
3 and
4 What's more
5 As well as
6 too
7 also
8 though

Exercise 4

Students' own answers.

VOCABULARY

Exercise 1

1 trip
2 transport
3 tour
4 journey
5 travel

Exercise 2

Students' own answers.

Page 18

GRAMMAR

Exercise 1

Campbell House has the best food.
Drumcraig Lodge is the smallest.
Hotel Glenross has the worst service.

Exercise 2

Drumcraig Lodge because it's not too noisy and it's fairly close to the city centre. The quality of food in the hotel doesn't bother them because they're planning to explore lots of different restaurants.

Track 009

Emma: Right, so, what about a hotel? We want to do lots of sightseeing, so we shouldn't stay anywhere that's too far from the city centre.

Tim: Yes, but we don't want anywhere too noisy. I hate it when you can't get enough sleep at night.

Emma: So do I. And we want somewhere that serves good food.

Tim: Do we? We're going to explore lots of different restaurants, aren't we? Edinburgh has such great places to eat. The hotel restaurant doesn't matter so much.

Emma: No, I guess it's not so important. Now, let's look at some reviews.

Exercise 3

1 such
2 so
3 too
4 enough

Exercise 4

1 so
2 such
3 enough
4 enough
5 too
6 too

Exercise 5

1 so
2 too
3 such
4 enough
5 too

Exercise 6

Students' own answers.

Exercise 7

They sound the same.

Track 010

too to

Exercise 8

to is shorter

Track 011

It's too far to drive.

Exercise 9

Track 012

It's too small to stay in.
It's too far from the city centre.
Do you want to go by car?
That's not too bad.

Page 19

LISTENING

Exercise 1

rainforest A
high and mountainous C
dry and rocky B

Exercise 2

Students' own answers.

Exercise 3

A the east
B the south
C the centre

Track 013

Hi, I'm Jo, and I want to tell you about my trip to the sunny island of Madagascar. I went there last year for a university geography project. The island has just two main seasons – a dry season, and a rainy season. But even in the rainy season, there's still plenty of warm sunshine, especially in the morning. Then in the afternoon, there are often storms. But the most interesting thing about Madagascar's climate is the incredible variety – in fact, it's completely different in every part of the island.

For example, the south of Madagascar is warm, dry and windy. The temperatures drop down to about twenty-three degrees in the dry season from May to October. And because there's so little rainfall in the south, the landscape is really dry and rocky. I took some photos of scenery that looks exactly like the moon! It was amazing.

That's very different from the northwest of the island, where it rains a lot. It's especially wet at the beginning of the year. But then, from May to October the northwest is pretty dry too. And because it's not so windy, it's warm all year round.

Then there's the east coast, where there's plenty of rain all year, with an average of two or three hundred millimetres of rain a month. So it's always warm and wet on the east coast. And because the weather is so humid, there are thick rainforests in this part of the island. These are home to lots of fantastic wildlife, especially monkeys!

Finally, there's the centre of the island, which is different again. Here, the temperatures are only around twenty-two degrees in the warmer part of the year, and it's fairly cool between May and September. It rains quite a lot from December to March, and then much less in the dry season. The island's high and mountainous in the centre, and there are farms on the hillsides. I went on a trip to a rice farm, which was really interesting. Madagascar is a truly amazing place!

Exercise 4

1 False. The island has two main seasons.
2 True
3 False. It's warm, dry and windy in the south of Madagascar.
4 False. It's warm all year round in the northwest.
5 True
6 True

Exercise 5

Students' own answers.

VOCABULARY

Exercise 1

1 cool
2 showers
3 breeze
4 climate
5 dull
6 humid
7 fine
8 lightning
9 chilly
10 damp

Exercise 2

1 lightning
2 showers
3 climate
4 humid
5 cool

Exercise 3

1 damp
2 chilly
3 dull
4 fine
5 breeze

Exercise 4

Students' own answers.

Page 20

PUSH YOURSELF B2

Exercise 1

Students' own answers.

Exercise 2

1 fossil fuels
2 environmentally friendly
3 Conservation
4 waste
5 carbon footprint
6 Climate change

SPEAKING PART 3 TRAINING

Exercise 1

Students' own answers.

Exercise 2

The answer is yes to all three questions.

Track 014

Man: So, a group of teenage students want to go away on a weekend trip. What do you think?
Woman: OK, let's take a look. Well, I think the city is the best place for them to go.
Man: Sorry, but I don't agree with you. I think it costs a lot to take a weekend break in a city. The teenagers might not have enough money for city hotels, restaurants and theatres and so on.
Woman: Yes, you're right. It is expensive. So, let's see what the other possibilities are. Well, I think they'd enjoy going to the seaside.
Man: Do you think so? I think the seaside's more for children. I don't think there's much they could do at the seaside.
Woman: Really? I think there are lots of things that teenagers can do at the seaside: beach volleyball, windsurfing, all sorts of things.
Man: That's true. They could have fun at the seaside.
Woman: More fun than in the countryside, I think.
Man: Yes, I agree.

Exercise 3

Column 1
I think they'd enjoy going to …
I think the … is the best place for them to go.
Column 2
What do you think?
Column 3
Yes, you're right.
I agree (with you).
That's true.
Column 4
Sorry, but I don't agree (with you).
Do you think so?
Really?

Exercise 4

Column 1: making a suggestion
Column 2: asking for an opinion
Column 3: agreeing
Column 4: disagreeing

Exercise 5

1 might
2 agree

3 a great idea
4 you agree?

Page 21

Exercise 6

Students' own answers.

SPEAKING PART 4 TRAINING

Exercise 7

1. Do you like holidays in the city or at the seaside?
   I prefer holidays in the city because I love shopping and visiting museums.
2. What's your ideal holiday destination?
   My ideal holiday destination is somewhere lively that has good nightlife because I really enjoy dancing.
3. Do you prefer to go on holiday with your family or with friends?
   I'd rather go on holiday with my family than with my friends because we have a lot of fun together.
4. What time of year do you like to go on holiday?
   Autumn is my favourite time of year to go on holiday because I prefer cooler weather and there aren't so many people.
5. What do you think about camping holidays in the countryside?
   I like the countryside, but I'd rather stay in a hotel than a tent because the weather might be cold and wet.

Track 015

1

Examiner: Do you like holidays in the city or at the seaside?
Candidate: I prefer holidays in the city because I love shopping and visiting museums.

2

Examiner: What's your ideal holiday destination?
Candidate: My ideal holiday destination is somewhere lively that has good nightlife because I really enjoy dancing.

3

Examiner: Do you prefer to go on holiday with your family or with friends?
Candidate: I'd rather go on holiday with my family than with my friends because we have a lot of fun together.

4

Examiner: What time of year do you like to go on holiday?
Candidate: Autumn is my favourite time of year to go on holiday because I prefer cooler weather and there aren't so many people.

5

Examiner: What do you think about camping holidays in the countryside?
Candidate: I like the countryside, but I'd rather stay in a hotel than a tent because the weather might be cold and wet.

Exercise 8

Students' own answers.

Page 22

EXAM FOCUS READING PART 2

1 C
2 H
3 A
4 D
5 G

Page 23

SPEAKING PARTS 3 AND 4

Students' own answers.

Page 24

REAL WORLD

Exercise 1

Students' own answers.

Exercise 2

A bed and breakfasts and homestays
B campsites
C hostels
D DOC huts
E motels

Page 25

Exercise 3

1 DOC hut
2 apartment
3 bed and breakfast/homestay
4 hotel
5 hostel

Exercise 4

1 twin
2 en suite
3 single
4 dormitory
5 double

Exercise 5

a 3
b 1
d 2

Track 016

1

Man: Hi. Can I help you?
Traveller: Yes. Do you have any information on accommodation?
Man: Yes. Sure. What kind of accommodation are you looking for?
Traveller: Probably a hostel. And we're looking for somewhere close to the city centre.
Man: OK. Are you happy with a dorm? A dormitory?
Traveller: Yes, that's fine.
Man: And is it just for one night?
Traveller: No. For three nights.
Man: OK. There's Queen Street Backpackers. It's very popular, and it's in a great location, right in the city centre. They've got some spaces.
Traveller: OK. Is there a kitchen?
Man: Yes, there are two kitchens and a room where all travellers can relax, and it has hot showers 24/7. There's also free wi-fi.
Traveller: And how much is it?
Man: It's 27 dollars for a bed in a six-bed dorm. There's a choice of a mixed dorm or an all-female one.
Traveller: OK. That sounds good. We'll go for that. And we'd prefer an all-female dorm.
Man: Great. OK, if you could just fill in your details here, I'll get that booked for you.
Traveller: Thanks.

2

Receptionist: Hello. Auckland City Hotel. How can I help you?
Traveller: Hello. Do you have any rooms available for tonight, please?
Receptionist: Let me just check. Is it for two people?
Traveller: Yes.
Receptionist: And would you like a double room or a twin room?
Traveller: A twin room, please.
Receptionist: OK. We have a room available. It's a standard room at $150. All our rooms are en suite, and they all have air conditioning. There's free wi-fi too.
Traveller: Does the price include breakfast?
Receptionist: No, breakfast is extra. It's $10 per person. Would you like to go ahead with that?
Traveller: Yes, please.
Receptionist: OK. So, if I can just take your name?
Traveller: It's Jones. Sam Jones.
Receptionist: And can I take a contact number for you?
Traveller: Yes, it's 07760 453782.
Receptionist: OK, Mr. Jones. That's all booked for you. We'll see you later today.
Traveller: Thanks. Bye.
Receptionist: Bye.

3

Receptionist: Hi. How can I help you?
Traveller: Hello. We've got a room booked for tonight.
Receptionist: OK. What's the name, please?
Traveller: It's Edmund. Sophie Edmund.
Receptionist: Ah, yes. I've got you down for a value twin – is that right?
Traveller: Yes.
Receptionist: So, the value rooms have a shared bathroom. Is that OK for you?
Traveller: Yes, it's fine.

Receptionist: That's great. Breakfast isn't included in the price, but we have an on-site restaurant where you can get breakfast and also a meal this evening, if you want.
Traveller: OK.
Receptionist: Right, I'll need you to fill in these forms with your name and address, passport number and car registration number. And how would you like to pay?
Traveller: I'll pay by card, please.
Receptionist: Right. If you could just pop your card in there for me? Thanks. So that's $110. If you could put your PIN number in? And that's all gone through for you. So, you'll be in room 46. That's on the first floor. Check out time tomorrow is eleven o'clock.
Traveller: That's fine.
Receptionist: Thank you. Enjoy your stay.

Exercise 6

1 True
2 False. There are mixed dorms and all-female ones.
3 True
4 True
5 False. The value rooms have a shared bathroom.

Exercise 7

1 information on
2 looking for
3 how much
4 sounds; go for
5 rooms available
6 price include
7 booked for
8 by card

Exercise 8

1 c
2 e
3 f
4 a
5 d
6 b

Exercise 9

Suggested answers

The country: made up of two islands, the North Island and the South Island. Auckland is on the North Island; lots of beaches
Wildlife: sea lions and whales
Camping: camping is very popular, especially from December to February, which is summer there; campsites are in beautiful areas; in many places wild camping is also allowed in the mountains and on the beaches
Hostels: popular with young people because they are cheap. You can wash your clothes and use the internet; places where you can meet other travellers
Homestays: good place to stay if you want to experience real New Zealand family life. They are popular with students
Motels: quite cheap and they're close to the road, but they don't provide food

Exercises 10 & 11

Students' own answers.

UNIT 2

Page 26

SPEAKING

Exercise 1

Students' own answers.

Exercise 2

1 A
2 B
3 E
4 F

Track 017

1
I can't stand big crowds, but last Saturday my favourite band played live in my town. I'm crazy about their music, so of course I went to see them. They were amazing. The only problem was that I couldn't see the stage very well. There were too many tall people in the audience, and I'm very small.
2
Sometimes, I enjoy just staying in and relaxing. So, last Saturday I caught up with a new series that I'm watching. I'm really into detective shows and this one is set in Copenhagen. I've never been there, but it looks great on the screen!
3
I usually watch films on my tablet. I'm comfortable on my sofa, and I don't mind having only a small screen. However, last Saturday my friends wanted to see a new comedy at the cinema, so I went with them. I'm not a fan of comedies, but this one was really funny, and it had a great soundtrack, too. I've decided to get off the sofa more often!
4
Parties are not my thing, and I have to work on Sunday mornings. That's why I'm not bothered about going out on Saturday nights, and I often stay at home with a good book. The book I read last Saturday was a really exciting thriller. I read it from beginning to end in one night. Of course, I was tired at work on Sunday.

Exercise 3

1 stand
2 crazy
3 enjoy
4 into
5 mind
6 fan
7 thing
8 bothered

Exercise 4

I'm into …
I'm crazy about …
I really enjoy …

I don't mind …
I'm not bothered about …

I can't stand …
I'm not a fan of …
… is not my thing

Exercises 5 & 6

Students' own answers.

Page 27

READING

Exercise 1

Students' own answers.

Exercise 2

Binge-watching means watching lots of episodes of a programme one after another.

Exercise 3

B

Exercise 4

1 spoiler(s)
2 download
3 catch-up TV
4 back to back

Exercise 5

1 True
2 False. She and her school friends all watched the same things.
3 True
4 False. She watches a lot of episodes back to back.
5 True

Exercise 6

Students' own answers.

Page 28

GRAMMAR

Exercise 1

used to

Exercise 2

1 used to sit
2 did; use to enjoy
3 didn't use to watch
4 used to tell

Exercise 3

Students' own answers.

VOCABULARY

Exercise 1

1 a concert
2 a detective series
3 a book
4 an opera
5 a radio programme
6 a film
7 a play
8 a biography

Page 29

Exercise 2

1 audience
2 stage
3 thriller
4 comedy
5 soundtrack
6 episodes
7 documentary
8 bestsellers

Exercise 3

Students' own answers.

LISTENING PART 2 TRAINING

Exercise 2

B

Exercise 3

1 C
2 A
3 B

Track 018

Narrator: One. You will hear a girl telling her friend about a theatre trip.
Girl: I was outside talking to Mark and Aiden, and then my dad shouted out the window "Angelina, sweetie, it's theatre time!" Of course, the boys laughed and my face turned bright red! I just wanted to crawl into a hole!
Boy: Poor you! And was it boring at the theatre with your parents?
Girl: Well, it's amazing, but I wasn't bored at all. The performances were fantastic. And the theatre itself is a beautiful building. Next time, I'll wear a smart dress.
Boy: Next time?
Girl: Yes! I couldn't believe how much I enjoyed it all. I want to go again! You should come too!
Narrator: Two. You will hear two friends talking about a film they've seen.
Man: I'm really sorry. It was my idea to see that film.
Woman: But it wasn't so bad. I can't believe all those strange events would happen in real life, but they were fun to watch in a film.
Man: No. It was all too silly. And Gary Power's performance was no good at all.
Woman: Oh, come on! He was fantastic. And he's such a good singer, too. I loved that final song.
Man: Well, yeah, me too. Actually, the songs and the soundtrack were great.
Woman: Yes, they were. See? You chose a good film and we've had a lovely evening.
Narrator: Three. You will hear a man telling his friend about a music festival.
Woman: Have you ever been to Glastonbury?
Man: Yes, I have. I went last year. I had such a good time. The bands were a bit disappointing, though. I wasn't really into the performers.
Woman: I don't understand. If you didn't like the music, then why was it so good?
Man: The atmosphere is great. There's lots of time just to hang out with mates. There's no stress and everyone's happy. Even camping there was OK. You know I never normally go on camping trips!
Woman: It sounds wonderful.

Exercise 4

Students' own answers.

Page 30

GRAMMAR

Exercise 1

1 present perfect
2 past simple

Exercise 2

1 Have you ever been
2 have seen
3 did you see
4 went
5 saw
6 did you enjoy
7 loved
8 have you seen

Exercise 3

Students' own answers.

Exercise 4

Have you/w/ever … ?

Track 019

Have you ever … ?

Exercise 5

1 Have you/w/ever been to England?
2 Have you/w/ordered a cup of coffee?
3 Have you/w/answered his two/w/ emails?
4 Have you/w/asked Tom to go/w/away?

Track 020

1 Have you ever been to England?
2 Have you ordered a cup of coffee?
3 Have you answered his two emails?
4 Have you asked Tom to go away?

Page 31

Exercise 6

present perfect

Exercise 7

since	*for*
2016 January last Monday last year	a long time a week three years two hours

Exercises 8 & 9

Students' own answers.

PUSH YOURSELF B2

Exercise 1

Students' own answers.

Exercise 2

2 fall out with
3 keep on
4 let; down
5 chill out
6 get into
7 turn (it) down
8 live up to; expectations

Exercise 3

1 turned down
2 fall out with
3 got into
4 split up
5 let; down; didn't live up to
6 kept on; chill out

Page 32

GRAMMAR

Exercise 1

Students' own answers.

Exercise 2

print out the tickets
book the campsite
book train tickets
buy rubber boots

Track 021

Ethan: Have you printed out our tickets yet?
Mia: Yes, I've already printed them out, but I haven't found our tent yet. Where could it be?
Ethan: My brother has the tent, remember? Oh, I haven't booked the campsite yet.
Mia: Don't worry. I've already done it. And I've already booked train tickets, too.
Ethan: Great!
Mia: Oh, have you bought rubber boots yet? I've bought a pair for myself because it's going to rain.

Ethan: I've already got some.
Mia: Great, so we've done everything!
Ethan: Well, we haven't packed our backpacks yet. Let's do it now!

Exercise 3

1 already
2 yet
3 yet

Exercise 4

1 I haven't booked the campsite yet
2 I've already done it
3 I've already booked train tickets
4 have you bought rubber boots yet
5 I've already got some
6 we haven't packed our backpacks yet

Page 33

WRITING

Exercise 1

Students' own answers.

Exercise 2

Hi Tina,
Hi,
Dear Tina,

Exercise 3

1 See you soon.
2 Looking forward to seeing you.
3 Bye for now.

Exercise 4

1 Thanks for your message.
2 Hi / Are you into … ? (Thanks also possible.)
3 I'm / you're coming / There's / We'll have
4 and/ too / as well as
5 Would you like to go?
6 we could see a play and then hear some music.

Exercise 5

1 c
2 a
3 b
4 a

Exercise 6

Saying yes: I'd love to / … sounds great / That's a good idea.
Saying no: I wouldn't like / Sorry, but … / That's a nice idea, but …

Exercise 7

Students' own answers.

Exercise 8

Model answer

Hi Martin,
Thanks for your email and your interesting suggestions. I'm really looking forward to our weekend together, too!
I'd love to go to the festival in your town. I'm into music from around the world so I think the African band sounds great. Actually, I think live music is always fun and I'd like to see any band. I'm not really into theatre, though. It's a nice idea but let's just see a band, or maybe a few bands. What do you think? Make sure we see some bands that you like, too.
See you soon,
(name)

Page 34

EXAM FOCUS LISTENING PART 2

1 A
2 B
3 B
4 A
5 C
6 B

Track 022

Narrator: For each question, choose the correct answer. One. You will hear two friends talking about a television drama.
Man: Did you see that drama on TV last night? You know, about that family in the nineteenth century?
Woman: Hampden Hall? Yes, I loved the two main actors in it. They played their roles so well.
Man: Do you think so? I wasn't too impressed, actually. The story was brilliant, though. I really wasn't expecting what happened at the end!
Woman: Neither was I! That was such an original idea. Great music, too.
Man: Mmm. It was good, but didn't you think it was a bit loud and too modern? I did.
Woman: I thought it went perfectly. In fact, I thought the whole thing was amazing.
Narrator: Two. You will hear two colleagues talking about jazz music.
Man: Hi, Meena.
Woman: Ah, Paul, you're just the person I wanted to see.
Man: Really?
Woman: Yes! Listen, you're into jazz music, aren't you?
Man: Yes, I am.
Woman: Well, the thing is … my cousin really likes jazz, too, and I want to take him to a concert for his birthday. And I was wondering … if I send you a link to some jazz concerts that are on next weekend, would you be able to tell me which one is the best?
Man: Of course. I'd be glad to. I'll take a look.
Narrator: Three. You will hear two friends talking about going to the cinema.
Woman: Do you go to the cinema?
Man: Not any more. I used to, when I was a student.
Woman: Cinema tickets cost less then. They charge so much nowadays, don't they?
Man: Yes, but it's still cheaper than a concert or a show. The thing is, I work late most evenings, so finding a few spare hours to see a film at the cinema can be hard. I'd rather download films and watch them when and where I want. And there's such a wide choice now. Some of them are boring, but I can always find something I want to watch.
Narrator: Four. You will hear a woman telling a friend about a concert she attended.
Man: How was the concert you went to? Rocky Simpson, wasn't it?
Woman: Yes, that's right.
Man: Did you enjoy it?
Woman: It was OK. Like with most big outdoor concerts, it wasn't perfect! There were some technical problems with the speakers, so what we heard right at the back wasn't great. But you expect that, don't you? And Rocky only sang for an hour, which isn't much, but it's what he usually does. I was hoping he'd sing some of his old hits, which are my favourites, but in fact he only did stuff from his latest album. That was a shame.
Narrator: Five. You will hear two friends talking about a computer game.
Woman: Have you played the new Fireball game?
Man: Yeah, it's cool. Really good fun, and not too expensive, either.
Woman: Hmm, I didn't think it was worth the price, actually. But I did enjoy playing it. I liked the special effects – they were amazing – and it wasn't too hard to win. I get bored if games are too difficult.
Man: I found it pretty challenging, actually. Maybe I need to practise some more!
Woman: Well, I'm pleased they've updated it, anyway.
Man: Me too. It's definitely an improvement on the old one.
Woman: The old one was full of bugs, wasn't it?
Man: I'm glad they've got rid of them.
Narrator: Six. You will hear two friends talking about a TV talent show.
Woman: That TV talent show was great, wasn't it? All those singers, dancers and musicians. I couldn't believe how brilliant they all were.
Man: Mmm, I really wasn't expecting to see so many talented people.
Woman: The way they organised the contest was annoying, though, wasn't it? It was boring listening to people talking before and after each performance.

Man: I didn't mind that, actually. Anyway, what did you think of the girl who won?
Woman: Definitely not the best. I wonder why the judges chose her.
Man: No idea. There were plenty of people better than her.
Woman: Oh well, at least it was fun to watch.

Page 35

WRITING PART 1

Model answer

Hi Alex,

I'm really looking forward to the music festival, too!

I'd like to go just for two days. Unfortunately, I have to work on Friday. We can go early on Saturday morning and then come home on Sunday evening.

I think we should take the bus. It stops very close to the park where the festival's going to take place. The bus is quite cheap, too.

You don't need to bring your tent. I'm going to take mine, and it'll be big enough for both of us.

See you on Saturday!

Jan

Page 36

REAL WORLD

Exercise 1

Students' own answers.

Exercise 2

A Getting there
B Coachella mobile
C Eat and drink
D Festival rules and general information
E On-site camping

Page 37

Exercise 3

1 False. There are regular shuttles.
2 False. Ins and outs are allowed.
3 False. You can have as many people camp in your spot as you like.
4 True
5 False. They are throughout the venue and camping ground.
6 True

Exercise 4

1 attendees
2 line-up
3 hit the stage
4 venue
5 pick-up and drop-off
6 set times

Exercise 5

b 1
c 2
d 3

Track 023

1

Official: Hi. Do you need some help?
Festival-goer: Yes. My phone's out of battery. Is there somewhere I can charge it?
Official: Not in the main festival area. Are you camping on site?
Festival-goer: Yes.
Official: OK. Which zone are you in? Are you tent only, or are you in one of the teepees?
Festival-goer: We're in the tent camping area.
Official: So, your nearest charging station is on Broadway, that's a wide avenue running down the centre of your camping area. As you go on to your camping area from the main site, you'll see a shower block on your left, and then the main avenue running down the centre. Do you know where I mean?
Festival-goer: Yes, I think so.
Official: Well, the charging station is in a small tent just off the main avenue. If you can't find it, just ask at the information kiosk in that area.
Festival-goer: OK. Thanks.

2

Festival-goer: Hi. Can you help me?
Official: Sure. What can I do for you?
Festival-goer: My wristband is broken. Can I get a new one?
Official: Sure. Do you still have the original one?
Festival-goer: Yes, it's here.
Official: That's good. You'll need it to get a replacement. You need to go to the wristband help tent. It's near the Sonora stage. Do you know where that is?
Festival-goer: Uhh, no.
Official: OK. Well, if you head for the camping area over there, to your left. There's the big wheel, there, can you see? And the entrance to the camping area is just behind that. So, make for that area, and when you get over there, carry on past the big wheel. You'll see wristband help on your right. They'll fix you up with a replacement.
Festival-goer: That's great. Thanks.
Official: You're welcome. Have a nice day.

3

Official: Hi. Are you OK there?
Festival-goer: Yes. We're looking for a supermarket. Is there one here?
Official: There are no supermarkets on the main festival site, but there's a shuttle service that goes every thirty minutes from car camping zone A.
Festival-goer: OK. Can you tell us where that is?
Official: Yeah. It's at the back of the camping area. So, as you go into the camping ground, keep on the red path down the centre, as if you're going towards the Eldorado area, you know, where the teepees are. Then you'll see Lake Eldorado on your left, but just keep going and you'll eventually get to the shuttle stop. The shuttles go on the hour and the half hour.
Festival-goer: OK. Thanks.

Exercise 6

1 out of
2 charge
3 Can I
4 looking for
5 Is there

Exercise 7

1 c
2 f
3 a
4 e
5 d
6 b

Exercise 8

Suggested answers

Venue: Coachellla Valley of the Colorado Desert; temperatures over 40 degrees and there is lots of space; 250,000 attendees

Kinds of music: rap, rock, and pop; famous names and new bands and singers

Getting there: fly to Los Angeles Airport and take a shuttle bus or drive and use car-share service, Carpoolchella

Food and drink: stalls with food from all over the world; open air restaurant 'Outstanding in the field' for four-course meals

On-site camping: bring your own tent or rent a tepee or safari tent; don't need to bring sleeping bags or pillows

Exercises 9 & 10

Students' own answers.

Page 38

PROGRESS CHECK 1

Exercise 1

1 gardener
2 journalist
3 chef
4 sales assistant
5 mechanic
6 hairdresser

Exercise 2

1 I go
2 we usually have
3 she's studying
4 isn't enjoying
5 She's always borrowing
6 they never invite

Exercise 3

1 My friends and I usually meet up on Saturday evenings.
2 We sometimes eat out.
3 My brother never goes to bed before midnight.
4 He is hardly ever at home.
5 I usually get up very early.
6 I am always tired!

Exercise 4

1 climate
2 fine
3 cool
4 showers
5 breeze
6 lightning

Exercise 5

1 Greenland is colder than Iceland.
2 Ireland is not as warm as Madagascar. / Ireland is colder than Madagascar.
3 France has the most tourists.
4 Hiking holidays are not as expensive as skiing holidays.
5 Beach holidays are more relaxing than city holidays.
6 The beaches in Brazil are the longest.

Page 39

Exercise 6

1 c a concert
2 e a film
3 a a book
4 h a series
5 b a comedy
6 f a play
7 d a documentary
8 g a radio programme

Exercise 7

1 have written / 've written
2 wrote
3 went
4 Have … visited
5 have been / 've been
6 have not visited / haven't visited
7 didn't write
8 lived

Exercise 8

1 When I was a child, I used to watch television with my family.
2 We used to sit together in the living room.
3 My sister and I used to argue about what programme to watch.
4 My father didn't use to enjoy watching television.
5 He used to read his book while we were watching our favourite shows.
6 Did you use to spend evenings with your family when you were younger?

Exercise 9

1 into
2 crazy
3 fan
4 stand
5 enjoy
6 thing

Exercise 10

1 Martin enjoys / enjoyed playing football.
2 I like Katrin because she is very kind.
3 She is always happy.
4 I never go to the theatre. / I've never been to the theatre.
5 We had such a great holiday.
6 He has been here since last week. / He's been here since last week.
7 I have never seen a musical.
8 I used to go to work on foot but now I go by car.

Exercise 11

1 most
2 has
3 is
4 already
5 worse
6 yet
7 than
8 since

UNIT 3

Page 40

LISTENING

Exercises 1 & 2

Students' own answers.

Exercise 3

A smart; stylish
B family run; good value for money; home-cooked; traditional
C cheap and cheerful; junk food

Track 024

1

My favourite place to eat is a nice family-run Italian restaurant. It's quite a traditional kind of place. The food is home-cooked, and it always tastes really good. My favourite dish is beef lasagna. It isn't expensive, so it's good value for money, too. But the best thing about it is the friendly service and the welcoming atmosphere – and it's wonderful to be able to sit outside in the summer. No wonder it's always full.

2

Sometimes, when we're in a hurry – like before going to the cinema, for example – my friends and I go to Tommy's. We usually have a quick meal of burger and chips there. It's cheap and cheerful, with plastic tables and bright lights, and you have to collect your food from the counter. The food's basic, but it's tasty. I guess it's junk food really, but, well, once in a while is OK, isn't it?

3

It was our wedding anniversary last month, so we decided to go out for dinner to celebrate. Hampton's quite a stylish place, and it's beautifully decorated. It's the kind of restaurant where everybody is smart – you know, women in nice dresses, and men in jackets and ties, and the staff are very polite. It costs quite a bit, so people usually go there for a special occasion.

Exercise 4

Restaurant A

Track 025

Hampton's is very popular because it serves good food, so we reserved a table for 8 o'clock. I'd been there once before, in fact, for a business dinner, but this was Sarah's first time. She was very impressed. It's a very smart place, with nice furniture, fresh flowers, soft music and everything. When we arrived, the waiter took our coats and showed us to our table. Then another waiter brought us the menu. We couldn't believe how much choice there was. At first, we didn't know what to choose. But we finally decided what we wanted and we ordered our meal. When the food came, it looked amazing. But it didn't just look good – it smelled great as well. And, what's more, it tasted delicious. Our dinner began with a nice starter. We both had a bowl of really tasty vegetable soup, which we enjoyed. Then for our main course we had a large plate of grilled fish with a fresh tomato salad. It was excellent. Sarah and I agreed that was the best part of the meal. For dessert, Sarah chose ice cream and I had apple pie. That was fantastic, too. Finally, we had coffee, and then I asked for the bill. Actually, the bill was quite big, and because the service was good, we also left a tip for the waiters. So it was quite an expensive evening. We had a lovely meal, but, to be honest, I didn't think it was worth the price we paid. We might go somewhere else next year.

Exercise 5

1 b
2 a
3 b
4 b
5 a
6 b

Exercise 6

Students' own answers.

Page 41

VOCABULARY

Exercise 1

Students' own answers.

Exercise 2
1 meal
2 starter
3 dish
4 main course
5 bowl
6 plate
7 bill
8 tip

Exercise 3
1 go
2 serves
3 reserved
4 took
5 showed
6 brought
7 ordered
8 asked
9 left

Exercise 4
Students' own answers.

READING PART 4 TRAINING
Exercise 1
Students' own answers.

Exercise 2
Customers eat in the dark.

Exercise 3
1 Sentence C

Exercise 4
2 A
3 E
4 B

Page 42
GRAMMAR
Exercise 1
1 horrible
2 disappointing
3 all right; OK
4 nice; enjoyable
5 delicious

Exercise 2
1 c
2 e
3 b
4 a
5 d

Exercise 3
A jackfruit; tropical regions
B haggis; Scotland

Exercise 4
1 A
2 B

Page 43
Exercise 5
1 haggis
2 jackfruit

Track 026

1
Man: It doesn't look very nice, does it?
Woman: No, it doesn't. It looks like a fat, grey sausage.
Man: It smells extremely strange.
Woman: Shall we try it?
Man: Yeah, why not?
Woman: Right, here goes.
Man: Mmm … it isn't too bad. I can taste the onions and pepper.
Woman: Hmm, quite tasty.
Man: Yeah. Actually, it tastes OK.
2
Woman: It smells very unpleasant.
Man: Yeah. It smells quite disgusting. It's really strong …
Woman: So, are you brave enough to eat it?
Man: Only if I hold my nose!
Woman: OK, one, two, three.
Man: Mmm. Wow. That tastes really delicious … and sweet. It tastes like pineapple and … bananas maybe. I actually really like it.
Woman: I think it tastes absolutely horrible. Yuck, I don't want anymore.
Man: Can I have your piece?
Woman: You certainly can!

Exercise 6
Words like: quite; fairly; very; really; extremely; absolutely

Exercise 7
1 really
2 quite
3 very
4 really

WRITING
Exercise 1
a paragraph 2
b paragraph 1
c paragraph 3

Exercise 2
The order of events

Exercise 3
1 c
2 e
3 a
4 b
5 f
6 d

Exercises 4 & 5
Students' own answers.

Page 44
GRAMMAR
Exercise 1
Students' own answers.

Exercise 2
Countable: restaurant(s); special ones; places; minutes; students; memories
Uncountable: food, time, money; imagination, music

Exercise 3
Uncountable	Singular	Plural
a little a lot of any much no some	a/an	a few a lot of any many no some

Exercise 4
1 some
2 any
3 any

Exercise 5
1 much/many
2 much / many
3 much
4 many
5 a lot of
6 a few / a little
7 a little / a few
8 a little
9 a few
10 no

Page 45
Exercise 6
1 many
2 no
3 much
4 few
5 any
6 some
7 little
8 lot

Exercises 7 & 8
1 much; U
2 some; U
3 any; U
4 a; C
5 few; C
6 an; C

Exercise 9
Students' own answers.

PUSH YOURSELF B2

Exercise 1

Students' own answers.

Exercise 2

1 c
2 a
3 e
4 b
5 f
6 d

Page 46

VOCABULARY

Exercise 1

Students' own answers.

Exercise 2

Photo C

Track 027

Man: So, tell me, Bella. What's your favourite dish?
Bella: Welsh rarebit's definitely my favourite dish. And it's so simple to make. It's basically cheese on toast, but much tastier! I love cheese, so that's why I like Welsh rarebit so much.
Man: So how do you make it?
Bella: Well, you need cheese, butter and milk. First, you take the cheese, and you grate it. After that, you put it in a small saucepan, mix it with the other ingredients, and heat it gently. You then add salt, pepper and a little Worcester sauce. Next, you grill a slice of bread on both sides, pour the mixture over the bread, and then put it back under the grill for a few moments until it goes nice and brown. If you like, you can get an egg and fry it. Then finally, you put the egg on top of the Welsh rarebit.
Man: Mmm, sounds good.

Exercise 3

1 grate
2 put
3 mix
4 heat
5 add
6 grill
7 pour
8 fry

Exercise 4

A fry
B grate
C grill
D pour
E mix
F heat

GRAMMAR

Exercise 1

Because she's talking in general about these things. Because we know which specific cheese/egg she's talking about.

Exercise 2

1 Ø
2 a; an
3 the

Exercises 3 & 4

1 I prefer to drink coffee ~~without the sugar~~ without sugar / without any sugar.
2 Please could I have ~~glass of water~~ a glass of water?
3 correct
4 Would you like ~~a bread~~ bread / some bread / any bread with your meal?
5 correct

Exercise 5

Students' own answers.

Page 47

Exercise 6

Track 028

a
slice
of
bread

Exercise 7

Track 029

Would you like <u>a</u> slice <u>of</u> bread?

Exercise 8

<u>a</u> cup <u>of</u> tea
<u>some</u> fries <u>to</u> go
<u>a</u> table <u>for</u> two
<u>a</u> piece <u>of</u> cake

Track 030

a cup of tea
some fries to go
a table for two
a piece of cake

SPEAKING PART 2 TRAINING

Exercise 1

Suggested answers

Adjectives	People/things
large tall big white	students kitchen man vegetables chef knife glass table pepper

Position	Verb
on the right on the left in the middle at the front behind	look wear stand cut

Exercise 2

1 This is a photo of
2 I think
3 In the middle, there's
4 on the left of the photo
5 I can see
6 he's wearing
7 He's holding
8 I'm not sure what it is, but
9 at the front of
10 I don't know what they are called, but

Track 031

This is a photo of a large kitchen. I think it's in a restaurant or perhaps in a college. In the middle, there's a large black table and there are some pots and knives on the left of the photo. I can see a man behind the table. Maybe he's a chef or teacher because he's showing the other people something and he's wearing a white apron. He's holding a knife and he is cutting something. I'm not sure what it is, but it looks like a small onion. Some people are standing at the front of the photo and they're watching the chef. There are some big wooden things in front of the people. I don't know what they're called, but people use them when they're cutting up vegetables.

Page 48

EXAM FOCUS READING PART 4

1 C
2 F
3 A
4 H
5 E

Page 49

SPEAKING PART 2

Students' own answers.

Page 50

REAL WORLD

Exercise 1

Students' own answers.

Page 51

Exercise 2

1 B
2 C
3 A

Exercise 3

1 TP
2 V
3 SF
4 TP
5 SF

Exercise 4

1 b
2 b
3 a
4 a

Exercise 5

1 b
2 e
3 a
4 d

Track 032

1

Woman: Hello. Issaya Siamese Club Restaurant.
Customer: Hello. I'd like to book a table for tonight, please.
Woman: OK. How many for?
Customer: Five people.
Woman: And what time would you like to eat?
Customer: Seven thirty, if possible.
Woman: Hmm. Seven thirty's a bit difficult. We could do 8 o'clock if that would suit you.
Customer: Yes, 8 o'clock is fine.
Woman: Good. Can I take your name?
Customer: Yes, it's Ferrari. That's F-E-R-R-A-R-I.
Woman: OK. Thank you very much. We'll see you this evening.
Customer: Thank you. Bye.

2

Customer: Excuse me.
Waiter: Yes?
Customer: I'm not very happy with my meal. My meat is really tough, and it isn't cooked properly, look.
Waiter: Oh, Yes. I'm sorry about that. Is it just the meat? Is everything else OK?
Customer: No. The vegetables are cold, too.
Waiter: No problem. I'll take this back to the kitchen and I'll get it sorted for you. I'm really sorry about this. I'll bring you a fresh meal in a few minutes, and we'd like to offer you a complimentary dessert as an apology.
Customer: OK. Thank you.

3

Waiter: Are you ready to order?
Customer: Not quite. Can you help me with the menu, please?
Waiter: Of course. What do you want to know?
Customer: Oh, thanks. What's this?
Waiter: It's a kind of omelette.
Customer: And what does it come with?
Waiter: It comes with crispy noodles and a sauce.
Customer: Is it suitable for vegetarians?
Waiter: No, it's got a bit of meat in it. But this one is meat-free. It's an omelette too, but just with vegetables.
Customer: OK. And is it gluten free?
Waiter: The omelette is gluten free, but the noodles have gluten in them. We could do you a fresh salad instead, if you prefer.
Customer: Thanks. And my brother has a nut allergy. Which dishes have nuts in them?
Waiter: Err, just these two.
Customer: OK. Thank you.

4

Customer: Excuse me. Can we have the bill, please?
Waiter: Of course. I'll get it for you. Here you are. Was everything OK for you?
Customer: Yes, the food was lovely, thanks. Err, can I pay by card?
Waiter: Sure. I'll get the machine. Can I take your card, please? Thank you. If you could just check the details, and then put in your PIN. Thank you. It just takes a while to go through. Right. That's all authorised.
Customer: Thank you.
Waiter: You're welcome. Enjoy the rest of your evening.

Exercise 6

1 to book
2 fine
3 very happy
4 isn't cooked
5 help me
6 suitable
7 gluten
8 the bill

Exercise 7

1 c
2 f
3 d
4 e
5 a
6 b

Exercise 8

Suggested answers

The best place for street food is the old city; you can buy fish or noodles, or ready-made food; you can watch people preparing the food; there are special street food tours for tourists; restaurants often specialise in one kind of food, a lot have a buffet; local restaurants are often simple but the food is delicious; typical dishes are Tom Yum soup and Pad Thai noodles; all kinds of special dining experiences are on offer, such as a dining cruise on the river, a sunset dinner next to Wat Arun temple, an open-air meal with traditional Thai dancing

Exercises 9 & 10

Students' own answers.

UNIT 4

Page 52

READING

Exercises 1 & 2

Students' own answers.

Page 53

Exercise 3

Suggested answers

1 His friend suggested it.
2 He loved the scenery and the animals.
3 When he was walking in the forest and saw a mother moose with her calf.

Exercise 4

Suggested answers

1 Her aunt invited her to go there.
2 She loved the buildings, lots of different neighborhoods (American spelling), and the views.
3 When she was standing on Brooklyn Bridge looking at the amazing skyline.

Exercise 5

Students' own answers.

Page 54

VOCABULARY

Exercise 1

Usually in cities	Usually in the country
apartment block food truck neighbourhood signpost, skyline skyscraper subway	nature reserve scenery stream valley waterfall

Exercise 2

1 apartment block
2 stream
3 skyscraper
4 scenery
5 food truck
6 subway
7 waterfall
8 neighbourhood
9 nature reserve
10 valley
11 signpost
12 skyline

Exercises 3, 4 & 5

Students' own answers.

GRAMMAR

Exercise 1

1 continuous
2 simple

Exercise 2

1 was waiting
2 was reading
3 heard
4 looked
5 was playing
6 arrived

Page 55

Exercise 3

1 drawing
2 talking
3 was writing
4 were laughing
5 was; doing
6 was sleeping

Exercise 4

1 while
2 When
3 when
4 while

Exercise 5

1 six
2 five
3 five
4 six
5 four

Track 033

1 I was working when he arrived.
2 Who were you talking to?
3 Toby was cooking all afternoon.
4 We were sleeping when you called.
5 Why was she crying?

Exercise 6

Track 034

1 I was reading when she called.
2 Why were you laughing?
3 I made dinner while Lisa was sleeping.
4 They were reading all day in the library.
5 Who was shouting so angrily?

Page 56

LISTENING PART 1 TRAINING

Exercise 1

C

Track 035

Narrator: Where does the woman live now?
Man: So, do you enjoy living in the big city?
Woman: It's fun and there's lots to do, but I grew up on a farm, so it's a big change. Some things are hard.
Man: What's hard?
Woman: Well, I'm an outdoors person, so I don't really enjoy living in an apartment block. I would prefer to have a house with a garden.
Man: You can have a house and garden in a city too, you know.
Woman: You can if you're rich! Do you know what houses cost in this city? I can't afford one.

Exercise 2

1 Yes, she has.
2 Yes, she would.
3 It's too expensive.

Exercise 3

1 A
2 A

Track 036

Narrator: One. What has the girl bought for Lisa?
Boy: Have you bought a birthday present for Lisa?
Girl: Yes, but it isn't the present I wanted to get her. The book shop didn't have that new book by Scott Sorrento …
Boy: Well it's lucky you didn't get that because I've bought it for her!
Girl: Really? But you wanted to buy her some jewellery from the new shop in King Street.
Boy: Yeah, but it was too expensive. So what did you get her?
Girl: A scarf in lots of nice colours. Do you think she'll like that?
Boy: Of course!
Narrator: Two. Where is the boy now?
Boy: Hi, Dad, why aren't you answering your phone? Anyway, we're having a great holiday. We've been to the beach every day. The weather's perfect and the water's really warm. I'm just having breakfast at the beach café, and then it'll be time for the first swim of the day. Listen, we're going to the shops in town later on, so I'll send you a postcard, OK? I know you always like getting postcards. Talk to you soon, bye Dad!

GRAMMAR

Exercise 1

before

Exercise 2

Jason: I'd never been so close to a wild animal before. I knew that something had changed.
Monica: I had never seen so many people in one place.

Exercise 3

1 The party had already started when Sam arrived.
2 Fiona felt nervous because she had never been on a plane before.
3 I didn't meet Henry because when I arrived at the café he had just left.
4 Had you ever tried sushi before you ate it yesterday?

Exercise 4

Marta's Aunt Katrin met her at the airport.	4
Katrin sold her car.	1
Katrin prepared a room for Marta.	3
Daniel moved to Los Angeles.	2
Marta looked out a window and felt happy.	5

Page 57

Exercise 5

1 flew
2 had visited
3 had been
4 was
5 felt
6 had travelled

Exercise 6

Students' own answers.

PUSH YOURSELF B2

1 was
2 had; slept
3 had happened
4 I was lying
5 heard
6 hadn't finished
7 did; do
8 had left
9 looked
10 were sleeping
11 was reading
12 decided

Page 58

WRITING PART 2 TRAINING

Exercise 1

It is a little too short and could be more interesting. There are no paragraphs.

Exercises 3, 4 & 5

My friend did not look happy. I saw her *when I was walking home from college* and called her name. *She had heard me but* she didn't answer. What was the problem?
At first I walked away, but then I decided to go and talk to her. 'What's wrong, Stefanie?' I asked. 'Nothing' she said, but *she wasn't smiling and* I knew it wasn't true. Then my phone went 'ping!' I looked at the words on the screen: 'Stefanie's birthday.' Finally I understood. 'I'm so sorry!' I said. 'I forgot, again. Happy birthday!'

Later we went out together and had fun. Next year, I won't forget.

Exercise 5

1 While
2 after that
3 finally
4 At first
5 the next day

Exercise 6

Students' own answers.

Page 59

SPEAKING

Exercise 1

1 nightclub
2 monument
3 shopping mall
4 art gallery
5 covered market

Track 037

1

Girl 1: I love this place!

Girl 2: What?

Girl 1: I said I love it here!

Girl 2: Oh, yeah, me too. There's always a great atmosphere and dancing here is so much fun!

2

Man: It really makes you think, doesn't it?

Woman: Yes, all the history that this represents. I love visiting historical places like this.

3

Woman: Is there a chemist's here?

Man: I'm sure there is, but I don't see one. Oh, look. There's one down there past the shoe shop, opposite the music store.

4

Man 1: I just don't understand it. I mean, it's ugly and it looks like a child did it. Even I could do better than that!

Man 2: Oh, I don't think it's ugly! But I know you don't like the modern stuff. Let's go upstairs and see something older.

5

Man: That cheese looks good. Do you make it yourself?

Woman: Yes, I do. Would you like to try a bit?

Man: Yes please. Mmm, it's fantastic! But it's quite strong. I'll just take a little.

Exercise 2

Students' own answers.

Exercise 3

we could …
I'm not sure
let's …
I think that's a better idea
what about … ?
that sounds good
shall we … ?
… is a nice idea

Track 038

Man: OK, so what shall we put right in the centre of the town, in the square?

Woman 1: We could put our department store there.

Woman 2: Oh, I'm not sure. Let's have the shopping area away from the square. We could have the department store in it. Here, on the right, opposite the sports centre and next to the covered market.

Man: Yes, and people will have more space to park their cars there, so I think that's a better idea.

Woman 1: OK. So, what about the square? I know. Let's have a café in the square and also a playground, in the middle. Then parents can relax and have coffee while their children play.

Woman 2: That sounds good. So, the café here, and the playground in the middle of the square. And, shall we have the bookshop in the square, too? Or do we want it near the department store?

Man: No, I think a bookshop in the square is a nice idea. Here, on the left, maybe?

Woman 1: Yes. Now, what about our police station…

Exercises 4 & 5

Students' own answers.

Page 60

EXAM FOCUS
LISTENING PART 1

1 C
2 B
3 C
4 A
5 A
6 B
7 C

Track 039

Narrator: For each question, choose the correct answer. One. Where will the man and woman go for the weekend?

Woman: So, where shall we go for our weekend away?

Man: We could go on a city break. Somewhere lively, where we can go shopping, and go to the cinema.

Woman: I fancy going somewhere quiet. Maybe the countryside. We can go walking. Or how about the seaside? We could go swimming in the sea.

Man: OK. Nice idea. Let's look at the weather.

Woman: It doesn't look too good for the weekend. I think your idea was the best.

Man: Yeah, let's do that.

Narrator: Two. Where is the girl at the moment?

Woman: Hi, it's Kerry. Listen, I'm going to be late home. I had to stay behind in class to do some extra work, so I left college quite late. Then I got to the station and guess what? My train was cancelled! I was there on the platform, waiting and waiting for ages. Finally, another one came and I've even got a seat. So, I'm on my way and I'll be back in about half an hour. Bye!

Narrator: Three. Where did the family spend the first night of their holiday?

Woman: Where did you camp?

Man: Well, the first night, Dad said we should camp by the river, but we persuaded him it'd be more fun in the forest, so we put the tent up under the trees. But there were so many insects that we had to take it down and go back to the spot which Dad had chosen. By the time we put up the tent again, we were so exhausted we fell asleep immediately! For the rest of the holiday we stayed at a nice comfortable campsite.

Woman: I don't blame you!

Narrator: Four. Which place did the woman like best?

Man: You went to Southminster yesterday, didn't you?

Woman: Yes. It's a beautiful town.

Man: Is there much there for tourists?

Woman: Plenty. We went to a brilliant art gallery and saw lots of great pictures. But it was the museum that really impressed me – they had some amazing stuff there. Of course, Southminster's most famous thing is its covered market.

Man: Yes, it's fantastic, isn't it?

Woman: The market's certainly the top attraction. It was a bit crowded yesterday, though, so we didn't stay long.

Narrator: Five. Where will the boy meet his friends?

Man: Hi. Aiden here. Hey, remember how we said we'd meet at the café to have a drink and a snack? You know, before we go to see the baseball game? Well, the problem is, I need to go the college library to take back a book I borrowed. And I don't know how long that's going to take, so I think I'd better just go straight from the library to the game. Anyway, I'll see you there. We can maybe go for something to eat or drink after that. See you later!

Narrator: Six. What will the family do this afternoon?

Woman: Right. So we've got places where we can take the children today.

Man: It's going to be a busy day! How about going to the castle this morning?

Woman: That doesn't open until midday. So we could go to the zoo first. See some animals!

Man: Good idea. The kids love going to zoos. And then after that spend a bit of time at the park, maybe?

Woman: That's where we could have our lunch.

Man: Great. I'll go and make a picnic.
Woman: And I'll go online and book our tickets for the castle. So, that's our day organised!
Narrator: Seven. Where will the coach pick up the visitors?
Man: Ladies and gentlemen, we're just coming towards the theatre now. We can stop there for a short time only, so please be ready to get off the coach. We hope you enjoy the show. When you leave the theatre, turn left and go to the car park, which is a five-minute walk away at the end of the road. The coach leaves from there at 4 p.m. And if the traffic isn't too bad on the way home, we expect to get you back to the coach station by 5 p.m. OK. Here we are!

Page 61

WRITING PART 2

Model answer

John looked out of the train window and saw the bright lights of the city. As he got off the train, he felt excited because he was going to start a new life in the capital.

At first, John enjoyed walking along the busy city streets. He loved looking at the huge department stores, the tall apartment blocks and giant skyscrapers. Everything seemed so big and exciting. However, after a while, John noticed that everybody looked unhappy and stressed. Before long, he started to miss the relaxed, friendly faces of the people in his village.

So he packed his suitcase, went back to the station, and said goodbye to the bright lights of the city.

Page 62

REAL WORLD

Exercise 1

Students' own answers.

Page 63

Exercise 2

The City Card photo is not mentioned.

Exercise 3

1 It has a lot of canals.
2 You can get off to visit sights and then get on again.
3 It's over 200 years old.
4 Historical paintings and Dutch culture.
5 Fruit, vegetables, cheese and fish.
6 Rembrandtplein

Exercise 4

1 c
2 b
3 a
4 e
5 d

Exercise 5

a 3
c 1
d 2

Track 040

1
Assistant: Hi. Can I help you?
Tourist: Yes. We've just arrived in Amsterdam, and we have two days here. Can you recommend some places to visit?
Assistant: Sure. It depends on your interests. Are you interested in art?
Tourist: No, not art, but we'd like to learn about the history of the city.
Assistant: OK. Well, I think I'd recommend some of the smaller museums. Here's a list: The Museum Van Loon is amazing. It's a 17th century house, and when you go in it's like stepping back in time. You can really see how people lived. Then there's Anne Frank's house. Do you know the story of Anne Frank? Her family hid in this house during the Second World War.
Tourist: That sounds interesting.
Assistant: And of course, you can't leave Amsterdam without going on a canal trip. There are loads of points around the city where you can pick one up. It's really worth it.
2
Tourist: Hi. Can you tell me how to get to the Albert Cuyp Market?
Assistant: Sure. Are you on foot?
Tourist: Yes. How far is it?
Assistant: Well, you can walk, but it's a bit of a hike. It would take a good half hour. The quickest thing would be to hop on a tram in the square. You want the number four tram, and the stop is Stadhouderskade. Here's a map, so you can see where it is.
Tourist: OK. Thank you.
Assistant: You're welcome. Have a great day.
3
Assistant: Hi. Can I help you?
Tourist: Yes. What's the best way to get around the city?
Assistant: Oh, there are lots of options. You can hire a bike – Amsterdam's perfect for cycling because it's flat. Then there are buses and trams. They go all over the city, and they're quick. This is a map of all the public transport showing bus routes, trams, and the metro.
Tourist: Oh, that looks good.
Assistant: You might want to consider getting an 'I Amsterdam' City Card. How long are you here for?
Tourist: Just the weekend.
Assistant: OK. So, you can get a 48-hour card for 67 euros. That gives you free use of all public transport, and you can also get free entry to lots of attractions. They're good value for money.
Tourist: OK, that sounds like a good idea. Can we buy a City Card here?
Assistant: Yes, of course. I can sort that out for you.

Exercise 6

1 recommend
2 learn about
3 get to
4 far
5 get around
6 buy

Exercise 7

1 e
2 b
3 c
4 a
5 d
6 f

Exercise 8

Suggested answers

Seeing the old city: best way to see the old city is by canal
Getting around the city: can be done on foot; cycling is a good option if the weather's fine. Buy an 'I Amsterdam' Card if you're using buses and trams as it's much cheaper; buy it online before you come
Museums: Rijksmuseum has works of art from all over the world - old and modern; Museum Van Loon shows life in a traditional house 200 years ago; some museums get very busy, so it's a good idea to book tickets in advance
Street markets: they offer good prices; try some local foods such as cheeses or pickled fish; buy tulip bulbs
Eating and drinking: cafes and restaurants in the main squares are nice, but expensive; smaller restaurants in streets behind the main squares or by the canals for better prices

Exercises 9 & 10

Students' own answers.

UNIT 5

Page 64

VOCABULARY

Exercise 1

Students' own answers.

Exercise 2

1 Anna is the fittest
2 Callum is the least fit.
3 Students' own answers.

Track 041

1
I'm Callum and I'd say I'm more of a stay-at-home kind of person, really. I can swim, but I only go swimming about once a year, when I'm on holiday, although I know it's really good for your muscles and lungs and general fitness. I can't ski or

snowboard, or anything like that. Some sports can be dangerous, can't they? And I don't want to break a bone. In winter, I prefer to keep warm, sitting in front of a good film on TV. And I'd rather drive than walk. It's more convenient, isn't it?

2

I'm Anna, and I like to keep active. I do yoga for an hour before breakfast, and go to the gym for a workout a couple of times a week. Then, every Saturday and Sunday morning I go cycling, or running. I actually had a cycling accident a couple of years ago. It was a bit nasty because I twisted my left ankle, cut my knees and bit my tongue, but I still love my bike! It's hard to get up on a cold morning and go out for a run – there are times I'd rather stay in bed – but I always feel better when I've done it. I just love being outdoors, especially in summer when I can feel the sun on my skin.

3

I'm Greg. I work long hours in an office in New York, riding the subway to work, so I don't get much exercise most weeks. I don't like water much, and I can't swim, but I'm really into winter sports. I can ski and snowboard pretty well, and I can skate a bit, too. I do freestyle skiing, which can be dangerous, but I always protect my elbows, shoulders and wrists and I've never broken anything. I love going to the mountains when it's snowy, it's just a shame I can't do it as often as I'd like.

Exercise 3

Callum: bone; muscles; lungs
Anna: ankle; knees; skin; tongue
Greg: elbows; shoulders; wrists

Exercise 4

1 True
2 False. One of our lungs is bigger and heavier than the other one.
3 False. There are more bones in a baby's body than in an adult's body.
4 True
5 False. We need 200 muscles to take just one step.
6 True
7 True
8 True
9 True
10 True

Track 042

1 It's impossible to kiss your elbow.
2 One of our lungs is bigger and heavier than the other one.
3 There are more bones in a baby's body than in an adult's body.
4 An average man has almost two square metres of skin.
5 We need 200 muscles to take just one step.
6 Shoulder injuries are the type of injury that doctors see most often.
7 Many more people wear their watch on their left wrist than on their right wrist.
8 Every person has different-looking knees!
9 The biggest problem among sportspeople is ankle injuries.
10 A person's tongue can be over 10 centimetres long.

Exercise 5

1 muscles
2 bone
3 wrist
4 knees
5 ankle
6 shoulders
7 lungs
8 tongue
9 skin
10 elbows

Page 65

READING PART 6 TRAINING

Exercise 1

Suggested answers

He's fit/strong/healthy/athletic/sporty. He's running.

Exercise 2

shoulder; knees; muscle

Exercise 3

1 He ran nearly 1,400 km. / He ran the whole length of Great Britain.
2 It took him only 31 days.
3 He did this run to raise money (for a charity) (which helps young people and their families).
4 He was fine apart from sore knees and a torn muscle.

Exercise 4

2 as
3 ago
4 which/that
5 from

Exercise 5

Students' own answers.

Page 66

GRAMMAR

Exercise 1

C

Exercise 2

1 can
2 able
3 could

Exercise 3

present perfect; I haven't been able to sleep for months now!

Exercise 4

1 can
2 couldn't
3 can't
4 haven't been
5 was

Exercise 5

Students' own answers.

Exercise 6

ought to

Exercise 7

1 shouldn't
2 ought
3 should
4 should

Exercise 8

Model answer

Hi Emily,
I'm sorry to hear about your problem.
I think you should stop drinking coffee and get some thick black curtains for your bedroom.
I hope this helps.

Page 67

VOCABULARY

Exercise 1

1 B
2 H
3 G
4 A
5 C
6 E
7 F
8 D

Track 043

1 I always have backache when I get up in the morning. I ought to buy a more comfortable bed!
2 My tooth hurts when I drink anything hot. I ought to go to the dentist.
3 I've got a cough. Can you pass me some water, please?
4 I think I injured my ankle running yesterday.
5 I won't come swimming with you today. I've got a cold and don't want it to get worse.
6 I've got a pain in my stomach. I think I ate my dinner too fast!
7 I think I'm getting ill. I've got a really sore throat and it's difficult to talk.
8 My knee has been really painful since I cycled 15 km at the weekend.

Exercise 2

1 pain
2 hurts
3 injured

4 sore
5 backache

Exercise 3

1 make
2 off
3 four
4 skirt
5 plane

Ache and *pain* have the same vowel sound.

Track 044

1 ache make
2 cough off
3 sore four
4 hurt skirt
5 pain plane

Exercise 4

a emergency
b infection
c patient
d prescription
e tablets

Track 045

Receptionist: Good morning. Can I help you?
Mr. Baker: Oh, hello. I've got an appointment to see the doctor at 9 o'clock. My name's Ron Baker.
Receptionist: Take a seat, Mr. Baker. You're the doctor's first patient today, so you won't have to wait long.
Doctor: OK, Mr. Baker. I'm just going to listen to your chest. Yes, you've got a chest infection. You need to take some tablets for that. I'm going to give you a prescription. Just take it to the chemist's and they'll give you your tablets.
Mr. Baker: Thank you.
Doctor: And I'm also going to send for an X-ray, just to make sure that everything's all right with your lungs. Is that OK?
Mr. Baker: Yes, of course.
Receptionist: Hello?
Doctor: Hello, it's Doctor Ali here. I'd like to send Mr. Baker to the hospital, so that he can have an X-ray.
Receptionist: Oh, I see. Shall I call an ambulance to take him there?
Doctor: No, we don't need an ambulance. It isn't an emergency. But if you could call him a taxi?
Receptionist: Yes, of course.

Exercise 5

1 prescription
2 emergency
3 patient
4 infection; tablets

Exercise 6

Students' own answers.

Page 68

PUSH YOURSELF B2

Exercise 1

1 B
2 D
3 E
4 G
5 F
6 H
7 A and C

Track 046

A
Man: Oh, those children outside are making such a noise! My head really hurts.
Woman: Yes, same here. I've got a splitting headache, too. It's really painful.
B
Man: So, you're not feeling well?
Woman: No, I feel really hot and ill. I think I'm coming down with flu.
Man: Let's see. … Oh, 39 degrees. Yes, you should go home and get into bed.
C
Woman: That was a long walk. My feet are killing me.
Man: Why don't you take your shoes off?
Woman: Yeah, I will. Ahhh. That's better.
D
Man: Are you coming running tomorrow morning?
Woman: No, I don't think I will.
Man: Oh, is anything wrong? Are you ill?
Woman: No, not really. But I don't feel very well, either. I haven't slept well these last few nights. I just feel a bit under the weather, you know?
E
Woman: You can't go to work tomorrow. You're not well enough.
Man: You're right. I'll call in sick.
Woman: Good idea. A day off work will do you good. Stay home and keep warm.
F
Woman: I can't stop coughing. And my throat hurts.
Man: That doesn't surprise me. Everyone at college has coughs and colds at the moment.
Woman: Yes, there's a bug going round, definitely.
G
Woman: How are you feeling?
Man: Not too bad, today. I can eat normally, and my temperature is going down. I think I'm on the mend, anyway. I hope to be back at work some time next week.
Woman: That's good to hear.
H
Man: I haven't seen you for ages!
Woman: That's because I haven't been well. I was in bed with terrible flu for two weeks. It was awful. Anyway, I'm back on my feet now and I feel fine, thank goodness.
Man: Oh, I didn't know you were ill. I'm glad you're OK now.

Exercise 2

Suggested answers

1 I think I'm coming down with flu.
2 I'm a bit under the weather.
3 I'll call in sick.
4 I'm on the mend.
5 There's a bug going round.
6 I'm back on my feet.
7 I've got a splitting headache. / My feet are killing me.

Exercise 3

Students' own answers.

SPEAKING

Exercise 1

Students' own answers.

Exercise 2

1 He wants to go to his friend's party.
2 He can't go because he has a sore throat.
3 She tells him to go home and have some tea with lemon and honey.
4 She tells him to take some tablets for five days.

Track 047

Woman: Hi, Tom. How are you doing? Are you coming to my party tonight?
Tom: Umm, I don't feel very well, actually. I really want to come to your party, but I can't. I need to rest. I'm sorry.
Woman: Oh. You don't need to say sorry. What's wrong?
Tom: I've got a sore throat. It's really painful.
Woman: Oh, poor you. You ought to go home.
Tom: Yeah, I think I will.
Woman: And how about having some hot tea? It's a good idea to add lemon and honey, too.
Tom: Yeah, I might try that. That's what my grandma always used to give me.
Woman: Mine too! It always works. Anyway, I hope you feel better soon.
Tom: Thanks. I've made an appointment to see the doctor tomorrow.
Woman: Good idea. Look after yourself.
Tom: Thanks. I will.
Doctor: So, Tom, isn't it? Now, what seems to be the problem?
Tom: My throat's really sore.
Doctor: Let's take a look … Mmm, yes, I can see that you have a throat infection. Now, here is a prescription for some tablets.

Tom: OK.
Doctor: You have to take these tablets four times a day.
Tom: And do I have to take them with food?
Doctor: No, you don't have to take them with food. You can have these at any time of day. But you mustn't forget to take your tablets. That's important.
Tom: Right.
Doctor: And you must take them for five days, and don't stop until you've had all the tablets in the bottle. Is that clear?
Tom: I see. Thank you.

Exercise 3

How are you doing?
What's wrong?
Poor you.
You ought to …
How about having …
It's a good idea to …
I hope you feel better soon.
Look after yourself.

Track 048

Woman: Hi, Tom. How are you doing? Are you coming to my party tonight?
Tom: Umm, I don't feel very well, actually. I really want to come to your party, but I can't. I need to rest. I'm sorry.
Woman: Oh. You don't need to say sorry. What's wrong?
Tom: I've got a sore throat. It's really painful.
Woman: Oh, poor you. You ought to go home.
Tom: Yeah, I think I will.
Woman: And how about having some hot tea? It's a good idea to add lemon and honey, too.
Tom: Yeah, I might try that. That's what my grandma always used to give me.
Woman: Mine too! It always works. Anyway, I hope you feel better soon.
Tom: Thanks. I've made an appointment to see the doctor tomorrow.
Woman: Good idea. Look after yourself.
Tom: Thanks. I will.

Exercise 4

1

1 Asking about problems
2 Showing sympathy
3 Giving advice

2

How are you doing?; How are you?
What's the matter?; What's wrong?
Get well soon.; I hope you feel better soon.
Take care.; Look after yourself.

Page 69

Exercise 5

1 are you / are you doing
2 well
3 What's
4 hurts
5 hear that
6 don't you
7 care

Exercise 6

Students' own answers.

GRAMMAR

Exercise 1

1–3 must, need to, have to (in any order)
4 & 5 don't need to, don't have to (in either order)
6 mustn't

Exercise 2

1 don't have to
2 mustn't
3 must
4 don't need to

Exercise 3

1 don't have to
2 must
3 mustn't
4 need

Exercise 4

Model answers

1 People can swim, dive and have saunas at the swimming pool.
2 People have to take a shower before they go in the pool.
3 People with short hair don't have to wear a swimming hat in the pool.
4 You mustn't take food or drink into the pool.

Page 70

READING PART 1 TRAINING

Exercise 1

Suggested answers

1 You might see it in a sports centre.
2 People who want to keep fit might be interested in it.
3 People would need to know about places, times, prices, levels, and if you need to book.

Exercise 2

Necessary; essential
Not necessary; no need

Exercise 3

C

Exercise 4

1 B
2 B

LISTENING PART 3 TRAINING

Exercise 1

Students' own answers.

Exercise 2

A time: gap 2
A place: gap 5
Something you can learn to do: gaps 1 and 4
Something to eat or drink: gap 3

Exercise 3

Students' own answers.

Track 049

In the mornings, we normally have a tennis class, but unfortunately the tennis court is out of use today. So instead we have an hour's yoga outside in the garden – that class will be taught by Annie, one of our fitness instructors.

Page 71

Exercise 4

1 yoga
2 12
3 honey
4 Diving
5 beach

Track 050

Good morning and welcome to Oasis Health Club. We hope you'll have a relaxing and enjoyable weekend with us. There are two swimming pools, a sauna and steam room here, as well as two well-equipped gyms. In the mornings, we normally have a tennis class, but unfortunately the tennis court is out of use today. So instead we have an hour's yoga outside in the garden. That class will be taught by Annie, one of our fitness instructors. It's an excellent way to stretch your muscles and relax your mind. Lunch is a self-service salad bar, and this will be available in the cafeteria from 12 until 2 o'clock.
Following lunch, we have one in a series of talks from an expert on foods and drink that are good for your health. Today's is on honey, and tomorrow's will be on lemons. They're both very interesting talks.
The afternoon is a good time to enjoy our swimming pools. The pool in the garden is ideal for swimmers of all abilities. Meanwhile in the indoor one, our diving instructor Mike will be holding a class for anyone who'd like to learn this skill. You don't need to book, just go along there at three o'clock.
Then, later, there's a choice of outdoor activities. If you like jogging, you can go for a run in the woods with one of our instructors, or you can join a cycling trip down to the beach if bicycles are more your thing. Then in the evening …

Exercise 5

Students' own answers.

WRITING

Exercise 1

He wants advice on how to get fitter and healthier.

Exercise 2

Advice:

The best way to get healthier is …

Why don't you try cooking your own food?

You shouldn't eat too much sugar …

How about joining a gym to get fitter?

If I were you, I'd join Lifestyle Fitness on High Street.

expression to start email: Thanks for your email.

expression to end email: Write soon!

Exercise 3

Punctuation errors:

~~Thank's~~ **Thanks** for your email.

~~Theyre~~ **They're** much better for you

Spelling errors:

its ~~swiming~~ **swimming** pool is fantastic

The staff who work there are ~~realy~~ **really** friendly people

Preposition error:

because it's not good ~~on~~ **for** your health

Modal verb error:

You shouldn't ~~to~~ eat too much sugar

Exercise 4

Students' own answers.

Page 72

EXAM FOCUS

READING PART 1

1 B
2 C
3 C
4 A
5 B

Page 73

READING PART 6

1 have
2 us
3 who/that
4 than
5 of
6 the

LISTENING PART 3

1 October
2 blue
3 password
4 bus stops
5 75
6 biketopia

Track 051

Narrator: For each question, write the correct answer in the gap. Write one or two words or a number or a date or a time. You have twenty seconds to look at Part 3. You will hear a radio announcement about a new bike hire club.

Speaker: Are you tired of waiting for buses? Or want to get some exercise when you're going round the city? Well, the City Bike Hire Club could be just the thing for you! Brightly coloured bikes are going to start arriving in the city towards the end of September, and you can sign up as a club member from the first week of October.

There'll be bikes for all ages. And because they're different colours, they'll be easy to recognise. For the smallest riders, up to the age of 10, there'll be children's bikes. These are going to be red. Then, the next size up is green, for young teenagers. And there'll be full-size blue bikes suitable for anyone in their late teens or older.

Hiring the bikes will be very easy. Unlike older bike hire schemes, where you used a coin or needed a key to unlock the bikes, the City Bike Hire Club is all electronic, and you just put in your own special password to get your bike.

So, where will you find the bikes? Well, you can pick them up and drop them off at bus stops all over the city. You can pay by phone, online, or else contact the Bike Hire offices at the station or town hall.

And finally, the price. You can hire a bike for €10 per day, or if you want to hire bikes regularly, you can pay a fee for the whole year, which gives unlimited use for only €75, which is good value.

If you want to find out more information, just go to the club's website at www. biketopia. That's double you double you double you dot B.I.K.E.T.O.P.I.A.

So, we're all looking forward to a cleaner, healthier city, with more cyclists, fewer cars and fitter people!

Page 74

REAL WORLD

Exercise 1

Suggested answers

It's an old city; there is a big market; you can buy lots of interesting things; you can stay in nice hotels

Exercise 2

Suggested answers

Check the weather forecast of the place you're going to; check the emergency numbers in case you need to call an ambulance; find out how to see a doctor if you need to; check if there are any specific dangers in a place, e.g. crime or insects

Page 75

Exercise 3

1 antiseptic
2 vaccination
3 travel insurance
4 filtered water
5 sanitiser
6 painkiller
7 sunscreen

Exercise 4

1 when there is nowhere to wash your hands
2 food that has been in the sun for a long time
3 the plastic causes pollution
4 filtered water

Exercise 5

2; 3; 5; 6; 8

Track 052

Travel agent: OK. So, I think that's all the details sorted. You're going to have an amazing trip! Do you have any questions?

Tourist 1: Yes. Do we need any vaccinations?

Travel agent: No, you don't need any special vaccinations for Morocco, but it's always a good idea to make sure all your regular vaccinations are up to date. You don't need to worry about malaria, either, because you're staying in Marrakesh. The cities are fine – it's only an issue in the very rural areas.

Tourist 2: Oh, that's good to know. Thanks. Is there anything we should take with us for our health?

Travel agent: Definitely sunscreen– lots of it! The sun's very hot, and you'll burn really quickly if you're out in it all day. Go for a good, strong sunscreen, factor 50 or something like that, and put it on regularly. The other thing it's a good idea to take is something to keep insects away. There aren't any dangerous insects in Marrakesh, but they can be a nuisance.

Tourist 1: OK, thanks. And I have another question. Is the water safe to drink?

Travel agent: Well, I think wherever you go on holiday it doesn't hurt to be cautious about drinking the tap water. There's no big problem with the water in Marrakesh, but it's obviously different to the water you have at home, so your body isn't used to it. The hotel you're staying in has filtered water, which is absolutely fine to drink. Remember, you must drink plenty – dehydration can be a real problem when it's very hot.

Tourist 1: OK. We'll remember that. And what's the food like in Morocco?

Travel agent: The food is brilliant – lots of really tasty dishes. I think there are some recommendations in the guide here … yes, you must try a tagine. You'll find the food's cooked to very high standards in most hotels and restaurants. If you're worried about sickness, stick to hot dishes and avoid raw vegetables, and you should be fine. With street food, it's the same advice, really. If someone's just cooked it, and it's nice and hot, it'll be fine to eat. I've had some great street food in Marrakesh!

Tourist 2: OK. One more question. What should we do if we're ill?

Travel agent: Well, your hotel's your first port of call for any problems, including health problems. They'll be able to advise you on where the nearest pharmacy is, and how to see a doctor. There are plenty of doctors, so you don't need to worry. As with any trip, make sure you have travel insurance to cover any costs.

Exercise 6

1 Do we need
2 Is there anything
3 safe to drink
4 the food like
5 we do

Exercise 7

1 a
2 b
3 a
4 b
5 a
6 b

Exercise 8

Suggested answers

Old city: dates back to 1062, lovely in the evenings

Hotels: choose a traditional style hotel and get an idea of Moroccan way of life, or a modern hotel.

Restaurants and cafes: lots of restaurants, serving traditional dishes like tagine, made with fresh vegetables, cafes serve mint tea

Street food: very popular, lots of street food, especially in the evenings; buy where you can see people cooking

Health advice: ask at your hotel if you're ill; don't forget health insurance

Exercises 9 & 10

Students' own answers.

Page 76

PROGRESS CHECK 2

Exercise 1

1 saucepan
2 slices
3 put
4 grate
5 oven

Exercise 2

1 delicious
2 bowl
3 course
4 meal
5 bill
6 tip

Exercise 3

1 e
2 a
3 g
4 f
5 h
6 b
7 d
8 c

Exercise 4

1 library
2 campsite
3 apartment block
4 art gallery
5 stream
6 neighbourhood
7 department store

Page 77

Exercise 5

1 went
2 had been
3 happened
4 was taking
5 had happened
6 had
7 were travelling
8 broke

Exercise 6

1 sore
2 prescription
3 shoulder
4 painful
5 patients
6 emergency

Exercise 7

1 can
2 couldn't
3 must
4 ought to
5 been able to
6 mustn't

Exercise 8

1 I'd like some rice, please. / I'd like rice, please.
2 I need a little time to finish my homework. / I need a few more minutes to finish my homework.
3 Last weekend we had a party.
4 Sarah gave Chris a present that he had always wanted.
5 You must do your homework!
6 It's Saturday so I don't have to go to work.
7 Sorry, but I can't go to the English lesson today.
8 You shouldn't/mustn't eat too many sweets.

Exercise 9

1 b
2 c
3 d
4 a
5 d
6 b

UNIT 6

Page 78

LISTENING

Exercises 1 & 2

Students' own answers.

Exercise 3

1 next weekend
2 to get information to plan the weekend

Track 053

Hi! It's Dylan. I can't wait to see you all next weekend! I want to make sure you love London, so tell me what you most want to do or see, OK? And I know one or two of you may have other people to visit here. Can you tell me when you're going to meet them? See you soon.

Exercise 4

A Rafi
B Sue
C Megan

Track 054

1

Hi all, Rafi here. Well, I'd like to see some famous places of course. Covent Garden, Trafalgar Square, maybe the Tower of London, you know … I've got one plan already. I'm meeting my cousin Meera on Saturday afternoon and she's taking me to some Asian shops. My friends say I have to bring back lots of Asian food because, you know, we can't get anything where we live! Oh, and she says we should have a meal at Brick Lane – there are lots of Indian and Bangladeshi restaurants there, right? OK, see you, bye!

2

Hi it's Megan. Yes, Covent Garden, Trafalgar Square and the Tower all sound great. The National Gallery is in Trafalgar Square, isn't it? You know I love art, so can we go there? Actually, I can go on my own if you don't want to. And then, yeah, dinner on Brick Lane on Saturday evening would be fantastic! Dylan, I'm visiting my aunt and uncle on Sunday evening, and staying another night with them, so I'll say goodbye to you all on Sunday afternoon at the station. Can't wait! Bye.

3

Hi, Sue here. Listen, I've got a problem: I'm not coming on Friday evening. My dad's in hospital and I have to pick him up and bring him home. But I've booked a train for Saturday morning. I arrive at ten thirty. But there's one good thing about this. I actually don't like spicy food, so why don't you all go to Brick Lane on Friday evening? Then I don't have to! Oh, and how about the theatre on Saturday, or is that too expensive? Well, anything we do is fine, Dylan, we're coming because we want to see you! Bye.

Page 79

Exercise 5

1 Sue
2 Rafi
3 Megan
4 Megan
5 Sue

Exercise 6

A 4
B 5
C 1
D 2
E 3

Track 056

Hi all, thanks for your messages. So Rafi and Megan, your train gets in at five o'clock on Friday, right? I'm going to meet you at the station and then we're going to have our spicy Brick Lane dinner. Oh, I forgot to book a table! I'll call the restaurant later. Anyway, on Saturday, when Sue arrives, we can do the West London sights – you know, Trafalgar Square and all that. Oh, and Sue, you'll be happy about this: my Dad got us tickets for a West End theatre show! We're all seeing a play on Saturday night, but I'm not telling you what play, it's a surprise! And Megan, everyone except Rafi is interested in the National Gallery, so let's go together on Saturday afternoon when he's shopping with his cousin. The Tower of London is further east, so let's all go there on Sunday morning. OK? Have I forgotten anything? This will be so much fun!

Exercise 7

Students' own answers.

SPEAKING PART 1 TRAINING

Exercise 1

1 This is too short.
2 The information does not answer the question.
3 This is a relevant answer, but the candidate could say more.
4 This is good.

Track 056

1

Examiner: Cristina, where do you live?
Cristina: In Spain.

2

Examiner: Daniel, where do you live?
Daniel: Yes, I'm Daniel and I have two brothers and a sister, and I live in an apartment and…

3

Examiner: Cristina, where do you live?
Cristina: I live in a town in Spain.

4

Examiner: Daniel, where do you live?
Daniel: I live in Toledo. It's a small town not far from Madrid. It's nice.

Exercise 2

Students' own answers.

Exercise 3

1 so (C)
2 well (D)
3 let me see (C)
4 repeating part of the question ('… a teacher that I liked …') (D)

Track 057

1

Examiner: Can you tell us about your family?
Cristina: OK. So, I come from a big family. I've got three brothers and two sisters. So, that's quite unusual. Big families were common in my country in the past, but they're unusual now.

2

Examiner: What does your family do together?
Daniel: Well, to be honest I don't see my family much at the moment. My parents and brother live in another city and I don't have a family of my own yet. I mean, I don't have a partner or children. So I do more things with my friends.

3

Examiner: Where do you meet your friends?
Cristina: Oh, lots of places. Let me see. We often meet in a café that we like in the town centre. Or sometimes we go running together, so we meet in the park. We rarely invite each other home. More often we go out.

4

Examiner: Tell us about a teacher that you like or liked.
Daniel: Hmm, a teacher that I liked. I really liked my Maths teacher, Mr. Meyer. I used to find Maths difficult, but when Mr. Meyer became my teacher everything changed. I don't know why, but I understood things better when he explained them. He was a bit strict, but that's OK.

Exercise 4

Students' own answers.

Page 80

GRAMMAR

Exercise 1

1 be going to
2 will

Exercise 2

1 to
2 won't
3 going
4 Will
5 will

Exercise 3

1 are you going to
2 'm not going to
3 'll
4 won't
5 'm going to
6 'll
7 Will
8 will

Exercise 4

1 continuous
2 simple

Page 81

Exercise 5

1 arrives
2 'm seeing
3 finishes
4 Are; going (to go)
5 'm staying
6 'm not doing
7 is/'s playing
8 does; start

Exercise 6

Students' own answers.

VOCABULARY

Exercise 1

Students' own answers.

Exercise 2

1 selfies
2 follow
3 tagged
4 unfriend
5 blocked
6 filters

Exercise 3

1 requested
2 update
3 stories
4 posting
5 status

Page 82

GRAMMAR

Exercise 1

Students' own answers.

Exercise 2

1 will
2 won't
3 will
4 won't
5 will
6 is going to

Exercise 3

Students' own answers.

Exercise 4

Track 058

1 It's going to rain.
2 Be careful! You're going to fall!
3 I'm not going to be on time for the meeting.
4 Are we going to see you at the party?

Page 83

PUSH YOURSELF B2

Exercise 1

a 2
b 1
c 5
d 6
e 3
f 4

Exercise 2

Students' own answers.

WRITING

Exercise 1

C

Exercise 2

Suggested answers

For most people: B and C.

A sounds too dry and formal. D suggests the writer is going to list personal problems and possibly insult people.

Exercise 3

Let me tell you a story …
Have you ever been in a similar situation?
What did you do?

Exercise 4

Model answer

Friends. Who can live without them? I don't need to have a huge group of friends, but my close friends are the people who make my life great! I love spending a relaxing evening with one or two other people. They should be friends I've known for a long time so that we can talk about things that are really important. Of course, I like getting to know new people, but old friends are the best.

However, it's not all about sitting together and talking. My friends and I want to have fun! I need to be with people who have a sense of humour, and a sense of adventure, too. I hit it off with people who want to try new things and go to new places. Friendships are for the good times and the bad times. You need people you can rely on, but you also need people who are just good fun. That's what I think, anyway. What do you think?

Page 84

READING PART 3 TRAINING

Exercise 1

Students' own answers.

Exercise 2

Answer 2

Page 85

Exercise 3

A

Exercise 4

B

Exercise 5

A Kath Moore uses a lot of different social media. <u>Here, she explains which social networks are best for friends, and which are best for families</u>.
C Kath Moore once had an argument with her mother. <u>Here, she tells us how we can use social media more for better relationships within families.</u>
D <u>Parents never respect their children's privacy online.</u> Kath Moore tells us why she was angry when her mother shared a photo of her.

Exercise 6

1 C
2 A

Exercise 7

Students' own answers.

VOCABULARY

Exercise 1

1 get on with
2 positive

Exercise 2

1 positive
2 positive
3 negative
4 positive
5 negative
6 positive

Exercise 3

1 They hit it off as soon as they met.
2 They sometimes fight but then they make up.
3 I can (always) rely on my parents (when I need help).
4 You can turn to me (if you need support).
5 Lucy and Lee have broken up.
6 Mary and Pia were school friends but at college they grew apart.

Exercise 4

Students' own answers.

Page 86

EXAM FOCUS READING PART 3

1 D
2 B
3 A
4 A
5 C

Page 87

SPEAKING PART 1

Model answers

1 Hello. My name's Chiara.
2 I live in Latina. It's a large town near Rome.
3 I've lived there all my life. I was born there, in fact.
4 I'm a student. At the moment, I'm studying economics at university.
5 Yes, I do. I go to English classes twice a week.
6 Yes. It's an interesting language and it'll be useful for me in my work.
7 I usually meet up with them at the weekends. We often go out together on Saturday night.
8 I met a friend for a coffee on Friday after work, and then on Saturday I met my family and we celebrated my grandmother's birthday together.
9 I live with my two flatmates. Maria is a chef and Gianni is a student.

Page 88

REAL WORLD

Exercise 1

Students' own answers.

Exercise 2

1 Travelmates
2 Freesofas
3 Localfriends
4 Travelmates

Page 89

Exercise 3

1 a
2 a
3 b
4 a
5 a

Exercise 4

Students' own answers.

Exercise 5

Suggested answers

It's important because some people use websites like these for bad purposes, so you need to be careful. Other possible advice: go with a friend when you meet someone for the first time, always have your phone with you, always tell a friend or family member where you are going.

Exercise 6

a 3
b 1
d 2

Track 059

1

Jamie: Hi. I'm Jamie. Are you Melanie? Have we got the right address?
Melanie: Yes. Come in. It's Jamie and Ian, isn't it?
Ian: That's right. I'm Ian. Nice to meet you.
Melanie: Come on in, both of you. This is my husband, Paul.
Jamie: Hi. I'm Jamie.
Paul: Nice to meet you both.
Jamie: Wow! You have a lovely apartment. It's very kind of you to offer us a room.
Melanie: Not at all. We enjoy meeting new people. There's only one room, I'm afraid. Is that OK?
Ian: Yes, we're happy to share a room.
Paul: So, where are you guys from?
Jamie: We're from London. We're going travelling round Europe for a month, and Paris seemed like a good place to start. We've already seen some of the main sights – the Eiffel Tower and Notre Dame.
Paul: Well, tomorrow morning I can show you round some of the little backstreets if you like. The real Paris.
Jamie: Yeah. That would be amazing! Thank you.
Melanie: And will you be eating with us this evening?
Jamie: If that's OK with you, we'd love to.
Melanie: That's settled then. Let me show you to your room.

2

Xavier: Hi. Are you Kasia and Magda?
Kasia: Yes. You must be Xavier. Thanks for coming. Sit down and join us. I'm Kasia, and this is Magda.
Xavier: It's great to meet you. Where are you from?
Magda: We're from Poland.
Xavier: And how long have you been in Paris?
Magda: We arrived two days ago. We've done all the main sights, like the Louvre and the Champs Elysees, and we decided we wanted to find a music event. It's really difficult when you're a tourist because you don't know the best places to go, so we went on the website and found you.
Xavier: Well, I'm glad you did. It's going to be a great concert tonight, and you'll meet all my friends, so you can get to know them, and see what life's really like for young people in Paris.
Kasia: Cool! Are you from Paris?
Xavier: Yes, I was born here, and now I'm studying Chemistry here.
Kasia: Oh great. We're students, too. I'm studying history, and Magda's studying French.
Xavier: Oh, that's great. Well, you'll get plenty of opportunity to speak French later, when you meet all my friends. So, shall we order a coffee?
Magda: Yes, good idea.

3

Eve: How long have you been in Paris?
Fredy: Three days. It's a great city. I've met lots of people from all over the world, but not many from Paris.
Eve: Yeah, I know. It's the same in any city. But there's this fantastic website I often use called Localfriends. Do you know it?
Fredy: No.
Eve: Well, it's basically a social media site, and you can use it in any city in the world when you're travelling. And basically, it's a way to find local people who are happy to meet you and show you around the city. I've met some really cool people using it.
Fredy: That sounds really good.
Eve: Hang on, I'll show you. Here we go. Here are some people who are keen to meet travellers and show them around. Look at this one, Emilie – and see, you can look at the person's profile and find out a bit about them. So, she's a student, studying biology. Or there's this guy , Louis, he says he loves meeting people from other countries and chatting to them. But he's only available at weekends, so that's no good.
Fredy: Well, shall we contact Emilie? She looks really friendly, and look, she lives quite near here.
Eve: OK. I'll message her and see if she can meet up later today.

Exercise 7

1 d
2 f
3 b
4 a
5 h
6 g
7 c
8 e

Exercise 8

1 Are you Jamie and Ian?
2 Come in
3 Where are you from?
4 Would you like to eat with us this evening?
5 That's agreed, then.

Exercise 9

Suggested answers

Over 15 million visitors per year; the Eiffel Tower is the most popular tourist attraction, built in 1885; the Champs Elysees is one of the most expensive shopping streets in the world; the Louvre is home to the Mona Lisa; you can use social networking sites to meet local people, who can help you find the best cafes and restaurants, the best places to shop, and the best local foods to try

Exercise 10 & 11

Students' own answers.

UNIT 7

Page 90

VOCABULARY

Exercises 1, 2 & 3

Students' own answers.

Exercise 4

He scores five points; Students' own answers.

Track 060

Man: OK, first question. Hmm, I'd say 'c'. I do like to keep up with fashion.
Woman: What about number two, then?
Man: I'd say 'a'. I only wear fashionable clothes if they suit me. If I look awful in them, I won't wear them. I mean, I don't wear clothes with patterns very often. I don't mind striped clothing, like a shirt or top, but I'd never wear checked trousers, or something like that. I think plain clothes with one colour suit me best.
Woman: How about the third question?
Man: Oh, 'a' definitely. I look around, I try things on, and I see how I look in them. If they fit me – they're not too loose, not too tight – and they're my kind of style, I'll buy them. If I need to buy a shirt for work, for example, I try it on. I want to know that the sleeves aren't too long and that I can do up the button on the collar, for example.
Woman: And then the last question? Do you buy clothes you like immediately?
Man: Oh, no, I don't buy clothes that I can't afford. If they're really expensive, I'll wait until the sales, when the prices go down.
Woman: OK, let's see what your score is … Right, it's five, so that means 'You care about your appearance, but there are things that matter more to you than wearing the latest fashion'. Is that right?
Man: Yeah, that's probably true.

Exercise 5

1 d
2 e
3 a
4 c
5 b

Exercise 6

1 Patterns
2 checked
3 loose
4 striped
5 sleeves
6 tight
7 button
8 plain

Exercise 7

Students' own answers.

Page 91

LISTENING PART 4 TRAINING

Exercise 1

Students' own answers.

Exercise 2

Matt's way of dressing could be described as casual, cool, on trend and stylish.

Exercise 3

Students' own answers.

Exercise 4

B; But the best thing is getting to know my audience

Track 061

Woman: Today I'm talking to Matt Davies, who's a fashion vlogger. Hi, Matt.
Man: Hi there.
Woman: So, tell us about the life of a vlogger. Is it fun?
Man: Yeah, it is. I have my own vlogging channel, where I give advice on tailoring, men's fashion and style basics. I like doing things my way, and I like the fact that it's my own channel, so nobody tells me what to do! And of course, I love it when the fashion companies send me new clothes to wear on my vlog. I get to wear them even before they're in the shops, which is cool. All I need to do is write a product review about them. But the best thing is getting to know my audience: all the guys who watch my vlogs and follow my channel. We chat, they tell me what they like and don't like. They tell me how I helped improve their image. And that's great.

Exercise 5

1 A
2 B
3 C

Track 062

Woman: So, how did it all start?
Man: Well, first of all I had a job working in a clothes store, which was OK, but I realised I had lots of ideas of my own about looking good. And I wanted to let people know about them, so I began making videos, showing my way of putting clothes together. At first I was just at home on my smartphone. It went on from there. A lot of people start vlogging just because they want to be famous, but that's not the reason I got into it.
Woman: So, what makes a successful fashion vlogger, in your opinion?
Man: Well, you need to give plenty of style tips. Some vloggers talk about lots of kinds of styles, while others focus on just one. The important thing, though, is to be an individual. If you look and sound the same as everyone else, you'll never get many people subscribing to your channel. There are thousands of vloggers posting videos every day, so you need to do or say something interesting, so that people remember you and follow you.
Woman: And do you have plans for the future?
Man: Well, people who like the way I look always tell me I should be a professional model. I'm not sure I'd enjoy that, though. Some vloggers dream of becoming TV presenters, but I don't think that's for me, either. I prefer to be creative, you know? In fact, I'd love to create some cool shirts, as well as jackets, trousers and stuff in my own style and see them in the shops. That'd be brilliant.

Exercise 6

Students' own answers.

Page 92

VOCABULARY

Exercise 1

1 return
2 refund
3 receipt
4 exchange
5 order
6 deliver
7 damaged
8 complain

Track 063

Man 1: Nice jacket, Mike! Is it new?
Man 2: It's a long story, actually. I bought it last month, but I didn't like it at first. So, I went back to the shop and tried to return it. I said that I wanted a refund. But I'd lost my receipt, so they told me that they couldn't give me my money back.
Man 1: That's a pity. So what did you do?
Man 2: Well, they said they would exchange it for another style of jacket. But there wasn't one of the same price in the shop, so I asked if they could order it for me. They said they could deliver it to my house the next day, but when it arrived, I opened the bag and saw that it was damaged!
Man 1: Oh, what a pain! Did you complain?
Man 2: Yes, of course. I told them that I wasn't happy. But in the end, I decided to keep the first jacket. It's OK. I quite like it now.

Exercise 2

1 order
2 complain
3 refund
4 deliver
5 return
6 exchange
7 damaged
8 receipt

Exercise 3

1 return
2 refund
3 receipt
4 exchange
5 order
6 deliver
7 damaged
8 complain

GRAMMAR

Exercise 1

Because he's reporting what was said and therefore uses a past tense instead of a present tense.

Exercise 2

1 present continuous
2 past perfect
3 past simple

Exercise 3

1 I said that I wanted a refund.
2 They asked if I wanted to exchange it.
3 I asked if they could order one for me.
4 They said that they would deliver it to my house the next day.
5 I explained that I'd changed my mind.
6 I told them that I was going to keep it.

Page 93

Exercise 4

1 he could; my
2 she was
3 they had
4 if/whether; wore
5 she didn't; that
6 he had; his

Exercise 5

1 Correct
2 Can you ~~say~~ **tell me** the price of this?
3 I said 'Good morning' to the sales assistant.

4 Correct
5 They ~~said~~ **told us** that the TV would arrive next week. / They **said** ~~us~~ **that** the TV would arrive next week.

PUSH YOURSELF B2

Exercise 1

1 c
2 a
3 b
4 a
5 c

Exercise 2

1 to show me/us
2 me/us not to wear
3 me/us to come/go shopping with them.
4 me/us not to go
5 (me/us) how much

Page 94

READING PART 5 TRAINING

Exercises 1 & 2

Students' own answers.

Exercise 3

1 C
2 A
3 B
4 B

Page 95

Exercise 4

1 colours
2 music
3 how goods are displayed
4 smells

Exercise 5

1 False. They just needed a pair of socks.
2 True
3 True
4 False. Shoppers are often keen to search through a messy pile of clothes, thinking that they might find a bargain.

VOCABULARY

Exercise 1

a bargain/very good value
customers/shoppers
display/arrangement
goods/products
messy/untidy
price reductions/special offers
shops/stores

Exercise 2

1 goods/products
2 price reductions/special offers
3 display/arrangement
4 a bargain/very good value

Exercise 3

Students' own answers.

Page 96

SPEAKING

Exercise 1

Students' own answers.

Exercise 2

1; 3; 4; 5

Exercise 3

1 a
2 a
3 b
4 a
5 a
6 b

The response 'Do you?' in Item 3 shows the speaker doesn't agree.

Track 064

Woman: So, do you prefer shopping online or in ordinary stores?
Man: Hmm, it depends. I'd rather buy clothes in ordinary shops.
Woman: Yeah, so would I. I want to know if they suit me or not, and I like trying things on before I buy them.
Man: Same here! Especially with shoes. I prefer to buy shoes in normal shops.
Woman: So do I. What if they don't fit, or they're uncomfortable? It's so annoying when you have to send things back to online stores for a refund or an exchange. I don't like returning things.
Man: Neither do I.
Woman: Anyway, I think it's more fun to go shopping in a real place. You know, walking about, browsing in different shops and chatting to people. I love going to big shopping malls.
Man: Do you? I hate them, especially when there are sales on, or at holiday times. I can't stand crowded shops.
Woman: I know what you mean.
Man: So, what kind of things do you buy online?
Woman: Oh, books and games. Technology stuff, like headphones and so on.
Man: Me too. There's more choice online, so there are more bargains.
Woman: That's a good point. There are some great prices out there. And of course, it's much quicker.
Man: It is more convenient, isn't it? It only takes a few minutes to buy something online.
Woman: Yeah, and the other advantage of online shopping is that you can read lots of reviews from other customers. So you know which products and sites are good.
Man: Absolutely. Other people's comments can be really helpful.

Exercises 4 & 5

Students' own answers.

Exercise 6

Track 065

clothes
close

Exercise 7

1 close
2 clothes
3 clothes
4 close

Track 066

1 close
2 clothes
3 clothes
4 close

Page 97

WRITING

Exercise 1

Students' own answers.

Exercise 2

1 A
2 C
3 B

Exercise 3

1 range of goods/variety of items
2 What I like most about this website
3 My only complaint
4 I'd certainly recommend this site.

Exercise 4

Positive: amazing value; excellent quality; incredible variety; very reasonable
Negative: not the cheapest; quite limited; rather disappointing

Exercise 5

1 but
2 and; as well
3 Although
4 though

Exercise 6

1 excellent quality
2 difficult
3 The best thing about it is
4 take quite a long time to arrive
5 fairly expensive
6 easy
7 My only complaint is
8 take quite a long time to arrive

Exercise 7

Students' own answers.

Page 98

EXAM FOCUS READING PART 5

1 B
2 C
3 D
4 A
5 C
6 B

Page 99

LISTENING PART 4

1 C
2 B
3 A
4 C
5 B
6 B

Track 067

Narrator: For each question, choose the correct answer. You now have 45 seconds to look at Part 4. You will hear an interview with a woman called Tina Mackay, whose job is to write reports on the service she receives in different shops.

Man: Can you imagine a job where you go shopping all day? Well, that's exactly what today's guest Tina Mackay does. You're known as a 'Mystery Shopper,' aren't you, Tina?

Woman: That's right. I'm employed by a research agency that helps shops to find out how good their service is. If a department store wants to know about their standard of service, I go to the shop, look round, buy something, then send them a report. Of course, the sales staff don't realise what I'm doing – they just think I'm an ordinary customer. It's almost like being a detective, really.

Man: What kind of things do you look for?

Woman: Basically, I check how clean and tidy the shop looks, see if the goods are laid out well, note if the staff seem polite and helpful, and how good they are at selling their products, that kind of thing.

Man: And what do you think makes a good sales assistant?

Woman: Being friendly and helpful, of course – that's what any customer wants from sales staff. Not jumping on the customer as soon as they walk in, but not leaving them too long wondering if anyone's going to serve them. It's a question of timing.

Man: So, what's the main goal for a mystery shopper?

Woman: Well, the main purpose of my job is to provide a fair, honest view, from someone outside the company, finding the good things as well as the bad. I always try to balance the positive and negative points. I think some people just make complaints, to get people into trouble, but I don't do that.

Man: Do you find your job hard at times?

Woman: It is, sometimes. There's a lot you have to notice in a short time. Fortunately, I've got a good memory – that helps me a lot. I'm naturally a very warm, open, sociable person, but I mustn't show it. I need to keep a certain distance from the people I'm reporting on, and that's not always easy. But I still think it's a great job for me – because I love going out and buying stuff so much!

Man: What kind of things do you buy?

Woman: All sorts, really. The company provides the money, and I choose what I want. I love trying on fashions, the latest styles of clothes. And perfume too. I bought some lovely French perfume last week. Unfortunately, I don't get to keep any of it! Apart from magazines, that is. I don't have to return those. Everything else is sent back the next day. I still enjoy buying it, though!

Page 100

REAL WORLD

Exercise 1

Ceramics; lanterns; leather goods; Students' own answers.

Page 101

Exercise 2

1 False. There is an amazing range of shopping malls.
2 True
3 True
4 False. There are spice shops all over Istanbul.
5 False. Leather goods are very affordable.

Exercise 3

1 b
2 d
3 c
4 e
5 f
6 a

Exercise 4

1 b
2 c
3 a

Track 068

1

Assistant: Can I help you?

Tourist: Yes. Do you have these jeans in a size 36?

Assistant: Let me have a look. There are some more over here. Yes, here's a size 36. Was it the darker ones you were interested in, because we've also got them in this lighter colour.

Tourist: Yes, it's the dark ones I want. Can I try them on?

Assistant: Of course. The changing rooms are just over there.

Tourist: Thanks. Can I try these tops on, too?

Assistant: Of course. You're only allowed six items at a time in the changing room, so if you've got more than six, you'll have to leave some outside. But someone over there will sort that out for you.

Tourist: OK. Thank you.

Assistant: How did you get on? Any good?

Tourist: Hmm, the jeans are a bit tight.

Assistant: Would you like to try the next size up?

Tourist: No, I think they'll be too big. I'll leave it. But I'll take this top.

Assistant: OK. Let me take the other things for you. This top's beautiful, isn't it? If you just come this way, I'll get it wrapped for you.

2

Tourist: How much is this wallet?

Stallholder: It's 120 lira. It's real leather. One hundred percent genuine leather.

Tourist: I think that's too expensive. I'll give you 60 lira for it.

Stallholder: No. Look, it's real leather. You can't find this quality in any other shops here. If you see cheaper ones in the bazaar, they're not real leather, but this one is the best quality leather.

Tourist: I'm not sure.

Stallholder: OK. I'll say 100 lira. That's a really good price. I guarantee you won't do better than that anywhere in the bazaar.

Tourist: Mmm, I think that's still too much. I'll give you eighty lira.

Stallholder: No, how can you be serious? It's worth much more than 80 lira. Look, it's handmade.

Give me ninety lira. I can't do any more than that.

Tourist: Eighty five. That's a fair price.

Stallholder: OK. Eighty five. Thank you very much.

3

Tourist: Excuse me. What's this one?

Stallholder: That's ground cumin. It's very fresh. Here, you can smell it.

Tourist: What do you use it for?

Stallholder: Cumin is a typical Turkish spice. If you want to cook Turkish food, you can't do without it. You can use it with meat, especially lamb. It gives a very nice, warm, spicy flavour.

Tourist: Thank you. And what are these?

Stallholder: These are red pepper flakes. You know red peppers? Like chilli peppers? These are very popular in Turkey. You sprinkle them on your food, to make it a bit hot, a bit spicy. Some people add a lot, and some people just add a little. It's up to you.

Tourist: OK. What's the difference between these three kinds of pepper flakes?
Stallholder: They're from different kinds of pepper, so the flavour is different. This one is very hot, this one is medium hot, and this one is mild and a bit sweet.
Tourist: Can I taste some?
Stallholder: Of course. Which one would you like to taste?
Tourist: The mild one, please.
Stallholder: Here you are.
Tourist: That's nice, and it isn't too hot. Mmm, yes. Can I have a small packet of that, please?
Stallholder: Of course.

Exercise 5

1 in a size
2 Can I
3 I'll leave
4 I'll take
5 How much is
6 I'll give you
7 a fair
8 do you use
9 taste
10 a small packet

Exercise 6

1 d
2 f
3 a
4 c
5 b
6 e

Exercise 7

Suggested answers

Currency: the Turkish Lira – about 5 lira to one euro
Forum Istanbul: one of the largest shopping centres in the world; open 10 am to 10 pm; popular with families, 10-screen cinema and an aquarium
Istiklal Street: known for designer shops, expensive goods, and also local crafts; goods have prices so no need to haggle; tram that goes along centre of the street
Grand Bazaar: 61 streets and over 4,000 shops, open every day except Sunday; sells many things such as lanterns and scarves; spice sellers are happy to talk about how to cook with spices

Exercises 8 & 9

Students' own answers.

UNIT 8

Page 102

VOCABULARY

Exercise 1

Suggested answers

A ice; a river/lake; someone kayaking
B a forest; a waterfall, palm trees
C a boat sailing on the ocean
D sand; the desert
Students' own answers.

Exercise 2

1 A
2 C
3 D
4 B

Track 069

1
Paul: This one looks exciting.
Liz: It looks freezing! Is that an iceberg?
Paul: No, it's a glacier. I've always wanted to see one. You can go into caves of ice. It must be amazing.
Liz: Well I think it sounds dangerous, and much too cold!
2
Liz: What about this one? It's a sailing race.
Paul: To be honest, that picture makes me feel a bit scared. I like being on the water, but I want to be near a beach or a riverbank. We can't see any shore at all here. And the big waves would make me feel sick.
Liz: But there aren't any big waves in this picture! I agree, though. We're not really sailors. It's not for us.
3
Liz: Here's a race through a desert. It looks beautiful.
Paul: But there's nothing there!
Liz: What? Don't you see those beautiful sand dunes?
Paul: Yeah, but I don't see any trees with branches and leaves that could give us some shade. Those little bushes wouldn't help. Sorry, but that's too much sun for me.
4
Liz: OK, how about a race through the rainforest, then? If it gets too hot, we could have a shower under this waterfall.
Paul: Yeah or we could fall down that cliff, or break a leg on those stones. But OK, we want an adventure, so let's read more about it. Actually, I think it looks cool!

Exercise 3

1 iceberg
2 glacier
3 caves
4 riverbank
5 shore
6 waves
7 sand dunes
8 branches
9 leaves
10 bushes
11 rainforest
12 waterfall
13 cliff
14 stones

Exercise 4

dense/empty
dry/humid
noisy/quiet

Suggested answers

dense B
dry D
empty A; C; D
humid B
noisy B
quiet A; C; D

Page 103

READING

Exercise 1

A Manu National Park, Peru
B The Gobi desert, Mongolia
C Alaska
D Four oceans around the world

Exercise 2

1 the Volvo Ocean Challenge
2 the Jungle Ultra
3 the Alaska Mountain Wilderness Classic
4 the Gobi March

Exercise 3

1 The humid air of the dense jungle, and the thin air of the mountains will be a new challenge.
2 You probably won't see a Gobi bear as, like some other animals here, this is an endangered species.
3 Respect nature! That's the key to completing this amazing challenge.
4 Your family may be very worried about you, and there are good reasons for this.

Exercises 4 & 5

Students' own answers.

Page 104

LISTENING

Exercise 1

Suggested answers

Why did you want to run the Jungle Ultra?
Did you enjoy it?
Did you have a problem with a jaguar?

Exercise 2

Student's own answers.

Track 070

Jack: Lisa, why did you take part in this really tough race, the Jungle Ultra? How did you even get the idea?
Lisa: Well, Jack, I've always been a runner. I've run lots of marathons, including the New York marathon, for example.
Jack: And that's too easy for you?
Lisa: No, no, it's very tough. I wasn't looking for something harder. I actually found out about the Jungle Ultra after I had watched a documentary about disappearing rainforests. I knew the

rainforests were in danger and I wanted to see them. In a few years, it could be too late! I looked for interesting events around the Amazon, and I found the Jungle Ultra – perfect! I immediately registered to take part.

Jack: It's five days of running in the jungle, and you weren't frightened. You must be a very brave person!

Lisa: Actually, as soon as I'd registered, I thought, what a mistake! I might not be fit enough. I may have problems with the temperature, or a snake might bite me! That was the most frightening thought!

Jack: But then you did it, and you were fit enough and you weren't bitten by a snake. Was it easier than you had feared?

Lisa: No, it was unbelievably hard, but I loved it. You soon feel exhausted and think you may not be strong enough to keep going. But you do keep going, and it's a great feeling at the end of each day, even if the race is exhausting.

Jack: And did you love the rainforest?

Lisa: No! Sorry, but there are too many scary animals. One day I was running with a man from Canada when he suddenly stopped and whispered, 'a tiger!' 'It can't be a tiger,' I said. 'There aren't any tigers here.' But honestly, I was terrified. We stayed very still for a long time and then a jaguar walked past. Later, people said we had been very lucky to see a jaguar, but it was a terrifying experience. I think I'm lucky to be alive!

Jack: So, you're not a jungle fan.

Lisa: Well, it's not for me, but we have to save the rainforest, Jack, it's so important! That's why I'm talking to you today. I want to ask people to support my new environmental project …

Exercise 3

1 c
2 a
3 d
4 b

Exercise 4

Example answers

1 She had run a lot of marathons including the New York marathon.
2 She was scared and thought she had made a mistake.
3 She felt great, and happy that she had kept going.
4 It was a jaguar.
5 She doesn't like the scary animals, but she knows it's important to save it.

Exercise 5

Student's own answers.

VOCABULARY

Exercise 1

1 -ed
2 -ing

Exercise 2

1 challenging
2 worried
3 confused
4 encouraging
5 relaxed
6 amazing
7 surprising
8 satisfied

Exercise 3

Suggested answers

1 I'm worried / It's worrying because the situation is getting worse.
2 I'm annoyed. / It's annoying. I'm trying to read and I can't.
3 I'm surprised / It's surprising, but it's very nice of her.
4 I'm relaxed and happy! / It's relaxing and I feel happy!

Page 105

GRAMMAR

Exercise 1

1 must
2–4 could; may; might
5 can't

Exercise 2

1 might
2 can't
3 could
4 may
5 could
6 might
7 may not
8 must

Exercise 3

1 Peru must be an exciting country.
2 I might/may/could go there next summer.
3 But the flights can't be cheap.
4 I may not / might not have enough money.
5 I might/may/could ask my parents to pay for the flights.
6 But then they may/might/could want to come with me.

Exercise 4

No, the *t* isn't pronounced.

Track 071

It must be true.
It might be true.
It can't be true.

Exercise 5

(Sounds that disappear are in brackets.)

1 You're the firs(t) person to arrive.
2 I don'(t) want eggs.
3 See you nex(t) week.
4 You cou(ld) be a star!
5 He bought a use(d) car.

Track 072

1 You're the first person to arrive. (firs(t) person)
2 I don't want eggs. (don'(t) want)
3 See you next week. (nex(t) week)
4 You could be a star! (cou(ld) be)
5 He bought a used car. (use(d) car)

Page 106

VOCABULARY

Exercise 1

A arctic wolf
B green iguana
C hedgehog
D orangutan
E penguin
F red deer
G red squirrel
H giraffe
I polar bear
J kangaroo

Exercise 2

Suggested answers

Grassland animals: Giraffes are found in Africa, and kangaroos in Australia.

Tropical forests: There are iguanas in Mexico and Central and South America (the green iguana prefers forest but some other types don't). Orangutans are native to Indonesia and Malaysia.

Temperate forests: Hedgehogs are native to Europe, Asia and Africa. Red deer are native to Europe, Asia and North Africa. The red squirrel is found in Europe and Asia.

Polar regions: Arctic wolves and polar bears are found in the arctic. Penguins live in the southern hemisphere, not only in the Antarctic but also in South America, southern Africa, Australia and New Zealand.

Exercise 3

Students' own answers.

Page 107

PUSH YOURSELF B2

Exercise 1

1 C
2 A
3 D
4 E
5 B
6 F

Track 073

1

I think I just like them because they are so large and look so calm. And the trunk is cool, though I'm not sure exactly what it is, to be honest. Well, it's a kind of nose, I suppose, but they can also use it for carrying things. It makes me angry that some people kill them for their tusks.

2
I love the beautiful red colour of their fur and their bushy tails. They look so sweet with their furry little paws, but I wouldn't like to have a fight with one. I'm sure they can bite you hard and scratch you with their claws.
3
I like all birds, but especially the ones that live on water, and these are my favourites. Their white feathers make them look so elegant. Don't make one angry, though. A bite from that sharp beak can really hurt you.
4
I love them because they are so strong and fast, but also so gentle. Of course, they could kick you with a hoof and really hurt you, but they don't want to. Some people cut their manes very short, which I don't like. They need a mane, and it's beautiful, too.
5
They look very gentle, but they can also fight with their impressive antlers. Some hunters kill them and take the antlers home, but that's not my thing. I don't know why they have such a small tail. Other animals' tails are much longer.
6
They have really pretty stripes on lovely dark orange fur, and I love their long, white whiskers. These animals are very dangerous, though, and if you see one in the wild, you shouldn't go near it. Their claws are very sharp!

Exercise 2

1 paw
2 fur
3 antlers
4 tail
5 trunk
6 tusks
7 beak
8 feathers
9 hoof
10 mane
11 claws
12 whiskers

Exercise 3

Suggested answers

1 deer and horses
2 birds
3 all of them
4 fur
5 dogs and cats

Page 108

SPEAKING PART 2 TRAINING

Exercise 1

Students' own answers.

Exercise 2

She includes all the points in the list.

Track 074

This is a picture of an interesting place. There is a beautiful lake with a yak resting beside it. This can't be a lake in Europe as we don't have yaks. On the right we can see a man with a backpack. He looks European, so he must be a tourist. He could be on a hiking holiday because he's wearing comfortable walking shoes. There is snow on the mountains in the background. It could be a cold country, or the mountains may be very high. But on the other hand, the man is wearing a T-shirt and no jacket. It must be a warm day, or it might always be warmer away from the mountains. The sun is shining, anyway. Umm … what else? Oh, the yak is wearing something colourful on its back. I don't know the name of the thing, but it's made by people and it shows us that the yak is not wild. It might be waiting to carry the man or his bags. I like this photo because it makes me think of exciting journeys.

Exercise 3

1 e
2 b
3 d
4 a
5 c
6 f

Exercise 4

Suggested answers

A: There's an elephant in the middle of the picture.
B: So this might be Asia or Africa. We can see a large old building.
A: Yes, so this could be a historic town that tourists visit. The man isn't wearing a coat.
B: It must be a warm day. The man is wearing something colourful on his head. I don't know the word in English.
A: I think he could be Indian. And the elephant is painted with colours and patterns that look Indian.
B: I agree. This must be India. The elephant has something on his back where people can sit.
A: It could be an elephant that tourists can ride.
B: Yes. I think that must be true.

Exercise 5

Students' own answers.

Page 109

WRITING PART 2 TRAINING

Exercises 1 & 2

Students' own answers.

Exercise 3

Sardinia: island; beaches; cliffs; coast; wildlife

Things you can do there: camping; sailing; swimming; eating fish; look at moon and stars

Exercise 4

My favourite part of Italy is Sardinia. Sardinia is an island, so it has a long coast. You can find __________ cliffs as well as __________, sandy beaches. The landscapes are __________ and you can see __________ wildlife. Although it's popular, Sardinia is not as full of tourists as many parts of Italy. For me, the best thing to do in Sardinia is swimming in the __________ sea. Then, when you're really hungry from the exercise, you can eat __________ fish. What's more, there are excellent campsites on the coast. At night, you can look at the moon and stars over the water and feel very happy!

Exercise 5

Suggested answers

1 high; rocky
2 long; relaxing
3 amazing; fantastic
4 interesting; fantastic
5 clear; cool
6 fresh; delicious

Exercise 6

so; as well as; although; then; what's more

Exercise 7

Students' own answers.

Page 110

EXAM FOCUS
WRITING PART 2

Exercise 1

Model answer

From polar bears in the Arctic to penguins in the Antarctic, the world is full of fantastic animals.
When I was on holiday in Greece last year, we took a boat trip on the Mediterranean. We were admiring the beautiful scenery, when suddenly a family of dolphins appeared out of the clear blue sea. They swam next to our boat and seemed so playful and friendly.
Although that was an amazing experience, I think it is better to see wildlife on TV documentaries. I believe it is cruel to keep animals in zoos and visiting animals in the wild can disturb their habitats and damage the environment.

Page 111

SPEAKING PART 2

Exercise 1

1 a
2 a
3 b
4 a
5 b

Exercise 2

Model answer

I think this photograph was taken on a lake, maybe in the USA or Canada. I can see a wide river or lake with a lot of trees on one side of it. The water is browny-green and quite still. There is a canoe on the water, and there are three people in the boat, two children and a man. I think the man might be the children's father. The girl is looking at something. She's using something, but I don't know what's it's called in English. The boy and the man are smiling. They could be on holiday or enjoying themselves at the weekend.

Page 112

REAL WORLD

Exercise 1

Suggested answers

You can see: someone hiking; a hot spring; a geyser; bears; bison

Activities: walking; hiking; skiing; watching wildlife

Need to be careful of: wild animals; getting lost; cold temperatures in the mountains

Page 113

Exercise 2

1 f
2 g
3 d
4 e
5 b
6 a
7 c

Exercise 3

1 c
2 f
3 a
4 b
5 e
6 d

Exercise 4

1 d
2 a
3 b

Track 075

1

Ranger: Hi. Can I help you?

Visitor: Yes. We want to go hiking near Clear Creek. Are there any bears in that area?

Ranger: There haven't been any reports of bears in that part of the park for the last three weeks, so you should be OK.

Visitor: That's good. Can you give us any tips about bears?

Ranger: Well, of course the best thing to do when you're hiking is to avoid seeing them. That means watching for things like footprints or other signs that a bear has been there. If you see those kinds of signs, think about turning around and coming back. When you're hiking, you should also call out every so often – a lot of people call: 'Hey, bear!' That just lets them know you're around, and with any luck they'll go off in the opposite direction.

Visitor: OK. And what should we do if we see a bear?

Ranger: That depends. If it's in the distance and hasn't seen you, stay out of sight and hopefully it won't see you. Then gradually back off, never taking your eyes off the bear. If a bear comes towards you, slowly back away, and if it carries on, or if it runs at you, use your bear spray on it. Do you have bear spray?

Visitor: Yes, we do.

Ranger: That's good. The chances are you won't need it, but better safe than sorry.

Visitor: OK. Thanks.

Ranger: You're welcome. Have a good trip.

2

Official: Hi, there. Can I help you?

Visitor: Yes. We want to go hiking on this trail here. We want to go up this mountain, and then back down this trail, by the river. Will it be easy to follow the trail?

Official: Hmm, I'm not sure. It's not a very well-used trail, because it's quite steep and a bit tricky in places. So, it may not always be clear exactly where the trail goes. Are you planning to do this in a day?

Visitor: Yes.

Official: Hmm. I think that might be pushing it a bit. It's not an easy trail.

Visitor: Oh. Is there an easier one we could follow?

Official: Sure. This one here is part of the Thorofare Trail. That's one of the most popular trails in the park, so a lot of people follow it.

Visitor: Oh, that looks good. Do we need to take a map with us?

Official: You certainly do. The trail is well-marked, but we always advise that people have a map and a compass with them, just in case they get lost. And a cell phone, of course.

Visitor: OK. Thank you.

Official: You're welcome. Have a great day.

3

Official: Hi, there. Are you OK? Do you need some help?

Visitor: Yes. We're going to spend a few days in the National Park, and we read that there are a lot of mosquitoes at the moment. Is that true?

Official: Yeah, this is the summer, so it's the time of year for all kinds of insects.

Visitor: Are mosquitoes a problem?

Official: Yeah, but you can avoid them. The mosquitoes tend to be around lakes and streams, where it's warm and not in the wind. So, if you stick to the high ground and keep away from the water, you should be fine.

Visitor: OK, thanks. And what about ticks? Are they a problem?

Official: Yeah, they can be. You find ticks anywhere where there are low bushes growing, but again, they especially like the lower ground, where it's warm. So, keep your clothes well tucked in, and don't expose any skin.

Visitor: OK. And what do we do if we find a tick on our body?

Official: You need some of these – they're just normal tweezers that you can use for picking up any small objects. You take hold of the tick firmly and then, very gently, just remove it from your body. You'll see a small mark on your skin where it's been. Clean that carefully and put some antiseptic on. But if you're careful and use repellent, hopefully that won't happen.

Visitor: OK. Thank you.

Official: You're welcome. Have a nice day.

Exercise 5

1 go hiking
2 any tips
3 easy to follow
4 need to take
5 a problem
6 find a tick

Exercise 6

1 a
2 a
3 b
4 a
5 b
6 a

Exercise 7

Suggested answers

Camping: 12 camp sites with showers, and 300 sites for wild camping where there are no facilities; need to buy a permit

Bears: if you meet a bear in the distance, keep out of site and move away; if it sees you, move backwards slowly, don't run; get your bear spray ready, if the bear runs at you, spray it when it is about 20 metres away

Hot springs: some water is perfect for bathing, but most is too hot, sometimes 95 degrees; geysers are where water shoots up into the air, most famous is Old Faithful

Streams and rivers: need to be careful because they become fast moving after rain, impossible to cross

Park rangers: trained to give first aid if someone is injured, help people who get lost, and give advice

Exercises 8 & 9

Students' own answers.

Page 114

PROGRESS CHECK 3

Exercise 1

1 request
2 comments
3 posts
4 tag
5 block
6 update

Exercise 2

1 I'm going to spend / I'll send
2 Are you going to / I'm flying
3 is seeing / it leaves
4 We're going to be / won't

Exercise 3

1 tight
2 good value
3 plain
4 messy

Exercise 4

1 goods
2 damaged
3 refund
4 receipt
5 complain
6 exchange

Exercise 5

1 … there was a new clothes shop in town.
2 … if I had been there yet.
3 … that it had a lot of nice things.
4 … me if I liked her dress.
5 … that she had bought it at the new clothes shop.
6 … me when I would go shopping with her.
7 … me if I could lend her some money.
8 … me (that) she had spent all (of) her money on new clothes.

Page 115

Exercise 6

1 branches; leaves / leaves; branches
2 sand
3 cliff; waterfall
4 waves
5 icebergs

Exercise 7

1 True
2 False; giraffes
3 False; penguins
4 True
5 False; hedgehogs

Exercise 8

1 c; relaxing
2 a; worried
3 e; amazing
4 b; disappointing
5 f; challenging
6 d; surprised

Exercise 9

1 must
2 might
3 can't
4 could
5 might not
6 can't

Exercise 10

1 I ~~will~~ **'m going** to visit my grandmother tomorrow.
2 We're going to see a film this evening.
3 Are you going to ~~ate~~ **eat** with us?
4 We ~~meet~~ **'re meeting** our friends later this evening.
5 Noel ~~say~~ **told** me that he liked fish.
6 She said that she ~~is~~ **was** reading a good book.
7 My dad asked me if I ~~have~~ **had** enough money.
8 You ~~can~~ **may/might** think this is easy, but I think it's difficult.

Exercise 11

1 social
2 species
3 trend
4 must
5 fall
6 on
7 going
8 filter

UNIT 9

Page 116

READING PART 3 TRAINING

Exercise 1

Students' own answers.

Exercise 2

A formal; strict; traditional
B informal; lively; relaxed

Track 076

Man: That looks like the kind of school I went to, where students have to sit behind desks and listen to the teacher. The atmosphere's quite formal; like, you have to raise your hand if you want to speak. It's a very traditional way of learning, isn't it? My school was quite strict, too. You had to do exactly what the teachers told you to.

Woman: That's quite a modern type of school, isn't it? The students are working together and learning from each other. It's quite a lively sort of place, and the atmosphere looks fairly relaxed. You don't have to sit still or keep quiet, and you can move around and talk to people. It's quite an informal kind of class, I think.

Exercises 3 & 4

Students' own answers.

Page 117

Exercise 5

A

Exercise 6

2 C
3 B

Exercise 7

4 D

Exercise 8

Students' own answers.

Page 118

VOCABULARY

Exercise 1

1 education
2 curriculum
3 attend
4 grades
5 essay
6 skills
7 rules
8 qualifications

Exercise 2

1 curriculum
2 attend
3 essay
4 qualifications
5 skills
6 rules
7 grades
8 education

Exercise 3

Students' own answers.

GRAMMAR

Exercise 1

First sentence: present tense
Second sentence: past tense
Third sentence: present tense / negative
Fourth sentence: present tense

Exercise 2

1 No, we don't know who stole the phone. Because the phone is more important. / We're more interested in the fact that the phone was stolen than in the identity of the person who stole it
2 My new phone is the subject of sentence a. Somebody is the subject of sentence b.

Page 119

Exercise 3

1 is
2 are
3 is
4 are
5 was

Exercise 4

1 was taken
2 was shown
3 were told
4 were called
5 weren't allowed
6 was shown
7 was asked
8 were given
9 were sent

Exercise 5

Students' own answers.

PUSH YOURSELF B2

Exercise 1

1 d
2 g
3 a
4 i
5 b
6 e
7 j
8 f
9 c
10 h

Exercise 2

1 is being built
2 will be taught
3 were being painted
4 have; been published
5 should be given
6 can be found

Page 120

VOCABULARY

Exercise 1

Students' own answers.

Exercise 2

1 graduate
2 degree
3 terms
4 fail
5 pass
6 topic
7 research
8 revise
9 lectures
10 tutor

Page 121

LISTENING PART 2 TRAINING

Exercise 2

A M
B W
C B

Track 077

Man: So, what did you think of that lecture?

Woman: Hmm, I didn't learn much.

Man: Me neither. I wanted to know about the subject, but the guy who was giving the lecture made no effort to help us understand what it was about. I couldn't follow what he was saying at all.

Woman: I thought he made things pretty clear, actually, but I just found the subject a bit dull and boring. And it went on for about two and a half hours, didn't it? Nobody can concentrate for that amount of time.

Man: Well, I certainly can't! It was awful.

Exercise 3

1 A
2 C
3 A

Track 078

Narrator: One. You will hear two university students talking about a book.

Woman: Are you using that world history book that Dr Jones recommended?

Man: Yeah, I am. I like it. It covers everything in our course, which is good.

Woman: Do you think so? I thought there were some things missing. A good thing about it, though, is that I don't have any trouble following what it's saying.

Man: Neither do I. It's all very clear. And I also like the way that each chapter's about a different country.

Woman: Hmm, I find it more useful when books deal with things in the order that they happen. You know, different periods of history.

Narrator: Two. You will hear a student telling his friend about an exam.

Woman: I'm sorry to hear you failed your biology exam last term. What do you think went wrong?

Man: Well, there are lots of different topics in biology … you know, humans, animals, plants, bacteria and so on. Then, in the exam, there were lots of questions and it was clear enough what we had to do: answer one from each section. Now, the one on plant biology looked easy, so I decided to do that one, even though I don't know so much about that topic.

Woman: Oh, well, we all make mistakes sometimes. I'm sure you'll pass next term.

Man: I hope so.

Narrator: Three. You will hear a sixth form student talking about her future plans to a classmate.

Man: So, what are you going to do after sixth form?

Woman: Well, I definitely want to work in IT, probably as a computer programmer, but I haven't decided which route to take.

Man: OK.

Woman: I could apply for a job as soon as I leave, and then study part-time, and get a qualification in IT while I'm working. Or I could go to university and do computer studies, then apply for a better job after I've graduated. So I'm not sure what to do.

Man: Why don't you ask one of the teachers?

Woman: I think I will.

VOCABULARY

Exercise 1

1 c
2 b
3 a
4 a

Exercise 2

1 make
2 do
3 taken
4 pay
5 take
6 get

Exercise 3

Students' own answers.

Page 122

SPEAKING

Exercise 1

1 geography
2 chemistry
3 history
4 economics
5 maths

Track 079

1

I was brilliant at geography and I always got good grades in it. That was definitely my favourite subject. I loved drawing maps and finding out about different countries. I thought geography was absolutely fascinating.

2

Hmm, I wasn't keen on chemistry, I remember that. I didn't like the smells in the school science lab and didn't like doing experiments. I found chemistry pretty dull, really. I couldn't wait to give it up.

3

Oh, I remember I couldn't stand history! All those dates, and battles and wars. Kings and queens and stuff like that. I was useless at history. And I failed all my history exams!

4

It wasn't a popular subject, but I didn't mind economics, actually. I quite liked all the facts and figures, graphs and things. I found economics fairly interesting.

5

You know, I hated maths when I was at school. When we did maths exams, I always made mistakes in my calculations and got all my sums wrong. Yeah, I was really terrible at maths.

Exercise 2

1 I was brilliant at / I loved / I thought … was absolutely fascinating
2 I wasn't keen on / pretty dull
3 I couldn't stand / I was useless at
4 I didn't mind / fairly interesting
5 I hated / I was (really) terrible at

Exercise 3

1 c bored
2 a terrible
3 b dull

Exercises 4, 5 & 6

Students' own answers.

Exercise 7

biology o O o o
economics o o O o
education o o O o

Track 080

biology
economics
education

Exercise 8

1 a
2 c
3 c

Exercise 9

archae**ol**ogy
cor**rec**tion
ge**ol**ogy
imagi**na**tion
mathe**mat**ics
trans**la**tion

Track 081

archaeology
correction
geology
imagination
mathematics
translation

Page 123

WRITING

Exercise 1

Students' own answers.

Exercise 2

2; 3; 5

Exercise 3

1 Dear Ms Bolton,
2 I am writing to enquire about …
3 Please could you tell me if … / please could you let me know if …
4 I'd also like to know if…
5 Yours sincerely,

Exercise 4

1 b
2 b
3 b

Exercise 5

1 … know when the course starts.
2 … me if accommodation is provided.
3 … know if under-18s can do the course.
4 … know how I should pay for the course.

Exercise 6

Model answer

Dear Mr Collins

I am writing to enquire about your driving courses at Rock Valley Race Track. I'd like to know what the prices are and whether there is a minimum age for students.

Please could you also tell me how I can get to Rock Valley Race Track?

I look forward to hearing from you.

Yours sincerely

(name)

Page 124

EXAM FOCUS
READING PART 3

Exercise 1

1 360
2 articles
3 attitudes
4 five
5 whole
6 four

Exercise 2

1 B
2 D
3 A
4 C
5 D

Page 125

LISTENING PART 2

Exercise 1

In this part, you have to answer **six** questions. For each question, you listen to **two people** talking, and look at some **sentences/words/phrases** to find the correct answer.

Each question has **three possible answers**. You hear the recording **two times/twice**.

Exercise 2

1 C
2 A
3 B
4 B
5 A
6 B

Track 082

Narrator: For each question, choose the correct answer. One. You will hear a girl talking to a classmate.
Girl: Hi, Ethan.
Boy: Oh, hi, Gemma.
Girl: Listen, have you got a moment? It's about tonight's homework.
Boy: Yeah?
Girl: You know the geography essay we've got to do for tomorrow? For Mrs. White?
Boy: OK?
Girl: Well, do you remember what Mrs. White said we should write about in the essay? I wasn't really concentrating in the lesson, I'm afraid. I think she said we had to write something about climate change in Antarctica, but I'm not quite sure.
Boy: Umm, I'll need to go and look at my notes. I can text you a bit later, OK?
Girl: Sure!
Narrator: Two. You will hear two university students talking about a lecture.
Woman: Were you at that lecture about the cotton industry this morning?
Man: Yes, I was, but I didn't find it very useful.
Woman: It covered far too many things, didn't it?
Man: That was fine, actually. But one moment the lecturer was explaining about technology, then the next she was talking about the business side of the industry, then cotton in ancient history, then modern business again! She presented it in a way that was just, well, confusing.
Woman: I see what you mean.
Narrator: Three. You will hear two students talking about a visit to a college.
Young man: It was interesting going to visit that college yesterday, wasn't it? Do you think you'll apply to go there?
Young woman: I might. It's in a very convenient position. It's close to the town centre and easy to get to by bus. And they teach all the things I want to study, like science, arts and languages. I liked it.
Young man: Yeah, I agree. The staff seemed very welcoming, and I thought there was a nice friendly feeling in the college. That was my favourite thing about it.
Young woman: Mine too. I think it would be a good place to study.
Narrator: Four. You will hear a woman talking to a friend about a problem with her studies.

Man: So, how's your course going?
Woman: Hmm, not too well. You know I'm doing a general science course, which is physics, chemistry and biology?
Man: Yes?
Woman: Well, I'm finding the physics part of it really hard.
Man: Could you stop studying physics?
Woman: I'm not sure. I'm wondering whether it might be better to do a totally different course. I've spoken to my tutor and she actually suggested taking some time off – going away for a while and coming back next term.
Man: Rather than making any decisions now about changing courses or dropping subjects?
Woman: Yes.
Man: Sounds like a good idea.
Narrator: Five. You will hear two students talking about an IT exam.
Woman: What did you think of that IT exam?
Man: It was too hard! I couldn't answer most of those questions. And there were so many of them, it took me about ten minutes just to read them all.
Woman: It had the same number as usual, I thought. But the thing was, they all seemed to focus on finding bugs in programs. So if that's something you know about, it's fine. But if that's not an area you're interested in, well, it's just not fair.
Man: It needed a bit more variety, didn't it? I don't think I'm going to get a very good grade.
Woman: Me neither.
Narrator: Six. You will hear a boy talking to a friend about a teacher.
Girl: Do you know Mrs. Baxter?
Boy: The Maths teacher? Yes. Do you like her?
Girl: I do. I like the way she doesn't let anybody behave badly. You've really got to work hard and pay attention in her lessons, haven't you?
Boy: Yes, but she's funny too, which is good. If you enjoy a lesson, and can have a laugh, you remember things better, don't you?
Girl: Yes. And, if you get something wrong first time, she doesn't get angry. She just explains it again really calmly, until you get it right!
Boy: Absolutely. For me, that's the most important thing. That's what's great about her.

Page 126

REAL WORLD

Exercise 1

Suggested answers

You have English lessons and also do activities, Oxford is a beautiful place.

Exercise 2

1 False. Students have language classes in the mornings and activities in the afternoons.
2 False. The course is great for students who want to improve their exam technique.
3 True
4 False. There is one excursion a week to a place of interest.
5 True

Page 127

Exercise 3

1 c
2 d
3 e
4 f
5 b
6 a

Exercise 4

1 d
2 a
3 c

Track 083

1

Receptionist: Hello, Acorn School, Oxford. How can I help you?
Boy: Hello. I'd like some information about the English Plus course, please.
Receptionist: OK. No problem. What would you like to know?
Boy: I'd like to come on a course in August. What dates can I start?
Receptionist: Is this for an individual booking or a group booking? Is it just you, or are you coming as part of a group?
Boy: It's just me and two friends.
Receptionist: OK, so, you can normally join the course any Monday in August, but let me just check the availability. Yes, the week beginning the 13th of August is fully booked, and the week before that, beginning the 6th of August is looking fairly full, so you'd need to book pretty quickly to get onto that one. Other than that, the weeks beginning the 20th of August and the 27th of August still have plenty of spaces.
Boy: OK. Thank you. Also, one of my friends can't eat any gluten. Is this a problem for the school?
Receptionist: No, that's fine. When you fill out the booking form online, just fill in the information in the 'special dietary requirements' section, and they'll make sure there's food that's suitable for your friend.
Boy: OK. Thank you.
Receptionist: You're welcome. Bye.

2

Boy: Well played. That was a good shot. That's game to you, I think.
Girl: Thanks. I think it was a bit lucky, actually.
Boy: Well, maybe. You have good skills.
Girl: Thank you. I practise a lot. I play for a club and we practise twice a week. I love tennis!
Boy: Me too! I play for a team too, but we aren't very good.
Girl: Are you enjoying the course?
Boy: Yes, it's really good. Our teacher is very nice, and the lessons are interesting.
Girl: And the activities are amazing! Last week I did history, and that was really interesting. We learned all about the history of London.
Boy: I'm doing tennis this week, and photography next week. How long are you staying here?
Girl: Four weeks. OK, shall we continue?
Boy: Yes. It's you to serve, I think.

3

Receptionist: Hello. How can I help you?
Girl: Hello. It's my first day today. I don't know which class I'm in.
Receptionist: OK, let's have a look. What's your name?
Girl: It's Lucia Bianchi.
Receptionist: Bianchi, ah, yes. Here we go. You'll be in the Lower Intermediate class, that's with Poppy. She's really nice, you'll like her. So, that's in room 10B, on the first floor. If you go up these stairs here, then head right, you'll find it.
Girl: OK, thank you. And this afternoon I'm doing art. Where is this class?
Receptionist: Well, it'll be in one of the art rooms, but as it's the first day of the course, we ask all students to meet back here at 1.45. All the teachers will be here at that time, so they'll get everyone together who's signed up for their class and take you to the right place.
Girl: OK. Thank you.
Receptionist: You're welcome. Anything else?
Girl: Yes. My friend wants to change her course and do art with me. Is that possible? She's doing photography at the moment.
Receptionist: Probably, yes, but it'll depend on the group numbers. The best thing is for her to come along at 1.45 and have a word with the art teacher. If she's happy, and the numbers aren't too high, then it should be possible. OK?
Girl: OK, thank you.
Receptionist: Bye.

Exercise 5

1 some information
2 can't eat
3 the course
4 are you staying
5 Where is
6 possible

Exercise 6

1 a
2 b
3 a
4 b
5 a
6 a

Exercise 7

Suggested answers

The city and university: about 90 km from London, the university is one of the oldest universities in the world. 38 individual colleges make up the university, with 23,000 students, who still study in the old buildings. There is punting on the river

Language schools: lots of language schools, can study Business English, university entrance courses, General English; classes are small, focus on speaking and fun activities, many schools also offer English with another activity, such as art, cooking, tennis, football

Things to do: shopping, exploring the city, e.g. visiting buildings used in the Harry Potter films, visiting Stonehenge

Exercises 8 & 9

Students' own answers.

UNIT 10

Page 128

VOCABULARY

Exercise 1

Students' own answers.

Exercise 2

1 A
2 B
3 D
4 C

Track 084

1

I quite like flying but I don't like all the time you spend at the airport. You have to wait in the departure lounge for a long time and then you only have a few minutes to get to the gate. I never know what to show where – sometimes they want to see my boarding pass and sometimes they want to see my passport. But when I'm in my seat in the cabin, I start to enjoy the flight.

2

I like driving my car, but it can be stressful. In the city it's really hard to find a parking space. I prefer motorways to narrow roads, but the petrol stations on motorways are expensive and I always forget to fill up before I start my journey. Sometimes I travel by bus in my city. In a traffic jam, a car isn't any faster than a bus, but at least on the bus I can read my book.

3

Travelling by train is great. It's comfortable and fast and not too damaging to the environment. But you often have to wait for your train because there are delays. In my country, railway stations are not always nice. Sometimes there's no waiting room, so you have to stand for a long time on a cold platform. However, the trains are comfortable, and I also think they're quite a safe way to travel.

4

I've only travelled on a ship once and I really enjoyed it. We went on an overnight car ferry from Ireland to France. I was afraid I might feel sick, but I didn't. I loved being on the water and seeing the coast get smaller and further away. It was lovely to arrive at a busy port early in the morning. The lights over the water were beautiful.

Exercise 3

1 boarding pass
2 flight
3 petrol stations
4 traffic jam
5 delays
6 platform
7 ferry
8 port

Exercise 4

Students' own answers.

Page 129

READING PART 4 TRAINING

Exercise 1

Students' own answers.

Exercise 2

Suggested answers

A man and woman were the only two passengers on a flight from Manchester to Dublin.

They were treated like stars by the cheerful cabin staff.

Normally, they don't like flying but this experience was very enjoyable.

Exercise 3

Sentence 2 is correct. *Them* refers to the couple's parents. In sentence 1, *she* doesn't refer to anyone from the previous sentence. In sentence 3, the idea does not logically fit. *Luckily* does not link this sentence to the previous one.

Exercise 4

2 B
3 C
4 F
5 D

Exercise 5

1 cabin staff
2 flight attendant
3 gate
4 airline
5 check-in
6 departure lounge
7 cockpit
8 business-class seat

Exercise 6

Students' own answers.

Page 130

VOCABULARY

Exercise 1

1 f
2 d
3 e
4 c
5 a
6 b
7 g

Exercise 2

1 got into
2 got out of
3 got on
4 get off
5 got to
6 get around
7 get back

GRAMMAR

Exercise 1

generally true

Exercise 2

1 go
2 is
3 don't feel
4 rains
5 get

Exercise 3

Suggested answers

1 If the train is late, people get angry. / People get angry if the train is late.
2 If you fly business class, the food is better. / The food is better if you fly business class.
3 If people travel by bike, they get fitter. / People get fitter if they travel by bike.
4 If I travel by ferry, I get seasick. / I get seasick if I travel by ferry.

Page 131

Exercise 4

1 take; 'll arrive late
2 won't buy; lends
3 park; will give

4 's; won't get
5 will; pay; fly
6 will; do; is

Exercise 5

Students' own answers.

Exercise 6

1 We'll go; doesn't rain
2 Unless I have; I'll visit
3 goes; is
4 takes; feels
5 I'll go; gives
6 I'll call; get

PUSH YOURSELF B2

Exercise 1

Students' own answers.

Exercise 2

Speaker one; 2
Speaker two; 1
Speaker three; 5
Speaker four; 3

Track 085

1

I use public transport and I can get everywhere I want to go, but I find it annoying how long it takes. Buses get stuck in traffic jams, especially in the morning rush hour when everyone is going to work. What a city this big needs is an underground. Now that would be fast and efficient! It's just a dream, though. They'll never build one – it would be too expensive.

2

Well, there are a lot of buses and some local trains, so you can get everywhere on public transport. That's great. I take buses every day and they're usually on time and not too full. However, ticket prices are crazy. They cost much too much. I think people would use public transport if it was cheaper, and that would be better for the environment.

3

Public transport here certainly isn't perfect, but it's OK. The other options are no better. If you take a car, parking is always a problem, and it's incredibly expensive to park in the city centre. Some people cycle, but it's dangerous. We should really improve things for cyclists, but until we do, public transport is the way to travel. It's the best option.

4

Public transport? It's useless! Well, I never use it anyway. I have a lot of appointments in a day, in different places, and I can't wait for a bus to get me there, I'd be late for everything. And in our city, public transport isn't even cheap. I feel sorry for the people who have to use it. Personally, I love my car.

Exercise 3

1 e
2 d
3 b
4 c
5 a

Page 132

LISTENING

Exercise 1

Students' own answers.

Exercise 2

be green; turn off the lights

Track 086

It's not too hard to be green at home. We can make sure to turn off the lights and the TV when we're not using them. All of our rubbish can go to the right recycling bin. We can try to buy things that don't have too much packaging, and get food from local producers. However, when we're out and about, things change. We buy drinks in plastic bottles, and eat meals in plastic packaging, which we throw away. And of course, the fuel that we use when we travel is so bad for our air. Transport causes air pollution, and that pollution causes global warming and climate change.

So what about people who are hardly ever at home? Bands on tour can be a disaster for the environment. Max Carver of the band *Yellow Ducks* tells us what they can do about it.

Exercise 3

rubbish 1
recycling bin 4
packaging 5
local producers 3
pollution 6
global warming 2

Exercise 4

Students' own answers

Track 087

Hi! Well, there's a lot that we can do and there are some great organisations that help us do it. For a start, we use environmentally-friendly tour buses. We use only biofuels. It's not as easy as stopping to get normal petrol whenever you need to, but it can be done. And on the buses, we can have our own water bottles that we reuse all the time. That may not sound like a big thing, but we're a huge team on tour and touring work makes you thirsty! If we all threw away the bottle every time we'd finished a drink, that alone would be a mountain of waste every day! Of course, if we used glass bottles, we could leave them at a bottle bank, but reusing our own bottles is best.

We can also do some things to help our fans be more environmentally friendly. Fans would come to concerts on public transport if we always performed in cities. However, we often play at festivals in the country, so we organise special concert buses. If everybody went to festivals in cars, we would have terrible traffic jams, and that would cause terrible pollution. We also encourage car sharing on our website. If you really have to drive, at least make sure the car is full! There are recycling bins at all concert sites and we don't serve snacks in plastic packaging. Oh, and if it's possible, we try to get our own food from local producers.

All in all, it makes a difference and we wish that more bands would do it. We have to stop climate change and talking isn't enough. We need to act now.

Exercise 5

1 True
2 False. They are a big team and they drink a lot on tour so it is a big thing.
3 True
4 True
5 False. There are recycling bins at all concert sites.
6 False. Their own food often comes from local farms.

Exercise 6

1 car sharing
2 environmentally friendly
3 bottle bank
4 reuse
5 gas

The word not in the interview is *gas*.

Exercise 7

Students' own answers.

Page 133

GRAMMAR

Exercise 1

1 b
2 c
3 e
4 d
5 a

Exercise 2

1 had
2 would be
3 wouldn't
4 would be
5 drove
6 Would
7 bought
8 wouldn't

Exercise 3

1 bought; would be
2 were; would reduce
3 would help; used

4 would stop; knew
5 increased; wouldn't use

Exercise 4

1 are
2 go
3 will solve
4 make
5 were
6 would
7 would be
8 could

Exercise 5

Suggested answers

1 There will be more air pollution if more people fly abroad.
2 More people would use their bikes if the streets were safer.
3 Sea levels will rise if global warming gets worse.

Exercises 6 & 7

1 shortened would
2 shortened will
3 shortened will
4 shortened would
5 shortened will
6 shortened would

Track 088

1 I'd take you to the station.
2 I'll take you to the station.
3 He'll go by bike.
4 He'd go by bike.
5 She'll drive the car.
6 She'd drive the car.

Page 134

WRITING PART 2 TRAINING

Exercise 1

I **went** to the cinema yesterday.; past simple; finished past actions and actions that were repeated in the past
While I **was walking** down the street, my friend phoned me.; past continuous; things in progress at a certain time in the past, or while another action took place
After I **had seen** the film, I went to my friend's house.; past perfect; things that happened *before* other actions in the past

Exercise 2

1 was waiting
2 hadn't seen
3 saw
4 was waving
5 ran
6 was looking

Exercise 3

1 three
2 1: to introduce the situation; 2: to describe what happened; 3: to say how things ended
3 when; then; suddenly; while; finally
4 old; long; cheerful; lively; confused; late
5 excitedly; angrily; suddenly; quickly

Exercise 4

1 comma; exclamation mark; question mark
2 said; called; asked; cried

Exercise 5

1 shouted
2 told
3 asked
4 whispered

Exercise 6

Students' own answers.

Page 135

SPEAKING

Exercises 1, 2 & 3

Students' own answers.

Exercise 4

She would make people pay if they used too much water.

Track 089

If I were the leader of my country, I would make people pay for water. Everybody needs water to live, of course, so some water should be free. However, if you used too much of it, you would have to pay. Some people use a huge amount of water just to have very green grass in their gardens, for example, and I'm completely against that. People in this country should only have garden plants that can live in our dry climate.
If I were the leader, I would make sure that new houses were environmentally- friendly. We have a lot of sunshine in our country, so we can use it for the energy that a house needs. Oh, and new houses would not have air conditioning. Just open the windows at night, it's cool enough!
But the first problem I would deal with if I were the president is definitely the water problem.

Exercise 5

Students' own answers.

Page 136

EXAM FOCUS READING PART 4

Exercise 1

1 H
2 D
3 B
4 A
5 F
6 G
7 E
8 C

Exercise 2

1 E
2 B
3 A
4 H
5 F

Page 137

WRITING PART 2

Exercise 1

1 article
2 around
3 past
4 linkers
5 adjectives
6 spelling
7 capital

Exercise 2

Model answer

By the time I got on the bus with my luggage, there were very few seats left. Fortunately, I found a comfortable double seat right at the back. I was tired, so I lay down across the seat, and soon went to sleep.
A few minutes later, I was woken by the words 'Is this seat taken?' I was on my way to university, feeling stressed and nervous, so I didn't want to share my seat or talk to anyone. The stranger sat down and said cheerfully, 'Hi, I'm Alex. I'm on my way to university.'
Unwillingly, I shook hands. That handshake was the beginning of a lifetime of friendship.

Page 138

REAL WORLD

Exercise 1

Students' own answers

Exercise 2

A check-in desk
B security
C passport control
D departure lounge

Exercise 3

1 Book your flight, check in online and print out your boarding pass.
2 Your baggage allowance and the size and weight of your bag.
3 make sure they are under 100 ml, put them in a clear plastic bag
4 coat; shoes; anything made of metal
5 at the departure gate
6 your passport

Page 139

Exercise 4

1 b
2 c
3 f

4 e
5 a
6 d

Exercise 5

1 b
2 d
3 a

Track 090

1

Officer: I'll need you to take your coat off, please.
Tourist: Oh, sorry.
Officer: It needs to go in a separate tray.
Tourist: OK.
Officer: Any liquids in your luggage?
Tourist: No. I've put my liquids in here.
Officer: I'm afraid you can't take this one. It's over 100 ml.
Tourist: Oh. What can I do with it?
Officer: I'm afraid I'll have to take it off you. Are you wearing a belt?
Tourist: Yes. Shall I take it off?
Officer: Yes, please. Anything else made of metal? Anything else in your pockets? Any loose change?
Tourist: You mean money?
Officer: Yes, coins.
Tourist: Yes, I have some.
Officer: OK. Best to take it out, to be on the safe side. Just pop it in there. Any electronic devices? Phones? Tablets?
Tourist: Just my phone, and I've already put it in here. Shall I put my passport in here, too?
Officer: Yes, please. OK. Come through. If you could step this way, please. Put your arms out. My colleague will just conduct a search.

2

Officer: Next.
Officer: Can you just confirm your name for me?
Tourist: It's Tessa Janssen.
Officer: And your date of birth?
Tourist: The 15th of July, 1998.
Officer: And what's the purpose of your visit?
Tourist: Sorry, I don't understand the question.
Officer: What are you here for? For a holiday? Or to study, or work?
Tourist: Oh, for a holiday. I'm visiting my uncle. He lives in London.
Officer: And how long are you staying?
Tourist: For three weeks.
Officer: Are you staying with your uncle?
Tourist: Yes. I'm staying in his flat.
Officer: OK. Do you have your return flight booked?
Tourist: Yes. I'm going home in three weeks, on the 18th of September.
Officer: Thank you. That's all fine.

3

Tourist: Here's my ticket.
Clerk: Thank you. And your passport, please?
Tourist: Yes. Here it is.
Clerk: Any checked-in bags?
Tourist: Yes, I have one bag to check in.
Clerk: OK. Can you pop it on here for me? Thank you. Did you pack your bag yourself?
Tourist: Yes, I did.
Clerk: It's overweight by two kilos. There will be a charge of £32 for that. Is that OK?
Tourist: Oh, no. Can I take some things out?
Clerk: If you can do it quickly, then that's fine.
Tourist: OK. There. Is that OK now?
Clerk: Yes. That's under the limit now. And how many items of hand luggage do you have?
Tourist: Just one. This bag.
Clerk: That's fine. Here's your boarding pass. It'll be gate number 12.
Tourist: Thank you.
Clerk: You're welcome. Enjoy your flight.

Exercise 6

1 passport
2 understand
3 home
4 Here's
5 check in
6 OK

Exercise 7

1 d
2 f
3 c
4 a
5 e
6 b

Exercise 8

Suggested answers

The airport: 5 different terminals, some deal with goods, not passengers; unusual goods include lions, racehorses and sharks
Flights: over 1,200 flights a day; flights stop at 11.30 pm
Passengers: over 75 million passengers per year, over 200,000 passengers a day; 45 minutes to get through passport control and collect luggage
Baggage: 200,000 bags a day, over 60 kilometres of conveyor belts
Security: body scanners, all bags are checked, around 6,500 security cameras watch people everywhere in the airport
Shops and restaurants: lots of shops and restaurants, breakfast is the most common meal served at the airport; almost 5 million eggs used per year

Exercises 9 & 10

Students' own answers.

UNIT 11

Page 140

VOCABULARY

Exercise 1

Students' own answers.

Exercise 2

A convenient; suburbs; terraced; two-storey house
B block of flats; brand new; business district; top floor
C cosy; old-fashioned

Track 091

Man: Hiya, Jessica. How was your trip to England?
Woman: It was really good, thanks.
Man: You were staying with English relatives, right?
Woman: Yes, three different relatives, in fact.
Man: Yeah?
Woman: Mmm, all really different places, too. The first place I stayed was my uncle's home, which is in a really modern block of flats in the middle of London. It's in the business district, so it's surrounded by modern offices and lots of smart buildings. The flat's brand new and very stylish. It's full of modern equipment and has got fantastic air conditioning. And it's really high up, too – it's on the top floor of the building, so there are some amazing views of London from up there.
Man: Wow! Lucky you. So where did you go next?
Woman: Next, I spent some time at my cousin's house in the countryside. She and her husband live in a kind of old-fashioned cottage, with a big garden, surrounded by trees. Inside, it's quite small, but there's a big fireplace, so it's lovely and warm. You know, really cosy and comfortable.
Man: Sounds nice.
Woman: It was. It's very pretty in the countryside, but a bit quiet for me.
Man: OK, then what about the third place?
Woman: Well, that was different again. At the end of my trip, I stayed for a few days with my aunt and her family in the suburbs of London. They live in a terraced house. You know, in a street, with a line of homes all joined together.
Man: Right.
Woman: It's a typical two-storey house. There's a kitchen, living room and dining room downstairs, and bedrooms and bathroom upstairs. It's a nice house, and it was convenient for the airport, but a long bus ride from anywhere else. It's not really in a tourist area.

Exercise 3

B. Jessica only says positive things about her uncle's flat.

Track 092

Man: So, which place did you like best, Jessica?

Woman: Well, they were all nice in their way, but …

Man: But?

Woman: … but I definitely liked my uncle's place best. It was a cool flat in a great location!

Man: I thought you were going to say that.

Exercise 4

1 block of flats
2 cosy
3 top floor
4 terraced
5 business district
6 two-storey house
7 convenient
8 suburbs

Exercise 5

Students' own answers.

Page 141

READING

Exercise 1

Students' own answers.

Exercise 2

1 C
2 B
3 C
4 B
5 A
6 B

Page 142

GRAMMAR

Exercise 1

1 which/that
2 that/which
3 who/that
4 that/who
5 when
6 where
7 whose

Exercise 2

1 where
2 which/that
3 who/that
4 when
5 whose

Exercise 3

Suggested answers

1 garage
2 washing machine
3 babysitter
4 evening
5 gardener

Exercise 4

1 a; b
2 b; a
3 c; d
4 d; c

Exercise 5

1 non-defining
2 defining
3 defining
4 non-defining

Exercise 6

1 which
2 that/who
3 that/which
4 who

Exercise 7

1 subject
2 object

Rule: object

Exercise 8

Sentence 3

Exercise 9

1 How long have you lived in the flat ~~which~~ where you live now?
2 Have you ever met anyone ~~who~~ whose home is a boat?
3 Do you get on well with the people who/that live next door to you?
4 Correct

Exercise 10

Students' own answers.

Page 143

VOCABULARY

Exercise 1

Students' own answers.

Exercise 2

1 D
2 B
3 H
4 F
5 C
6 I
7 E
8 G
9 A
10 J

Exercise 3

1 wardrobe
2 cabinet
3 sink
4 kettle
5 rug
6 tap
7 duvet
8 cushion
9 heating
10 chest of drawers
11 bin

Exercise 4

1 False. The cabinet is above the sink.
2 False. There is no bin underneath the desk.
3 True
4 True
5 False. The hole in the wall is behind the wardrobe.

Exercise 5

Students' own answers.

Page 144

Exercise 6

Track 093

rug
cup
cut

Exercise 7

Students' own answers.

Track 094

rug rag
cup cap
cut cat

Exercise 8

1 same
2 same
3 different
4 different

Track 095

1 rug rug
2 cat cat
3 cap cup
4 hut hat

LISTENING PART 1 TRAINING

Exercise 1

1 The building in picture C has a black door.
2 The buildings in pictures A and B both have a white door
3 In picture B, there's a tree in front of the building.

Exercise 2

The door has been painted white and the tree has been cut down. / The door is white now and there is no tree any more. The correct answer is A.

Track 096

Narrator: What does the woman's block of flats look like now?

Man: Hi, it's Jim here. I'm just on my way to your flat!

Woman: Great. You've got the address, haven't you? Silverdale House on Park Street?

Man: I actually know that building. I used to work just opposite it. It's a six-storey building with a black door, isn't it?

Woman: Well, in fact they've just had it painted white.

Man: OK. Now, there's a tree just in front, isn't there?

Woman: There used to be one. But it was cut down not long ago.

Man: Oh, that's a shame. Anyway, I know where it is.

Woman: Excellent. Flat four, on the second floor. See you soon!

Exercise 3

1 B
2 C
3 B
4 A

Track 097

Narrator: One. Where is the woman's purse?

Woman: Hi, John, this is Stella. Sorry to bother you, but I left my purse at home this morning. I forgot to put it in my bag before I left for work. I remember I took it from the cupboard next to the washing machine, and I had it with me when I sat down to have breakfast. I meant to pick it up off the table, but I forgot! Silly me! So could you bring it when you pick me up from work this afternoon, please? Thanks. See you later!

Narrator: Two. Which cushions do the friends decide to buy?

Man: So, should we get some cushions as a housewarming present for Annie, then?

Woman: Good idea. Let's look online.

Man: Right. How about those ones with the flowers? They're nice.

Woman: They are, but we don't know what other patterns Annie has. They might not go with her room.

Man: That's true. Let's get plain ones instead. They've got round or square. Which ones do you like?

Woman: I prefer the round ones. Let's see.

Man: Oh. They haven't got any left.

Woman: Ah, that's a shame. Oh well, we'll get the other plain ones, then.

Man: OK.

Narrator: Three. Which product costs less than usual at the moment?

Man: Good afternoon to all our customers. We have some great offers in our homeware department on the first floor at the moment. Just arrived today are some beautiful rugs, at the fantastic price of only £30 each. They're a real bargain – and really soft, too! We also have quality curtains, in a range of colours and styles, all reduced in price by twenty percent for this week only. And finally, we have a special offer on duvets. Buy one and get two free pillows, worth £20 each. So come along and …

Narrator: Four. What does the study in the man's flat look like?

Woman: So, have you got a study in your flat?

Man: Yes, it's small, but it's got everything I need to do work at home. There's a computer and some shelves, as well. And also lots of books, like textbooks and manuals, and things. There are bookshelves above the desk, and some more underneath the desk, as well. I can concentrate really well in my study.

Woman: That sounds perfect. But do you have a printer?

Man: Yes, I just bought one recently. It's on one side of the room, opposite the window.

Woman: OK.

Page 145

GRAMMAR

Exercise 1

b

Exercise 2

1 We've had our doors painted.
2 We haven't had much else done to our house.

Exercise 3

1 had/got your eyes tested
2 have/get your hair cut
3 have/get your teeth checked
4 had/got clothes made
5 have/get it fixed
6 having/getting it delivered

Exercise 4

Students' own answers.

PUSH YOURSELF B2

Exercise 1

Students' own answers.

Exercise 2

1 stunning
2 unique
3 picturesque
4 delightful
5 residential
6 spacious
7 luxurious
8 furnished

Exercise 3

1 luxurious
2 delightful
3 stunning
4 picturesque

Exercise 4

Students' own answers.

Page 146

WRITING PART 1 TRAINING

Exercise 1

Students' own answers.

Exercise 2

Suggested answers

To invite her to a party. A housewarming is a party to celebrate a new home.

Exercise 3

1 and 3

Exercise 4

Suggested answers

She likes it. No, she isn't.

Exercise 5

1 Thank you for your email
2 congratulations on your new home
3 Your flat looks beautiful!
4 I'd love to come to the party, but unfortunately I can't.
5 I'm afraid I'll be away next weekend on a sailing course.
6 Perhaps I could come and visit you another evening soon?
7 I'm really looking forward to seeing your flat.

Page 147

Exercise 6

Model answer

Hi Chris,
Thanks for your email. I'm really looking forward to next Saturday, too.
Swimming and hiking both sound fun, but I'd prefer to go hiking. I swim every day in the sea, but I don't often go hiking in the hills, so I'd enjoy that more.
Thanks for inviting me to stay for the whole weekend. I'd love to stay, but I need to come home on Saturday evening because I'm playing in a football match on Sunday morning.
See you on Saturday!
All the best
(name)

SPEAKING

Exercise 1

Students' own answers.

Exercise 2

They find it interesting that someone lives in such a small space, but they wouldn't want to live there.

Track 098

Woman: Hey, have you seen that video of that guy who lives in Paris who's got a flat that's only eight square metres in size?

Man: Eight square metres? You're joking!
Woman: No, honestly. His whole flat is only eight square metres.
Man: No way!
Woman: It's true. He's got everything he needs, though. Furniture and kitchen equipment, and everything.
Man: How incredible!
Woman: It is. I couldn't believe it either until I saw the video.
Man: So, what's it like?
Woman: Well, there's a kind of shelf. It opens out and can be used as a table. And he's got a fridge and a cooker and even a tiny dishwasher.
Man: Wow. That's unbelievable.
Woman: And there's, like, a big door that slides out and turns into a bed.
Man: Really?
Woman: Yes. And there are some stairs, and inside them there's a sort of chest of drawers which he keeps lots of things in. He's got music, books, games, and stuff like that …
Man: Sounds cool.
Woman: It is. There's even a type of cupboard in the floor, where he keeps brushes and those kinds of things.
Man: That's amazing. I wouldn't want to live there, though!
Woman: Neither would I!

Exercise 3

2 M
3 M
4 W
5 M
6 W
7 M
8 W
9 W
10 W
11 W
12 M

Exercise 4

1 b
2 a

Exercise 5

1 joking
2 kind/sort/type of
3 way
4 like
5 like that
6 That's/How

Exercise 6

Students' own answers.

Page 148

EXAM FOCUS LISTENING PART 1

Exercise 1

1 seven
2 one
3 pictures
4 three
5 twice

Exercise 2

1 B
2 C
3 C
4 B
5 B
6 A
7 B

Track 099

Narrator: For each question, choose the correct answer. One. Where is the poster now?
Woman: Great poster, Harry. I like the cool racing car.
Man: So do I. I've moved it a few times, though. When I first got it, I had it above my bed, but then I moved it to above my desk. But I found I couldn't concentrate on my work. So I put it between the window and the door, but then realised I couldn't see it when the door was open. So finally, I moved it back to where I'd put it in the first place.
Woman: It looks good there.
Man: Thanks.
Narrator: Two. What do the man and woman need to buy soon?
Man: Do we need to buy any kitchen equipment for the flat before we move in?
Woman: Well, it's all there, but it's quite old. The washing machine isn't working, but we can have that repaired. The fridge isn't working, either. I don't think we can get it fixed, so we'll have to replace that before we move in.
Man: OK. What about the cooker?
Woman: We'll probably need to get a new cooker some time, but it's OK for the moment.
Man: Right. So that's just one thing we need to buy straightaway.
Narrator: Three. Where did the man put the key?
Man: Hi, Sam. Listen, I won't be there when you get to the house, but I've left a key. You'll see there are two plants in pots by the door. Now, just between them, there's a statue of a cat, made out of stone. I've hidden it underneath that, OK? It's small, but if you look for the plants, you won't miss it. Anyway, I hope you enjoy your stay, and before you leave, could you drop the key in the letter box on the left of the door? Thanks!
Narrator: Four. What are the girl's parents going to bring her?
Man: Is your room at college OK?
Girl: It's a bit cold at night. Can you bring an extra blanket when you and Mom visit tomorrow?
Man: Aren't those provided? Look in the wardrobe. There might be a spare one in there.
Girl: Oh you're right. There is.
Man: Should we bring a heater?
Girl: It's all right. I'll be fine with the extra blanket.
Man: OK.
Girl: What is annoying is I've got to share a bin with my roommate. I'd like one of my own.
Man: No problem. We'll pick one up on our way.
Girl: Thanks!
Narrator: Five. What does the woman's home look like?
Man: Is that a photo of your house?
Woman: Yes, it was taken this summer. You haven't visited our house for ages, have you?
Man: No, I haven't. Can I have a look?
Woman: Yes, of course.
Man: That's odd. I was sure the apple tree was next to a garden seat, on the right of the house.
Woman: It was, but the seat broke last winter. It was really old and it fell to pieces.
Man: Oh, dear.
Woman: So we had another one built on the other side of the garden. We wanted to give the tree more space to grow.
Man: I see!
Narrator: Six. Which piece of furniture belonged to the first owner of the house?
Tour guide: We'll now move on to the bedroom of the eighteenth century author Edward Pryor, who was the first owner of this house. The bed here is an exact copy of one owned by Edward Pryor. We know what the bed looked like from paintings of the period. The chest of drawers in the corner is the original one which Edward Pryor was given as a present in 1742. Meanwhile, the matching wardrobe was actually made for Pryor's grandson, who lived in the house in the mid-19th century. Moving on now …
Narrator: Seven. Which flat will the man and woman rent?
Man: So which flat do you like?
Woman: The ground floor one's nice, because it's got a garden. Or how about that one on the fourth floor? It's a bit dark because of the tree, but it's got lots of rooms.
Man: But we don't need such a big flat. And it's expensive. What about that one on the second floor? It costs less than the other two. We could even put flowers on the balcony.

Woman: I guess it's good to save some money on the rent.
Man: So we'll go for the cheapest one?
Woman: Yes, good idea. Then we'll be able to spend more on nice furniture.

Page 149

WRITING PART 1

Exercise 1

1 True
2 True
3 False. You must use all of the notes.
4 False. You can put the information in the order you choose, as long as all the information is included.
5 True
6 True

Exercise 2

Model answer

Hi Alex,
It's great that you can come to my housewarming party.
The best way to get to my house is by bus. Take the number 52 bus from the station and get off at King Street. My flat is in a four-storey block next to the petrol station. It's got a green door.
Thanks for offering to bring something, but it's really not necessary. My mum is making lots of food, so there'll be plenty to eat and drink.
Finally, you can wear what you want. Everyone's going to wear casual clothes, like jeans and T-shirts.
See you at the party!
Anna

Page 150

REAL WORLD

Exercise 1

One is very simple, with just one bed and one desk. It looks like a single room for one person, and there aren't any personal possessions. It looks quite basic.
The other has a couple of desks and two beds or a sofa bed. It looks like a shared room and there are lots of personal possessions around the room. It looks cosy.

Exercise 2

1 False. You should start looking two months before you arrive in the city.
2 True
3 True
4 True
5 False. It's up to you to find your flatmates.

Page 151

Exercise 3

1 b
2 c
3 h
4 g
5 a
6 e
7 f
8 d

Exercise 4

1 c
2 d
3 a

Track 100

1

Estate agent: Hello. Can I help you?
Student: Yes, I'm a student at the University of Grenoble and I'm looking for a flat.
Estate agent: Is it just for you?
Student: No, I have two friends, and we want to share a flat.
Estate agent: OK, no problem. Let's see what we've got. There's a lovely flat close to the city centre. It's got three bedrooms, so it would be ideal for the three of you. It's very modern, too.
Student: Yes, that looks very nice. How much is the rent?
Estate agent: It's 1500 euros a month, so that would be 500 each. Then there's electricity on top of that. So, you might be looking at a total of 550 euros per person per month.
Student: Oh, that's OK. And how far from the university is it?
Estate agent: Well, it's not within walking distance. It would be about a 20-minute bus ride. But on the other hand, it's close to all the shops and restaurants in the city centre. Would you like to arrange a viewing?
Student: Yes, please.

2

Male: Hello?
Student: Hi, I'm here to see the room in your flat.
Man: OK. Come up. We're on the first floor.
Man: Hi. I'm Toby. Come in.
Student: Thanks. I'm Ana. It's nice to meet you.
Man: And you. So, have you just arrived in Grenoble?
Student: Yes. I arrived last week.
Man: Cool. I've been here for nine months now. It's a great city. Anyway, this is the flat. There are two of us here – there's me and Maxine – she's French too. And we're looking for a third flatmate. So, as you can see, we've got quite a big sitting room.
Student: Yes, it's really nice.
Man: Yes, and we try to keep on top of the cleaning, so it never gets too messy. And over here is the kitchen. We've each got our own cupboard for food, but we often cook and eat together.
Student: Oh, that's nice. I like cooking.
Man: Cool. I'm not very good, but Maxine's a fantastic cook. Now, if you come this way, I'll show you the third bedroom.
Student: Oh, it's really nice. It's nice and light, and clean.
Man: Yes. And it's a lovely warm flat.
Student: Is there wi-fi?
Man: Yes. We've got wi-fi, and that's included in the rent. So, do you think you're interested?
Student: Yes, definitely.

3

Student: Hello. Do you speak English?
Official: Of course. How can I help you?
Student: I'm starting a course at the University of Grenoble next week. I'm looking for some accommodation.
Official: OK. No problem. What are you going to study?
Student: Business management.
Official: And do you want a room close to the Business School?
Student: Yes, please, if possible. That would be best for me.
Official: Is it a single room that you want?
Student: Yes.
Official: And do you want your own kitchen and bathroom, or are you happy to share?
Student: I'm happy to share.
Official: OK. So there are rooms at a hall of residence close to the Business School. For a basic student room, the rent is 290 euros per month, with one month's rent as a deposit. You share a bathroom and kitchen with six other students.
Student: OK. That's quite expensive.
Official: Yes, but this is a new hall of residence, with very good facilities. Everything is included in the price: water, electricity and heating, and wi-fi, so there are no additional costs. We do have cheaper rooms, but they're all booked now. They get booked up quite quickly.
Student: Yes, I know. I'm a bit late.
Official: Yes. But in this hall of residence you'll probably be sharing with other business students, so it's a good opportunity to make friends, too.
Student: That's true. OK, I'll take a room there. Thank you.

Exercise 5

1 looking for
2 share
3 rent
4 room
5 happy
6 expensive
7 take

Exercise 6

1 a
2 b
3 a
4 b
5 a
6 b

Exercise 7

Suggested answers

The city: in the south east of France, in the Alps, in beautiful countryside with mountains all around, old city is beautiful, lots of old buildings, and a river

The university: started in 1339, one of the best in Europe, science and technology subjects

Accommodation for students: thousands of student rooms, 100 to 400 euros per month, a good way to make friends because you share a kitchen, also can get help if you can't pay your rent, help available 24/7 if you lose your key or have problems. Flats in the city are more expensive, but closer to cafes and restaurants, and students are more independent, lots of students move into shared flats in second or third year

Places to eat: university restaurants, cheap and good food, and a place to meet your friends, or can order a pizza

Exercise 8

Students' own answers.

Page 152

PROGRESS CHECK 4

Exercise 1

1 c
2 d
3 a
4 f
5 b
6 e

Exercise 2

1 I was given a desk and a computer.
2 My new colleagues were asked to introduce themselves.
3 I was shown around the office.
4 I was taken to a nice cafe at lunchtime.
5 The employees are paid well at this company.
6 However, we are expected to work very hard.

Exercise 3

1 delays
2 departure lounge
3 platform
4 boarding pass
5 check-in
6 air pollution
7 fuel
8 get on

Exercise 4

1 is
2 isn't
3 'll give
4 if
5 Unless
6 'd
7 wouldn't be
8 lived

Exercise 5

1 accommodation
2 top floor
3 block of flats
4 drawers
5 sink

Page 153

Exercise 6

1 We have our house painted every 10 years.
2 I get the windows washed once a month.
3 We can't go out now because we're having a pizza delivered.
4 I had the carpet cleaned last month and now it's dirty again!
5 If you can't read this, you should get your eyes checked.
6 I've never had the grass cut. I can do it myself!

Exercise 7

1 where
2 who
3 that
4 whose
5 where
6 who
7 which
8 –

Exercise 8

1 Sally's favourite film **is** called *Avatar.*
2 A lot of clothes **are** made in Asia.
3 My best friend ~~it~~ **is** called Gerry.
4 This house ~~is~~ **was** built 100 years ago.
5 ~~When~~ **If** I have any questions, I'll ask you.
6 He'll visit me later if ~~he'll have~~ **he has** time.
7 I like people ~~which~~ **who/that** have a sense of humour.
8 We played tennis, ~~that~~ **which** is a sport we really enjoy.

Exercise 9

1 c
2 a
3 d
4 b
5 d
6 a

UNIT 12

Page 154

VOCABULARY

Exercise 1

Students' own answers.

Exercise 2

1 programmer
2 astronaut
3 plumber
4 accountant
5 architect
6 lawyer
7 lecturer
8 pharmacist
9 electrician
10 politician

Exercise 3

Nora: architect, electrician
Mia: politician, lawyer
Rory: pharmacist, pharmacist
Fiona: astronaut, tour guide
Patrick: plumber, accountant

Track 101

Narrator: Nora

Nora: When I was little, I used to love drawing interesting houses and trying to build them in my bedroom. I wanted to be an architect because my dad said that was a good job for people who like drawing and building. Later, I understood that you have to study to be an architect, and I didn't want to study for years. I still work in new buildings, though, which is great. I'm an electrician.

Narrator: Mia

Mia: When I was a child, I wanted to change the world, and I thought the best way to do that was to be a politician. Actually, I wanted to be the Prime Minister. Now I still want to make the world a better place, but I don't like politics. I'm a lawyer and I work in environmental law. I want to support the people who are trying to save our planet.

Narrator: Rory

Rory: I wanted to be a pharmacist, and now I'm studying pharmacy. How did I know what I wanted to do when I was so young? To be honest, nearly everyone in my family is a pharmacist, or something to do with medicine – there are some doctors too. I thought about other jobs, but really, pharmacy is perfect.

Narrator: Fiona

Fiona: I wanted to be an astronaut. Now, I don't know why, it sounds much too scary! Actually, I don't really know what I want to do. I've finished school, and I'm working as a tour guide just because it was easy to find this kind of work. But it's not forever. I know I have to decide and to start studying or training for some other kind of job, but what? It's such a hard decision.

Narrator: Patrick

Patrick: I remember I loved repairing things. I used to play 'plumber'. I knocked on our door and said to my mother, 'Good afternoon Madam, is your shower broken? I can fix it for you!' And now? Well, I'm an accountant. I sit at a computer all day and I never repair anything! I suppose I wanted a good salary and I do earn quite a lot of money now.

Exercise 4

1 Mia
2 Nora
3 Patrick
4 Rory
5 Fiona

Exercise 5

Students' own answers.

Page 155

LISTENING PART 3 TRAINING

Exercise 1

1 degree
2 employment opportunities
3 salary
4 shifts

Track 102

I'm from a very small town in an area full of rivers and lakes. It's beautiful, but there are few employment opportunities, except in tourism. When I finished school, I tried to get a job in a tourist office but that wasn't possible. So, I started to work in a hotel. I had to work long shifts and the employers made me work every weekend because I didn't have children. It was awful. I decided to get a degree in Business, moved to the city and started studying. I didn't really enjoy it, but I knew someday I would have a good salary.

Exercise 2

hotel

Exercise 3

Students' own answers.

Exercise 4

1 the internet
2 university
3 year
4 boss

Track 103

Then, a boat rental business opened an office in my town. I saw a report on TV about their big, comfortable motor boats. The next day I saw an advertisement on the internet for someone to run their office and show the tourists how to drive the boats. You didn't need a university degree for the job, but you needed quite a lot of skills. Well, I'm able to drive a motor boat and repair one, too. I've been boating all my life. And at university I learned a lot of useful office skills. I can deal with bills, I can use all the necessary software … all the things you need to do in a small office where you have lots of different responsibilities. Oh, and I'm good at customer service, after working in a hotel. I applied for the job and I got it right away.

So, after just one year in the big city, I came home, and after just one week in the new job, I knew I had made the right decision. My parents were furious because I wanted to stop studying. In the end, I agreed to finish my degree, but part time. That'll take years, but I'm really happy now. My boss is cool. She trusts me with everything, so I can get lots of useful work experience. Also, she lets me take a boat out whenever I want to. I'll never get rich in this job, but I don't care!

Page 156

GRAMMAR

Exercise 1

1 can/may
2 may/can
3 could
4 mustn't
5 allowed

Exercise 2

1 may; mustn't
2 can; can't
3 can't; may not

Exercise 3

1 a
2 b
3 a

Exercise 4

1 is allowed to
2 wasn't allowed to
3 were allowed to
4 wasn't allowed to

Exercise 5

Students' own answers.

Page 157

VOCABULARY

Exercise 1

Suggested answers

1 Mark
2 Martha
3 Cathy
4 George

Exercise 2

1 line manager
2 director
3 employees
4 freelancer
5 Co-workers
6 employer
7 personal assistant
8 staff

Exercise 3

Students' own answers.

Exercise 4

1 two
2 two
3 three

Track 104

1 business
2 different
3 interesting

Exercise 5

(The letters with brackets around them are not pronounced.)

1 cam(e)ra
2 choc(o)late
3 fact(o)ry
4 fav(ou)rite
5 rest(au)rant
6 temp(e)rature
7 veg(e)tables

Track 105

1 camera
2 chocolate
3 factory
4 favourite
5 restaurant
6 temperature
7 vegetables

Page 158

GRAMMAR

Exercise 1

1 let
2 make

Exercise 2

1 made
2 lets
3 makes
4 let
5 let

Exercise 3

1 lets; borrow
2 made; walk
3 make; feel
4 let; pay
5 made; promise

Exercise 4

Model answer

My school was not very strict. They didn't make us wear a uniform, for example, but they didn't let us wear whatever we wanted, either. We weren't allowed to go to school in T-shirts and shorts. We had to wear a shirt or blouse and trousers or a skirt. I don't remember many other rules. I'm sure we weren't allowed to behave badly but the teachers let us have a lot of freedom.
I thought it was a very good school.

SPEAKING

Exercise 1

Students' own answers.

Page 159

Exercise 2

agreeing: I agree with you; I'd agree with that; exactly!
disagreeing: I'm afraid I disagree; Perhaps, but … ; I don't think that's true

Track 106

Man 1: There is no better job than teaching young children.
Woman: I agree with you.
Man 2: I'm afraid I disagree. I've never done it, but it must be really stressful working with little children. And you don't get paid enough for doing it.
Man 1: Well, yes, I'd agree with that. The salary should be better. But the job makes you happy. And it's so important.
Woman: Exactly! And when you do something that's important, you feel good about it.
Man 2: Perhaps, but I think you can only feel good about your job if other people respect it, too. And people in jobs with a high salary are always respected the most.
Woman: Oh, I don't think that's true! But anyway, what job do you think is better than teaching children?

Exercises 3 & 4

Students' own answers.

PUSH YOURSELF B2

Exercise 1

1 d
2 b
3 a
4 f
5 e
6 c

Exercise 2

Students' own answers.

Page 160

READING PART 5 TRAINING

Exercise 1

A lawyer
B judge
C teacher/professor
D pilot

Exercise 2

B make

Exercise 3

1 make an announcement
2 send a message
3 say a word
4 tell a lie

Exercise 4

1 D been
2 B experience
3 A matter
4 D encourage

Exercise 5

Students' own answers.

VOCABULARY

Exercise 1

the programmer: intelligent; patient
the lecturer: organised; friendly
the wedding planner: flexible; reliable
the yoga teacher: calm; creative

Track 107

Narrator: The programmer
Woman: I went to university and after three years of studying I got a bachelor's degree in Computer Science and then it was quite easy to find a job. My boss thought I was very intelligent, so he gave me interesting projects. I think for my occupation you need good problem-solving skills, and you also have to be quite patient. You have to find solutions for complicated problems and you don't always find them quickly.
Narrator: The lecturer
Man: I'm a lecturer in history at a famous university. How did I get this job? Well, of course, I studied history and got a PhD. So, I'm a doctor. For my job I need to be good at presenting information and to be friendly. I don't think all lecturers are friendly, but we should be ready to talk to our students and help them. And we should be organised, but I'm afraid I'm not very organised at all!
Narrator: The wedding planner
Woman: Actually, I don't have any special qualification for my job. I got a normal high-school diploma, and then I helped my cousin to organise her wedding and she said, 'You should start a business doing this!' So I did! You need really good communication skills for my job, as you're dealing with stressed people. And you have to be flexible and 100 per cent reliable. It's somebody's special day so you can't let them down.
Narrator: The yoga teacher
Man: I have lots of different certificates for teaching different types of yoga. It's always good to do a course and learn something new. You need to be good with people in my job, and you should be a calm person. I think you also have to be quite creative. You have to create a beautiful room and a good atmosphere so that people love learning with you.

Exercise 2

the programmer: have problem-solving skills, a bachelor's degree
the lecturer: good at presenting information, a PhD
the wedding planner: have good communication skills, a high-school diploma
the yoga teacher: be good with people, a certificate

Page 161

Exercise 3

1 at
2 with

Exercise 4

1 high-school diploma
2 bachelor's degree
3 master's degree
4 PhD/doctorate
5 certificate

Exercise 5

Suggested answers

dentist: as per activity
astronaut: calm; intelligent; fit/healthy; probably a degree in some kind of science
plumber: reliable; good with your hands; problem-solving skills; a high-school diploma and a diploma or certificate in plumbing
journalist: flexible; good communication skills; a degree in journalism, communications or similar

WRITING

Exercise 1

1 verb
2 noun
3 noun

Exercise 2

1 application
2 apply
3 applicants

Exercise 3

1 a high-school diploma or higher qualification
2 driving and high-quality photography
3 good with animals, calm, patient, a team player

Exercise 4

1 C
2 B
3 A

Suggested answers

1 Fortune-cookie writers think of and write the messages that we find on the slips of paper inside fortune cookies.
2 Line standers need to wait in a line for other people for a long time, for example to buy tickets for a concert that will be sold out quickly.
3 Dog surfing instructors teach dogs how to ride a surf board. The dogs may take part in a competition like the World Dog Surfing Championships in California.

Exercise 5

Students' own answers.

Page 162

EXAM FOCUS READING PART 5

Exercise 1

1 vocabulary
2 six
3 a text
4 four
5 nouns

Exercise 2

1 D
2 A
3 C
4 B
5 B
6 C

Page 163

LISTENING PART 3

Exercise 1

1 False. You listen to one person giving information.
2 False. You have to fill in six gaps in some notes or sentences.
3 False. You have to write one or two words or a number/date/time in the gaps.
4 True
5 True
6 True

Exercise 2

1 painter
2 sister
3 IT
4 radio
5 football
6 music

Track 108

Narrator: For each question, write the correct answer in the gap. Write one or two words or a number or a date or a time. You have twenty seconds to look at Part 3. You will hear hear a woman called Lara McGee talking to a group of students about her job.

Woman: Hello, I'm Lara McGee, and I'm a digital artist. I design graphics for video games. I've enjoyed drawing since I was a child. There was always art equipment around at home, because my dad's a designer. My earliest ambition was actually to work as a painter, because I loved doing pretty landscapes, that kind of thing. Then, I got into video games as a teenager, but I was disappointed by the poor quality images. I was playing a game one day with my sister, and I said, 'These graphics are rubbish. I could do better ones myself'. Then she said, 'Why don't you? You could do that as a job.' So I spoke to my teacher and asked her for some advice.

I left school and went to uni. Many people in my profession did art at university, but I did a degree in IT, because I felt I needed some technical background. I still did lots of drawing in my spare time, though.

After graduating, I got a job with a small games company in my home town. The best place to find jobs is generally the internet. That's where most adverts are. Unusually, I heard about my company when I was listening to the radio one day – local firms were offering jobs and inviting people to apply, so that's how I started.

I've worked on loads of games since then. The one I'm most proud of is a football game. That's my favourite, even though another one – a racing car game – has been more successful.

I love my job, but I'd like to move on soon. The big money for designers is in doing graphics for the cinema, and maybe I'll do that someday, but before that, I'm keen to move to the music industry, you know, videos and things. Now if anyone …

Page 164

REAL WORLD

Exercise 1

Students' own answers.

Exercise 2

A Teaching a child archery (activity leader)
B Supporting children (camp counsellor)
C Working as a chef/in the kitchen (support staff)

Exercise 3

1 AL
2 SS
3 CC
4 SS
5 CC
6 AL

Page 165

Exercise 4

1 b
2 d
3 e
4 c
5 f
6 a

Exercise 5

1 d
2 a
3 c

Track 109

1

Manager: Hello, everyone. It's great to have you here at our summer camp. Thank you all for coming, I'm sure you're all going to have an amazing summer. First, I'd like to introduce a few people. On my left here is Ellie. She's the go-to person for any problems you might have. She's usually in her office, or you can call her cell phone and fix up an appointment. Next to her are the three people who will be running your training sessions: Gino for the activity leaders; Sam for the camp counsellors; and Teddy for the support staff. You'll get to know these guys over the next few days, and they'll help you with any problems you have with your particular roles. So, are there any questions up to now? Yes?

Woman: Is it possible to try a different role during the summer?

Manager: That's a very good question, and the answer is, we'll do our best. Obviously, we need to make sure we have enough people doing each job in the camp, but if you'd like to get involved in a different job, we'll see what we can do. Any more questions?

Man: Yes. Do we get any days off?

Manager: Yes, of course. We don't work you to death! It's all in your terms and conditions, but basically you get one day a week off, so don't worry. OK, then, let's start by …

2

Manager: Hi. Right. That's all for today. I hope you've enjoyed your first day of training, and I hope you're looking forward to your summer as Camp Counsellors. Are there any questions before we stop for today? Yes?

Man: How many kids will there be in my group?

Manager: There are usually between 10 and 15 in a group, depending on the age of the kids. Younger kids are in smaller groups because they need more attention, but if you're working with 11 or 12 year olds, they'll be in slightly bigger groups.

Man: OK. Thanks.

Manager: Yes, over there?

Woman: Some of the activities look quite dangerous. Are there many accidents?

Manager: The short answer to that is no. We're very proud of our safety record here, and we have very few accidents. Tomorrow, when we give you your training for the different activities, we'll teach you how to make sure that you keep the kids safe at all times. If you follow the guidelines for each activity, you shouldn't have any problems.

Woman: And what should we do if a child becomes ill?

Manager: That's a good question. Basically, you will call the camp nurse and get the child back to the camp. But we'll go into all that on day three. OK, everyone, have a great evening, and see you tomorrow!

3

Man: Hi. Is it OK if I sit here?

Woman: Sure.

Man: Oh, it's nice to have a bit of peace and quiet while they eat.
Woman: Yeah. I know what you mean. What job are you doing?
Man: Camp counsellor. It's really tiring! The kids in my group are all about eight years old, and they basically want to play and have fun all day! What about you?
Woman: I'm an activity leader.
Man: That's pretty cool. What's your activity?
Woman: Tennis. It's my favourite sport. I play a lot back home. I think my job isn't quite as difficult as yours. The kids who come to me want some serious coaching, and they work hard. It's a great feeling when they learn something new. It makes them so happy. And I get to play tennis all day, which is great.
Man: I know. It's an amazing way to spend a summer. I love being outdoors all day. It's much better than an office job.
Woman: You can say that again. What are you going to do at the end of the summer?
Man: I want to go travelling for three weeks. I'd like to see a bit of the country – maybe visit Yellowstone National Park.
Woman: That sounds good. I want to go to New York! See the big city!
Man: Cool! Well, I guess I'd better get back to work. See you around!
Woman: Yeah, see you!

Exercise 6

1 possible
2 Do we get
3 will there be
4 Are there many
5 should we do
6 What's your

Exercise 7

1 b
2 a
3 a
4 b
5 a

Exercise 8

Suggested answers

The activities at summer camps: painting, sports, watersports, learning about animals and insects, building campfires and cooking
The advantages of working at summer camp: learn skills that might help you get a job, such as teamwork, communication, planning, organisation, you are in charge so become more confident, may work with disabled kids, so learn about different lives, travel and see the US when camp finishes

Exercises 9 & 10

Students' own answers.

UNIT 13

Page 166

VOCABULARY

Exercise 1

Students' own answers.

Exercise 2

Lizzie: DJing
Neil: Geocaching
Dan: Playing basketball

Exercise 3

1 D
2 N
3 D
4 L
5 D
6 L
7 D
8 N
9 L
10 D

Track 110

Interviewer: So what's your name?
Dan: I'm Dan.
Interviewer: Hi, Dan. Do you mind if I ask you some questions?
Dan: Sure, go ahead.
Interviewer: Can you tell me about your favourite hobby?
Dan: That's got to be basketball! I've always been keen on trying out different sports, and a few years ago, a friend of mine said, 'Do you fancy joining a basketball club?' So I went along with him and I joined. It was the best thing I ever did!
Interviewer: Yeah?
Dan: Yes. I'm on the local basketball team now. I train after college a couple of evenings a week, and we play matches against other teams most weekends. And last year, my team represented our city in a national tournament, which was brilliant.
Interviewer: Great. And what's the best thing about taking part in a basketball match?
Dan: It's always a fantastic feeling when you score a point. It makes you feel great. And if you don't, well … sometimes you lose, and I try not to feel upset when another team beats us. I just try harder to win next time. My friends come and support me at every game I play, which is cool.
Interviewer: Thanks.
Interviewer: And what's your name?
Lizzie: I'm Lizzie.
Interviewer: Could I ask you what you do in your free time, Lizzie?
Lizzie: I'm a student at uni, and when I'm not studying, I'm a DJ.
Interviewer: Cool. So, how did you start doing that?
Lizzie: Playing music has always been a hobby of mine. When I was younger I experimented with music a lot at home, you know, mixing different songs. Then, a few years ago, a local radio station was holding a competition, so I decided to enter. The owner of a club heard me on the radio, and he invited me to play my music on Saturday nights at his club.
Interviewer: Great. Then what?
Lizzie: Well, that gave me some experience, and I soon started getting some fans. And then after I won a national talent contest, even more people came to listen to me.
Interviewer: So, what do you enjoy most about it?
Lizzie: The music! I love going out in the evenings and having fun. And it's great to hang out with friends while I'm doing something I love.
Interviewer: Thanks, Lizzie.
Interviewer: What's your name?
Neil: I'm Neil. It's nice to meet you.
Interviewer: Nice to meet you, too, Neil. Could I ask you about any hobbies that you have?
Neil: Certainly. In fact, I've got quite an unusual hobby. I go geocaching.
Interviewer: That is unusual. Could you explain what geocaching is?
Neil: Well, I took it up because I really enjoy discovering new places. Geocaching involves going to a forest, or a beach, or a cave, or maybe even somewhere in a city, and hiding a small box or jar there. Inside it, you put some paper and a pencil, and maybe some other little things, like a coin or a small toy.
Interviewer: OK. And then what do you do?
Neil: You note the exact location using GPS – you can use an app on your phone to do that – and you go to a website and record it. Then someone else sees what you've written, and goes searching for the thing that you've hidden. It's like a hunt for treasure. It's really quite exciting. And it's something that the whole family can take part in.
Interviewer: And what's your favourite part of being a geocacher?
Neil: Well, spending time outdoors is really enjoyable. I love being outside in the fresh air and I love the adventure.
Interviewer: Thank you, Neil.

Exercise 4

1 take up
2 beat
3 score
4 hang out with
5 support
6 go out
7 hold
8 join
9 take part in
10 represent

Exercise 5
Students' own answers.

Page 167

LISTENING

Exercise 1
his fitness; his friends; his studies

Track 111

Basketball is a big part of my life. I play on my local team and we travel all over the country to play matches. And soon, we're going to start going to different countries to play against their teams. I can't wait to do that, it's going to be great.

Taking up basketball has helped me in lots of ways. For a start, it's a brilliant way for me to get strong and keep fit. But what's even better is that it's taught me how to work with other people and be part of a team. It's a really useful skill in life.

I get on well with my teammates, especially the captain, but there are plenty of other people involved. We've got a good coach, who always makes sure we're playing well. And when we're playing matches, there are other competitors, too. These are our opponents – the team we're trying to beat. And there's the referee, who makes sure both teams are playing fairly. Then finally there are the spectators – the supporters who come to see the game. Some players don't like it when the crowd shout and cheer, but it doesn't bother me. In fact, I like it. It makes a good atmosphere.

Training is very important. I practise with the team two or three evenings a week, and on other days I train on my own, with a ball and basketball hoop in the garden. As you can imagine, this doesn't leave me a lot of free time. So I often can't hang out with my friends. I have to say 'no' to a lot of fun things. But my mates understand the situation. In fact, I don't mind spending so much time training. I love playing basketball, so it's worth missing a few parties.

Of course, I have to do my college work as well. But basketball has helped me with that, too, because it teaches you to concentrate. So I've found that I can focus on my studies much better than I could before. And I'm getting higher grades than I did. So that's all good!

Exercise 2
1 True
2 False. The main benefit is learning to work with other people and be part of a team.
3 True
4 False. Some days he trains on his own.
5 False. He loves playing basketball, so it's worth missing a few parties.
6 True

VOCABULARY

Exercise 1
1 c
2 h
3 g
4 d
5 f
6 a
7 b
8 e

Exercise 2
Students' own answers.

Page 168

GRAMMAR

Exercise 1
1 a/e
2 e/a
3 b/d
4 d/b
5 c
6 f

Exercise 2
Students' own answers.

Exercise 3
after certain verbs: sentence 2
after prepositions: sentences 1 and 4
when the verb is a subject or object: sentence 3
after certain adjectives: sentence 5

Exercise 4
1 imagine
2 love
3 recommend
4 involve
5 practise

Exercise 5
Students' own answers.

SPEAKING PART 1 TRAINING

Exercise 1
Students' own answers.

Exercise 2
She prefers outdoor sports.; Yes, she does.

Track 112

Man: What do you enjoy doing in your free time, Elena?
Elena: Well, as I live in the mountains, I love mountain biking. It's so much fun!
Man: How often do you do go mountain biking?
Elena: I go mountain biking every weekend if the weather is good enough.
Man: And do you have any other hobbies?
Elena: I like keeping fit, so I play tennis two or three times a week. I do that in summer, in the park.
Man: How long have you been playing tennis?
Elena: For about five years. I usually play with my brother and sister, and I really enjoy it.
Man: Why do you like playing tennis?
Elena: It's fun, and I like getting plenty of fresh air and exercise. Because I work in an office all day, I'm not keen on spending time indoors at weekends. I'd rather be outside.
Man: What do you like doing in the evenings?
Elena: I usually hang out with friends in the evenings. I can't stand being in crowded places, which is why I never go to clubs. I'm going to a large festival this summer, though, since my favourite band is playing there. I like music and dancing.
Man: Can you play a musical instrument?
Elena: Yes. I enjoy playing the piano, because I find it relaxing after a busy day at work. I'm not very good at it though!

Page 169

Exercise 3
1 a
2 e
3 f
4 b
5 d
6 c

The words Elena uses to give reasons are *as*, *so*, *because*, *which is why* and *though*.

Exercise 4
1 What do you enjoy doing in your free time?
2 How often do you go skiing?
3 Do you have any other hobbies?
4 How long have you been playing tennis?
5 Why do you like playing tennis?
6 What do you like doing in the evenings?
7 Can you play a musical instrument?

WRITING

Exercise 1
Students' own answers.

Exercise 2
a strategy game

Exercise 3
1 Paragraph 2
2 Paragraph 1
3 Paragraph 3

Exercise 4
Students' own answers.

Exercise 5
Suggested answers
1 I've been playing *Go* for about ten years; In my view, playing *Go* is an excellent way to develop thinking skills.

2 ill; excellent; simple; complicated; interesting; carefully; fun
3 taught; was; couldn't go; 've taken part in; 'm going to enter
4 since then; in fact; although; actually; and also; this is because; too

Exercises 6 & 7

Model answer

My favourite hobby is playing the violin. A violin is a wooden musical instrument with strings which you hold against your neck and play by moving a bow across the strings. You can play both classical and folk music with this instrument.

I started learning to play the violin three years ago. At the beginning, I found it quite difficult, but it became easier after the first few months. Last year, I joined a youth orchestra. I like playing in this orchestra because I've made lots of good friends there.

I think that playing an instrument has many advantages. Music makes you feel good and it also helps to reduce stress. It's an enjoyable social activity, too.

Page 170

READING PART 2 TRAINING

Exercise 1

Students' own answers.

Exercise 2

2 outdoor activity; with their son; souvenir of their weekend
3 class; indoor; can also do on her own
4 watersports; never done before; several different sports

Exercise 3

1 D
2 F
3 C
4 B

Exercise 4

Students' own answers.

Page 171

VOCABULARY

Exercise 1

football; swimming; a workout; tennis; athletics; skateboarding; ice skating; golf

Track 113

Hello everyone, and welcome to our town. If you like sports, you've chosen a good place to come and study, because we have some excellent facilities here. If you're keen on team sports, and you want to play football, why not go down to the sports centre, where there's a full-sized football pitch, as well as several smaller five-a-side pitches. The sports centre also has a large swimming pool, if you fancy going swimming, either before or after your lectures, as well as a gym for anyone who feels like doing a workout. Or, if you go down to the park, you'll find some tennis courts – they're always popular in the summer – and for anyone who enjoys going running, they've got an athletics track. Also in the park, there's a skateboarding ramp for any of you who like going skateboarding, and a newly opened ice rink for those of you who prefer ice skating. So there's really something for everyone there. And, finally, if playing golf is your thing, you'll be pleased to hear that we've got a really good golf course, only a few miles outside town. OK, so if anyone has any questions …

Exercises 2 & 3

1 play
2 go
3 do

A *go*	B *play*	C *do*
running ice skating skateboarding swimming	*basketball* football golf hockey tennis	*yoga* athletics a workout

Exercise 4

2 swimming
3 tennis
4 athletics
5 skateboarding ramp
6 ice-skating
7 golf

Exercise 5

Students' own answers.

PUSH YOURSELF B2

Exercise 1

She's go-karting.

Exercise 2

She found it easy at the beginning but then kept coming last.

Exercise 3

1 picked up
2 chill out
3 wind down
4 got into
5 have a go
6 get the hang of
7 cheers up
8 stuck at

Exercise 4

1 pick up
2 have a go
3 stuck at
4 got into
5 wind down
6 chill out

Page 172

GRAMMAR

Exercise 1

a to do
b to warm up
c to go
d to exercise

Exercise 2

1 a
2 d
3 b
4 c

Exercise 3

1 to join
2 to play
3 to beat
4 to go
5 to do
6 to win

Exercise 4

1 swimming
2 to keep
3 to go
4 spending
5 to come
6 being
7 relaxing
8 studying

Exercise 5

Model answer

My favourite hobby is running. I do it to be healthy, and also because I enjoy being in the fresh air. If possible, I'd like to be able to run in a marathon in the future. If I had more free time, I'd learn to sail because I've always dreamed of crossing the Atlantic by boat.

Page 173

SPEAKING PARTS 3 AND 4 TRAINING

Exercise 1

Students' own answers.

Exercise 2

a skateboard ramp; a playground; a fountain; a café; a tennis court

Exercise 3

A café. All the phrases appear except phrase *h*.

Track 114

Man: So, what's your opinion?
Woman: I'm not sure. Let's look at the pictures. Hmm, well, I think they should build a skateboard ramp.
Man: Really?
Woman: Yes. Skateboarding's fun. Everybody would use it.

Man: I'm sorry, but I don't agree with you. Skateboard ramps are good for teenagers, but not for small children or adults.
Woman: Yes, that's true. So, what do you think?
Man: Perhaps they could build a playground for small children.
Woman: I'm not sure that's the best idea. I think they should build something that people of different ages can use.
Man: How about a café? Everyone would enjoy that!
Woman: Yes, you're right. That's a good idea.

Exercise 4

1 a; e
2 b; g
3 h; i; j
4 c; d; f

Exercise 5

Students' own answers.

Exercise 6

Stressed: *What; think*
Unstressed: *do; you*

Track 115

What do you think?

Exercise 7

(Stressed syllables in bold)
Where did they **meet**?
What does it **mean**?
How do you **know**?
When will they **go**?
The wh-word and the main verb are stressed.

Track 116

Where did they meet?
What does it mean?
How do you know?
When will they go?

Exercise 8

They need to be fuller and provide examples and reasons.

Track 117

Examiner: Are there many sports facilities near your home?
Student: A swimming pool.
Examiner: Do a lot of people use the sports facilities in your neighbourhood?
Student: I think so.
Examiner: What about you? Do you use the sports facilities near where you live?
Student: Not really.
Examiner: Are there any other sports facilities that you'd like to have in your neighbourhood?
Student: A skateboard ramp.

Exercise 9

1 a is better because it uses sentences; b is just a list
2 a is better because it answers the question using different but appropriate vocabulary; b is OK but it repeats the language of the question
3 a doesn't answer the question; b is better because it gives a response and an explanation
4 a doesn't answer the question; b is better because the student has understood question

Exercise 10

The answers are fuller and show the examiners a better range of language, e.g. grammar and vocabulary.

Track 118

Examiner: Are there many sports facilities near your home?
Student: Yes, there are. We've got an excellent leisure centre with a well-equipped gym and a fantastic swimming pool. There's also a small skateboard ramp and a large football pitch.
Examiner: Do a lot of people use the sports facilities in your neighbourhood?
Student: They do. The gym is really popular and so is the swimming pool. And I think that more people would go skateboarding if the ramp were bigger.
Examiner: What about you? Do you use the sports facilities near where you live?
Student: I go swimming two or three evenings a week after college. I find it really relaxing. And I go for a workout at the gym from time to time.
Examiner: Are there any other sports facilities that you'd like to have in your neighbourhood?
Student: Well, it would be really good if we had some tennis courts. The nearest tennis courts are ten kilometres away, and it's really annoying when we have to go so far just to play tennis. Oh, and I'd love to have a skating rink. That's my favourite sport!

Exercise 11

Students' own answers.

Page 174

EXAM FOCUS
READING PART 2

Exercise 1

1 e
2 d
3 c
4 b
5 f
6 a

Exercise 2

1 D
2 H
3 G
4 E
5 B

Page 175

SPEAKING PART 3

Exercise 1

1 b; c; d
2 a; e; f; g

Exercise 2

Students' own answers.

SPEAKING PART 4

Exercise 1

1 three minutes
2 the same topic as
3 not all
4 won't
5 a variety of structures and tenses

Exercise 2

Students' own answers.

Page 176

REAL WORLD

Exercise 1

Students' own answers.

Exercise 2

1 B
2 C
3 A
4 D

Exercise 3

1 False. All watersports equipment is free for guests to use.
2 False. Life jackets are recommended for guests.
3 True
4 True
5 True
6 False. Diving is allowed in the diving pool.

Page 177

Exercise 4

a not permitted
b deposit
c supervise
d help with fitting
e appropriate footwear
f must be accompanied
g There is no charge
h on demand

Exercise 5

1 b
2 d
3 a

Track 119

1

Receptionist: Hi. Can I help you?
Tourist: Yes, please. I'd like to book a tennis court.
Receptionist: Sure. When would you like to play?
Tourist: This afternoon at four o'clock, if possible.
Receptionist: Let's have a look. Yes, there's a court free. What's your room number?
Tourist: Three, five, four.
Receptionist: Three, five, four. OK that's all sorted for you. It'll be court number four. Are you familiar with the courts? Have you played before?
Tourist: No.
Receptionist: OK. So, they're behind the swimming pool. Just follow the path past the swimming pool, and you'll see them, and court number four is the one on the far right. Do you need rackets and balls?
Tourist: Yes, please. We need four rackets. Do you have smaller rackets, for young children?
Receptionist: Yes, we have junior rackets.
Tourist: OK. So, two adult and two junior, please. And some tennis balls.
Receptionist: Anything else I can help you with?
Tourist: No, that's all, thanks.

2

Assistant: Hi. How are you doing?
Tourist: Fine, thanks.
Assistant: What are you looking to do today?
Tourist: I'd like to try a paddle board, please.
Assistant: OK. Have you used one before?
Tourist: No.
Assistant: OK. No problem. Let's get you sorted. I'll give you a slightly smaller board, because they're a bit easier to manage. There, this one looks good. This is the part you fix round your arm, so you don't lose the board if you fall off. And then a paddle. Here we go. There, if you take that for me?
Tourist: Thanks.
Assistant: Now, let's find you a life jacket.
Tourist: Do I have to wear a life jacket? I can swim quite well.
Assistant: It's not compulsory, but we do recommend it. The thing is, if you fall off, the life jacket will keep your head above water, so it's good to have the life jacket as a backup, just to be on the safe side.
Tourist: OK. No problem.
Assistant: So, here we go. This one should fit you. Can you just pop that on for me? That looks perfect.
Tourist: Are there any rules about where I can go?
Assistant: No, no real rules, but we recommend that you don't go beyond those two red things in the water, over there. If you stay in the area inside those, and stay clear of the rocks over on the right. Can you see?
Tourist: Oh, yes. Thank you.
Assistant: OK. All set?
Tourist: Yes, thanks.
Assistant: No problem. Enjoy!

3

Owner: Hello.
Tourist: Hi. We'd like to hire some bikes.
Owner: OK. For both of you?
Tourist: Yes, please.
Owner: A whole day or half day?
Tourist: A whole day, I think. How long is a half day?
Owner: A half day is four hours. So, it's 10 o'clock now, so you'd have to bring the bikes back by 2 o'clock.
Tourist: OK, that's not enough time, so I think we want a whole day.
Owner: No problem. So that's ten euros per bike per day, plus a thirty euro deposit per bike. Do you want helmets?
Tourist: Yes, please.
Owner: OK. Two helmets. And where are you planning to go?
Tourist: We want to go along the coast.
Owner: OK, so off-road cycling?
Tourist: Yes, off-road.
Owner: Right. If you just hop on this bike. How does that feel? Is the saddle too high?
Tourist: No, it's fine.
Owner: OK. And for you? Can you hop on here? Yes, that's perfect for you. And here are the helmets.
Tourist: Thanks.
Owner: Right, let's see. That's two bikes and two helmets for one day, …

Exercise 6

1 to book
2 rackets
3 try
4 have to wear
5 any rules
6 some bikes
7 How long

Exercise 7

1 a
2 b
3 a
4 b
5 b
6 b
7 a
8 b

Exercise 8

Suggested answers

Beaches: popular, attract tourists from all over the world
Sea: deep blue, usually calm, sailing is popular, can sail from one island to another and stay there for the night
Holiday resorts: sports facilities, such as swimming and tennis, may pay for lessons; water sports, such as windsurfing and paddle boarding, might want to pay for a lesson, fun water activities such as banana boat and jet pack
Biking: hire bikes for exploring and getting away from resorts, mopeds for steep hills

Exercises 9, 10 & 11

Students' own answers.

UNIT 14

Page 178

READING PART 1 TRAINING

Exercise 1

Students' own answers.

Exercise 2

disappointed; text 2
excited; text 1
worried; text 3

Exercise 3

1 B
happened at work; I can't wait to tell you about it!

Exercise 4

2 A
3 C

Exercise 5

Suggested answers

A–C could probably all be phone messages but there are also reasons to choose written messages. For example, in text 1, Alicia may know Toni is busy and not want to interrupt her. In text 2, Pete may feel too sick to talk, or not want Sarah to try to persuade him to go to the party. In text 3, Lou might not want to risk his father saying 'no' if he asks to spend the evening at his friend's house, or may not want to bother him at work.

Page 179

READING PART 6 TRAINING

Exercise 1

Suggested answers

Emojis are symbols for facial expressions, originally created by using punctuation marks, letters and numbers on a keyboard, now pre-made for various apps. The original emoji was the *smiley*.

Exercise 2

1 I; he; me; them; your; our, etc.
2 that; which; who; where, etc.
3 in; on; at; during; after; under; into; towards; up, etc.
4 and; but; however; although; finally, etc.

Exercise 3

1 my
2 where
3 but
4 on

Exercise 4

1 True
2 False. You can hear how the person is feeling.
3 False. We seem to be cheerful on social media but we might not feel cheerful.
4 True
5 True

Exercise 5

Students' own answers.

VOCABULARY

Exercise 1

1 delighted
2 disappointed
3 shocked
4 cheerful
5 depressed
6 miserable

Exercise 2

1 jealous
2 satisfied
3 guilty
4 nervous
5 amused
6 impressed
7 embarrassed

Exercise 3

Students' own answers.

Page 180

GRAMMAR

Exercise 1

1 zero conditional; C
2 second conditional; B
3 first conditional; A

Exercise 2

1 have
2 don't answer
3 won't know
4 knew
5 would be
6 saw

LISTENING PART 4 TRAINING

Exercise 1

Students' own answers.

Exercise 2

How did Mara feel about playing Lady Georgina Bentley?

A worried because Georgina was not a nice person
B excited because this was Mara's first big part
C nervous because Georgina was a complicated person

Exercise 3

C is correct
A she was worried, but not because Lady Georgina was not nice
B Mara has had big parts before this one

Track 120

Mike: Here to talk to us about her new film, *A Lady*, is actress Mara Clark. Thanks for coming in, Mara.
Mara: Great to be here.
Mike: Mara, *A Lady* is a very serious film about a woman with a difficult personality. Most people didn't like Lady Georgina Bentley. How did you feel about playing this part?
Mara: Well, it's never disappointing, obviously, when a director offers me a big role. I was a little nervous about this one though, because I hadn't done a film in ages and I was also a bit worried about playing Georgina. She helped a lot of people, although she wasn't charming or cheerful. I wasn't sure I could show all the sides of her special personality.
Mike: You managed it perfectly.

Exercise 4

1 A
2 B
3 B
4 C

Track 121

Mike: Here to talk to us about her new film, *A Lady*, is actress Mara Clark. Thanks for coming in, Mara.
Mara: Great to be here.
Mike: Mara, *A Lady* is a very serious film about a woman with a difficult personality. Most people didn't like Lady Georgina Bentley. How did you feel about playing this part?
Mara: Well, it's never disappointing, obviously, when a director offers me a big role. I was a little nervous about this one though, because I hadn't done a film in ages and I was also a bit worried about playing Georgina. She helped a lot of people, although she wasn't charming or cheerful. I wasn't sure I could show all the sides of her special personality.
Mike: You managed it perfectly. And of course, everyone is saying how amazing you look in the film! Is it hard work to look so beautiful all the time?
Mara: Yes, actually, it is! And I always hope that people will talk about my performance in a film and not what I look like, but that never happens. I'm really satisfied with both my performance in *A Lady* and how I looked in it, but everyone else seems to be more impressed with my hair and wants to have a chat about that!
Mike: Oh, I'm sorry, Mara. You are an excellent actress. What do you think makes someone a great actor, like you?
Mara: Thanks. Well, I suppose you need a mix of talent and hard work to be good at any job. Actually, people think that actors are always thinking about themselves and looking for attention, but I would say, that above all, actors need to care about other people. You need to be able to imagine other people's lives.
Mike: Interesting. How do you feel about people's interest in your life? It must be hard to have a private life.
Mara: It's very hard to get time alone when you're well known, and sometimes that does make me a bit miserable, but not always. I understand what it means to be a celebrity: your fans want to know about you and that's fine. If I wanted my whole life to be private, I'd do a different job. But I love being an actress, and I love films.
Mike: What type of films do you like best? I mean, what do you like watching?
Mara: I've played in a lot of romantic comedies, but when I go to the cinema I often want to see something serious or historical. A drama like *A Lady*, in fact. But I think the very best films mix a serious subject with an exciting story, so a really good political thriller would always be my first choice.
Mike: Again, thank you for talking to us.

Exercise 5

Students' own answers.

Page 181

VOCABULARY

Exercise 1

cute; clear; curly; fashionable

Exercise 2

1 fashionable
2 clear
3 stupid
4 cruel
5 cute
6 brave

7 rude
8 curly
9 generous

Exercise 3

Students' own answers.

Exercise 4

The *t* is not heard as /t/. Followed by vowels, it indicates a /ʃ/ sound.

Track 122

essential
patient
relations

Exercise 5

Students' own answers.

Track 123

education
information
station
emotion
efficient
social
special
delicious

Page 182

GRAMMAR

Exercise 1

1 loved; past simple
2 was saying; past continuous
3 had played; past perfect
4 had helped; past perfect
5 would talk; would

Exercise 2

1 where Owen was
2 didn't know
3 hadn't seen him
4 hoped he was OK
5 why she was worried
6 had posted an embarrassing photo
7 had been furious
8 he was feeling good that day
9 would be home soon

PUSH YOURSELF B2

Exercise 1

1 noun
2 verb

Exercise 2

1 She's a kind-hearted teacher.
2 She's a well-known actress.
3 He's a highly respected author.
4 She's a brown-eyed girl.
5 He's a badly behaved child.
6 He's an open-minded person.

Page 183

WRITING

Exercise 1

1 paragraph 2
2 paragraph 4
3 paragraph 1
4 paragraph 3

Exercise 2

1 tall, short, dark, fashionable, well-made
2 generous, kind-hearted, ambitious, clever
3 he's clever and has interesting conversations with the writer; he's fun and knows how to have a good time

Exercise 3

Students' own answers.

Page 184

GRAMMAR

Exercise 1

1 b
2 c
3 d
4 e
5 a
6 j
7 f
8 h
9 i
10 g

Exercise 2

1 no alternatives
2 You must wear sports shoes in the gym.
3 Sorry but you mustn't eat or drink in this theatre.
4 May/Could I sit down here?
5 You ought to eat more fish. It's good for you!
6 no alternatives
7 no alternatives
8 I don't know where Jill is but she may/could be at home.
9 Fred mightn't be at work today.
10 no alternatives

Exercise 3

1 She wasn't able to talk when she was a year old.
2 We're allowed to use the school computers during our lunch break.
3 We're not allowed to eat in the classroom.
4 Did your parents allow you to play computer games when you were five? / Were you allowed to play computer games when you were five?
5 My father is able to speak six languages.

Exercise 1

1 who; that; whose
2 that; which
3 where
4 whose

Exercise 2

1 who/that
2 –
3 that/which
4 where
5 –
6 whose

Page 185

SPEAKING

Exercise 1

1 Carmen
2 Martin
3 Martin
4 Ben
5 What would you do if you heard a robber in your house in the middle of the night?

Track 124

Carmen: Martin, what's the biggest city you've been to?
Martin: I think it's Paris. I don't know how many people live there but it's really huge.
Carmen: And Ben, what's the biggest city you've been to?
Ben: Well, I've been to London, and I think that's bigger than Paris, so I win!
Carmen: No you don't! I've been to Istanbul and nearly 15 million people live there so I'm the one who has been to the biggest city. Now what about shoes? I'm not interested in shoes and I've only got three or four pairs. How many pairs of shoes have you got, Ben?
Ben: Oh, about the same. Three or four pairs.
Martin: What? That's not enough! You need summer shoes and winter shoes and sports shoes and smart shoes. I can't even count how many shoes I have!
Carmen: OK. Martin, then you are definitely the person who has the most shoes! Now, when are you next having a holiday?
Martin: Well I'm going to Manchester on Friday for a long weekend. Is that a holiday?
Carmen: I suppose so, yes. I haven't planned any holidays for the moment. What about you, Ben?
Ben: Well, I'm going to Ibiza in September, but that's a long way away.
Carmen: OK, so it's Martin again. Now, the last question. Martin, what would you do if you heard a robber in your house in the middle of the night?
Martin: Oh, I think I would stay in bed and very quietly phone the police.

Carmen: That's what I'd do too. Ben?
Ben: That's crazy. Anyway, I don't keep my phone next to my bed. I think I'd jump out of bed and open the bedroom door and shout very loudly 'get out of my house!'
Carmen: OK so that answers my final question. Ben is the bravest person in the group.
Martin: What? No, hang on, who says that's the bravest thing … ?

Exercises 2 & 3

Students' own answers.

Exercise 4

Suggested answers

What do you think is the best way to spend an evening with friends?
Which would you prefer, a trip to a city or a holiday in the countryside?
Can you play a musical instrument?
Why do you like your school/college?
Do you prefer to go shopping in shops or to buy things on the internet?
How often do you play a team sport?
How do you get to school or work every day?
How long have you lived in your home?

Exercises 5 & 6

Students' own answers.

Page 186

EXAM FOCUS
READING PART 1

Exercise 1

1 f
2 a
3 d
4 e
5 b

Exercise 2

1 A
2 B
3 A
4 C
5 A

Page 187

READING PART 6

Exercise 1

1 grammar
2 text
3 six
4 options

Exercise 2

1 than
2 our
3 make
4 who/that
5 In
6 as

LISTENING PART 4

Exercise 1

1 c
2 b
3 a
4 e
5 d

Exercise 2

1 B
2 C
3 B
4 C
5 A
6 C

Track 125

Narrator: For each question, choose the correct answer. You have 45 seconds to look at Part 4. You will hear an interview with a woman called Alisha Bennett, who teaches yoga.
Man: So, Alisha. Tell us a bit about what yoga is.
Woman: It's a form of exercise where you put your body into different positions to get fit and flexible. Some people think it's easy, but it isn't. You've got to do it right. But because it's gentle, anybody can do it: young, old, strong, weak – anyone at all! I think it's going to get even more popular over the next few years.
Man: Why did you start doing yoga?
Woman: Well, about ten years ago, I wanted to meet new people, so I joined a squash club. Unfortunately, I damaged a leg muscle playing a match, and it felt sore for a long time. So my doctor suggested that yoga might help. And it did. What's more, I just loved how yoga made me feel relaxed all over. It was wonderful.
Man: And then you decided to become a teacher?
Woman: Yes, a few years later, I hired a studio and started giving lessons. I'd worked in an office for quite a while and felt it was time to do something different. It was scary working for myself at first, but I soon got used to it. Now, I get more money than I did before. It's amazing, I never actually imagined I'd earn quite this much.
Man: So, tell us about your students.
Woman: They get a lot out of doing yoga. All the things they expect, like getting fitter and stronger, and also more energetic. Plus some things that they often don't think will happen. Like, students often arrive feeling depressed or negative about things, then after a term or two of yoga, they feel really good and really positive.
Man: And do you enjoy your job?
Woman: I do! I'm a naturally happy kind of person, and I enjoy helping other people feel better about themselves. I love it when we can share a laugh or joke together. And it's helped me too. I used to be quite unsure of myself, and I felt nervous standing up in front of people, telling them what to do. But I'm fine with all that now.
Man: And what are you intending to do next?
Woman: Well, a real ambition of mine is to write a book about yoga. That's something I'm going to do when I've got some more experience. Also, I think that having my own internet channel will be a great way to reach a big audience. But first, I'm planning to get some classrooms in a nearby town and hire some yoga instructors to teach there. So, I've got lots of ideas for the future.
Man: Sounds good! Thank you, Alisha, for …

Page 188

REAL WORLD

Exercise 1

Suggested answers

holiday rep; waiter
You can get work experience, improve your language skills and have fun.

Page 189

Exercise 2

1 practise answering
2 feel comfortable
3 interested and enthusiastic
4 anything that isn't true

Exercise 3

1 hire
2 punctual
3 relevant
4 referees
5 available
6 academic qualifications
7 strengths
8 weaknesses
9 reliable

Exercise 4

Students' own answers.

Exercise 5

1 waiter
2 holiday rep

Track 126

1

Interviewer: Come in.
Lucy: Hello.
Interviewer: Ah, hello. Lucy White?
Lucy: Yes, that's right.
Interviewer: Come in and take a seat. I'm Adam Greenwood and this is Emma Valdez.
Lucy: Hello. Pleased to meet you.
Interviewer: Did you find the office OK?
Lucy: Yes, no problem.
Interviewer: So, we'd like to ask you a few questions, and then you'll get the chance to ask us some questions.

Lucy: OK, fine.

Interviewer: So, first. Why are you interested in this job?

Lucy: Well, I like working in restaurants, and I enjoy serving food to people and making sure everything is OK for them. And I like this restaurant because it has good food and it gets good reviews online. I think I would enjoy working here, and I always do my best, so I think I could do the job well.

Interviewer: Thank you. And can you give me an example of your ability to work in a team?

Lucy: Yes. Last year at school I had to plan a school trip with three friends. So, we had a meeting and agreed what each person would do. And it was all very easy, because we all worked together to find the information we needed and plan the trip. I think I did well because I can pay attention to detail. I think that's quite important.

Interviewer: Thanks. Finally, when are you available to start?

Lucy: I'm available on the 31st May, and I can work until the end of August.

Interviewer: That's great, thanks. Now, do you have any questions for us?

Lucy: Yes. I'd like to ask about accommodation. Is it difficult to find a place to live in Tenerife?

Interviewer: No, it isn't difficult. I think it's quite easy. We don't provide accommodation, but there is plenty of accommodation available.

Lucy: OK. Thank you.

Interviewer: Thanks, Lucy. We'll be in touch.

Lucy: OK. Thank you for the interview. Goodbye.

2

Interviewer: Hello. Come in. It's Tobias, isn't it?

Tobias: Yes. Tobias Schmidt.

Interviewer: Hi. I'm Stella Jones.

Tobias: Nice to meet you.

Interviewer: So, thank you for applying to work for our company in Tenerife. Your academic qualifications are very impressive. What are your other strengths?

Tobias: Well, I work very hard in my studies and at work, and I'm very reliable. I learn quickly, so I don't need to spend a lot of time on training, and I get on well with everyone.

Interviewer: That's good. Do you have any relevant work experience?

Tobias: Yes. Last summer I worked as a tour guide in my town, so I showed tourists around the old city centre and explained the history of the town. This gave me experience of working with tourists.

Interviewer: That's good. You say in your letter that you can start on the 14th June. How flexible can you be on dates?

Tobias: Well, a little bit flexible. My course ends on the 29th May, so I thought I could have little break before I start work, but I could start at the beginning of June.

Interviewer: That's good. Because usually we ask our holiday reps to start at the beginning of June.

Tobias: OK, that's fine.

Interviewer: Good. OK. Do you have any questions?

Tobias: Yes. How many holiday reps do you have at this resort?

Interviewer: We have around 20. I think 12 are staying on from last year, so we need eight more this year.

Tobias: OK, thanks.

Interviewer: Right. Thanks for coming in, Tobias, and we'll let you know. We'll need to follow up on your references, so it might be a week or so before you hear from us.

Tobias: OK, that's fine. Thanks for the interview. Bye.

Exercise 6

1 would enjoy
2 my best
3 pay attention
4 hard
5 quickly
6 get on

Exercise 7

1 b
2 a
3 a
4 b
5 a
6 a

Exercise 8

Suggested answers

Things you should do: wear smart clothes or smart casual clothes, smile as you introduce yourself, sit straight and still, look calm and relaxed, look interested, listen to what people are saying, make eye contact, be confident, relaxed and interested, shake hands at the end and thank the person for your interview

Things you shouldn't do: don't wear clothes that are too informal, don't fold your arms, don't look too casual, don't look down all the time, don't get up and walk out

Exercises 9 & 10

Students' own answers.

Page 190

PROGRESS CHECK 5

Exercise 1

1 co-workers
2 freelancer
3 salary
4 patient
5 with
6 organised
7 at
8 calm

Exercise 2

1 could
2 aren't allowed
3 can't
4 may not
5 can I
6 mustn't

Exercise 3

1 e
2 g
3 a
4 h
5 d
6 b
7 f
8 c

Exercise 4

1 to keep
2 Joining
3 to take up
4 to go
5 doing
6 being
7 to find
8 Talking

Page 191

Exercise 5

1 False; guilty
2 True
3 False; depressed
4 False; generous
5 True
6 False; brave
7 False; amused
8 False; satisfied

Exercise 6

1 do
2 who
3 should
4 didn't
5 went
6 had
7 which
8 must

Exercise 7

1 She asked her dad **to** let her go to the party.
2 We're going to arrive late tomorrow night, but I'm sure ~~we can~~ **we'll be able to** find a taxi.
3 I love ~~swim~~ **swimming / to swim** in the sea.
4 Would you like **to** go to the cinema with me?
5 Tim enjoys ~~to help~~ **helping** his co-workers.

Exercise 8

1 who/that
2 degree
3 able
4 subject
5 unless
6 have
7 guilty
8 told
9 with
10 make

GRAMMAR REFERENCE

Page 196

STARTER

PRESENT SIMPLE AND PRESENT CONTINUOUS

Exercise 1

1 are taking up
2 helps
3 use up
4 walk
5 go
6 'm training
7 spend/'m spending

ADVERBS OF FREQUENCY

Exercise 1

1 I go to the gym twice a week.
2 I hardly ever spend more than an hour there.
3 I sometimes run for half an hour.
4 I usually listen to music while I'm running.
5 When he gets home, he's always exhausted.
6 We go out with our friends every Friday.
7 You rarely watch TV during the week.

PRESENT CONTINUOUS WITH *ALWAYS*

Exercise 1

1 He is always forgetting my birthday.
2 My friends are always ringing me late at night.
3 Our tennis trainer is always telling us to train hard.
4 She is always talking about her job.
5 They are always eating crisps.

WH- QUESTION WORDS

Exercise 1

1 Where
2 Who
3 How
4 When
5 Why

Exercise 2

1 What
2 Where
3 What
4 Where
5 How much
6 How

SHORT ANSWERS TO *YES/NO* QUESTIONS

Exercise 1

1 Is she living in England at the moment?
2 Does he work in a bank now?
3 Could you help me with my project?
4 Are they on holiday at the moment?
5 Do you like the taste of the soup?

Exercise 2

1 I am; I'm not
2 they are; they aren't/ they're not
3 he has; he hasn't
4 he can; he can't
5 she is; she isn't
6 I/we did; I/we didn't

Page 199

UNIT 1

COMPARATIVE AND SUPERLATIVE ADJECTIVES

Exercise 1

1 the thinnest
2 nicer
3 lazy
4 more comfortable
5 the best
6 worse
7 far

Exercise 2

1 the wettest
2 the most beautiful
3 heavier
4 better
5 worse
6 further/farther

Exercise 1

1 Josh isn't as tall as Roman.
2 My new phone is / was much more expensive than my old phone.
3 Fruit is a lot healthier than burgers.
4 Spain is a bit smaller than France. (It's 505,370 km^2, but France is 643,801 km^2.)
5 The new shopping centre is far nicer than the old shopping centre.

COMPARATIVE AND SUPERLATIVE ADVERBS

Exercise 1

1 more clearly
2 the best
3 faster
4 harder
5 more seriously; better
6 the most carefully

Exercise 2

1 dances more beautifully
2 writes the best of all
3 the most patiently
4 work harder
5 to bed earlier than you did last night
6 runs faster than me

TOO ... TO .../ TOO ... FOR ...

Exercise 1

1 The room was too dark to see anything.
2 He is too unfit to play football.
3 The project was too difficult for the students to do.
4 I arrived too late to catch my flight.
5 Jane's too ill to go to school today.
6 This book is too hard for my child to read.

ENOUGH, SO, SUCH

Exercise 1

1 Are you warm enough?
2 We have enough books for all the students.
3 They aren't strong or fit enough to be firefighters.
4 It was so hot that I couldn't concentrate on my work.
5 She's such a good teacher.

Page 202

UNIT 2

USED TO

Exercise 1

1 I didn't use to like hot weather (but I do now).
2 My brother used to play football (regularly) (until he broke his leg).
3 I used to have blond hair / My hair used to be blond (but now it's brown).
4 Did you use to go on holiday with your friends (when you were a child)?
5 When I was younger, I didn't use to get up late.

PRESENT PERFECT OR PAST SIMPLE?

Exercise 1

1 went; 've/have just woken up
2 arrived; haven't seen her yet
3 've/have already seen; saw
4 've/have ever bought; cost; 've/have never spent
5 Have, ever done; 've/have never done
6 did, go; went; 've/have never visited

Exercise 2

A: Have you heard? My oldest sister's getting married to a guy called Elliot.
B: Really! How long ~~did she know~~ **has she known** him?
A: Only six months. Apparently ~~they've~~ **they met** at work.

B: Have you met Elliot ~~already~~ **yet**?
A: No, not yet, but my sister's told me a lot about him.
B: When ~~have you seen~~ **did you see** her?
A: ~~I've seen~~ **saw** her last week. She drove me to school one day.

SINCE AND *FOR*

Exercise 1

1 for
2 since
3 since
4 for
5 since

YET AND *ALREADY*

Exercise 1

1 already
2 already
3 already
4 yet
5 yet

Page 204

UNIT 3

COUNTABLE AND UNCOUNTABLE NOUNS

Exercise 1

Countable: diet, cereals, biscuits, things, vegetables, glass
Uncountable: energy, sugar, food, ice cream, chocolate, fruit, milk

SOME, ANY WITH COUNTABLE AND UNCOUNTABLE NOUNS

Exercise 1

1 some
2 some
3 some
4 any
5 any
6 any
7 some
8 some

MUCH, MANY, A LOT OF AND *LOTS OF*

Exercise 1

1 We haven't got ~~many~~ **much** time.
2 I drink ~~much~~ **a lot** of water when I wake up.
3 There are ~~lot of~~ **lots of** / **a lot of** things we need to talk about.
4 How ~~much~~ **many** friends do you have online?
5 We have driven ~~a lots~~ **a lot of** / **lots of** miles today.

FEW, A FEW / LITTLE, A LITTLE / ALL/ALMOST ALL/MOST

Exercise 1

1 I'd like **a little** advice about going to university, please.
2 They only gave us ~~few~~ **a little** information about the trip.
3 ~~Little~~ **Few** people in my class are hard-working.
4 We only had **a** ~~few~~ **little** water left at the end of the day.
5 **Almost all** / **Most** cars have four doors.
6 She's ~~most~~ **almost** 20 years old.

VERBS + ADJECTIVES

Exercise 1

1 That car looks expensive.
2 He appears sad.
3 The engine sounds loud.
4 This room feels cold.
5 Your socks smell bad.

ARTICLES

Exercise 1

1 a; the
2 the; a; a; the
3 a; the; ø
4 the
5 The; ø
6 a; the

Exercise 2

1 the
2 The; The; the; the
3 The; the
4 The; the; the; the
5 a
6 ø; ø

Page 206

UNIT 4

PAST SIMPLE AND PAST CONTINUOUS

Exercise 1

1 was watching
2 often phoned
3 realised
4 was shining; were singing
5 won

Exercise 2

1 was tidying; found
2 was leaving; realised
3 was watching; was cooking / cooked
4 heard; stopped; were doing; walked
5 crashed; was updating

PAST PERFECT AND PAST SIMPLE

Exercise 1

1 had rained; had stopped; was
2 had planned; had to
3 had been; started
4 could not / couldn't; had made
5 went; had seen

Page 208

UNIT 5

TALKING ABOUT ABILITY AND INABILITY / *BE ABLE TO* / TALKING ABOUT POSSIBILITY

Exercise 1

1 can't
2 could
3 was able to
4 can
5 couldn't

Exercise 2

1 d can
2 c can't
3 a was able to
4 e could
5 b couldn't

SHOULD/SHOULDN'T

Exercise 1

1 You should eat lots of fruit and vegetables.
2 You shouldn't eat too many burgers and chips.
3 Why don't you start jogging?
4 How about doing more exercise?
5 I recommend you start revising for your exam.
6 I suggest you stop getting up so late.
7 Consider eating more salads.

MODALS OF OBLIGATION

Exercise 1

1 mustn't/can't
2 can/must; can't
3 can
4 can't
5 mustn't/can't

Exercise 2

1 didn't have to
2 could
3 had to
4 had to
5 could
6 couldn't

Page 210

UNIT 6

BE GOING TO, PRESENT CONTINUOUS FORMS FOR THE FUTURE, PRESENT SIMPLE FORMS FOR THE FUTURE, *WILL*

Exercise 1

1 're going to see
2 'll be
3 'm going to go
4 leaves
5 'll go

PROBABLY, DEFINITELY, THERE'S A GOOD CHANCE/NOT MUCH CHANCE THAT..., I DOUBT

Exercise 1

1 a
2 a
3 b
4 a
5 b
6 a

Page 211

UNIT 7

REPORTED SPEECH WITH MIXED TENSES / REPORTED COMMANDS

Exercise 1

2 'I'm sorry but I can't lend you any more money.'
3 'I still feel ill.'
4 'I'm older than you.'
5 'We'll come and see you later.'
6 'I left yesterday.'
7 'Stop worrying!'

Exercise 2

1 He said (that) he was leaving school at the end of the following year.
2 She said (that) she'd got a surprise for me.
3 She told him to shut the door.
4 They said (that) they'd all passed their English exam.
5 He said (that) it was his birthday the next day.
6 She said (that) I was the only person she knew who liked / likes classical music.
7 They said (that) they'd gone to / been to Italy for their holiday the previous year / the year before.
8 He told Max not to drink any more coffee.

REPORTED QUESTIONS

Exercise 1

2 'Are you enjoying your new course?'
3 'Has anyone / Have you found my keys?'
4 'What did you do yesterday?'
5 'Can you come to my party this evening / tonight, Veronika?'
6 'Can you tell us where the station is?' / 'Where's the station?'
7 'Who's your favourite actor?'
8 'Did you try to phone me?' / 'Have you tried to phone me?'

Exercise 2

1 My mum asked (me) why I was wearing my best clothes.
2 My dad asked (me) where I was going.
3 My brother asked (me) what I was going to do there.
4 My sister asked (me) if/whether I was going with anyone/someone.
5 My dad asked (me) if/whether he knew who I was going with.
6 My mum asked (me) what time I would be back.
7 My brother asked (me) how I would get home.
8 My sister asked (me) what I would do if I missed the last bus.

INDIRECT QUESTIONS

Exercise 1

1 Could you tell me where you live?
2 I was wondering if/whether you were doing anything at the weekend.
3 Can you tell me what they did last weekend?
4 I'd like to know what you thought of the film.

Page 214

UNIT 8

MUST / MIGHT, MAY, COULD / CAN'T

Exercise 1

1 a
2 b
3 a
4 b
5 b
6 a

Page 215

UNIT 9

PASSIVE: PAST AND PRESENT TENSES AND WITH MODALS

Exercise 1

1 was played; was watched
2 are taken; are driven
3 was written; were predicted

Exercise 2

1 Our cat is being seen by a vet this morning.
2 Last night, the roads were closed (by the police) because of the storm.
3 The book was written by a famous author.
4 All this fantastic food was cooked by six women.
5 I had been taught how to sing by my grandfather.

FUTURE PASSIVE: *WILL*

Exercise 1

1 Will the kids be picked up by her husband from school tomorrow?
2 Al the food on the table in the garden will be eaten by the birds.
3 The race will be watched by millions of people.
4 The town will be flooded by the next heavy rain because the river is so high.
5 Will the road be repaired by the council's workmen?

Page 216

UNIT 10

ZERO CONDITIONAL / FIRST CONDITIONAL / SECOND CONDITIONAL

Exercise 1

1 d
2 g
3 a
4 h
5 c
6 b
7 e
8 f

Exercise 2

2 If she spoke English, she could study in Canada.
3 If I had enough free time, I'd learn to play a musical instrument.
4 If I had enough money, I'd buy a laptop.
5 If we were at home this evening, we would watch the new comedy programme on TV.

WHEN, IF, UNLESS

Exercise 1

1 Unless
2 unless
3 If
4 if
5 unless
6 If/When
7 If
8 when

Page 217

UNIT 11

RELATIVE CLAUSES

Exercise 1

1 whose
2 that/which
3 who/that
4 where
5 that/which
6 where
7 that/which
8 when

Exercise 2

Sentence 7

Exercise 3

1 The music that/which Gisela was playing last night was by Mozart.
2 The violin that/which Gisela was playing in the concert was not hers.
3 James, whose violin Gisela borrowed, is her music teacher.
4 We've just listened to Gisela's latest recording, which is number 1 in the classical charts.
5 Gisela's mother, who was in the audience tonight, is very proud of her.
6 Tomorrow, Gisela is going back to Vienna, where she goes to music school.

HAVE/GET SOMETHING DONE

Exercise 1

1 Have you had your hair cut?
2 I might have my bedroom painted blue.
3 Has Michael had his bike fixed yet?
4 I get my teeth polished every six months.
5 You should have your computer checked for viruses.

Exercise 2

1 He has had his computer repaired.
2 She had her car washed yesterday.
3 He has had his shoes cleaned.
4 They're having their house painted.
5 He had his tooth taken out this morning.
6 She'll have her eyes tested tomorrow.

Page 219

UNIT 12

MODALS OF PERMISSION: *CAN/CAN'T*

Exercise 1

1 can't
2 can
3 can't
4 can't
5 may not
6 Could

MAKE/LET

Exercise 1

1 make
2 let
3 let
4 made
5 let
6 let

MIGHT BE ABLE TO, WILL BE ABLE TO, COULD/WAS ABLE TO

Exercise 1

1 b/c
2 c
3 b/c

Page 220

UNIT 13

GERUNDS VS INFINITIVES

Exercise 1

1 going
2 to have
3 going
4 to go
5 doing
6 living
7 to have
8 spending

Exercise 2

1, 2, 4, 5 have the same meaning.
3 Different meaning. (In A, Ben stopped what he was doing in order to phone. In B, Ben no longer phones his parents.)
6 Different meaning. (In A, the next thing they told us about was their holiday. In B, they didn't stop telling us about their holiday.)

GERUNDS AFTER PREPOSITIONS/GERUNDS WHEN THE VERB IS THE SUBJECT / GERUNDS OR INFINITIVES WITH *TO* AFTER CERTAIN ADJECTIVES

Exercise 1

1 to be
2 Swimming
3 Smoking
4 stopping
5 watching

Page 222

UNIT 14

COMPOUND ADJECTIVES

Exercise 1

1 We were stuck behind a slow-moving vehicle.
2 We made a last-minute decision to change trains.
3 He finally managed to get a full-time job.
4 The teenagers were very badly behaved.
5 The thief was a middle-aged man with short black hair.

PHRASAL VERB BANK

Page 224

RELATIONSHIPS

Exercise 1

1 look after
2 get on with
3 bring up
4 split up
5 get together
6 go out with

Exercise 2

1 get together
2 get on
3 brought up
4 look after
5 split up

Exercise 3

Students' own answers.

TRAVEL

Exercise 1

1 take off
2 get back
3 set off
4 break down
5 turn up
6 check in

Exercise 2

1 set off
2 broke down; turned up
3 checked in
4 took off
5 got back

Exercise 3

Students' own answers.

COMMUNICATION

Exercise 1

1 hang up
2 switch (something) off
3 call (someone) back
4 fill in (something)
5 ring up (someone)

Exercise 2

1 switched it off
2 rang up
3 hung up
4 called back
5 fill in

Exercise 3

Students' own answers.

DAILY ROUTINES

Exercise 1

1 wake (someone) up
2 get up
3 pick (someone) up
4 tidy up
5 put (something) on

Exercise 2

1 get up
2 picks me up
3 wake up
4 put on
5 tidies up

Exercise 3

Students' own answers.

WRITING BANK

Page 226

MAKING YOUR WRITING MORE INTERESTING

Exercise 1

b 7
c 1
d 5
e 2
f 4
g 6
h 8

Exercise 2

adjectives
beautiful
delicious
modern
wonderful
adverbs
completely
easily
loudly
quickly
linking words
and
because
but
so
time expressions
later that day
the next day
this morning
yesterday

Exercise 3

(other possible answers in brackets)

1 suddenly (finally)
2 but
3 early the next morning (the next day; later that day)
4 large (delicious; small)
5 really (very; extremely)

Exercise 4

1 I was very tired, so I went straight to bed.
2 We all went to the party, and everyone had a great time.
3 Paul wanted to come with us, but he couldn't.
4 We all laughed because it was so funny.

Page 227

WRITING PART 1: AN EMAIL

Exercise 1

You have to respond to the news, say which month you can go, say which sport you would like to see, and suggest something you should buy as a souvenir.

Exercise 2

1 d R
2 a S
3 b O
4 c P

Exercise 3

1 **I'm** afraid I won't be able to come to your party.
2 Guess **where** I'm going next week.
3 I'm sorry, **but** Dan won't be here when you visit.
4 You'll be pleased **to** hear that I've now finished all my exams!

Exercise 4

1 so
2 also
3 but
4 because
5 and

Exercise 5

You should respond to the idea of a barbecue, say which day you'd like to come, suggest some ideas for food and explain what sport would be best.

Exercise 6

Students' own answers.

Exercise 7

Model answer

Hi Logan,

I think a barbecue sounds like a great idea, and I'd love to come! It will be lovely, especially if the weather's going to be warm and sunny. Friday would be great! Why don't we have some salads and potatoes to go with the meat? Also, make sure you remember that some people in our class are vegetarians, so you'll need some special dishes for them.

I agree that games are fun after a barbecue. We could play badminton. It's a very easy game, so everyone can play.

See you on Saturday!

Eva

Exercise 8

Students' own answers.

Page 230

WRITING PART 2: AN ARTICLE

Exercise 1

The article is about your favourite city. You should say what the city is, why you like it and what makes it so special. You should then explain which city you would love to travel to in the future.

Exercise 2

1 There are many benefits to keeping fit.
2 The internet has changed people's lives in many ways.
3 Teaching is a very difficult job.

Exercise 3

clothes
old-fashioned
tight
fashionable
expensive
films
amusing
frightening
exciting
boring
horror
food
delicious
tasty
spicy
salty
sweet
countryside
peaceful
quiet
beautiful
wild
empty
weather
freezing
stormy
hot
wet
cool

Exercise 4

The article is about your perfect job. You should say what makes a job perfect for you. Then give your opinion about how important it is to earn a lot of money in your job.

Exercise 5

Students' own answers.

Exercise 6

Model answer

For me, an architect is the perfect job because it is interesting, creative and very challenging.
For an architect, every day is different. You might design a modern house, then a new classroom for a school, then change an old factory into flats. So this job is never boring, because every building you work on is different. I think it would also be very satisfying to create beautiful buildings for people to live or work in.
I would say it is important to earn enough money so you don't have to worry about it. But if you enjoy your job, you don't have to be rich to be happy.

Exercise 7

Students' own answers.

Page 232

WRITING PART 2: A STORY

Exercise 1

2 is the best because it talks about what was in the letter, and suggests that something is going to happen in the story.

Exercise 2

1 called
2 was waiting
3 had passed/'d passed
4 was walking
5 had forgotten/'d forgotten
6 closed

Exercise 3

1 First
2 Then
3 Next
4 An hour later
5 Finally

Exercise 4

1 curly
2 smart
3 spicy
4 entertaining
5 messy
6 disappointed

Exercise 5

Students' own answers.

Exercise 6

Model answer

A day at the zoo
We had decided to spend the day at the zoo. The day at the zoo began quite well. I was there with some friends, and the sun was shining.
First, we saw some baby elephants. Then we watched some very funny penguins.
By midday, we were getting hungry, so we decided to go for lunch. As we were walking towards the café, we suddenly heard people shouting. A tiger had escaped! We immediately ran to the café and shut the door behind us. It was quite scary, but fortunately the tiger was caught quickly and no one was hurt.
Finally, the café offered a free meal to everyone, so the day ended very well.

Exercise 7

Students' own answers.

SPEAKING BANK

Page 234

SPEAKING PART 1

Exercise 1

Yes, she does.

Track 127

Examiner: What's your name?
Maria: My name's Maria.
Examiner: What's your surname?
Maria: It's Moretti.
Examiner: Where do you come from?
Maria: I come from Rome, in Italy.
Examiner: Do you work, or are you a student?
Maria: I'm a student.

Exercise 2

Track 128

Examiner: What did you do yesterday evening?
Maria: Yesterday evening I went to the cinema with some friends. I often watch films with my friends because we all enjoy the same kinds of films.
Examiner: Do you think that English will be useful to you in the future?
Maria: Yes, I think it will be very useful. I want to work for an international company, so I hope I'll travel to different countries with my job, and I'm sure I will need English.
Examiner: Tell us about a place you would like to visit in the future.
Maria: I'd love to go to New York one day because it looks such an exciting city. Actually, my uncle lives there, so I hope I can go and visit him soon.
Examiner: Can you describe your house or flat?
Maria: My flat is quite small, because I just share it with one friend. The kitchen is very small, but the living room is quite big. Also, it's got a balcony, and I really like sitting there in the evening.
Examiner: What do you enjoy doing in your free time?
Maria: Well, I'm quite into sport, so I do quite a lot of sport in my free time. For example, I sometimes go running in the evenings and I often play tennis at the weekend. I also like spending time with friends. My friends are very important to me.

Exercise 3

1 often
2 and
3 because
4 but
5 Also
6 so
7 For example

Exercise 4

present simple	**past simple**	***be going to***
always sometimes usually	last night last weekend when I was younger	next weekend tomorrow tonight

Exercise 5

1 b + i
2 d + h
3 a + f
4 e + j
5 c + g

Exercise 6

1 because
2 for example
3 which
4 but
5 Unfortunately

Track 129

Examiner: Tell us about your English teacher.
Pablo: My English teacher is called Mr Adams, and he's from Manchester. He's really funny, and I like him because he always makes our lessons interesting. I think he's a really good teacher.
Examiner: Would you like to live in a different country?
Pablo: I'd like to visit different countries, for example the United States or maybe Australia, to get some experience of what life is like there. But I wouldn't like to go for long, because I'd miss my family and friends at home.
Examiner: Can you tell us about your home town?

Pablo: My home town is Barcelona, in the north-east of Spain. It's a big city, and there are lots of beautiful buildings which are very famous. I like it because it's very friendly, and there are lots of cafés where you can meet your friends. Also, it's on the coast, so you can go to the beach in the summer.

Examiner: How do you usually travel to school or work?

Pablo: I usually catch the bus to school. It takes about half an hour for me to get there. I'd prefer to walk, but it's too far for me to walk every day.

Examiner: What did you do last weekend?

Pablo: On Saturday I played football for my team. We usually have a match every Saturday. Unfortunately, we didn't win last week. Then on Sunday I met my friends, and we went to the beach because it was very hot.

Exercise 7

Students' own answers.

Page 236

SPEAKING PART 2

Exercise 1

They might be in a car park. They are probably friends.

Track 130

The picture shows two teenagers playing basketball outdoors. I think they might be in a car park or something like that. It isn't a very attractive place, because there are no flowers, and there isn't any grass. It's a cloudy day, and it doesn't look very warm because one of the boys is wearing long sleeves. The two boys are at the front of the photo, in the middle, and at the back we can see a basketball net, and some buildings. They look like garages or sheds, something like that. On the left, you can see some houses in the background. The boys aren't actually playing a game, but they're practising. One of the boys is wearing a stripy top, with a hood, and he's holding the ball above his head. He seems to be aiming for the net, which is quite a long way away. The other boy, who's short and has dark hair, is running forwards. I think maybe he's going to catch the ball. I guess the two boys are probably friends because they don't look like brothers.

Exercise 2

1 at the front
2 right
3 left
4 behind
5 In the background

Exercise 3

1 are travelling
2 are smiling
3 is showing
4 is looking; is thinking
5 standing; is talking

Track 131

The picture shows some people who are travelling by bus. There are two women at the front of the picture, on the left. They're smiling, and one woman is showing the other one something on her phone. On the right, there's an older man. He's looking forwards. I'm not sure what he's looking at, but maybe he's thinking about where to get off the bus. In the background, at the back of the bus, there's a man. He's standing up and I think he's talking to another passenger.

Exercise 4

1 probably
2 might
3 looks
4 seem
5 guess

Exercise 5

Students' own answers.

Track 132

The photo shows two people sitting in a living room in a house, a teenager and an older man. I think they're probably father and son. The teenager, who's on the right, is wearing a pullover and jeans, and the older man is wearing a blue shirt and jeans. He's got grey hair. The sitting room looks quite modern, and the sofa looks very comfortable. In the background, on the left, you can see some photos on a table. On the right, you can see some books. They might be watching TV because you can see that they're looking at something, and there is a remote control, or something like that on the sofa on the right. They're eating something from a box, some kind of a takeaway. It looks like pizza. They seem to be quite relaxed. I guess they're probably having a relaxing evening at home.

Exercise 6

Students' own answers.

Page 241

SPEAKING PART 3

Exercise 1

Yes, they do. They agree on two cinema tickets.

Exercise 2

1 think
2 sure
3 agree
4 opinion
5 idea
6 so
7 OK
8 go

Track 133

Maria: So, shall we start with the book? What do you think about that idea?

Pablo: I'm not sure. Some people enjoy reading, but a lot of people don't like it. And it's difficult to choose a book for someone else.

Maria: I agree with you. And I don't think flowers are a good idea because they're a bit boring, in my opinion.

Pablo: That's true. In my opinion, people buy flowers if they can't think of any other ideas. Would a T-shirt be a good idea? Most people wear T-shirts.

Maria: Well, I don't really like it when people buy me clothes, because I prefer to choose them myself.

Pablo: OK, so not a T-shirt. Would a concert ticket be a good idea?

Maria: Yes, I think that's a great idea. Everyone loves listening to live music.

Pablo: No, I disagree. There's only one ticket, and I don't think it would be fun to go to a concert on your own.

Maria: Yes, you're right. But there are two cinema tickets, so maybe they might be a better choice.

Pablo: Yes, I agree they would be a good choice. So, what else is there? Chocolates seem quite a cheap present. What do you think?

Maria: Yes, I agree. And I'm sure she'd love to get a necklace, so that's a possibility.

Pablo: OK. So, it's time to decide. What do you think?

Maria: Well, I would say either the cinema tickets or the necklace. Do you agree?

Pablo: Yes, but the necklace might be too expensive, so maybe we should choose the cinema tickets. Are you OK with that?

Maria: Yes, good idea. We'll go for that one, then.

Exercise 3

1 d
2 f
3 a
4 b
5 c
6 e

Exercise 4

Track 134

Pablo: So, shall we talk about the barbecue first? I think it's a good idea. A barbecue is relaxing, and everyone can enjoy it. What do you think?

Maria: Yes, I agree with you. The only problem is that someone has to organise everything, like buying the food and cooking it, so it's quite a lot of work.

Pablo: Yes, that's a good point. What do you think about going to watch a football match?

Maria: Well, it would be perfect for me, because I'm a football fan, but I don't think it's a good idea for a class celebration, because not everyone likes football.

Pablo: That's true. So, would the beach be a good idea? Everyone likes going to the beach. Do you agree?

Maria: I'm not sure. What if the weather's bad?

Pablo: Yes, you're right. The beach is great if the weather's good, but it's really boring if it's raining. So, what else is there? I don't think hiking is a good idea, because some people might not be fit enough to enjoy it.

Maria: Yes, I agree. What about going to a theme park? I'm sure people would enjoy that.

Pablo: Yes, that's a good idea. There are different rides, too, so not everyone has to go on the really scary ones. It's definitely more fun than a boat trip. That would be really boring, in my opinion.

Maria: I agree, because on a boat you're just sitting there for a few hours, but I prefer to be active.

Pablo: What about the zoo? That could be fun. And there are things to do indoors if it's wet.

Maria: Yes, that's true. And everyone loves animals.

Pablo: So, it's time to decide. I would choose the theme park or the zoo because I think everyone would enjoy them.

Maria: Yes. I think the theme park would be more fun, so I would choose that.

Pablo: OK. We'll go for that one, then.

Page 243

SPEAKING PART 4

Exercise 1

They give reasons, ask for each other's opinions, and use an expression to allow time to think about the answer.

Track 135

Examiner: Who do you most enjoy buying presents for?

Maria: Let me see. I would say my cousins. One is 14 years old, and the other is 12. I love buying presents for them because there are so many fun things that you can choose for children, like toys or games. What do you think?

Pablo: Yes, I agree with you, and it's also fun buying presents for children because they're always so excited when they open them. I've got a cousin who's ten, and I really enjoy buying things for him. He's really into football so it's easy to find things he likes. It's great.

Examiner: Which people in your family are the most difficult to choose presents for?

Pablo: That's an interesting question. My dad is definitely the most difficult to choose presents for. He never seems to want anything, and he doesn't have any hobbies, so I usually end up buying him something really boring, like socks. Do you agree that it's difficult to buy things for your parents?

Maria: Yes, I completely agree. It's much easier to buy things for people your own age, because you know what they like and what they're interested in.

Examiner: Do you like receiving money instead of presents?

Maria: Hmm, that's a difficult question. It's sometimes nice to receive money, because then you can buy something you really want, or you can save up to buy something bigger, like a new tablet. What do you think?

Pablo: Hmm, I'm not sure about that. When it's my birthday, I usually get money from three or four relatives, and it's good because I can use the money to buy something more expensive for myself. But in my opinion it's a bit boring if you don't get any presents on your birthday, just money. Do you agree?

Maria: Yes, I do. I love getting presents, but I think when it's relatives who don't know you very well it's better to get money, because sometimes they can give you things you don't really want.

Pablo: That's true. I prefer to get money from people who don't know me very well, but it's nice to get presents from people who know what I like.

Exercise 2

1 buying
2 is sometimes
3 usually get
4 to get
5 getting

Exercise 3

1 Do you agree?
2 That's true.
3 What do you think?
4 That's an interesting question.

Exercises 4 & 5

Students' own answers.

Track 136

Examiner: Would you like to have more social events with your class?

Pablo: Yes, I think that more social events would be great, because it would be an opportunity to get to know other students in the class better. I would like some trips to the cinema, or maybe visits to other towns and cities. What do you think?

Maria: Yes, I agree. I think it would be fun to have more social events, and in my opinion it would also help us to study, because it's easier to study when you're with people that you know, because you're more relaxed. I agree with you that trips to the cinema would be fun, because then we could talk about the films together.

Examiner: Do you think watching sports events can be more fun than taking part?

Maria: I'm not sure about that. I love sport, and in my opinion it's always more fun to take part than to watch. When you play a game like tennis or football, for example, you really want to win, so it's very exciting and it encourages you to make an effort and do your best. Do you agree?

Pablo: Yes, I do. I'm really into sport, too, and I agree that it's exciting when you play a match and you really want to win. But when I watch my favourite football team I also want them to win, so that's exciting too. I also love watching really good players, who are much better than me!

Maria: Yes, that's true. It's exciting to watch good players, but I would still prefer to take part.

Examiner: Do you prefer cooking a meal for friends or eating out in a restaurant?

Pablo: I think it depends. I enjoy cooking, and I often cook meals for a few friends. But if I want to have a big meal with a lot of friends, I prefer to go to a restaurant. What do you think?

Maria: Yes, I think you're right. It would be very stressful to cook a meal for 15 or 20 people. But cooking for a few friends is fun, and it's nice because you're at home and you're relaxed.

Pablo: Yes, I agree with you. The only problem is that you have to do the washing up.

Maria: That's true. I think it's only fun if you have a dishwasher!

ACKNOWLEDGEMENTS

The authors and publishers would like to thank the following contributors:
Grammar on the move: Lucy Passmore and Jishan Uddin
Grammar reference: Bryan Goodman-Stephens

The authors and publishers are grateful to the following for reviewing the material during the writing process:
Italy: Katia Santella, Jessica Smith; Portugal: Liliana Moreira; Spain: Tara Deakin, Julia McDermott

The authors and publishers acknowledge the following sources of copyright material and are grateful for the permissions granted. While every effort has been made, it has not always been possible to identify the sources of all the material used, or to trace all copyright holders. If any omissions are brought to our notice, we will be happy to include the appropriate acknowledgements on reprinting and in the next update to the digital edition, as applicable.

Key: ST = Starter, U = Unit, CA = Communication activities, GR = Grammar Reference, PVB = Phrasal Verb Bank, SPB = Speaking Bank.

Photography
The following images are sourced from Getty Images.

UST: hadynyah/E+; Westend61; Squaredpixels/E+; boonchai wedmakawand/moment; Didier MartiMoment Mobile; Richard Drury/Taxi; Johan Mård/Folio; andresr/E+; skynesher/E+; gilaxia/E+; Alex Potemkin/iStock/Getty Images Plus; Thomas Coex/AFP; VCG/Visual China Group; Media for Medical/Universal Images Group; Hero Images; Nick Dolding/DigitalVision; Caiaimage/Justin Pumfrey; AdiniMalibuBarbie/DigitalVision Vectors; **U1:** Matteo Colombo/DigitalVision; Sri Maiava Rusden/DigitalVision; Jordan Siemens/DigitalVision; Nick Dolding/DigitalVision; Betsie Van Der Meer/DigitalVision; Mary Rueda/EyeEm; Plume Creative/DigitalVision; John Howard/DigitalVision; Hans Georg Eiben/Stockbyte; John Hamilton/EyeEm; georgeclerk/iStock Unreleased; Tom Merton/Caiaimage; TheYok/iStock/Getty Images Plus; yorkfoto/E+; Pierre-Yves Babelon/Moment; John Seaton Callahan/Moment Open; Zi Wang/EyeEm; PeopleImages/E+; Hero Images; Paul Bradbury/Caiaimage; Michael H/DigitalVision; Hoxton/Tom Merton; Ascent/PKS Media Inc./DigitalVision; Lighthouse_Creative/iStock/Getty Images Plus; Pobytov/DigitalVision Vectors; aaaaimages/Moment; **U2:** franckreporter/E+; gilaxia/E+; Westend61; PhotoAlto/Ale Ventura; Chris Ryan/Caiaimage; BraunS/E+; Hollie Fernando/DigitalVision; The Washington Post; Image Source; Sergio Dionisio/Getty Images Entertainment; Susan Barr/EyeEm; Flashpop/DigitalVision; Neilson Barnard/Getty Images Entertainment; Frazer Harrison/Getty Images Entertainment; Mitch Diamond/Stockbyte; Klaus Vedfelt/DigitalVision; Sascha Kilmer/Moment; Caiaimage/Robert Daly; **U3:** YinYang/E+; Erik Snyder/Photodisc; Christian Science Monitor; © Santiago Urquijo/Moment Open; ArjyLondon/iStock/Getty Images Plus; Matt Dutile/Image Source; Tim Graham/Getty Images News; Jose Manuel Azcona/Moment; skynesher/E+; Dorling Kindersley; Joy Skipper/Photolibrary; The Picture Pantry/Alloy; Lartal/Photolibrary; digihelion/E+; Tony Robins/Photolibrary; 4kodiak/E+; HandmadePictures/iStock/Getty Images Plus; William Lingwood/StockFood Creative; Dmitrii Balabanov/iStock/Getty Images Plus; James Baigrie/Photolibrary; Steven Morris Photography/Photolibrary; Ian Lishman/Juice Images; MIB Pictures/UpperCut Images; Kirsty Lee/EyeEm; Claire Gunn; Hinterhaus Productions/DigitalVision; andresr/E+; Ray Laskowitz/Lonely Planet Images; VW Pics/Universal Images Group; kundoy/Moment; **U4:** Predrag Vuckovic/E+; Johannes Hulsch/EyeEm; Scott Suriano/Moment; S. Greg Panosian/E+; Mats Silvan/Moment Open; Anton Petrus/Moment; © Santiago Urquijo/Moment Unreleased; petek arici/iStock Unreleased; tunart/Editorial RF; Paulo Amorim/Moment Unreleased; I_Valentin/iStock Editorial/Getty Images Plus; filo/DigitalVision Vectors; Hero Images; martin-dm/E+; shomos uddin/Moment; Stephan D_tsch/EyeEm; **U5:** technotr/iStock Editorial/Getty Images Plus; AJ_Watt/E+; Steve Debenport/E+; marrio31/iStock/Getty Images Plus; BSIP/UIG/Universal Images Group; PeopleImages/E+; VasukiRao/E+; Renaud Philippe/EyeEm; apomares/E+; Science Photo Library; Peter Dazeley/Photographer's Choice; sturti/E+; mustafagull/E+; pilesasmiles/Editorial RF; Visions Of Our Land/Photolibrary; Richard T. Nowitz/Corbis Documentary; tbralnina/iStock/Getty Images Plus; Image Source/DigitalVision; Westend61; edge69/DigitalVision Vectors; 10'000 Hours/DigitalVision; Hollie Fernando/DigitalVision; Geber86/E+; **U6:** franckreporter/E+; jatuporn amorntangsati/Moment; Moussa81/iStock/Getty Images Plus; mirjanajovic/DigitalVision Vectors; Caiaimage/Robert Daly/OJO+; Tetra Images; B&M Noskowski/iStocl/Getty Images Plus; Vincenzo Lombardo/Photographer's Choice RF; David Buzzard-media-centre.ca/Moment; PeopleImages/E+; Hero Images; Westend61; Eric Audras/ONOKY; Chris Bell/EyeEm; Jozef Culák/iStock Editorial/Getty Images Plus; eli_asenova/E+; Jutta Klee; svetikd/E+; Ariel Skelley/DigitalVision; pawel.gaul/E+; PeopleImages/E+; **U7:** SolStock/E+; Hill Street Studios/Blend Images; Bob Krist/Corbis Documentary; Vostok/Moment; Rosmarie Wirz/Moment; Martin Child/robertharding; gilaxia/E+; Bonfanti Diego/Image Source; LeoPatrizi/E+; svetikd/E+; SolStock/E+; **U8:** Shobeir Ansari/Moment; Doug Demarest/Design Pics/First Light; ak_phuong/Moment; moodboard/Cultura; Pete Mcbride/National Geographic; Picavet/Photolibrary; Ippei Naoi/Moment"; Thorsten Vernik/EyeEm; Lee Frost/robertharding; Raimund Linke/Photolibrary; VVZann/iStock/Getty Images Plus; Joe McDonald/Corbis Documentary; Martin Ruegner/The Image Bank; "hphimagelibrary/Gallo Images; Gary Ombler/Dorling Kindersley; Roberta Olenick/All Canada Photos; David Clapp/Oxford Scientific; Christian Cabron/Biosphoto; Raimund Linke/The Image Bank; JoanBudai/iStock/Getty Images Plus; Duncan Shaw/VisitBritain; Manoj Shah/The Image Bank; Danita Delimont/Gallo Images; dominiquemills/RooM; Volanthevist/Moment; hadynyah/E+; MONTICO Lionel/Hemis.fr; Fuse/Corbis; Tom Montgomery/Aurora; Photo ©Tan Yilmaz/Moment; WITGOAWAY/Moment; Bryant Aardema-bryants wildlife images/Moment; Don Johnston/All Canada Photos; pixelfit/E+; Stephen Lux/Cultura; AlexvandeHoef/DigitalVision Vectors; Anton Petrus/Moment; Go Ga/500px Prime; Tambako the Jaguar/Moment Open; **U9:** Jetta Productions/DigitalVision; Hero Images; imagewerks; Shannon Fagan/The Image Bank; ImagesBazaar; Topic Images Inc.; William King/Taxi; Wavebreak/E+; Geography Photos/Universal Images Group; Westend61; Caiaimage/Robert Daly; Michael Dunning/Photographer's Choice; Juice Images; kali9/E+; **U10:** Grafissimo/E+; Alexander W Helin/Moment; Danita Delimont/Gallo Images; ChrisHepburn/E+; Westend61; Jason Black/EyeEm; DuKai photographer/Moment; Hinterhaus Productions/Taxi; AzmanL/E+; anouchka/iStock Unreleased; Loop Images/Universal Images Group Editorial; enjoynz/DigitalVision Vectors; vm/E+; malcolm park/Photolibrary; Klaus Vedfelt/DigitalVision; s0ulsurfing-Jason Swain/Moment; © Allard Schager/Moment; Samuele Seguso/EyeEm; **U11:** Richard Baker/Corbis Historical; David Clapp/VisitBritain; marg99ar/E+; Ray Kachatorian/The Image Bank; Sam Edwards/Caiaimage; adamkaz/E+; terng99iStock/Getty Images Plus; Astrakan Images/Cultura; bauhaus1000/iStock/Getty Images Plus; HUFTON + CROW/Corbis Documentary; sturti/E+; Hero Images; Westend61; Peathegee Inc/Blend Images; Pobytov/DigitalVision Vectors; MediaProduction/E+; phototropic/E+; Cavan Images; Caiaimage/Rafal Rodzoch; L. Toshio Kishiyama/Moment; Helen Cathcart/DigitalVision; **U12:** Westend61; Caiaimage/Trevor Adeline; Rodger Shagam/Moment; Vivid International/EyeEm; Idea Images/The Image Bank; Ezra Bailey/Taxi; Morsa Images/DigitalVision; Robin Skjoldborg/The Image Bank; sturti/E+; Hero Images; Hill Street Studios LLC/DigitalVision; Robert Daly/Caiaimage; Phil Boorman/Cultura; Colin Anderson/Blend Images; Raymond Liu , Hong Kong/Moment; A. Witte/C. Mahaney/Stone; martinedoucet/E+; Kat Gardiner/EyeEm; Luis Alvarez/DigitalVision; Caiaimage/Robert Daly/OJO+; Thomas Barwick/DigitalVision; Maskot; Comstock Images/Stockbyte; Ariel Skelley/DigitalVision; Philipp Walter/EyeEm; **U13:** Hill Street Studios/Blend Images; Paffy69/iStock/Getty Images Plus; endopack/iStock/Getty Images Plus; Georgette Douwma/Photographer's Choice; GoodmakerLee/iStock/Getty Images Plus; Hoxton/Sam Edwards; Juanmonino/E+; SensorSpot/E+; Thomas Tolstrup/Taxi; microgen/iStock/Getty Images Plus; Tony Anderson/DigitalVision; PeopleImages/DigitalVision; Maskot; Rick Gomez; Caiaimage/Paul Bradbury; Cultura RF/Benedicte Vanderreydt; yoh4nn/E+; Blend Images-Erik Isakson; Peter Kindersley/Photodisc; Suphanat

Wongsanuphat/Moment; Paul Bradbury/Caiaimage; **U14**: TerryJ/E+; ONOKY-Eric Audras/Brand X Pictures; Caiaimage/Tom Merton; Westend61; twomeows/Moment; Chris Hepburn/The Image Bank; Hinterhaus Productions/DigitalVision; Maskot; kali9/E+; Ariel Skelley/DigitalVision; **CA:** Hero Images; Dreet Production/Alloy; Adam Hester; Zero Creatives/Cultura; Sisoje/e+; Romy Tesei/Moment; JodiJacobson/E+; **GR:** Hero Images; PeopleImages/E+; LPETTET/E+; Blend Images/Michael DeYoung; Sollina Images/Blend Images; NurIsmailPhotography/RooM; FatCamera/E+; ksumano/iStock/Getty Images Plus; Fresh, amazing pictures make people look!/Moment Open; alexsl/iStock/Getty Images Plus; Feifei Cui-Paoluzzo/Moment; Newton Daly/DigitalVision; Philartphace/iStock/Getty Images Plus; Hybrid Images/Cultura; Radius Images/Getty Images Plus; skynesher/E+; Francesco Riccardo Iacomino/Moment; **PVB:** Eugenio Marongiu/Cultura; PeopleImages/E+; Deagreez/iStock/Getty Images Plus; RoBeDeRo/E+; **SPB:** HaizhanZheng/E+; Nikada/E+; Ronnie Kaufman/Larry Hirshowitz/Blen Images; Hero Images; Caiaimage/Chris Ryan; Blend Images-Mike Kemp; Dougal Waters/DigitalVision; Hill Street Studios/Blend Images.

The following images are sourced from other sources.

U1: rfranca/Alamy Stock Photo; Sam Dcruz/Shutterstock; Ilene MacDonald/Alamy Stock Photo; **U2:** Werner Otto/Alamy Stock Photo; **U3:** Martin Charles Hatch/Shutterstock; Vassamon Anansukkasem/Shutterstock; **U4:** Alexander Tolstykh/Alamy Stock Photo; **GR:** Bignai/Shuttetsock.

Front cover by Supawat Punnanon/EyeEm; Patrick Foto; fStop Images-Caspar Benson; Westend61; Blackstation.

Video Still photography
The following images are sourced from Getty Images.

U2: ROBYN BECK/AFP; hjurcik/iStock/Getty Images Plus; Gabriel Olsen/FilmMagic; The Lighthouse Film Co, Inc./; Michael Kovac/Getty Images Entertainment; Frazer Harrison/Getty Images Entertainment; **U7:** Bloomberg; **U9:** Loop Images/Universal Images Group; Jon Bower/LOOP IMAGES/Corbis Documentary; Juan Jimenez/EyeEm; **U10:** Westend61; **U11:** Alex Grimm/Bongarts; BSIP/Universal Images Group; Andia/Universal Images Group; GUIZIOU Franck/hemis.fr; **U14:** Justin Case/Taxi.

Video
The following videos are sourced from Getty Images.

U1: AhmetovRuslan/Creatas Video+/Getty Images Plus; Mageed/Creatas Video; Hal Bergman/Image Bank Film; NAZABB Photography/Moment Video RF; Schroptschop/Vetta; Nazar Abbas Photography/Moment Video RF; Doug Pearson/AWL Images; mgost/Creatas Video; basketman23/Creatas Video; piola666/Creatas Video; Caiafilm; Photokanok/Creatas Video; Siraphol/Creatas Video; WOWstockfootage/Iconica Video; WOWstockfootage/Iconica Video; Nazar Abbas Photography/Moment Video RF; tawattiw/Creatas Video; **U2:** AhmetovRuslan/Creatas Video+/Getty Images Plus; korudirect/Creatas Video; WireImage House/Getty Images Entertainment Video; www.devlomedia.com/Moment Video RF; SolStock/Creatas Video; **U3:** AhmetovRuslan/Creatas Video+/Getty Images Plus; jessikla/Creatas Video; Robert Harding Video/Photolibrary Video; Loungepark/Image Bank Film: Signature; danr13/Creatas Video+/Getty Images Plus; Chris Sattlberger/Image Bank Film; Nzb/Creatas Video; vijaifoon/Creatas Video; krissada/Creatas Video; Blacklight Productions LLC/Image Bank Film; Otto Stadler/Image Bank Film; intek1/Creatas Video+/Getty Images Plus; **U4:** AhmetovRuslan/Creatas Video+/Getty Images Plus; Schroptschop/Vetta; Jorg Greuel/Image Bank Film; RupertBritton/Creatas Video; vichie81/Creatas Video; danr13/Creatas Video+/Getty Images Plus; RupertBritton/Creatas Video+/Getty Images Plus; Frans Lemmens/Corbis Video; Stock KM/Image Bank Film; fredmantel/Creatas Video+/Getty Images Plus; BlackLight Films-Louie Schwartzberg/Image Bank Film; Calisproducties/Creatas Video+/Getty Images Plus; Kadri Alkan/Creatas Video; ReeldealHD Ltd./Verve+; primeimages; franckreporter/Vetta; ventdusud/Creatas Video+/Getty Images Plus; **U5:** AhmetovRuslan/Creatas Video+/Getty Images Plus; fStop/Verve+; Malorny/Moment Video RF; PBS Broadcast/Image Bank Film; RPM Media Inc-Roberto & Christina Mitrotti/Verve; opal2/Creatas Video+/Getty Images Plus; PBS Broadcast/DigitalVision; Pacific7 Productions London/Verve; Geoff Tompkinson/one80; Frans Lemmens/Corbis Video; Stereoscreen Audiovisual Productions GmbH/U/DigitalVision; GoldenBrown/Creatas Video+/Getty Images Plus; navigatorstudio/Creatas Video+/Getty Images Plus; **U6:** AhmetovRuslan/Creatas Video+/Getty Images Plus; zxvisual/Vetta; davidf/Creatas Video; Timestock22/Creatas Video+/Getty Images Plus; vichie81/Creatas Video; Geoff Tompkinson/one80; Mark Andersen/Verve+; The Lighthouse Film Co, Inc./The Lighthouse Film Company; Mark Andersen/Photolibrary Video; Radachynskyi/Creatas Video+/Getty Images Plus; Flame Media/Verve+; **U7:** AhmetovRuslan/Creatas Video+/Getty Images Plus; ABC Studios; ilkerdoser/Creatas Video+/Getty Images Plus; Aerial Filmworks; da-kuk/Creatas Video; Chris McGrath/Getty Images News; aerialcamturkey/Creatas Video+/Getty Images Plus; SahKartal/Creatas Video; yavuz sariyildiz/Moment Video RR; gokhantekin/Creatas Video; minemero/Creatas Video; Born To Explore With Richard Wiese/Image Bank Film; william87/Creatas Video+/Getty Images Plus; Craig McCourry/Verve; AhmetovRuslan/Creatas Video+/Getty Images Plus; ABC Studios; ilkerdoser/Creatas Video+/Getty Images Plus; Aerial Filmworks; da-kuk/Creatas Video; Chris McGrath/Getty Images News; aerialcamturkey/Creatas Video+/Getty Images Plus; SahKartal/Creatas Video; yavuz sariyildiz/Moment Video RR; gokhantekin/Creatas Video; minemero/Creatas Video; Born To Explore With Richard Wiese/Image Bank Film; william87/Creatas Video+/Getty Images Plus; **U8:** Ahmetov_Ruslan/Creatas Video+/Getty Images Plus; Guillaume749/Creatas Video; SkyworksFootage/Creatas Video; Buff Corsi Focus On Nature, Inc./DigitalVision; Multi-bits/DigitalVision; Phillip Suddick/one80: Signature; Ascent Xmedia/Image Bank Film: Signature; Gregory B Balvin/Photodisc; Galaxiid/Moment Video RF; Science Photo Library/Image Bank Film; Bryan and Wendy Mullennix/Verve+; thisnight/Creatas Video; WW News/Image Bank Film; **U9:** Ahmetov_Ruslan/Creatas Video+/Getty Images Plus; creuxnoir/Creatas Video+; alice-photo/Creatas Video; Sky News/Film Image Partner; ITN; John Ambrose/Image Bank Film; Bronek Kaminski/Iconica Video: Signature; ContentWorks/Creatas Video; SolStock/Creatas Video; Ariel Skelley/Iconica Video: Signature; Caiafilm; GalloAbraham/Corbis Video; Gary John Norman/Image Bank Film: Signature; Merlinus74/Creatas Video+/Getty Images Plus; Ridofranz/Creatas Video+/Getty Images Plus; **U10:** Ahmetov_Ruslan/Creatas Video+/Getty Images Plus; Flyingtv Ltd/Image Bank Film; Skyworks/Image Bank Film; Sky News/Film Image Partner; Hal Bergman/Photodisc; Multi-bits/Image Bank Film; John McBride & Company Inc./Iconica Video; footagefactory/Image Bank Film; Tivoli Entertainment LLC/one80: Signature; Big Ideas In Film/Image Bank Film; amornme/Creatas Video; Tivoli Entertainment LLC/Iconica Video: Signature; Siraphol/Creatas Video; Peter John Phipp/Image Bank Film; **U11:** Adriel/SoundExpress; Ahmetov_Ruslan/Creatas Video+/Getty Images Plus; creuxnoir/Creatas Video+; Skyworks/Image Bank Film; Jon Hicks/Corbis Documentary; Henryk Sadura; simonkr/Creatas Video; Assembly/Image Bank Film: Signature; Dangubic/Creatas Video; HeroImagesFootage/Creatas Video; Alex Potemkin/Vetta; Tomekbudujedomek/Moment Video RR; kimberrywood/Creatas Video; Ariel Skelley/Iconica Video: Signature; SrdjanPav/Creatas Video; **U12:** Ahmetov_Ruslan/Creatas Video+/Getty Images Plus; Thomas Barwick/Image Bank Film: Signature; FatCamera/Creatas Video; Go East/Image Bank Film: Signature; FatCamera/Vetta; SolStock/Creatas Video; kali9/Creatas Video; Sonya Farrell/Image Bank Film: Signature; SolStock/Vetta; The Lighthouse Film Co, Inc; Toshi Sasaki/Image Bank Film; thisnight/Creatas Video; selamiozalp/Creatas Video; **U13:** Ahmetov_Ruslan/Creatas Video+/Getty Images Plus; Gary Isaacson/DigitalVision; mbbirdy/Creatas Video; Slerpy/Creatas Video; MediaProduction/Creatas Video; Academic Media Network/Verve+; joakimbkk/Creatas Video; mladn61/Creatas Video; Ashley Cooper/Corbis Video; ImagesBazaar/Photolibrary Video; TRAVELXP HD/Image Bank Film; simonkr/Vetta; eakgrunge/Creatas Video; PBS Broadcast/Image Bank Film; Sarah Faubus/Verve+; Ascent Xmedia/Image Bank Film; Laurence Dutton/Vetta; Dkart/Creatas Video; Constantinis/Creatas Video; **U14:** Ahmetov_Ruslan/Creatas Video+/Getty Images Plus; Mark Andersen/Verve+; Blend Motion/Verve+;

FilmColoratStudio/Creatas Video; ReeldealHD Ltd./Verve+; freemixer/Vetta; gawrav/Creatas Video; Stereo Lab Films/Image Bank Film; Beyond Our Reality Productions Inc./Verve; Easy_Company/Creatas Video; Bronek Kaminski/DigitalVision; GCShutter/Creatas Video; Ariel Skelley/Iconica Video: Signature; FatCamera/Creatas Video; simonkr/Creatas Video.

Illustration
Steven Johnson; Chris Chalik; Denis Cristo.

Audio
Produced by Creative Listening and recorded at Tileyard Studios, London.

Speaking bank produced by Leon Chambers and recorded at The SoundHouse Studios, London

Grammar on the move audio produced by Dan Strauss and recorded at Triangle, Cambridge.

Real World documentary audio produced by Dan Strauss and recorded at Half-ton Studios, Cambridge.

The following audios are sourced from Getty Images.

U2: juqboxmusic/SoundExpress; **U3:** Richard Peikoff/SoundExpress; **U4:** You Bred Raptors/SoundExpress; **U5:** Cagdas Takmaz/SoundExpress; **U6:** Cuttlefish Music/SoundExpress; **U7:** You Bred Raptors/SoundExpress; **U8:** bjg1804/SoundExpress; **U9:** Michael Bierschenk/SoundExpress; **U10:** David Hughes/SoundExpress; **U12:** juqboxmusic/SoundExpress; **U13:** Cesar Paucar/SoundExpress; **U14:** Alexey Nikolaenkov/SoundExpress.

Page make up
EMC Design Ltd